D1524522

THE ECONOMICS AND
POLITICS OF HEALTH

This book was written under the
auspices of the Hoover Institution.

THE ECONOMICS AND
POLITICS OF HEALTH

RITA RICARDO-CAMPBELL

THE UNIVERSITY OF NORTH CAROLINA PRESS

CHAPEL HILL

© 1982 The University of North Carolina Press
All rights reserved
Manufactured in the United States of America
Library of Congress Cataloging in Publication Data

Ricardo-Campbell, Rita.
  The economics and politics of health.

  Includes bibliographical references and index.
  1. Medical economics—United States.   2. Medical
policy—United States.   I. Title. [DNLM: 1. Health
policy—United States.   2. Health services—Economics—United States.   3. Economics, Medical—United
States. W 74 R488e]
RA410.53.R53   338.4'73621'0973   81-13377
ISBN 0-8078-1509-8   AACR2

TO GLENN

ACKNOWLEDGMENTS

Invaluable insights about health and medical care from different perspectives have arisen during informative conversations with several of my colleagues and visiting scholars. I am especially grateful to my colleagues Sidney Hook, Martin Anderson, Alex Inkeles, and Dan Throop Smith for their thoughtful comments and encouragement, and also to my friends Mary Lee and Sidney Ingbar for their perceptive interpretations of the medical world.

During the writing of this book, I have been helped by several research assistants. Among them, I particularly thank Jim Gadsden, Paul Glassman, Ken Froot, and Doris Abrams, each of whom has contributed in a special manner. I am especially grateful to Gloria Watson and Omar El Sawy whose invaluable assistance in the use of the text editor made this book possible. Also, Lewis Bateman, of the University of North Carolina Press, has given helpful counsel.

I especially thank Dr. Glenn Campbell, Director of the Hoover Institution, for maintaining a work environment of intellectual curiosity and a home environment of encouragement and understanding.

CONTENTS

TABLES AND FIGURES

THE ECONOMICS AND
POLITICS OF HEALTH

I. INTRODUCTION

Americans are now spending $280 billion per year, nearly 10 percent of the gross national product (GNP), on health, which is a larger commitment to health than that made by any other nation. Predictions are that expenditures on health will soon be 12 percent of our GNP. This implies that health is treated as a desirable good in our culture and that "medicalization" will continue to increase. However, more medical care does not always improve health, and it is improvement in the level of health which must be the ultimate goal of medical care in society.

Television soap operas with medical themes became very popular during the 1970s, but this curious and sometimes exaggerated concern with all things medical has begun to subside, giving way to the more usual concerns of a vigorous, secular, and productive society. Sales of paperback books on death and dying, a reflection of our aging society, are, however, still in the millions. People no longer cling to the claim that more medical care is always better medical care and that the greater use of more expensive, newer technology is always desirable. The public is beginning to recognize that changes in life-style can promote better health, and admit that prolongation of life by medical intervention without consideration of the quality of the additional days of life is undesirable.

Dramatic technological advances in medicine, such as organ transplants and artificial insemination, continue to raise new questions of ethical concern. Solving the potential conflicts over values challenges scholars and policy-makers alike. New medical technologies do not always provide less expensive substitutes for existing medical technologies, unlike advancements made in other sectors of the economy. While medical innovations often add to quality, they can also add to costs by requiring additional, specially trained labor. Not all medical interventions result in a measurable benefit; many relieve anxiety about the uncertainty of whether one has a disease or not, and some may be harmful. The length of time for informational feedback on effectiveness may be very long, and the degree of uncertainty of medical outcomes remains large. A new drug often represents a medical advance which does not increase costs but substitutes for surgery and/ or hospitalization. New medical technology and new drugs pose similar questions. How can the risks and their benefits best be assessed? Should the marketing of a new drug be permitted when it has a therapeutical benefit demonstrated abroad above that of drugs already marketed in the United States even though the drug also carries an unknown but slight risk of a serious adverse effect for a few persons? Who should make such decisions?

The rational weighing of the costs, which include risks, and the benefits of medical interventions is needed because most medical goods and services do not compete in the normal economic markets. Cost-benefit analysis can help to clarify the assumptions and reasoning behind the present government regulations.

Cost reimbursement by other than the consumer has largely replaced the market determination of price and whether or not an additional unit of medical care or improvement in its quality is worth the additional cost to the buyer. Can consumer information about the value of medical interventions and about competitive sources of medical care be improved? Can more competitive markets replace some of the existing government regulations? Physicians who order x-rays and tests do not pay for them, and patients or consumers do not pay for the total cost of their office visits. Payments by third parties, insurers and government, account for 94 percent of all hospital bills and 66 percent of physician bills. Thus, the net cost to the consumer at the time of purchase is far below the actual resource cost of production. Costs reimbursed by third parties do not restrain consumer demand as do prices in the normal marketplace or time costs incurred by patients who wait. The credo of the physician implies the use of the "best" practices in medical treatment and often assumes that these are the newest and most expensive technologies available. For the physician to ration care on the basis of societal rather than the individual patient's benefits conflicts with his ethics. Rationing an adequate level of medical care in the face of expanding demand, supported by third party reimbursement, is the major health issue in all industrialized countries. Neither artificial restriction of the supply of medical resources in the name of high costs, "implicit" rationing, nor explicit rationing by government rules eliminates the problem. Because medical need cannot be defined, it is difficult to use to allocate medical care in those societies where a third party umbrella from tax money covers costs. Societies can no longer afford to provide all the types of medical care that might yield some medical benefit, especially if a benefit cannot be proven.

There are at least five methods of allocation or rationing, each with drawbacks: (1) market price, (2) waiting or time costs, (3) government regulations favoring one group of consumers over another, (4) medical triage on basis of medical need, as by multiphasic screening, and (5) cost-benefit analysis. The latter is an evolving approach, but it is rarely acceptable to physicians because of their intuitive aversion to monetary evaluations.

In common clinical practice, the physician evaluates risks and benefits, often without determining patients' preferences, and uses an implied, subjective estimate of the value of life. I support continuing explicit evaluations of costs and benefits, which in practice include the preferences of the patient, in order to improve the allocative efficiency of societal and personal decision-making. This method, however, will always be imperfect because the outcomes of medical intervention are often uncertain and because economics cannot precisely evaluate psychic benefits such as relief from pain or psychic costs such as those of anxiety. However, because ball-park estimates, through standardized quantitative methods, are better than either inconsistent, subjective estimates or no estimates at all, they can serve as guidelines for making societal decisions. Alternative methods of allocation are less desirable, and market allocation by money price is impossible. Time costs are neither responsive nor equitable when matching medical care use with individual medical need and, futhermore, cause a loss in society's market and household productivity.

Government regulation which favors one group of consumers over another without justification is unacceptable. Triage by health personnel does not eliminate time costs, and the recent scientific literature does not seem to justify multiphasic screening as a viable alternative. Moreover, the rules, written and unwritten, which are used by government and medical care providers to ration medical resources must depend ultimately on some form of cost-benefit analysis, whether implicit or explicit.

It is time to reassess the U.S. public's apparent desire to use one-tenth of the nation's resources for direct forms of health care under the present financial arrangements. If the third party umbrella were not so all-pervasive, might the public prefer an alternative allocation of its total product? There are alternative options to the existing distribution of GNP that can lead to better health and possibly less medical care. Goods and services other than medical care, such as housing, food, clean water, and clean air, contribute to good health. Moreover, all expenditures on medical care will not result in better health. The erosion of medical care markets by third party payments has transformed the question of allocation into a political issue. "Fairness" as an allocator of health care is difficult to define and involves tradeoffs of one individual's rights against another's.

We are at a crossroads. The Carter Administration had proposed a phased-in national health insurance program while others are pushing for comprehensive national health insurance. The U.S. budget is in financial deficit, and evidence of a taxpayers' revolt is mounting. Yet expenditures will increase for the already budgeted social security benefits and for national defense. In view of this situation, it is unlikely that Congress will, during the 1980s, pass an expensive program which would act to redistribute income and not accomplish its publicized purpose—to improve health. It is more likely that Congress will try to increase competition in the medical care market and encourage cost-benefit analyses in support of government regulations.

WHY HEALTH CARE COSTS CONTINUE TO RISE

Expenditures on all types of medical care have risen from $39 billion in 1965 to a projected $250 billion in 1980, and from 6 to 10 percent of the GNP. The rise in costs of medical care is a world-wide phenomenon among industrial countries irrespective of the method of financing care. In all of these countries, however, individuals do not pay an amount equal to the value of the actual resources used for the medical care they receive. Patients are often treated with new, expensive medical technologies which cost more to produce and operate. These advanced technologies are often supportive: they do not cure a disease, but preserve a particular level of personal health by creating a continual dependence on further medical treatment.

Saving persons' lives at early ages may mean that they will be more susceptible to illness later. Expensive treatment for serious heart disease saves an individual possibly for cancer, and successful treatment of that cancer may save him or her for pneumonia, which antibiotics cure, only for the patient to endure another type of cancer, possibly induced by the treatment of the first cancer. The costs of medical treatment over a lifetime for an individual have become progressively higher. The research focus is on the complex biological nature of chronic disease and prevention of the early onset of these diseases.

The increase in the number and level of costs of more routine diagnostic tests and x-rays has also been great. Medical care has become more scientific and thus more costly. A physician who performs surgical and other technical procedures receives greater monetary re-

wards than "the physician who provides a general medical service
. . . [hence] the 'style' of practice tends to lean toward doing more
and talking less. Many patients demand more tests and procedures,
thinking this gets them better medical care. Often the best service the
well-trained physician can offer a patient is to advise that nothing be
done."[1] Some of the increase in types and numbers of medical tests
is due to the practice of "defensive medicine," which helps protect
against malpractice suits. Other tests are necessary to make a differential diagnosis. However, it is difficult to decide which tests are
medically needed.

Our society is aging. In 1979, life expectancy at birth was 73.8
years, and for those who reached age 65, 81.0 years. Life expectancy
at age 65 has increased by 2.2 years from 1965 to 1979; white women
gained 2.1 years and all other women 2.6 years. Comparable data
for men were 1.5 and 1.8 years. However, life expectancy at age 75
has hardly changed since 1900. It is possible, therefore, that there
will be a slowdown in the increase in medical care costs for the aged
in the not too distant future. The cost of prolonging life at older ages
is usually higher than at younger ages and has become increasingly
higher since the introduction of life-saving antibiotics in the 1940s.

The medical care sector is probably the most regulated industry in
the United States. In order to build a new hospital, expand the number
of beds, or purchase expensive medical equipment, a "Certificate-of-
Need" from a regional government body is required. The costs created
by these regulations include administrative costs and the costs of
compliance by providers: hospitals and physicians. Estimates of these
costs range from 15 to 25 percent of hospitals' total costs. Mandated,
Professional Standards Review Organizations (PSROs), which restrain the use of hospital beds, cost more in 1977 than the dollars they
saved. Regulatory requirements to market new therapeutic drugs and
medical devices have become stricter and have increased the market
prices of those goods which are eventually marketed in the United
States. Licensure requirements, which restrict entry into allied health
jobs, regulate the supply of qualified workers and make health jobs
and personnel more specialized and less flexible. Moreover, they
hinder the substitution of inexpensive labor for more expensively
trained labor and thus drive up prices.

Accordingly, the demand for medical care continues to expand as
costs (i.e., patients' bills) are underwritten by private insurers, by
government under Medicare for the aged, and by Medicaid[2] for the
poor. Today, consumers have more real income to spend than twenty
years ago, and their anticipation of health gains from medical care

is greater, even though other factors such as heredity, diet, exercise, and standard of living may influence individuals' level of health more than would inputs of medical care. Education about the limitations of medical care is rare while glamorization of the new, spectacular medical technologies is common.

Efforts to contain costs, prices, and the utilization of health care services have not been successful. A major concern of government during the 1970s has been the creation of a method to retard the rising total costs of health care. Medical care prices continue to rise faster than the prices of all other consumer goods, as reflected in the Consumer Price Index (CPI), and even faster than prices of other services such as education and entertainment. Even though prices were successfully contained in 1971–74 by price control, the rate of utilization of medical services increased. Thus, expenditures on health care rose more than the prices of individual items which were restrained. The 1971–74 federal controls on prices in the health sector were successful in containing prices because providers voluntarily complied in a short-run period and regulators employed a method of delaying price increases in order to control prices. In the long run, however, there is no way to police about 400,000 clinical physicians.

Recently proposed government legislation favors prepayment of medical bills to physicians on a per capita basis rather than the traditional payment of a fee-for-service when that service is rendered. Insurance has been the traditional method of prepayment. Health Maintenance Organizations (HMOs) combine the insurance function with provision of medical care. The federal government has made large loans to many HMOs that have not always been repaid. Governments favor HMOs because they permit closer budgeting of health costs, that is, a given number of dollars for each person under government programs.

Government regulations attempt to control costs by reimbursing a percentage of the total bill, by limiting capital expansion of hospitals, and by investigating fraud in government programs. Insurers also reimburse only part of the billed costs. This practice makes prices higher to other than government payers than they would be if the providers of medical care were reimbursed for 100 percent of the billed costs. The reimbursement a provider receives is a percentage of only partially audited costs negotiated with the third party. Thus, those with lesser bargaining power pay higher prices than they would if actual total costs were fully reimbursed. The claimed and the actual costs may differ. Even under our system of partial market regulation, income is redistributed through the provision of medical care.

By 1975, the issue of cost containment overshadowed that of national health insurance. In April 1978, President Carter urged Congress to pass a controversial hospital cost containment bill because "daily hospital costs have jumped from $15 in 1950 to over $200 today. And, physicians' fees have gone up 75 percent faster than other consumer prices."[3] As of this writing, legislation to contain hospital costs has not been enacted. Without some type of cost containment feature, comprehensive national health insurance is only a remote possibility. The ineffectiveness of past government regulation to contain expenditures and the difficulty of enforcing additional rules, such as control over large capital expenditures by hospitals, are dividing public opinion. Congress has not solved the basic problem of allocation in a society where, because of tax subsidies for insurance payments and tax-supported health care programs, many individuals who believe that they need medical care also believe that they are entitled to unlimited amounts of it. Many of those who benefit from tax subsidies protest—at the same time—the high level of their taxes.

HEALTH OUTCOMES AND MEDICAL CARE INPUTS

Medical care is purchased in the hope that it will improve health. However, additional units of medical care do not always do this and, in some instances, they may even worsen health. Those who experience more ill health consume more medical care than those who are relatively healthy. The high utilization per person of medical care in the United States relative to other countries raises the question of whether or not additional dollars spent on medical care will, in the 1980s, yield additional benefits that are worth the costs. The answer depends on what type and level of medical care a patient consumes. It also depends on which groups of persons receive additional medical care. More medical care for minor illness, and in many cases for chronic illness, will not improve health although it may comfort the patient. More medical care can yield greater benefits if it is delivered to the rural poor instead of the suburban middle class.

The level of medical care provided cannot be the "best available" for everyone. The word "best" implies a comparison between *best* and a level of care that is *less than best*. Because no society can afford the best care for everyone, most industrial countries guarantee their citizens access to "adequate" medical care, yet "adequate" is rarely well defined. A 1965 British National Health Service report specified "adequate" as "the best service possible within the limits of the available resources."[4] This definition implies that the concept of adequate medical care is relative and may afford little comfort to some Americans in a period of public dissatisfaction with high taxes. Moreover, there is disagreement within the medical profession concerning the technological content of adequate care and optimal care in a given medical situation. Outcomes from given medical care inputs are uncertain. The natural course of untreated disease is not always known. Additionally, patients influence their own responses, and the practice of medicine is still an art as well as a science. Thus, the level or quality of "adequate" medical care for an individual patient varies, depending on who uses the term.

ALLOCATING SCARCE RESOURCES FOR HEALTH

Economics is concerned with the allocation of scarce resources to alternate, and often unlimited, wants in the most cost-effective manner. The mounting problem of the economics and politics of medical care today is the problem of resource allocation.

America's health industry developed primarily in response to market demand and, as a result, the interplay of supply and demand resulted in mutually acceptable prices that reflected the actual resource costs. In the past, individual decisions guided the medical industry's response in providing needed services so that if the demand for a certain type of care increased, then more resources would be allocated to provide that type of care through the market price mechanism. For this reason, symptomatic care took precedence over preventive care. Private health insurance covering hospital costs has grown faster than other types of health insurance.

But economic demand and medical need are not necessarily the same. Economic demand represents an intent to pay a given market price. The market economy presents a formal, rational framework for the problem of resource allocation constrained by economic demand. However, "medical need" is not easily defined; its meaning changes from person to person and varies for the same person over time. Physician and patient perceptions of an individual's medical need may not be equivalent. As medical technology improves and becomes more accessible, the definition of medical need becomes broader. There is no simple method to allocate medical care in accordance with medical need. Waiting or queuing, commonly used in the absence of price under different forms of national health insurance, does not necessarily allocate medical resources according to need. Great Britain, by limiting health resources to less than 6 percent of its gross national product, is using an implicit form of rationing: "first come, first served." Great Britain has also rationed by explicit regulations that give preference to emergency care and to certain medical procedures for persons under a given age.

In the United States, a combination of price and waiting allocates medical care resources, however imperfectly. If market forces alone were operative and if complete consumer information existed, then the difference between an individual's economic demand and his or her medical need would be minimized. But today the market process is by no means the only force at work in the health industry. The number of government regulations is all pervasive. The complexity of modern medicine may have outstripped the educational level of the consumer, and even of some providers, thereby making the possibility of a fully informed consumer remote. However, this is also true in other industries, such as stereo equipment and home computers. The growth of health insurance, both public and private, means that the price of care acts only partially in allocating medical resources. An increasing share of the nation's medical bills are paid by third parties: government, insurance companies, Blue Cross, and Blue Shield. In 1979, only 32 percent of personal health care bills were paid by patients themselves as compared with over 65 percent in 1950 and 81 percent in 1940. In the last 40 years the financing of health care in the United States has changed drastically, and in the last 10 years total per capita expenditures for health have more than tripled, although after correcting for inflation the increase is reduced by about 50 percent. By 1979, 94 percent of hospital bills were not paid by the patient, and the dictum that the supply of hospital beds creates its own demand had become widely accepted.

However, not all medical bills are paid by third parties. Many billions of dollars are still spent directly by private individuals for medical and dental care, drugs, and nursing home care (which is almost entirely privately financed). These expenditures affect what suppliers are willing to offer. Medical care markets in which substantial third party payments exist do not operate in the same way as other imperfect markets. For example, in the regions where the supply of physicians per capita is greatest, the price per unit of service is often the highest even after corrections are made for geographical differences in the cost of living. A 1978 U.S. government report states that "except for population growth, there is little evidence that physician fees are responsive to supply and demand forces operating in local medical care markets."[5] Third party payments create distortions in the allocation of medical resources that were absent in the past when patients dealt directly with their physicians. Insured persons may be less discriminating than non-insured persons about how often they visit their doctor and less interested in how much that doctor charges. Moreover, if a patient is covered by insurance, a physician may be less reluctant to prescribe expensive services. Thus, it is generally believed that all forms of third party payments, private insurance and government payments, increase the demand for medical care and inefficiently divert scarce medical resources from other worthwhile uses whose prices reflect their actual resource costs.

II. DEMAND FOR
MEDICAL CARE

EXPANSION

The demand for medical care is rising due to a variety of factors in modern societies. Individuals in urban areas incur greater stress created by the high concentration of people per acre. Crowding in large cities roughens the complex interface between different socio-economic, racial, and ethnic groups, increases travel time from home to work, and raises the level of urban noise. The fast pace and accelerated progress that characterize our society multiply the number and the required speed of decisions individuals must make. The overwhelming rapidity and abundance of information that bombards one's senses in metropolitan centers also generates a necessity for rapid adaptation to perceived changes. All these factors create mounting stress. The greater the stress with which individuals must live, the greater the health problems for which they will seek traditional medical care. Individuals and society are broadening the definition of medical care to include what is termed in the United States "preventive and community medicine" or "holistic medicine" and in the Soviet Union, "social hygiene."

A few years ago, the Office of Economic Opportunity (OEO) experimented with payment to four Health Maintenance Organizations (HMOs) for very broadly defined medical services to the poor. OEO provided more than the customary funding to support "specific services beyond the basic comprehensive physician's services to plan members, [and] regular plan members usually have restrictions on benefits such as prescribed drugs, outpatient mental health services, home health services, and eye glasses."[1] For the OEO-supported members, these services were paid in full. Also, the OEO-assisted families were provided with more additional benefits than those that traditional health services provide. A support staff advised and helped those families with their questions about obtaining public assistance, gave them information about employment opportunities, and identified useful community services. Family health workers from the community, newly trained, provided some home health care and provided information about nutrition. Transportation was made available to help get families to and from the health service. If this example of a much broader concept of health care were generally accepted, it would add 10 to 12 percent annually to the premium rates charged for more traditional medical care.

There is a tendency in most tax-supported, community clinics and some prepaid per capita groups, or HMOs, to provide a broader range of health services than does traditional fee-for-service medical practice. If the tendency to provide a wider range of services continues, some of which may be cost-effective but most probably not, and the level of quality of traditional medical care is maintained, then the total resource costs for health will increase. When the area of medical care is thus expanded, the resource costs rise even faster above what consumers would willingly pay out of their own pockets for traditional medical care. This is because consumers may prefer to purchase foods and services rather than the non-traditional health care offered. Where services seem free at the time of consumption because of prepayment or payment by others, there is little to restrain an expansionary concept of medical care that may include such diverse items as the "helping services" of social workers, biofeedback, control over environmental factors, and other non-traditional components of medical care.

Some consumers may prefer a more limited, less costly form of medical care while others may prefer a broader, more expensive form. The cost of the former, more traditional type of medical care will be less than that of the latter if the standards of quality for the common units of care are the same. By varying the kinds and qualities of services offered, many cost options are conceptually possible. The consumer and/or the voter—depending on how the options are presented—should be aware of the costs and benefits of each option and who actually pays for each.

As the average age of the United States population rises, the demand for medical care also increases because older persons, on the average, need more medical care. Due to medical improvements which keep persons alive longer as well as socio-economic changes in the family and environment, chronic disease requiring periodic medical care has become more widespread. This creates a greater demand for long-term nursing care facilities and innovative home care programs for the elderly that are only in small part medical care programs. The demand for medical care has also increased because physicians have become, to a degree, substitutes for ministers. Additionally, older persons, especially women who on the average outlive their husbands, are often lonely and may seek medical care to relieve their culturally isolated position. Our culture does not honor the aged as do many other societies.

Younger groups are also in increasing need of medical care as a result of medical successes. Diabetics are a rising percentage of the population: from 14.5 per 1,000 persons in 1965 to 20.4 per 1,000 persons in 1973,[2] an increase of 41 percent in an eight-year period. Among females under 45 years, the rate per 1,000 increased 79 percent in that eight-year period and among males, 16 percent. Most striking is a 150 percent increase among non-whites under 45 years of age, from 2.8 per 1,000 to 7.0 per 1,000. Diabetes mellitus[3] accounts for 2.8 million (or 5 percent) of all internist office visits. Only essential hypertension and chronic ischemic heart disease account for more visits: 9 percent and 8 percent respectively.[4] Moreover, diabetic mothers give birth to a higher percentage of infants with various birth defects than do mothers without diabetes.

New medical technology enables infants to survive who would not have lived a few years ago. Among infants needing a great deal of medical care are those suffering from spina bifida.[5] There are difficult ethical and religious problems involved in genetic screening, or amniocentesis, because it implies a presumption that some women, when informed that they have a high risk of bearing a seriously defective child, will choose to abort. If this is not assumed, genetic screening's benefit is usually limited to forewarning and counseling the parents. In rare cases, amniocentesis and ultrasound findings have permitted physicians to intervene medically to correct defects while the baby is still in the mother's womb.

It is impossible to cast arguments in this area solely in terms of costs and benefits. Given the political climate of the 1980s, to even advocate that decisions about these mothers are personal decisions becomes a political statement. The advance of medical technology has helped to provoke controversy that religionists, scientists, physicians, and economists are unable to resolve. This chapter is concerned only with the increasing demand for medical care and its rising costs, not solutions to ethical dilemmas.

Screening during the early period of pregnancy for diseases resulting from inborn deficiencies in metabolism, spina bifida, and other high cost (including psychic cost) congenital anomalies such as Tay-Sachs disease has the potential to contain costs but at a sacrifice of some individuals' beliefs. Although some pregnant women faced with potentially severely disabled infants choose to abort, others do not. To the extent that amniocentesis screening helps to prevent such births, it is cost-saving for the individual. Where the individual cannot pay the costs, it may also be cost-saving for society. Because of the rarity of these diseases, screening of all pregnant women could push the costs of an inexpensive procedure that has a small risk to the individual being screened beyond the benefits to society. In the case of Tay-Sachs disease, the population at risk is known and can be targeted, but potential carriers of other diseases, such as spina bifida, can be identified only when a woman has already given birth to a child with that disease. A simple blood test for spina bifida is being developed and it could become a preferred screening technique, but its rate of false negatives is still high and there are some false positives. Even a low level of the latter are probably unacceptable to many in our society. Although "only 47 percent of cases of spina bifida survive to the age of one year, . . . the lifetime cost of caring for the spina bifida cases born [in Scotland, 1973] . . . in one year would be more than £1 million.[6] These future costs are not discounted in the above estimate to obtain present values. If they were discounted, the present costs of later years would be less, the higher the interest rate that is used. In addition, psychic costs and benefits are not included.

Medical technology has the potential to reduce the costs of the medical care of a population by genetic screening of a specific subgroup at risk. There are, however, unresolved ethical questions in encouraging women who have a high probability of bearing defective children to abort. Societies and individuals differ in the degree of deviation from the norm that they will tolerate.

The rising level of medical technology also has created the ability to diagnose diseases and perform cures more easily. The latter has reduced substantially some types of demand. Antibiotics are a common example of cost savings because they replace surgery and hospitalization in some cases, such as ear infections. The incidence of polio has been greatly reduced by immunization, and individuals with tuberculosis are no longer hospitalized for lengthy periods because successful treatment with drugs is available. These are all cost-effective changes. Over a forty-five-year period, 1930–74, technological advances are estimated to have reduced the annual rate of health expenditures by 0.4 percent.[7] By attributing the influence of technology to an unexplained residual, another investigator estimated that over a shorter time period of twenty years, 1947–67 (this eliminates the large, initial effect of the use of antibiotics), technology accounted for an annual 0.6 percent *increase* in medical care expenditures.[8]

The cost-effectiveness of different medical technologies varies greatly. Kidney transplants are replacing the more expensive kidney dialysis, which is also a relatively recent treatment. Persons with successful transplantations need continuing medical supervision for the rest of their lives and also are more susceptible to other diseases. With Medicare paying for the treatment of end-stage kidney disease, the numbers of persons medically evaluated to need either kidney dialysis or a transplantation increased from under 5,000 persons in 1971 and 11,000 in July 1973 (the start of Medicare reimbursement) to 20,764 in March 1975 to about 60,000 in 1980, and an estimated 90,000 in 1995.[9] The 1975 congressional estimates of future caseloads of 50,000 to 70,000 patients by 1990[10] are clearly under-statements. Included in the estimate are patients whose chances for successful treatment are marginal but whose economic situtation qualifies them for care because of assured Medicare reimbursement. The end-stage, renal disease program of Medicare consumes about 10 percent of all of Medicare's Part B (physicians' fees) payments and about 1.3 percent of Part A (hospitalization). Although home dialysis costs less than in-hospital dialysis, political considerations—among other factors—have favored, by reimbursement policies, the latter over the former.

The decisive reason for the expanding demand for medical care is that consumers' out-of-pocket expenses are far less than the cost of the resources they consume. In comparison with most other goods and services for which the consumer pays a price at least equal to the cost of the resources, the low out-of-pocket price of medical care makes it a great bargain. Ninety-four percent of all hospital bills and 66 percent of physician services are paid by third parties (the government, the employer, or the insurance company), not the consumer at the time of consumption.

Economists agree that medical insurance (for a more detailed description of the varieties, see Chapter VII) and the payment of many medical bills by the government, in whole or in part, have shifted the whole demand curve (the amounts of medical care demanded at different prices) to the right, from DD to $D_1 D_1$ in the following diagram. If OP^1 is the price for consumers with health insurance, they will demand OA^1 units of care. The slope of the line $D_1 D_1$ is steeper than the line DD, which is to say that the elasticity of demand is less under health insurance because reimbursement makes the consumer less sensitive to price changes. The consumer with health insurance demands OA^1 units of care while the consumer without health insurance demands or prefers only OA units and at a lower

Figure 1. Demand for Health: Effect of Reimbursement

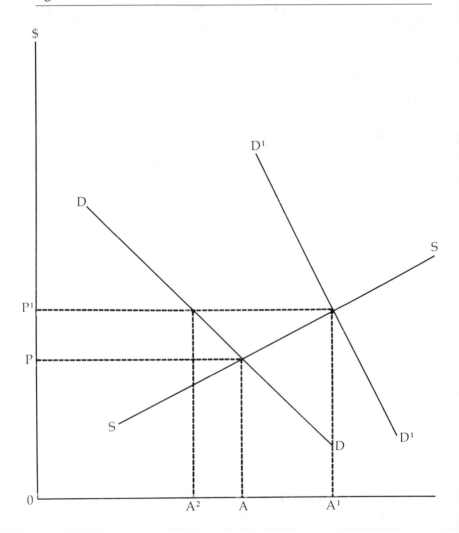

price, OP. However, the effective price that all consumers usually must pay is OP^1, and under those circumstances, persons without any reimbursement will demand only OA^2 units of care.

Although the preceding analysis makes some rigid assumptions about the uniformity of units of care and the prices charged, this does not invalidate the basic effects of extensive third party payments, that is, payments by another party than the buyer or seller.

The desire of individuals to reduce the uncertainty of high financial risk, the employee's advantage of having premiums paid out of income not subject to personal income tax, and the employer's ability to expense health insurance premiums as labor costs all account for the rapid growth of private third party payments. If only risk aversion were the major reason for purchasing health insurance, then catastrophic health expense and not first dollar coverage would be the more common form of health insurance. The prices of medical care covered by private health insurance are in the long run reflected by the insurance premiums, but these may be paid wholly or in part by employers, not by employees. Although the health insurance premiums are not taxable income as are the wages for which they substitute, the latter generally would be higher if employer-paid health insurance did not exist. Employees, however, have a larger total package with health insurance.

As private insurance and the government programs of Medicaid and Medicare have grown, the demand and prices of medical care have increased remarkably. But these higher prices do not restrain demand because for the past ten years the out-of-pocket real costs of medical care to the consumer have remained constant.

The sensitivity of demand to price, or the elasticity of demand, is not the same in all medical care markets. In emergency cases, individuals are quite insensitive to price even if they pay for the care. Definitions of emergency care vary, but when emergency care is defined as a life-saving procedure, price has no influence on demand. In the section of this book that examines the right to medical care, it is argued that emergency medical care (using the strict definition of "life-saving") is not, in the United States, denied to anyone because they lack the means to pay for it.

Economists have estimated the elasticity (or sensitivity) of demand for medical care with respect to price, but the estimates vary considerably. Joseph Newhouse and Charles Phelps of the Rand Corporation correct for differences in their estimates for such factors as the self-perceived status of health, the percent paid by the patient, and individual income levels. Their estimates yield an elasticity of

−0.33 for hospital expenditure and −0.22 for physician services.[11] Some other estimates of the price elasticity of demand for hospital bed days and physician visits are higher. The data available do not show precisely how much demand will increase for given decreases in price. The great variety of insurance financial offerings complicate empirical testing of response to changes in price. However, it is clear that the higher the out-of-pocket prices of hospital bed-days and physician visits, the lower is the demand. Medical care is subject to the rules of the marketplace.

Data indicate that, despite the historical trend of a rising price of a unit of time (and time is spent in obtaining and consuming medical care), individuals still demand greater quantities of medical care as the money price out-of-pocket falls. Additionally, increases in productivity have created increases in per capita real income. As real income rises, individuals change the portions of their income spent on different goods and services. As real income increases, the demand for services generally rises faster than the demand for commodities.

Medical care is primarily service-oriented, and some health care services can be viewed as luxuries because they receive a greater share of an increment to income than they do of the base income. Dental services, plastic surgery, prescription drugs, and frequency of physician visits may all fall into this category. The precise relationship between increases in income and the demand for medical care is unknown because of the distortions created by third party payers. It is generally believed that the demand for health care is more sensitive to changes in net price to the consumer than to changes in income. Figure 2, per Capita Personal Health Care Expenditures and Disposable Personal Income, 1950–1979, is presented in current dollars to compare the rapid rise in per capita health expenditures with increases in the disposable income of individuals, that is, their incomes after payment of taxes. Per capita personal health care expenditures have more than kept up with the increase in disposable income.

An analysis of California hospitals' number of days or lengths-of-stay by method of payment in 1971 (Table I) shows that the average (median and mean) length-of-stay was lowest for patients who "self-pay" and generally highest for those aged patients with both Medicare and Medicaid reimbursement. The latter group's total bill is paid by third parties; the former group has no reimbursement. The latter group also are probably sicker; they are all 65 years or older. The length-of-stay for all Medi-Cal (California's Medicaid) patients

Table 1. 1971 California Hospital Length-of-Stay Report

(By method of payment)

	All Diagnoses			All Operations Only		
	No. of Patients	Length of Stay Mean	Median	No. of Patients	Length of Stay Mean	Median
Method of Payment		(days)			(days)	
Medicare/Cal	29,481	10.2	7	8,656	11.7	8
Medicare	110,296	9.9	7	40,236	10.9	8
Workmens Comp.	13,927	6.5	4	8,207	6.6	4
Free	4,149	6.1	3	1,768	6.5	4
Other Government	20,922	5.9	3	8,304	6.2	4
Blue Shield	11,790	5.6	3	6,388	5.4	4
Blue Cross	103,672	5.4	3	54,285	5.5	4
Commercial Ins.	275,821	5.1	3	148,538	5.2	3
Medi-Cal	135,426	4.5	3	57,919	4.0	2
Self-Pay	81,331	3.4	2	32,940	3.2	2
Miscellaneous	179,210	5.5	3	61,133	6.3	4
TOTAL:	966,025	5.7	3	428,410	5.8	4

Source: California Medical Association. California Hospital Length-of-Stay compiled by California Health Data Corporation, Attachments 3 and 5, as reported on initially in CMA's *Socio-Economic Report*, June 1972. (Mimeo)

Figure 2. Per Capita Personal Health Care Expenditures and Disposable Income 1950–1979 (Current Dollars)

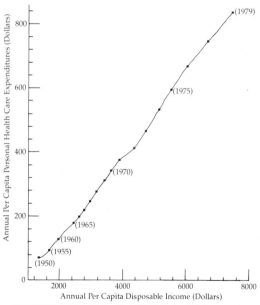

Sources: Economic Report of the President, 1981 (Washington, D.C.: Government Printing Office, 1981): p. 259, Table B-22. U.S. Department of Health and Human Services, Health Care Financing Administration, Health Care Financing Review, Summer 1980, Vol. 2 (Baltimore, Maryland, 1980): p. 23, Table 4.

is lower because the average age is younger and also there was the strict state review of the use of hospital days by Medicaid patients in 1971. When these data are broken down by the usual differential diagnoses, the same pattern of influence of the financial arrangements on the length of hospital stay repeats.

The cost of medical care for families of four averages over $3,000 a year. The rate of growth in health expenditures per capita has increased substantially since 1966. From 1950 to 1965, the average annual rate of growth in per capita disposable income was 4.2 percent and, for per capita health expenditures, 6.4 percent. From 1966 to 1970, these rates increased to 6.7 percent and 11.7 percent respectively. During the period of price controls from August 1971 to June 30, 1974, the increases were 9.1 percent and 11.6 percent respectively, and from June 30, 1979, to June 30, 1977, to 9.3 percent and 14.2 percent respectively. In other words, the growth rate of per capita health expenditures has out-distanced that of per capita disposable income since 1950. The differences in growth were especially great following the enactment of Medicare and Medicaid and after price controls on medical care were lifted. The unit prices rose in the latter period but also individuals, patients, and physicians used more medical care at the expense of other goods and services. Cost increases occurred not only in the private sector, but also under government health programs.

In the fifteen-year period prior to 1965, 44 percent of the increase in the total expenditures for health resulted from price increases, 21 percent from population growth, and 35 percent from improved technology, greater utilization, and other changes which are believed to have improved the quality of medical care.[12] In the ten-year period from 1965 to 1975, 53 percent of the increase in total expenditures for health resulted from price increases, 9 percent from population growth, and 38 percent from those factors believed to raise the quality of medical care. From 1971 through 1974, which closely corresponds to the period of price controls in the health sector, 42 percent of the total increase was due to price increases, 8 percent to population growth, and 50 percent to higher utilization of resources and improvement in quality. The latter also reflects the increase in breaking out and pricing more medical procedures so that, where prices were restrained, costs continued to rise. From 1974 to 1980, inflation or rising prices accounted for about 68 percent of the increase, population growth (continuing to reflect the decline in fertility rate) only 7 percent, and the catch-all of greater utilization, technological, and other changes in the system, about 25 percent.[13] Thus, whatever dampening effect price control had exerted was quickly wiped out. Despite this, the percentage of the country's real income or gross national product spent on health increased from 6 in 1965 to over 9 in 1979—a very substantial growth.

If physicians had as much influence on the demand for their services as they are credited with having, one would anticipate, in view of the rapidly increasing number of physicians and the prevalence of third party payments, that visits per capita would have been increasing. This, however, is not the case. In 1976, total physician office visits declined 1 percent from 1975 and another 1 percent from 1976 to 1977. Although this decline covered only a two-year period, it occurred when the population was increasing. Annual visits per capita have been declining for twenty years, from 5.3 in 1958 to 4.8 in 1977 and 4.7 in 1978. Over that same period, the number of physicians per 1,000 population increased, as has the number of diagnostic and radiologic procedures. Physicians who use an independent laboratory can, in most states, legally bill the patient for an amount higher than the laboratory fee. From 1975 to 1978, the number of laboratory tests increased by 20 percent and the number of x-rays by 36 percent. Among x-ray procedures done out-of-hospital, in physicians' offices and in their laboratory areas, the increase was 122 percent.[14] This figure reflects changing methods of medical practice.

Physicians have increased the number of tests for a variety of reasons. Some physicians may order a high number of tests when they are uncertain about a diagnosis and want to relieve their anxieties of otherwise not having done all that they could for a patient. Some physicians may order additional tests primarily to protect themselves from potential malpractice suits. Some physicians who receive income derived from tests, such as those in a group practice-run laboratory, have used a "target income" approach to compensate for lower incomes that result from fewer office visits.

The target income approach is usually described as follows: a provider sets an income goal, then increases the unit number of suggested return office visits and of ancillary services when prices of these items fail to rise in line with income expectations. Obviously, various tradeoffs are possible. Once the income target is met, it is claimed that physicians reduce their working hours because they value incremental amounts of leisure over income. The latter part of this theory may partially explain the decline in per capita office visits cited earlier. In addition, the higher cost to patients of their time spent obtaining and consuming medical care may have encouraged patients to substitute self-care and seek fewer office visits.

When either money or time costs increase, demand falls. In recent years, the time costs of receiving medical care have become more important than money costs for many persons.

It is possible that the providers of medical care are also substituting tests and x-rays for office visits in addition to substituting office visits for in-hospital bed days. The latter substitution effect is substantiated in the economic literature, but the former has not been proven. There has been a 109 percent increase in tests performed by independent laboratories and a 164 percent increase in hospital laboratories from 1970 to 1978. There are obvious economic incentives for physicians to order more procedures performed in-office. The same is true in group practice laboratories, where physicians share in the revenues. Although the empirical data are imperfect, one economist's careful analysis concludes that "there appears to be substantial evidence that physician decisions with respect to the frequency of tests, fees charged, and the decision to perform tests in-house are influenced and constrained by economic factors that affect demand for their services and input costs."[15]

If the tests and x-rays are beneficial, more frequent use of some medical procedures might be concomitant with a decline in morbidity and mortality rates. However, an analytical study of patients with hypertension performed at George Washington University found among the thirteen faculty internists in the study that there was "no positive association between a physician's frequency of lab use and either clinical productivity or outcomes of care."[16] The study does not substantiate that the physicians used a target income approach because they were "faculty members [who] were salaried and did not share income obtained from laboratory tests."[17] These are complex relationships and not enough is known to explain the expansion of some types of medical care and the decline in others.

ACCESS TO CARE

The major argument behind the political drive from the 1940s into the 1970s for compulsory national health insurance has been that the poor do not have access to adequate medical care. A recent (1977) Deputy Assistant Secretary of Health, Education, and Welfare wrote: "In 1976 an estimated 24 million people received services covered by Medicaid, a number similar in size to the poverty population, which was estimated at 25 million that year . . . [but] adjusting for movements in and out of Medicaid [this] suggests that perhaps no more than half of the poor population is covered by Medicaid at any one time."[18] Therefore, a "major reform of the current network of financing programs, public and private . . . can best be accomplished by the introduction of national health insurance . . . [which] is urgently needed if the low income population is to have access to adequate health care."[19]

The above conclusion, based on the estimate that about one-half of the poor experience a financial barrier to seeking medical care, assumes that everyone who is poor needs to visit a physician at least once a year. Figures show, however, that about one out of every four Americans do not see any physician during a given year. Although the poor, who may eat less well and live in inadequate housing, are believed to have greater medical needs than the non-poor, the assumption that every poor person *needs* to see a physician once a year is unrealistic. Perhaps the greater medical needs of the poor can be better combatted through preventive measures (school lunches, physical examinations upon entering school with followup medical care, and simple public health and sanitation measures) than through additional expenditures on traditional health care. Labor unions and others continue to press, through Senator Edward Kennedy, for some form of comprehensive national health insurance in order to remove a presumed financial barrier that may not exist.

In the opinion of many economists, the poor under Medicaid do have access to adequate medical care with the exception of some rural poor and children of a small number of urban poor.[20] Their analyses emphasize access barriers to medical care other than income. For example, Myron Lefcowitz and Michael Grossman emphasize the greater importance of the low level of education which is correlated with low income. "Education has a positive and statistically significant coefficient in the health demand curve"[21] because the more educated are more efficient in combining medical care, better food and housing, and other factors which affect health. Grossman also shows that higher income may mean poorer health because it makes easier the consumption of items which harm health. Lefcowitz states that "the share of income required for medical care is greater for the poor. Any policy which picks up the tab for services can, to that extent, redress the inequity. Clearly, however, this objective is more income-distributional than health-improving."[22]

Data on access to medical care by the poor prior to 1970 are not very pertinent to the 1980s. Aday and Andersen have updated to 1976 the University of Chicago's 1963 and 1970 survey data. They define family incomes below $8,000 as "low income." In 1976, 73 percent of all such low income persons had seen a physician during the previous year while 77 percent of urban Blacks had seen physicians. Rural Southern Blacks and low income, Spanish-surnamed persons in the Southwest were less likely (65 percent) to have seen a physician while only 68 percent of all rural farm inhabitants had seen a physician in the previous year.[23]

The percentage of the poor without access to adequate medical care in 1980 is likely to be between 10 and 15 percent. The numbers of poor have been declining steadily. Martin Anderson, in his book *Welfare*, states that "because government redistribution of income had grown so rapidly during the eight years preceding 1973, the net transfer of income to the poorest fourth of the population from the other three-fourths was so great that the 'total value of the resources consumed by the poor in 1973 was enough to raise every officially poor family 30 percent above its poverty line.'"[24] The Congressional Budget Office's estimates of the number of poor were as low as 6 percent of the population in 1976, or less than 14 million persons. Rural versus urban, not low versus high income, appears to be the most important differential.

The 1976 data in the federal government's ongoing *Health Interview Survey* also show that there has been a continuing decline in the number of poor who have not visited a doctor in two years: 1964, 28 percent of poor below $3,000 annual family income; 1973, 17.2 percent below $6,000; and 1976, 15.1 percent below $7,000.[25] In 1978, 12.9 percent below $7,000 were in this category.

Low income persons continue to use dentists less than middle and high income persons. In 1978, about 67 percent of those with incomes of $25,000 or more saw a dentist during the previous year as compared with only 37 percent of low income persons. In 1978, data from the federal government's continuing *Health Interview Survey* indicate that 79 percent of those earning $25,000 and 51 percent of those earning less than $7,000 had used a dentist in the previous two years.[26] The gap has been narrowing.

Sociologists such as Thomas Bice and Diana Dutton argue that, once Medicaid and Medicare were fully implemented, various cultural factors (lack of education together with the impersonal, mass-produced technology of hospital outpatient clinics and emergency rooms) act as greater barriers to physician care than does lack of income.[27] There is general agreement that the poor are more likely to receive medical care from lesser trained medical personnel—a general practitioner rather than a specialist and a resident or an intern rather than an established physician—in outpatient clinics and other settings less accommodating than the offices of private physicians.

The lack of medical facilities in rural areas may act as a special barrier to the rural poor. Non-English speaking individuals do not communicate well with medical professionals, most of whom speak only English. Only recently have interpreters become available in hospitals. In the ambulatory medical care sector, interpreters are even less common. Individuals who have a regular source of medical care (86 percent of the low income population in 1976) use more medical care than those persons who do not have a regular source of care.[28] U.S. *Health Interview Survey* data indicate that the principal, self-perceived barrier to medical care was, in 1974, "trouble getting [an] appointment." Only one-half as many people believed that the care would cost too much. Among families in that year with incomes less than $5,000, the percentage that had trouble getting appointments was identical with the percentage which stated that the care would cost too much. Only 10.4 percent of all families interviewed observed any barriers to receiving medical care.[29]

There are probably several million poor people just above the level of income that cuts off Medicaid who experience financial barriers to receiving adequate medical care. Many of the working poor do not receive a health insurance package at work that covers them and their dependents adequately. There are temporary, part-time, intermittent, and migrant workers who may have no health insurance coverage at all as well as an increasing number of illegal immigrants who do not seek medical care because they do not wish to reveal their presence. There are also some younger people who are no longer covered under their parents' health insurance plans but who, when their own employment does not automatically cover them, rarely purchase health insurance coverage because the nongroup premium is higher than its anticipated benefit. Similarly, many other people who work and live outside the system, such as artisans, workers in agricultural communes, and some of the self-employed in the more traditional lines of work, are less likely to purchase health insurance. The Congressional Budget Office estimates that in total there are 18 million persons who have no government or private health insurance expense coverage.

No one in the United States today would deny needed medical care to ill people. The situation for those relatively few poor and elderly who may need more medical care than they are getting and who are eligible for Medicaid or Medicare and/or Supplemental Security Income (SSI) will not improve until the real barriers to care are removed. The fact that a small percentage of the population may not have ready access to non-emergency medical care is not an argument for federal comprehensive health insurance.

It has been shown that medical care is least accessible in rural farm areas. Every country lacks physicians in rural areas. Some countries have more physicians per capita than the United States, and many have comprehensive national health insurance. Increasing the total number of physicians does not automatically make medical practice in rural areas more attractive to well-educated physicians and their families. However, the recent extraordinary increase in the supply of physicians, one for every 500 persons by 1990, will induce more physicians to practice in the rural areas. This will be true despite the lack of specialized medical facilities, and also the scarcity of museums, theaters, and other cultural centers in farm areas. The federal government may be too far removed from rural areas to solve unique regional and local problems. Specific solutions tailored to specific problems may be more helpful. For example, grants and loans made to small towns by wealthy foundations such as the Robert Wood Johnson Foundation and by large companies such as Sears, Roebuck have succeeded in attracting physicians.

Regional groups can play an important role. The Western Interstate Commission for Higher Education (WICHE) established a regional network of continuing education for physicians serving rural areas in the West. WICHE also expanded airlift ambulance services from rural mountain areas to the nearest university medical center and encouraged communication networks to link rural paramedics to physicians who supervise medical care at a distance.

A "RIGHT" TO MEDICAL CARE

It is only in relatively recent times and wealthy countries that medical care has been considered a "right" by some individuals. Relatively poor, underdeveloped countries do not have the luxury of guaranteeing their populations rights that are even more basic to life than medical care, such as the right not to starve. It is estimated that one of ten persons in the world face possible death from starvation. The higher a country's per capita income, the more generous can be that country's policy in establishing basic human needs as rights through legal action.

Rights based on economic needs are positive or legal rights. Legally awarded rights are not, however, what the philosopher categorizes as moral or natural rights.[30] The latter evolve from humanitarian feelings and reasoning, and are the antecedents to legal rights which do not necessarily encompass natural rights. It is a moral, not legal, right to guarantee the social condition of various freedoms on the condition that the pursuit of these freedoms does not interfere with other individuals' moral rights. Moral rights do not require others to do anything for an individual.

Some individuals believe that they have moral rights to economic goods or services provided by others. A pragmatic philosophy of life, or "the method of creative intelligence,"[31] recognizes that choices push individuals into a conflict between what they can achieve and what they hope and believe they can achieve. Such individuals may have a "tragic sense of life" because they realize that, having made their choices amid their conflict of values, they have sacrificed "the selves they might have been."[32]

To confuse equality of outcome with a moral right of equality of opportunity is to deny the conflict between two or more nearly equal good values. A right to emergency medical care places a higher value on the life of the patient than on the rights of choice of those who are obligated to provide the care. As long as the right is to "life-or-death care," this tradeoff between values among individuals is generally acceptable. However, to extend the right to emergency care to include all medical care, some of which may be paid for by others in greater need of food and shelter, offends many persons' values.

It is impossible to guarantee access to equal quality medical care because under the best of circumstances quality varies with the skills of physicians. In emergency medical care situations, the poor may often receive better care than the wealthy. Trauma centers and other specialized emergency care facilities are usually in a city or university hospital, and access to these may be by chance.

Governments may pass laws to provide equal opportunities to become rich but leave individuals to take advantage of these opportunities themselves. In order for a free economic marketplace to exist, the moral right to individual freedoms (such as the right to choose one's occupation and geographic location of residency) must already be present, guaranteed by the law. These individual freedoms do not exist in totalitarian countries. Moral rights exist outside the marketplace and are not assigned a price. Market prices for these freedoms and moral rights also do not exist.

Among the moral rights specified in the United States Constitution are the right to liberty, the right to freedom of speech and choice of religion, and the right to act for survival, to pursue "happiness," to enjoy equal opportunity, and to own property— providing that the pursuit of these rights is not unduly harmful to others. Among these, the right to acquire property has been challenged most frequently.

Traditional economists argue that without a right to property there is no incentive to work and produce necessities such as food, shelter, and emergency medical care, broadly defined. Some individuals acquire more property than others because of inheritance, natural ability, or family wealth and advantages (with or without a combination of hard work), and therefore the distribution of wealth is unequal. Taxation of inherited wealth and income may reduce inequalities of outcome and make more equitable each person's share. Some economists, however, state that this is not necessarily an optimal solution because, by levying high, progressive taxes that discourage work, redistribution may reduce the absolute shares of real goods and services (the GNP) that the poor receive. Economists generally support taxes on inherited wealth because they affect incentives to work less than do comparable taxes on income. Taxes on incomes are acceptable to some economists only if they are not so progressive as to discourage work. What level of each type of tax will not affect the size of the GNP is debatable because of differences in individuals' values and total output of goods among societies.

Some economists argue that, even though the total pie (all the goods and services produced in a year) may be reduced by redistributing income via taxation, this is acceptable because it also equalizes shares of the pie. Economists point out that high levels of taxation may inhibit the growth of real goods and services within a country so that there is less to divide up and the poor might not then fare as well as they would without such an extreme redistribution. Economists recognize that there is a tradeoff between the size of national income and the degree of equality of its distribution.[33] Value judgments, not one's mastery of economics, determine what may be that system of taxation in a given country which yields an ideal balance between the growth of the national income and its allocation.

Non-economists may criticize economic analysis for "its failure to provide for particular rights with sufficient specificity and emphasis. Indeed, I (John Rawls) have argued that the moral blindness, and therefore the unacceptability of the economic analysis of rights, cannot be cured solely by redistributing in the form of lump sum transfers the presumably efficiently allocated maximal social stock."[34] John Rawls, a philosopher, thus revived the dispute about the correct definition of moral (natural) rights in his book, *Theory of Justice*. Rawls presents an esoteric theory of non-coercive contracts negotiated by mythical persons who, because of a veil of ignorance, may refuse a contract that would help them because they are unaware of their own abilities and attributes and of the type of society in which they will live. In Rawls' theory, individuals initially arrive at fair or just contracts by trading off entitlements to economic goods against limits on their personal liberties, a tradeoff which would benefit, it is assumed, society as a whole.

Rawls' theories of both ethics and economics are questionable. He believes that a moral society should achieve total equality. With equality as his end-point, Rawls is willing to justify any means which creates a more equal distribution, even if it means denying some of Peter's moral rights to assure Paul a more equitable share or outcome. He assumes that societies can reach an idealized goal or nirvana of complete equality. His theory of initial contract negates the traditional economic assumption that, because resources are scarce, they should be allocated in the most efficient manner in order that the net, largest possible amount of goods and services is produced from the given resources. ("Net" is used because if the environment is spoiled in the process of production, such as by air pollution, then that is a societal cost.) If the allocation of goods and services favors some persons above others, society may correct for this by taxation and redistribution of income. Value judgments will determine how much redistribution might occur.

Others, such as Robert Nozick,[35] reject a solely egalitarian goal and support the more traditional distinction between moral rights and positive rights conferred by society's legal structure. Nozick believes that it is the historical development of redistribution which must be morally observed; that society evolves through making the moral rights of transfer and inheritance, legal rights. The rules of the game to achieve the end of more equal distribution of income and wealth are to be fair. The end-point of egalitarianism does not justify the means.

In some societies, moral rights to protect the integrity of a free and independent individual from external abuse exist. In other societies, positive or legal rights to enforce these moral rights do not exist. Moral rights become legal rights when there is a consensus to make them so.

Legal rights often take the form of human "needs," and some societies may grant them at the expense of other persons' antecedent moral rights. Emergency medical care in many societies can be defined as a legal right to medical treatment for a life-or-death matter. However, if the legal right to emergency medical care were extended to include rights to all types of medical care, then some of the moral rights of physicians might be eroded. Physicians could no longer choose where they prefer to work, what specialty they prefer to practice, and how many patients they want to accept.

If emergency medical care is defined as a strictly lifesaving action, it can be considered a legal right in the United States. For centuries many of the world's great religions have taught that such limited emergency care is a moral right. Some argue against this concept because it requires the physician to be "his brother's keeper."

It is difficult to define emergency medical care precisely. Definitions of emergency medical care vary over time, even in the same country. During the May–June 1975 strike (in California and New York State) by anesthesiologists against the very high increases in malpractice premiums, the definition of "emergency" varied among hospitals. However, "in most hospitals, 'emergencies' [were] defined by the doctors as life-or-death cases. Cancer patients, fracture victims, have had to be transferred to public hospitals or have their surgery deferred."[36] The AMA's House of Delegates voted, in June 1975, to expand "the degree of care they would provide patients during a walkout from 'emergency and urgently needed medical care' to . . . doctors would not 'jeopardize the medical care of their patients.'" They also voted to retain the provision that each physician has an "inalienable right" to decide " 'the circumstances in which he can and cannot continue to practice his profession.' "[37]

Emergency medical services have been defined very broadly for reimbursement purposes under Medi-Cal, California's Medicaid program for the poor. California regulations say that emergency medical care is that which is "required for alleviation of severe pain or immediate diagnosis and treatment of unforeseen medical conditions which, if not immediately diagnosed and treated, would lead to disability or death."[38] The head of Medi-Cal at the time this policy was made was a physician. Despite the broader definition under Medi-Cal than under private health insurance contracts, there has not been (to my knowledge) any legal test decided in the courts of whether an individual's right to medical care was abrogated during the 1975 strike.

There are state laws in California and Illinois which require public or tax-supported hospitals to supply emergency care. California statutory law requires all licensed hospitals which maintain and operate emergency care facilities to provide emergency care for any person in danger of losing his or her life. The Illinois law is broader, covering severe injury or serious illness. Federal law requires that hospitals that received tax stipends under the Hill-Burton Act of 1946 must provide medical care to the poor. The federal government tried to enforce this during the period of 1971–74 price controls. Although most hospital bills of the poor are paid by Medicaid, not all hospitals readily accept the poor who apply. This is because, under Medicaid, provider reimbursement is almost always a lesser percentage of costs than under Medicare, commercial insurers, or Blue Cross.

Under the equal protection clause of the Fourteenth Amendment, state and lower federal courts have held that hospitals which have received state and/or federal money must deliver health care to the poor, despite the fact that the poor are a "suspect classification." The United States Supreme Court, however, has not accepted this reasoning. A "right to life" argument based on equal protection has also been used to support the right to basic emergency medical needs. This argument charges the government with failure to provide "due process" in cases where an indigent person dies from lack of medical care. However, again this is not a legally accepted argument.

Heart transplants that were unknown only a short time ago today save lives. Is this expensive medical procedure, of which 213 had been performed by mid-1981 at Stanford University Medical Center, accepted emergency medical care? Do heart transplants belong in the category of experimental, research medicine? Some may accept the procedure as established therapeutic treatment but object to the use of about $100,000 worth of scarce medical resources to benefit primarily one individual when alternative uses of those resources may help hundreds of other people.

There was no legal right to a heart transplant in the United States in 1980. An administrative regulation of the Department of Health, Education, and Welfare permitted payment for a large part of the costs for heart transplant patients performed by Stanford University Medical Center during a few months in 1979. As of this writing, this policy is being reviewed.

As medical technology improves and public opinion concomitantly changes, experimental treatments gradually become accepted as good medical practice. In 1972, a legal right to kidney transplants was created by Congress, which provided reimbursement under Medicare. Individuals in the United States with renal failure thus have a "right" to receive such a transplant, subject to the medical realities and the availability of a compatible donor kidney, irrespective of financial ability to pay for it. This is not true in some other countries.

At times, some costly medical procedures have been used without proof of their efficacy. Scientific, hard data about the benefits and costs of surgery are only recently appearing in the medical literature. Here, as in controlled trials of new drugs, the studies do not always agree and the numbers involved are often too small for reliable conclusions. There are many controversial issues about the efficacy of some medical procedures, and the public should not assume that all medical intervention even of an emergency nature is beneficial. The comparative records of different trauma or specialized emergency care centers that handle most accident victims (accidents are the primary cause of early death) vary greatly, as measured by lives saved.

Insurance companies that can be liable for the high costs of new technologies are likely to view them as experimental for a longer period than they would less costly care. If the federal government does not pay for organ transplants under Medicare, private insurers are likely also to exclude these procedures from reimbursement coverage. Governments that might have to pay high permanent disability benefits in lieu of the costs of some transplants may favor payment for the latter because in the long run they are less costly for the governments.

Emergency medical care can be defined strictly or broadly. If a broad definition is adopted, the right of medical care providers to practice where and as much as they please may be affected. If all types of medical care were a right, what percentage of the GNP should be allocated in order to make that "right" effective? All health expenses are already absorbing close to 10 percent of the GNP in the United States. Would a 15 percent level that would require higher taxes cause the GNP to fall? The level of taxation to support even the 40 percent financed by government is sizeable. Increases in taxation levels to support government financing of all kinds of health care would sharpen the conflict between moral rights that have not yet become legal rights and already-determined legal rights.

There is no common law practice which requires a physician to treat a person in need of emergency care unless the physician created the circumstances from which relief is sought. Others argue that in return for licensure, which in each of the fifty states restricts the practice of medicine to only those who are licensed, the physician should be required to perform emergency medical care. The argument is strengthened because individuals' taxes may have provided a considerable part of the physician's education. The person seeking care is likely to have paid taxes that are compulsory levies.

Although in practice the legal right to medical care, broadly defined, is restrained because many individuals are unwilling to vote to pay taxes to supply all forms of medical care to everyone in the United

States, Medicaid gives to the poor a statutory right to medical care. There are also some legal decisions which in recent years have supported a limited concept of a right to broadly defined medical care for the poor. Once a hospital accepts an injured person as a patient, it has a duty to provide "reasonable care."[39] The Supreme Court of Delaware held that a private hospital which maintains an emergency ward has a duty to determine whether or not an "unmistakable emergency exists."[40] The court argued that the patient relied on a previously established availability of emergency services and if he had sought help elsewhere the patient might further worsen his condition in view of the time lost during the refusal process. However, the court also stated that "a private hospital is under no legal obligation to the public to maintain an emergency ward."[41] Since then, other courts have used this "reliance" argument, in some instances, to cover more than life-or-death care. To the degree that there is a common law duty to provide emergency care for indigent patients, all persons have, in effect, a positive "right" to emergency medical care.

III. SUPPLY OF
MEDICAL CARE

Over the last two decades, government decisions have become increasingly important for the United States health industry. Government legislation and regulations have increased the supply of health personnel and, until 1974, the supply of hospital beds as well. Since 1966, government cost-reimbursement of medical expense through Medicare and Medicaid has increased the effective demand for health services beyond what it would have been in the absence of these programs. Further, assured payment has encouraged the rapid diffusion of new and costly medical technology. Cost-reimbursement rewards, not penalizes, inefficient hospital administrators and encourages them to make unwarranted expenditures, whether the costs are reimbursed by government or private insurers. Because cost-reimbursement is now so pervasive, it cannot be eliminated without denying the poor and low income persons access to medical care. Thus, government regulations have multiplied to mitigate the effect. As the supply of health providers increases, higher costs are reimbursed, resulting in an upward spiral.

This chapter discusses the relationship between the supply of resources in the health sector and the expansion in demand. Medicare and Medicaid became effective in mid-1966. Total personal health care expenditures paid by the government surged from 21 percent in 1965 to 33 percent in 1967, and to over 40 percent in 1980.

Contrary to popular belief, the suppliers' responses to the growing demand have been significant. In 1977, 6.3 million workers, over 6 percent of the labor force, were employed in the health field as compared with 2.8 million in 1966, the year Medicare and Medicaid were passed. Most people are surprised that "health sector employees are the second largest employee group—after local government employees—in the United States."[1] For several years there has been a continuous increase in the numbers of allied health personnel and the kinds of tasks they do: x-ray technicians, physical therapists, nurses (registered and practical), licensed vocational nurses, radiology and clinical laboratory technicians, inhalation therapists, and others. In 1950 there were only 30,800 radiology technicians, but by 1960 there were over 60,000 and in 1976 over 100,000. In 1950 there were 218 registered nurses per 100,000 population; 364 in 1970, 448 in 1975, and 521 in 1979. Registered nurses working full time have more than doubled since 1960 while those working part time have tripled.[2] Physical therapists increased from 4,600 in 1950 to over 32,100 in 1976.[3] One hundred twenty-six medical schools are graduating about 16,000 new doctors annually, the largest number in United States history. However, since 1950 the number of physicians has increased less than 40 percent while the number of nurses has increased 140 percent. There are nearly 450,000 professionally active physicians, including nearly 30,000 interns and residents, and about 1.5 million registered nurses. The change in manpower mix reflects primarily the rapid changes in hospital technology. As technology becomes more complex and specialized, a larger number of more highly trained hospital personnel are required per patient. In 1951, less than 20 percent of non-profit hospitals with 100 beds or more had intensive care recovery rooms; by 1974, 66 percent did. Of hospitals with 300 beds or more, 90 percent had diagnostic radioisotope facilities as early as the 1960s.

The spread of this new technology, as with most others, has been more rapid in large hospitals than in smaller hospitals with fewer beds. Hospitals have adopted new medical techniques rapidly even though sometimes little substantiation of their cost-effectiveness exists. By 1978, the number of full-time equivalent employees per patient in non-federal, short-term, community hospitals was 3.79 as compared with 2.26 in 1960.[4] Some of the new medical technology substitutes sensitive electronic monitoring equipment for personnel, but most of the new technology requires more personnel for effective operation. The increased complexity of the new technology requires new categories of specialized personnel, each to perform a special function. The technical personnel are licensed by the states to perform only limited tasks. Their licensure, in some states' accreditation, has increased the rigidity of the manpower structure and costs of hospitals. Only large hospitals can keep such a broad spectrum of full-time technical personnel busy.

ARE THERE ENOUGH DOCTORS?

The much-touted projections of a severe shortage of physicians in the United States by 1970 were wrong. In 1959, the Bane Committee had projected that there would be a shortage of 30,000 physicians in 1965.[5] By 1979, 20 years later, there had been a two-thirds increase in the number of active physicians.

A careful analysis made as early as 1970 explains the projection error as follows:

> This came about because more graduates were produced than has been anticipated, fewer physicians retired, and the inflow of foreign physicians into the U.S. continued to increase. . . .
> The adjusted projections of changes in requirements and supplies proved to be almost 20 percent too low over a period of only six years.[6]

There were over 15,000 graduates of medical schools in 1979 as compared with 8,367 in 1970 and 7,409 in 1965. It is estimated that by 1983, 16,500 new MDs will graduate annually from U.S. medical schools. In 1980, there were 125 medical schools; in 1975, 114; while in 1965, only 88. Many of the schools have expanded the size of their classes. The number of full-time medical school faculty increased from 26,504 in 1971 to 44,762 in 1978. The student to faculty ratio has declined from 1.5 to 1.3. Medical education has become increasingly expensive and is subsidized by federal and state governments.

The inflow of foreign-trained physicians has been continuing, but at a lower rate. By 1976, foreign-trained physicians comprised 21 percent of all practicing physicians as compared with only 12 percent in 1963.[7] Whereas in 1965 only 10 percent of physicians immigrating into the U.S. were from Asian countries, by 1980, 70 percent were. Because the number of first-year positions available for residency training is far greater than the annual number of United States medical school graduates, foreign-trained MDs were needed for staffing. However, by 1977 foreign medical school graduates filled only 18 percent of these vacancies as compared with 33 percent in 1970, and today those foreigners permitted to take resident training here must return to their country of origin upon completion of their training.

There are 10,000 to 12,000 Americans enrolled in medical schools abroad. They must have two years of clinical training in the U.S. in order to get a license. Control over the numbers of foreign-trained physicians permitted to practice in the U.S. has been influenced by the organized bodies of the existing members of the profession through their own programs and by lobbying Congress.

The rapid expansion in the supply of physicians in the United States occurred primarily because of direct federal government subsidization of medical schools. Under the 1971 Health Manpower Act, effective until June 30, 1974, medical schools received per capita federal grants. From fiscal 1974 until fiscal 1978, federal monies for health manpower programs were cut back; however, in 1976–77, 32.4

percent of the revenues of medical schools, or almost $1.3 billion, came from the federal government in the form of grants and contracts. An additional $1.4 billion in government funds was spent for all types of health training and education.[8] This amount increased to $1.7 billion in fiscal 1977, but was estimated to be $1.6 billion annually in the 1978–79 period of rapid inflation.[9]

A proposed repayment provision for medical students who had received government tuition aid was opposed in the late 1970s by would-be students, physicians, and especially the medical schools. Together they created enough pressure to kill the payback proposal. The bill (PL 94-484), finally signed into law by President Gerald Ford in October 1976, had authorized a total of $2.3 billion for three fiscal years (1978–80). It contained a modified version to expand the hospital residency training program and the number of primary care placements. It increased the scholarship programs for students who agreed to practice in a medically under-served area after graduation. The bill required that medical schools reserve third-year places for qualified U.S. students who had completed two years at a foreign school and who wanted to complete their training in the United States. Many medical schools objected to the latter provision, claiming that the law violated their academic freedom to select their own students. As a result, the law was modified in Fall 1977 to limit its effect to one academic year, 1978–79, rather than for three years, through 1980–81, to reduce the percentage by which schools were to expand their third-year classes, and to remove restrictions on the academic standards which the schools apply for admitting transfer students. Medicare and Medicaid payments for the services of physician assistants and general nurse practitioners in rural clinics and in a limited number of under-served urban areas were authorized, thus helping to increase the supply of medical providers in these areas.

Congress recessed in 1980 without passing a health manpower bill with respect to loans to medical and other health care students, grants to the schools that train them, or scholarship monies for those who would serve in the National Health Service Corps. The latter program, almost ten years old, has somewhat eased the shortages in rural areas as those who receive scholarships must serve a few years as federally employed physicians assigned to physician-short areas.

The bill (HR 7203) that passed the House in September 1980 clearly signaled an end to a federal policy of educating more physicians but supported continuing the National Health Service Corps and some per capitation grants to the schools. There is considerable congressional support for increasing federal support not only to the minority health professional schools, but all schools in which minorities enroll in health programs. Whereas Blacks are about 12 percent of the population, only 1.7 percent of physicians and 1.8 percent of dentists are black. Medical care is an intensely personal service and, although white physicians serve black patients, there are those who believe that more black physicians are needed.

The Reagan Administration has proposed a 40 percent targeted cut, 1982–86, of federal support from the Carter Administration's 1982 budget and would continue to train primarily registered nurses and the minorities who are under-represented, especially among physicians. Whether registered nurses are in short supply in an economic sense is debatable. Many who are trained leave nursing to take higher paying, higher status jobs with more convenient hours and less stress. Most economists point to the great increase in nurses' other occupational opportunities that have developed since 1969–70. It is data for that year that is often used to support the theory of "shortage" in the sense that higher wages and higher status will not result in sufficient supply, and hospital staff vacancies will continue over long periods. Over the past ten years, times have changed. If wages of registered nurses rise sufficiently, men will be increasingly attracted to this field, and some of the already trained nurses who have left the profession will return. The Department of Health and Human Services (HHS) has estimated that, over the 1950–90 period, "by far the greatest increase in supply will have been attained by registered nurses, with more than a four-fold increase."[10] Medical doctors will approach a three-fold increase.

In 1978, federal research funds were only 19 percent of all federal contracts and grants to medical schools, compared with one-third in 1968. Federal dollars for research, teaching, and training accounted for about 50 percent of all medical school revenues in 1968, but for only 32 percent in 1978.[11] A career in research and administration attracts some younger doctors who might otherwise become practicing physicians. Between 1963 and 1967, the number of physicians in teaching, administration, and research (both government and private) increased by 5,000 and the number of physicians in federal service increased by 6,000.[12] However, between 1968 and 1974, the number of physicians working for the federal government declined by 2,000. This downward trend continued into 1976 when 8 percent of all the active physicians worked for the federal government. Although federal money for health-related research in the public sector has been declining, the number of physicians holding administrative positions in government has been increasing. This reflects the increasing federal government regulation of the health sector, a trend expected to be reversed by the Reagan Administration.

State governments have been reducing the number of psychiatric beds in long-term hospitals during the past fifteen years, primarily because the use of prescription tranquilizers has permitted outpatient treatment of many mental patients who previously would have been hospitalized. This fact alone should have resulted in fewer physicians being hired for patient care by the state governments, but the decrease from this source has been more than offset by an increase in the number of physicians hired to administer state and local health programs.

In 1979, there was one physician for every 550 persons in the United States, or 1.85 physicians per 1,000 population.[13] About 80 percent of U.S. physicians are specialists. HHS has projected a rapid increase in the number of physicians relative to the population so that by 1990 there will be one physician for every 409 persons, or nearly 2.5 physicians per 1,000 population.[14] There is considerable geographic variation in the ratio of physicians to population. Physicians tend to settle in disproportionately high numbers in large metropolitan areas. In 1974, when there was 1.5 physicians per 1,000 population nationwide, there were 2.4 in New York and only 0.8 in South Dakota.[15]

One economist, using the assumption that maintaining the net income of physicians is probable, commented in 1974:

> If income were, say, $45,000 after professional expenses, then the ratio of roughly 300 physicians per 100,000 population proposed by Gerber would require an annual budget allocation of roughly $500 per family of four just to maintain physicians at their customary station in life. The true budget cost would, of course, be higher still, for in addition to the physician's desired net income, his professional expenses (office space, equipment, and automobile) must be ultimately borne by consumers as well.[16]

It is not money alone, however, that attracts physicians to urban rather than rural areas, or explains their tendency to practice specialties rather than primary care. Physicians and their families are attracted to the greater cultural opportunities of cities, and most physicians prefer the better-equipped large, urban hospital to a small, rural hospital. The Carter Administration's 1980 budget increased funds for rural clinics and for those urban clinics originally established in 1971 in under-served areas.[17] However, no nation has been able to overcome the rural/urban maldistribution imbalance.

The financing of medical care by the federal government without geographical mandates cannot solve the problem of rural/urban distribution of medical services. Within the United States, an increasing surplus of physicians may result in a decline but not elimination of the discrepancy between the urban and rural areas. West Germany, Denmark, and Israel have about two physicians per 1,000 population, which is very similar to that in the United States in the 1980s.

The increase in supply of physicians has created incentives for physicians to decrease the rural/urban and generalist/specialist maldistributions. For example, because the ratio of specialists to general practitioners is increasing rapidly, more specialists are acting as general practitioners. During 1973–76, 62 percent of internist, 65 percent of obstetrician-gynecologist, 58 percent of cardiologist, and 53 percent of rheumatologist visits were conducted by physicians acting in a primary care capacity. In addition, some rural areas are becoming suburbs, and some surplus physicians are moving out of the crowded metropolitan areas to the suburbs. The movement out of the cities that have a high number of physicians relative to the population appears to be growing. Young physicians who do not want to join a group practice cannot make a living in those cities. Additionally, semirural areas near large cities may offer better schooling and general living conditions, greater opportunities for outdoor living, and still permit easy commuting to the theater and the greater variety of restaurants that large cities offer. Still lacking in many rural areas, however, are specialized medical facilities and equipment. The increasing cost of gasoline may deter a continuation of this movement, but the increasing competition among physicians in many cities probably will offset the latter factor.

It is difficult to make an estimate of the future supply of and demand for physicians because of the multiplicity of variables that have to be projected. Most countries have predominantly government-financed or government-provided medical care. Even the countries that have centralized the delivery of medical care decisions have difficulty in making these estimates. In the United States, the National Science Foundation has had little success in estimating the supply and demand for other kinds of scientists, and the obstacles confronting forecasts of physician supply and demand are more complex than for the more theoretical scientist.[18]

A policy that uses a single ratio of physicians to population throughout the United States and makes that ratio equal to that existing in the locality where one physician serves the lowest number of persons anywhere in the nation would result in neverending expansion. Because physicians are not perfect substitutes for each other since they are becoming ever more specialized, and because the United States is so large and diverse, it is impossible to declare that there is a physician surplus or shortage nationwide that would have equal meaning throughout the country. An annual statistical index based on various measures of waiting by patients for appointments in physicians' offices might eliminate some of the guesswork, but whether it would be worth the cost is debatable. The concept that there is an optimum ratio of primary care physicians, or of all physicians to the population, implies a value judgment about medical needs.

The supply of manpower has responded to demand in the classical sense in the health sector in general as well as in the area of medical care services. This has occurred despite monopolistic practices by suppliers, such as licensure and professional trade union-type associations' efforts. The response occurred despite the federal government's regulation of medical care prices in the period 1971–74. The law of supply and demand works to a considerable degree in the health services market even though the demand is not wholly independent of the supply.

By 1976, there was a general consensus that no overall shortage of medical personnel existed and that some specialists, such as the general surgeon, are actually in over-supply. The AMA recommended in 1977 that "there should be no new efforts to increase the number of medical school graduates until such time as necessity for change is clearly evident."[19] The percentage of specialty board certificates issued for "primary care" specialties (internal medicine, pediatrics, and family practice) has increased substantially in the past ten years from 23.3 percent in 1966 to 45.3 percent in 1976. At the same time, the percentage of certificates issued for general surgery decreased from 44.3 percent to 26.3 percent.[20] Although the type of specialty board certification does not precisely reflect the nature of medical care given by clinical specialists who are certified, the trend indicates renewed interest by physicians in the delivery of primary care and a recent decline in the number of general surgeons, a category that is clearly in over-supply in 1980. Specialists are increasingly providing primary care. Non-physician providers, midwives, nurse practitioners, and others have begun to compete in independent primary care practice in response to consumer demand for more personal, less fragmented, and less costly medical care.

Legislation has also contributed to the increasing trend to primary care practice. Following the establishment by the AMA in 1970 of the new specialty "General Family Practice," Congress passed the Comprehensive Health Manpower Training Act of 1971 (PL 92-157) that authorized federal funds through June 30, 1974, to help hospitals and medical schools provide professional and technical training in family medicine. The Health Professions Educational Assistance Act of 1976 stressed the training of primary care physicians and their equitable numeric distribution. The Act required that by July 1977, 35 percent of all graduate students in university-affiliated, first-year residencies be enrolled in a primary care specialty. The schools that failed to comply would lose grant monies.

Although in September 1980 the U.S. House of Representatives passed a scaled-down version ($2.3 billion, 1981–83) of scholarships and grants for students and colleges in the various medical professions, the Senate, which had acted earlier, and the Carter Administration had substantial disagreement. The latter would have ended capitation grants entirely and eliminated most federal aid to nursing schools. Nursing graduates had increased substantially, but salaries and working conditions are such that a high percentage leave nursing for other jobs. It is anticipated that the more conservative 1981 Senate will pass a considerably less costly health manpower bill as selective cuts are made in the Reagan Administration's austerity program.

In only six years, 1970–76, the number of physician primary care residencies in hospitals increased from 290 to 4675.[21] An American Medical Association publication carries the statement that

> . . . there is no question that the tide has turned in favor of primary care, and if preliminary reports of the percentage of medical students indicating family practice as choice of specialty is meaningful, this deficit in the U.S. health care system is well on its way to being remedied.[22]

Some people point out that there will always be a shortage of physicians, albeit in a statistical sense. Physicians can and do create, to a degree, the demand for their services by telling their patients whether and how often to return for further treatment, by controlling decisions over the number and kinds of medical procedures used, and by deciding who is to perform the procedures. Estimates of the percentage of the demand for their services that physicians influence range from 60 percent to 90 percent. Often cited in 1980 as evidence of physician influence on demand is the 176 percent increase in the rate of Caesarean section (C-Section) deliveries from 5.5 in 1970 to 15.2 in 1978 per 100 live births.[23] This rapid increase is defended by some as evidence of higher quality care (infant mortality rates have fallen), but by others is criticized as primarily a result of the higher reimbursement of C-sections over natural delivery births. Higher surgical fees and longer hospital stays occur. However, C-section rates have increased in other countries where fee-for-service practice does not dominate. The regional variations in the percentage rise in the rate corresponds to the considerable regional variations of other surgical rates and length of hospital stays. However, there is no definitive analysis that explains these regional variations within the United States.

At current medical care prices and with more than 60 percent of the bills being paid by third parties, individuals' demands for physicians' services are being met in the United States without appreciable queueing. However, statistical data on queueing for all types of medical care are difficult to find. Several studies on waiting have appeared in the academic literature. Some are case studies, others are analyses of the 1973 AMA data base, and still others are descriptions of interview responses by a sample of patients and physicians about the time spent waiting in physicians' offices. The American Medical Association analyses of 1973 data[24] report that the average waiting time in physicians' offices was 22.6 minutes. The longest average waiting time was 30 minutes in the offices of general family practitioners and the shortest average waiting time was five minutes—predictably, in the offices of psychiatrists. The data support the belief that if there is a shortage of physicians by types of practice, it is in the area of primary care and suggest that "greater availability of examining rooms tends to increase average patient waiting time to see a physician, such longer waiting time possibly taking place within the examining rooms themselves."[25]

Technical analyses of the data confirm what many have believed without evidence, namely, "women and persons over 65 wait longer periods before seeing a physician" and that "whites tend to be kept waiting less."[26] To these, the AMA data also add persons at younger ages with average family incomes under $15,000 and Medicaid eligibility.[27] Physician characteristics that are correlated with increased waiting time for patients are: non-certified board status, over 49 years old, relatively low fees, and relatively high weekly workloads. Obviously, these variables are interrelated.

In order to evaluate whether the amount of waiting time might indicate a shortage or surplus of physicians, one needs a measure of the time each patient must wait for an appointment in addition to time actually spent waiting in a physician's office.[28] However, without trend data and in the absence of a resource cost price,[29] it is a value judgment to assess an average of one hour or one-half hour wait in a physician's office, or an average two-month or one-week wait for an appointment with a specialist as indicative of a shortage of physicians and/or specialists. In prepaid group practice or Health Maintenance Organizations (HMOs) where there is, by definition, no price identifiable by the consumer for any specific service, waiting for an appointment may be used to structure demand. By increasing the time, HMOs may consciously curtail demand for their medical services and ration demand for specialists until they have enough backlog to warrant hiring an additional physician. The longer the wait, the more likely persons will use physicians elsewhere and thus reduce the HMO's costs. The longer the wait for an appointment, *ceteris paribus*, the higher is the real cost of medical care. The latter includes the patient's psychic costs of anxiety and possible development of medical complications that might have been allayed by prompt attention by a physician.

In general, economists believe that the quality of medical care declines when long waits are required, either in the physician's office or for an appointment. To argue that a two-hour office wait for high quality care is medically preferable, and thus should be preferred by the consumer to a five-minute wait for a somewhat lower level of quality care, is to ignore the patient's alternative uses of time. Similarly, to argue that a two-month wait for an appointment with a better-trained specialist over a less qualified person yields automatically higher quality care ignores the patient's belief that he needs urgent medical care and thus increases his anxiety costs. In cases of long waits, there may develop adverse psychological effects that may change the nature of the patient-physician relationship.

There are both time costs and money costs, and they may be substitutes for each other. Increasingly in the United States, time costs are allocating medical care. The public generally believes that the higher the money price of medical care, the higher the quality of medical care. Many physicians believe that this relationship holds for time costs as well as money costs. They rationalize that people are willing to wait longer, or pay more, for higher quality care. But, if some illnesses have psychosomatic aspects, long waits *per se* can reduce whatever quality improvement that might have existed. High money prices do not have this negative aspect. Access to care can be allocated by either device.

The increasing demand for medical care traditionally delivered by physicians has created pressure to train physician extenders to deliver primary care, help in emergency rooms of hospitals, and perform some of the support functions that physicians have usually handled.

Increasing demand has also encouraged the establishment of multi-phasic screening units run by technicians and the development of consumer health education to aid would-be patients in finding the most suitable sources of medical care and to increase their use of self-care.

A higher degree of specialization may mean better scientific medicine, but it also may mean a decrease in the art of medicine because of the greater fragmentation of care and considerable patient confusion. Specialization *per se* does not ensure higher quality.

There is some evidence that every consumer does not prefer costly, specialized medical care in all circumstances. Where no life-saving emergency is involved, some consumers may prefer lower cost, impersonal, and generally more spartan medical care to high cost, luxury care. In the extreme circumstance of impending death from irreversible causes, a patient may prefer not to accept the advanced medical techniques that will prolong life at a high cost in both physical suffering and dollars.

An over-supply of physicians raises the question of whether there is over-doctoring. Professor Eli Ginsburg, a manpower specialist, comments that "given the alternatives of high average earnings for a taut supply of physicians versus a loose supply, lower fees, and over-doctoring, I opt unequivocally for the first."[30] Over-doctoring is already taking place and with high fees. Effective peer review by physicians of their colleagues from whom they may get referrals is difficult to achieve. It is naive to believe that colleagues, even in prepaid group practice where dependence on referrals is *de minimus*, will be as critical of each other's performance as they might be. Here, as in many areas of health services, better consumer education is sorely needed. Consumer ignorance is a major cause of the over-utilization of medical care resources.

A striking example in 1980 has been the advocacy by some physicians of "preventive mastectomies" for women who have benign cystic fibrosis breast disease. During the twenty-five years prior to 1980, radical mastectomies were often performed without first determining whether the cancer had spread making it unlikely that an operation would be beneficial. The patient was, and is, not always fully informed of the benefits and costs, including risks of alternative treatments. California law, as of January 1981, requires that this information be given in cases of breast cancer. Several physicians have observed that if the reimbursement rate for a radical were the same as for a modified radical mastectomy, the U.S. rate per 1,000 for the radical (Halstead) mastectomy would have dropped when the early British evidence indicated that it had no greater efficacy than a modified radical mastectomy. A needle aspiration instead of a biopsy (which is more painful) has been largely ignored in cases of suspected breast cancer in the United States.

Yet the paternalism of some physicians in respect to their women patients persists even into 1981. On May 19, 1981, KRON-TV (San Francisco) aired an interview with several physicians, most of whom agreed that they treat an otherwise "healthy, unsuspecting" wife whose husband has "gonorrhea through an extramarital affair" without letting that woman know that she is in the initial stages of an infectious disease that can, in its advanced stage, make her "crippled for the rest of her life." The assessment of the seriousness of the disease was made on the television program by Samuel Sherman, M.D., head of the California American Medical Association's Judiciary Committee. An urologist, Daniel Neustein, M.D., defended his placing greater importance on the existing marriage relationship with "It is my decision and her husband's decision." Irwin Braff, M.D., head of the Infectious Disease Department of Public Health (California), stated, "Now the patient, I would think, has the right to decide how much she wants to know about her disease," and then elaborated: "She is told she has been exposed to a communicable or infectious disease that her husband has. I mean, you have got to tell her something. And I think she should have that choice, of living her fantasy that her husband really isn't cheating on her." Robert Rowland, chairman of California's Board of Medical Quality Assurance, protested: "Personally I find that to be both paternalistic and manipulative." He implied, and Dr. Sherman stated, that "legal liabilities" on the part of physicians who do not tell the truth about diagnoses exist.[31]

Productivity and Supply

A 10 percent average increase in the productivity of workers equals a 10 percent increase in their numbers. Evidence indicates that the productivity of physicians has been increasing in many areas of medicine because of new drugs, new medical techniques, and the increasing use of different kinds of substitute, allied health personnel who are less expensive to train and whose services, to a degree, replace the services provided by the physicians. The productivity of physicians is difficult, if not impossible, to measure accurately. A considerable part of the new medical technology may increase life expectancy but may not cure a disease, and sometimes may not result in a level of activity that will permit a patient to work or even leave bed. Reassurance that a patient does not have a suspected disease is often of great value. Medical tests and procedures may have been used, but there is no change in outcomes of either life expectancy or relief from pain or other symptoms except that uncertainty has been eliminated. How can productivity be measured accurately when the output cannot be measured? Here, as in other service industries, the units of inputs consumed may be substituted. This is admittedly not a precise measure.

The economist is interested in what is produced in response to consumers' wishes. Common measures of medical productivity are: hospital days, physician visits, surgical procedures, number of x-rays, etc. These are intermediate products of varying usefulness that tell little about the final product of improved health. The data are often uncorrected and misinterpreted. "Hospital days" may include emergency room visits. Hospital days are used because the records are easily obtainable. However, they do not measure the end product of health levels, sick or well, or outcomes of life or death. The goal of medical care is not to produce hospital days and physician visits, but to improve health.

Physician Extenders (Reimbursement and Utilization)[32]

If the use of physician assistants (PAs) and general nurse practitioners were not so limited by licensure requirements initiated by the AMA, substitution by less expensively trained labor might have resulted in lower costs of medical care and, as a result, prices would have risen less rapidly. The AMA imposed its examination of this category of health worker in December 1974. The substitution of cheaper labor did not occur because of physician-controlled entry, which restricts the supply of allied health workers, and also because of the AMA's general rule that the price charged to the consumer or patient should be related to the service provided and not to the level of training of the provider. If this practice is strictly followed throughout the medical manpower ladder, it rules out maximum potential cost-savings to the consumer in the form of lower prices from the use of medical assistants (trained in six weeks) to give injections that Licensed Practical Nurses (LPNs) or Licensed Vocational Nurses (LVNs), trained in twelve months, used to give. Similarly, savings from LVNs performing services that Registered Nurses (RNs), with three years training, once performed are not realized. These examples could be extended throughout the manpower ladder of medicine.

Potential savings from the substitution of lesser trained and less costly health workers for the more highly trained and more costly professional could offer a way to deliver a given quantity of medical care assumed to be of the same quality (an assumption discussed below) at costs rising less rapidly than the average rate of inflation. Who benefits from the savings that would be created by the use of less costly labor inputs depends on several factors. The established suppliers of medical services such as physicians, HMOs, and hospitals may realize higher returns as a result of lower operating costs. The savings may go to patients in the form of lower prices or greater availability of more expensive medical technology. Third party payers, private insurers and the government, who in total pay three-fourths of the personal health bill, may also benefit from the substitution of less expensive labor. If the government benefits, the taxpayers may benefit. One way to contain Medicare and Medicaid costs is to encourage greater use of less expensively trained providers who can be directly reimbursed. This would make the medical care market more competitive.

Reduction of costs by the substitution of less expensive labor is usually accomplished by subdividing the professional's job into component tasks. Thus, a less skilled individual may perform one or more of the simpler tasks which are part of the more complex function of the professional. Labor inputs which substantiate the title of "professional" include training, native intelligence, experience, and judgment. These constitute a package of health skills so that the function performed cannot always be diluted into specialized tasks that can be delegated to less well-trained personnel with the assurance that quality will be maintained without being monitored.

How to maintain quality and contain costs involves questions of degree, and is an issue of continuing debate. Some believe that, in the health sector, direct supervision by a top professional is always necessary to maintain quality. Others argue that many tasks can be performed independently by someone other than a physician or a dentist because referral of a patient to the professional is always an option. If quality can be maintained without supervision, savings are obviously greater. The probability that the consumer will benefit from lower prices rather than the supplier from higher profits is greater when there is independent practice by labor substitutes. From society's point of view, a danger in containing costs through the substitution of less well-trained labor is that the quality of care may decrease and, given the current state of the art of quality control of services, the decline may not be detected.

The Colorado Nurse Practice Act of January 1, 1974, permits the independent "practice of professional nursing as the diagnosing and treating of human responses to actual or potential health problems." That Act has resulted in relatively low fee schedules by some corporations of nurses. For example, Creative Health Services, Inc., charged $16 per hour in 1974. On the other hand, a survey of general practitioners who employ PAs in rural northern California indicates that each of the eighteen physicians surveyed in 1974 charged the same fee regardless of whether the physician or assistant performed the service.[33] This is standard AMA practice. In December 1974, the AMA established an examination for the "physician's assistant," giving rise to the apt title of a paper, "The Importance of an Apostrophe," delivered in New York in 1975 at the American Association for the Advancement of Science meetings.

The physician's productivity or output per manhour is usually measured by the number of office visits, but these are not necessarily adjusted for the type of visits. There are initial office visits and followup office visits. These may be subdivided further into "brief," "routine," and "prolonged" office visits. The 1974 California Medical Association's (CMA) "Relative Value Schedules" use the terms "minimal, brief, limited, intermediate, extended comprehensive, unusually complex" to describe physician visits, further subdivided on the basis of whether the visit was made by a new or a long-time patient. An increase in the variety of visits for pricing was induced by federal price controls in 1971–74. The upgrading of a visit into a higher paid category is an effective method of technically "complying" while permitting actual charges to rise.

Since the usual productivity measure—the number of visits—does not recognize any qualifiers, productivity can be statistically increased without an increase in the units of labor input by the physician by simply reducing the average number of minutes per visit. Most observers believe that a reduction in office visit time, *ceteris paribus*, reduces the quality of care. Although productivity measured by the number of visits may increase, a drop in quality may offset it. Physicians differ in their abilities and training, and even with their patient case mix held constant, the quality of health care delivered cannot be judged solely by the average number of minutes each physician spends with a patient.

In the health sector, assurance of a given level of quality is virtually impossible. Quality control is usually sought through licensure and accreditation, that is, through control of labor inputs rather than through direct control of the quality of the service that the labor produces. Measures of health outcomes such as mortality, morbidity, or sickness and days of disability are not directly related to medical care inputs. Quality tracer controls depend on whether the prescribed tests and procedures that are monitored are optimally effective in diagnosis and treatment. The use of selected procedures as an optimum against which the quality of actual medical practice is measured is still in its infancy. Government-mandated Professional Standards Review Organizations (PSROs) have primarily used the practice profiles of physicians to find large deviations from the average utilization rates. PSRO *optima* are usually applied only to in-hospital and not ambulatory care.

There is no agreement on which of the great variety of tasks, each requiring different skill levels, can be performed by new health workers (child health associate, general nurse practitioner,[34] surgical associate, MEDEX, physician assistant, etc.) without any loss in quality. The first training programs for these types of workers began in 1965 with Duke University's program for PAs and the University of Colorado's program for child health associates. The functions that have gradually become recognized as ones that can be delegated include patients' health histories, triage of walk-ins, handling minor emergencies, routine checkups for well-baby care, and caring for patients with chronic diseases or terminal illnesses. There is no agreement on the degree of supervision that physician extenders require, but there is agreement that referral by physician extenders to a physician should always be an option.

The functions overlap between the new and the established occupations at all levels of the medical hierarchy. Registered nurses seem especially threatened by the different types of specialized licensed vocational nurses placed below them and by the PAs placed, in terms of economic rewards, above them. Unlike the situation in the industrial sector, an established manpower ladder permitting promotions does not exist in the health sector.

An overall assessment of the savings resulting from the substitution of the less well-trained for the better-trained health personnel is difficult until we have better data on who does what, what the commonly accepted measures of units of output are, and what the quality of that output is.[35] In some instances, the use of physician assistants or extenders may complement rather than substitute for physician care. It is not the lack of a measure of quality so much as the lack of a good measure of the quantity of the end product or service being produced that is the chief obstacle to an economic analysis.

The relatively few physician extenders of any type in the United States are scattered throughout the country. It is estimated that there were 12,000 nurse practitioners and 5,000 PAs in 1977.[36] The majority of all types of physician extenders are employed in primary care in the rural areas. The delegation of traditional medical tasks has been very recent and is not accepted by all physicians. The Bureau of Health Manpower's 1976–78 studies state that "the majority of adult ambulatory care office visits can be delegated safely to a nonphysician provider."[37] In pediatrics, the most commonly delegated tasks are the preventive medical care of well babies and of those with short-lived, acute illnesses such as a cold or stomach upset. These constitute 80 percent of pediatric visits. Such delegation is common in prepaid group practice where those visits are covered by the prepaid charge while, in the fee-for-service practice, insurance rarely covers children's checkups. For this reason, as well as the long-run trend of a decline in birth rates, there is a surplus of pediatricians developing along with a relative fall-off in their incomes. Kaiser-Permanente's documentation of their supervised use of non-physician providers also suggests that "80% of adult ambulatory care office visits can be delegated without detracting from the quality of care."[38]

A Canadian study of considerable interest is the "Burlington Randomized Trial of the Nurse Practitioner" that evaluates the independent or nonsupervised delivery of primary medical care by nonphysicians and physicians in a suburban town that in 1970 had 85,000 persons and only two physicians. Reports on this study that appeared in two prominent medical journals[39] indicated that nurse practitioners on the average can give about the same quality of primary care to a particular mix of cases as do general practitioners on the average. The study used both quality tracers and outcome measures. That the nurse practitioners handled two-thirds of patient episodes without consulting a physician and scored about the same as the physicians on the quality tracers suggest that, although the physicians handled the more difficult cases, substitution did not decrease the overall level of the quality of care. A comparison between the two differently treated groups of their health outcomes and their low, overall level of dissatisfaction supports this hypothesis.

Many United States studies indicate that patients accept physician extenders in supervised settings. The data on the extent to which consumers accept them as independent practitioners are limited. General nurse practitioners and midwives who perform duties independently under the nursing practice statutes, not the Medical Practice Acts, work usually in rural areas. The United States can save money not only by substituting less expensive health workers supervised by professionals, but also by permitting patients directly to hire PAs or nurse practitioners with third party reimbursement of their services at a lower price than paid by physicians for the same service.

In all the states of the United States where the licensure boards consist primarily of the professionals being licensed or competing professionals, the independent practice of medicine by PAs is prohibited. All states prohibit practice of "medicine" by anyone who is not an MD. However, the line between nursing practice and medical practice has become blurred and some physician extenders work under the Nursing Practice Acts. It has been reported that "Since 1971, 38 states have amended laws to allow nurses to diagnose, prescribe drugs, and perform other duties that were once barred to them by Medical Practice Acts."[40] These functions are beyond traditional nursing practices. Therefore they do affect the demand for physicians' services. Early in 1981, there was discussion in the California legislature about permitting registered nurses to prescribe medications. This was proposed to induce nurses to stay in their profession. Most economists argue that increasing their salaries would have more positive results.

Rigid licensure rules and union practices limit the number of persons who may perform a given function and thus drive up hospital and other institutional costs. Smaller hospitals cannot fully utilize their technical personnel when each individual is licensed to perform only a specific task. If the quality of medical services is not at issue, such restrictive practices run counter to the interests of the public. In February 1978, the federal government acted to increase competition on the supply side of the health care market by directly reimbursing personnel such as general nurse practitioners who treated Medicare patients. In 1980, federal legislation was enacted to permit Medicaid also to reimburse independently practicing nurse midwives and Medicaid and Medicare to reimburse directly optometrists and psychologists.

Federal legislation does not override the state professional practice acts and direct reimbursement of physician extenders is limited to those working in rural and selected urban areas. Costs to the consumer are lower only if the savings are passed on to the consumer, not added to the profits of the physician or the group that hires physicians.

The working environment of health workers (whether it is a hospital, group practice, physician's solo practice, or independent practice) determines in most cases whether third parties will pay for their services. Currently, about 60 percent of nurses of all types work in hospitals and less than 10 percent work in physicians' offices. Apparently, 30 percent work independently. Nurses working in a hospital or in group practice are salaried and their employers, who are responsible for their supervision, are reimbursed under Medicare, Medicaid, or by private insurers. As group practice increases, the numbers of physician assistants will increase.

If general nurse practitioners were reimbursed directly by all insurers, their use would be greatly increased. They seem especially suitable to make home care visits to the chronically ill. Legislation in 1980 dropped the prior hospitalization requirement for Medicare payment of home health care and also eliminated the limits on the number of home visits that Medicare would pay for. These are believed to be cost containment measures because they would postpone, and for some individuals eliminate, the need for nursing homes, a more expensive and less desirable option.

By 1985, there will be about 40,000 physician assistants and general nurse practitioners, and that number is likely to grow because about 250 educational programs for various types of physician extenders exist. About 15,000 nurses of all kinds are in independent practice. About 2,000 of these are midwives, some are public health nurses serving the chronically ill in their homes and the others serve the poor in health clinics. Although the new independence of the more highly educated nurses is being challenged, primarily by physicians, the upgrading of nurses for expanded roles is likely to continue in the 1980s.

Physicians, in general, tend to under-estimate the gains even from the supervised use of allied health labor. For example, recent studies using the AMA-University of Southern California data that unfortunately include secretarial-clerical workers as "allied health workers"

. . . suggest that physicians in general practice should approximately double their employment of aides, assuming physician labor input remains constant and that diversified groups should increase their employment of aides by about two-thirds, to maximize unit mark-up and by even more to maximize profits. Thus, increased utilization of allied health personnel can, for some specialties, produce significant cost savings, at least some of which are not passed along to consumers in the form of lower prices but which instead are retained by medical practices as higher unit profit.[41]

Estimates of the increase in the productivity of physicians derived from hiring additional aides range from 50 percent to 75 percent. Because the salaries of physician extenders are only about one-third of that of physicians, their cost-effectiveness after allowances for capital costs of office space and equipment and costs of supervision are substantial.

Although some specialty physicians welcome supervised physician assistants, physicians in the 1980s, in a period of physician surplus, will increasingly discourage their employment. Some prepaid group practices under-utilize PAs and many physicians state that they could delegate more tasks than they do in actuality. Kaiser-Permanente, an HMO which provides medical care to 3.7 million persons, primarily in the western areas of the United States including Hawaii and Colorado, has jointly and independently conducted research in this area. A basic study[42] of the first two years of experience of its Portland, Oregon, area facilities (July 1, 1971 to June 30, 1973) analyzes data on office visits to 50 MDs and 5 PAs in Kaiser's Portland Department of Medicine. The analysis found that 50 percent of potential savings would be lost under a state law requiring a one-to-one ratio, PA to MD. Even more restrictive would be a state requirement that the supervising physician must be physically available. If the K-P medical group had hired a PA only to reduce the physician overload in their noncomplex, primary care areas, savings in 1975 would have been (K-P estimate) $34,000.[43] K-P paid its PAs $19,576 per year in 1975. Total costs of medical care are affected by the relative value of the PA's time and the MD's time, and the latter's is worth more than twice the former's.

As more PAs are hired by a group, the returns at some point must begin to diminish. The Oregon study estimates that, with no restrictions on their use, the average annual savings would average $20,000 for each PA hired up to a total of 30. However, not all their physicians were willing, in 1975, to supervise PAs. Many physicians preferred a nurse while the others preferred a general nurse practitioner. The above estimates allow for 119 triage errors annually in non-referrals to a physician. The estimates also apparently assume a continuous growth in the demand for medical care and a continuing acceptance of PAs by consumers.

In 1975, K-P served about 18 percent of the population of Portland. The study allocates the same units of time for physicians and physician assistants to handle the various forms of office visits cross-classified by new or continuing patients' visits as follows: "walk-in" or no appointment, about 6 minutes; initial complete history, 30 minutes; complex illness, 15 minutes; and relatively simple illness, 15 minutes. The most common form of visit with both the MDs and the PAs was scheduled for 15 minutes for continuing patients.

The initial general policy was that PAs should not handle patients with chronic disease, physical examinations for patients over 40, and complicated or life-threatening situations. In Oregon, the PAs were initially limited to walk-ins, and every patient was to see a physician no later than the third visit for the same illness or complaint. As in other K-P settings, the PAs in Oregon gradually developed their own panels of patients, and the upper age limit on physicals and the third-visit rule became less firm. In 1975, the health plan of the Portland K-P Clinic employed 12 PAs: three in surgery, three in orthopedics, one in pathology, and five in medicine. Consultative physician time was less than 2 percent of the physician's total work schedule and, for general supervision of PAs, about 7 percent. Twelve percent of all PA visits included an MD consultation.

The study of K-P in Portland, Oregon, covers only variable costs. The study also assumes that the quality of care by the supervised PA is the same as that by the MD. Little can be added to the general conclusion of the study: "There appears to be a growing conviction among those in the system who make the policies which govern PAs that quality of care is best protected—once a competent PA has been recruited—by selecting a 'responsible supervisor.'"[44] It is worth noting, however, that in the same K-P group, five primary care nurse practitioners functioning under the nursing statutes and boards rather than the medical ones are providing health appraisals with only one internist as supervisor. Under the laws in most states, five PAs would require five MD supervisors.

The armed forces, because of the nature of combat duty, made early use of "physician extenders." Air Force Regulation 160-12, September 9, 1974, lists the duties of the certified nurse practitioners separately from those of the physician assistants. The latter are enlisted rank while the former are officer rank and are paid a higher wage. This distinction reflects in part the historical development of the earlier use of nurses within the armed forces and in part the differences in the levels of training required and in the functions which are performed by each. Although both the nurse practitioners and physician assistants in the armed forces may prescribe drugs and order laboratory tests, electrocardiograms, and x-rays, only the former may assess the results and manage "selected major illnesses."

In contrast, civilian physician assistants are paid higher salaries than either nurse practitioners or traditional nurses. Civilian PAs may order prescription drugs, laboratory tests, and x-rays in only the few states that permit them to do so. PAs, general nurse practitioners, and others are accepted as substitutes for MDs in the supervised delivery of primary care. The question remains whether physician extenders may practice independently, performing a restricted set of functions.

Nurses working in hospitals, as well as out of hospitals, have been protesting that the difference between their pay and that of PAs is largely discriminatory by sex and does not reflect differences in skills or education.[45] Physician assistants may have only one or two years of training, but theirs is highly specialized training. Nurses usually have three years of training. General nurse practitioners have additional intensive training; some are certified by specialty such as geriatrics, medical-surgical, and psychiatric. PAs may be trained to do minor surgery, such as suturing, and may work relatively independently in rural areas performing primary care. Such PAs may have had more on-the-job training as medical corpsmen in the army, but they usually lack the breadth of training in the biological sciences that nurses receive over a three-year period.

Even if the wage differential is justified by a difference in the job content, the latter, in itself, can be a form of discrimination by sex. A study for the Canadian Committee on the Healing Arts states that "males normally dominate the medical professions and seem to delegate to females jobs that require less responsibility and competence than their training would justify."[46] There may have been, in the 1970s, an under-supply of PAs relative to demand that pushed up the PAs' supply prices, though not to such levels as to absorb all of the economic returns that PAs appear to bring to their employers. With a physician surplus during the 1980s, PAs and general nurse practitioners are not likely to gain in income relative to physicians unless physician incomes fall.

Physicians who are at high levels of income and working long hours usually prefer more leisure to higher gross income. Therefore, it is worthwhile for these MDs to hire a PA because the PA increases a physician's productivity substantially. The physician gains more leisure (time income) and his money income also increases. The policies of the AMA and the California Medical Association (CMA) are that the price of a medical service should be related to the service rendered, not to who performs it. Thus, the physician receives an "economic rent" when he uses an assistant to provide a service that he otherwise would have performed. Under the AMA stricture, there is no fall in the price to the consumer. In the survey of the use of PAs by 18 physicians in rural northern California, some physicians indicated that they were considering offering a percentage of their profits to the PA in addition to an annual salary.

If the increased use of PAs can reduce costs, why is it that the physicians are not making greater use of them? Do some physicians fear their competitive potential? Are there more effective ways, without entailing the burden of increased supervisory duties, of reducing costs and increasing the leisure time and the income of physicians? The reduction in the physicians' work week from 54.8 hours to 46.3 hours in the Montreal metropolitan area when national health insurance became effective in Canada was made possible by the substitution of office visits and telephone calls for home visits. The reduction was not created by hiring a large number of PAs.[47] The home visit, however, is rare in the United States. The income of Canadian physicians also increased through a significant reduction in the percentage of previously written-off, unpaid bills; an increase in the utilization of various units of care; and a finer subdivision of tasks permitting more charges. These developments have already occurred in the United States. Also, because of the earlier under-reporting of Canadian physician income for tax purposes, the reported increase may be higher than that which actually occurred.

Malpractice suits, which are of great concern to U.S. physicians, may conceivably reduce their use of PAs. Almost 85 percent of nurse midwives carry their own malpractice insurance and one-third are covered both by their own policy and by that of their employers.[48] There is no evidence that malpractice suits in actuality interfere with employment of physician extenders, but that suspicion remains. If the only gain to the consumers from the use of PAs is less waiting time and not lower dollar cost, it cannot be assumed that all consumers will choose to accept the services of lesser trained personnel. Any tradeoffs between costs and quality of care will vary in each instance.

Physicians in group practice accept substitute manpower more readily than solo physicians. A physician's choice of group practice over solo practice indicates a relatively strong preference for a pre-established working schedule and a structured work environment where he or she can interact with colleagues. Those who prefer set working schedules are willing to give up some of the autonomy of an individual practice. Those physicians who draw salaries and bonuses from prepaid per capita funds of a group practice have an economic incentive to encourage patients to accept physician substitutes. They may encourage more of their patients than do fee-for-service physicians to accept services from less trained personnel who may in fact be better trained for the particular task.

Fee-for-service, solo practice physicians with a large practice also stand to gain from hiring physician extenders. The solo physician may thus eliminate doing routine tasks that require little training. Solo physicians may prefer nurse practitioners (NPs) to PAs because physicians can delegate a wider range of tasks to the more broadly trained NP, use her also as a nurse, and pay her a lower wage. The precise amount of savings depends on the supply and the demand in the various labor markets and in the medical care service markets.

The taxes used to subsidize the education of physicians and to pay Medicaid and Medicare fees might be better spent if more PAs were used, and if they were paid according to the services they render. Federal funding for PA education was first given to the University of Washington, Seattle, for their MEDEX program in 1969. Other federal funds to NP and PA programs have been available: the Comprehensive Health Manpower Training Act of 1971, the Nurse Training Act of 1975, the amended Health Professions Education Assistance Act of 1976, and the Rural Health Clinic Services Act of 1977. Obviously, Congress believes that the use of physician extenders is cost-effective.

The greatest barrier to their widespread use is opposition from physicians. In specialties such as radiology, where an oversupply of physicians probably exists, many physicians believe that there is little or no need for physician assistants.[49] The number of physicians per capita is increasing faster than that of many other groups of health workers.

Licensing practices are controlled in most states by physicians. Licensure legally restricts physicians in some states to the supervision of only one, and in other states, to two, PAs. Further, some states require the immediate, physical presence of an MD supervising any type of physician extender. Physicians have effectively limited independent practice by PAs and GNPs in rural areas to certified clinics that do not have a full-time physician. The non-physician is then paid by Medicare for "reasonable" costs and not the physician "prevailing" charge. Midwives were included in this limited category under December 1980 legislation.

In 1980, it was common among physicians, nurses, and some politicians to claim that there was a shortage of registered nurses. However, economists disagreed and argued that the apparent shortage in hospitals, where 60 percent of nurses work, was caused by the fact that registered nurses' (RNs) salaries were too low. These salaries were being squeezed down closer to the level of the lesser trained licensed practical nurses' salaries and at the same time, the income gap between RN and MD was widening. The increase in the number of RNs has been spurred by continuous federal government support of nursing education since 1956.

The tremendous growth in supply of nurses has depressed their wages and has also served to attract, in recent years, young women who may be interested in obtaining an education but not necessarily in making a career of nursing. As their supply has increased, demand has not kept up despite the growing complexity of medicine and the increased intensity of nursing care per day of hospital care because the length of hospital stay has fallen. This is primarily because the occupancy rate has steadily decreased under peer reviews to about 75 percent (on the average) since 1968, a nearly constant number of beds.

Unpopular hours, night and weekend shifts, pay that is lower than that for other jobs with similar requirements, increased stress (especially in intensive care units), and dissatisfaction with status make nursing in a hospital an unattractive profession. A recently published study, supported by the Public Health Service, Division of Nursing (admittedly using 1970 data), states that "increasing the flow of services from the existing stock of trained RNs (e.g., with wage incentives or expanded childcare programs)" is more effective than "increasing the rate at which additional nurses are trained."[50] Among ten industrialized countries, the United States (in the mid-1970s) ranked third, behind Canada and Sweden, in the number of registered nurses per 1,000 population but far ahead of such countries as England and Wales, the Netherlands, West Germany, France, and Japan.[51] If, as seems likely, federal funding of nursing education is continued under the present labor market conditions, the quality of women who will enter that field will fall and the wages of nurses will remain low as compared with wages in similar professions.

Licensure

For over 200 years, governments of various political persuasions have required physicians to be licensed in order to practice medicine. By 1830, all but three states in the United States had some form of physician licensure. The 1910 Flexner Report criticized the quality of many medical schools and, as a result, only graduates of approved medical schools from that time forward could get a license. The loss of approval reduced the number of medical students by one-third between 1910 and 1920.

Licensure developed to protect the public interest against low quality, an idealistic goal that also acts to give the members of any licensed profession considerable monopoly power. Licensure is more common in occupations that require education beyond the college level and where there are a substantial number of complex tasks. George Stigler analyzed occupational licensure data and found that the political power of an occupational group is significantly related to obtaining licensure early.[52] Physicians have substantial political clout because all people, including Congressmen, become ill and physicians, if they wish, can influence directly the votes of Congressmen when they are in the role of a patient. The lobbying by medical societies at the state and national levels is well-financed.

In almost every case of occupational licensure, it is the professional and not the consumer who has sought licensure. This implies that the provider benefits more from licensure than the consumer, and thus Stigler's "acquired regulation theory" over-rides the older public interest theory of licensure. The dominant economic interest of an individual's occupational role over-rides the more diffuse interest of a consumer. Individuals devote more time to affect legislation governing their occupations than to affect legislation governing the items that they consume.

Competition among professional suppliers is limited by state licensing practices. State licensing boards usually consist of the professionals whose occupation is being licensed, or their potential competitors. The public has only token members on a few licensing boards. The level of difficulty of a licensing examination is controlled by persons in that occupation who have an economic interest in keeping it high. For example, a class action suit was filed in Hawaii by those who applied for the dental examination in that state after August 1, 1974, and in behalf of those who "may be denied dental licensure . . . in the future" (Pekarsky et al. versus Ariyoshi et al., Civil No. 76-0455). "The plaintiffs claim that they were illegally denied their dental licenses because they were either of Caucasian ancestry or new/non-residents of Hawaii."[53] It was also stated that, during a two-year period, 30 out of 35 Orientals and only 28 of 74 non-Orientals passed the dental board examinations. Six of the seven members of the licensing board in Hawaii were of Asian ancestry.[54] This illustrates how an at-interest licensing board can keep outsiders from receiving a license to pursue an occupation for which they have been trained.

Reciprocity among the states is increasing, but Florida and California still do not accept examination results from the forty-nine other states as proof of ability to practice medicine in their states. In California, the Board of Medical Quality Assurance, which handles complaints of incompetence, has separate committees for physicians, acupuncturists, physician assistants, physical therapists, psychologists, podiatrists, speech pathologists, and others. There are licensing boards that cover registered nurses and vocational nurses, and there are also examiners of nursing home administrators, optometrists, pharmacists, and psychiatric technicians. Dentists, medical technologists, and persons selling hearing aids are licensed. About fifty health occupations are licensed by one or more states. In addition, there are over twenty types of technicians and assistants that require training in an approved program. National licensure is argued against by providers living in those states that have a high number of practitioners relative to the population and where there is a climate that attracts older providers, close to retirement.

The number of health licensure boards and health accrediting agencies that govern standards for institutions and personnel has been increasing. The Council of Medical Education of the AMA sets the credential requirements for many types of medical technicians and assistants. Credentialing often precedes the battle waged by allied health workers for more status through licensure. Although in the early 1970s health professionals criticized the multiple, rigid requirements of state licensure boards and accrediting agencies, the number of allied health jobs that are licensed has grown steadily. Moving up the manpower ladder of health care is difficult. Licensure increases costs of medical care because only large hospitals can fully utilize all the licensed personnel that they hire.

A recent experimental health manpower program in California (AB 1503) trained existing health care professionals for expanded roles. It also established career ladders so that whatever an individual learns at a lower level is credited as training towards a higher position. Career ladders had been proposed for many years because they would reduce costs of training. Although the expanded roles for registered nurses, physician assistants, and pharmacists to prescribe, dispense, and administer drugs (allowed until January 1, 1983, under the amended 1977 California Nurse Practice Act) have been opposed by physicians and others, they have not been opposed by consumers. Even though the initial project of the University of the Pacific, School of Dentistry, demonstrated increased productivity with the use of assistants supervised by dentists, the project was not continued. Once again the opposition was voiced by the competitive supplier, the dentist.

In May 1977, a survey was made of pilot projects established under AB 1503 (California) to educate trainees for expanded roles. Table 2 shows that, although many persons had completed their training, not all trainees were employed at the higher levels.

Whether or not physicians realize a substantial economic gain from restriction of entry by requiring licensure is still being debated in the economic literature. Physician licensure requires specific training:

Table 2. Utilization of Trainees In Expanded Roles
(May 1977, California)

Health Profession	Completed Training	Utilized Trainees (estimated)
Medical Auxiliaries	298	202
Nursing	2,201	1,073
Pharmacy	91	51
Dentistry	210	64
Mental Health	4	0
	2,804	1,390

Source: Dick Howard and R. Douglas Roederer, *Health Manpower Licensing: California's Demonstration Projects,* Fourth Annual Report (Lexington, Kentucky: The Council of State Governments, April 1978), p. 17.

three to four years of medical school and, depending upon specialty, one to four years of hospital internship and/or residency. In addition, a licensing examination must be passed. Further, subspecialty qualification requires two to three additional years of training and yet another board examination.

An analysis (Leffler) of the net, 1976 value of a career as a physician estimates that physicians who completed training prior to the introduction of Medicare and Medicaid (mid-1966) earn about $1,750 more annually than what would be expected according to the required years of training.[55] Physicians' returns, as computed by Leffler, nearly doubled in real dollars in 1973 as compared with years prior to 1966. It was during the later period when the government greatly increased its payments under Medicare and Medicaid for personal medical care that the economic rent or the monopoly return to physicians rose substantially.

Leffler's estimate of average annual return can be criticized as probably low because it uses the median income of a general practitioner with a one-year internship. About one-fourth of practicing physicians are general practitioners. Returns to the more common specialists, after corrections for costs of longer residencies, may differ.

Although other studies of physicians' incomes yield much higher returns than does Leffler's,[56] they do not correct for the higher number of hours worked by physicians as compared with the average hours worked by other professionals. Leffler assumes in his estimate that physicians work 55 hours per week and college graduates work 44. He does not compare the hours of physicians with those of other professionals who have completed several years of postgraduate education and are also likely to work 50 hours or more per week. Leffler's estimates have been reworked to partially correct for some of their deficiencies. There remains a "corrected rate of return of 17.4 percent, clearly higher than the return to a college education."[57]

The percentage of applicants accepted by medical schools has been decreasing slightly. Whereas prior to 1970 there were 2.1 or less applicants for each person accepted, in all subsequent years there has been 2.2 to 2.8 applicants for each place.[58] About 21 percent of the physicians in 1980 are foreign medical graduates as compared with 9 percent in 1959. Although foreign medical graduates, on the average, do less well on specialty board examinations than do the U.S.-trained medical graduates, many of the United States Nobel Laureates in medicine are foreign-trained. Obviously, an increase in the supply of foreign-trained physicians tends to lower the economic returns to the U.S.-trained physicians.

It can be argued that a part of what may appear to be a monopoly return to medical education is, in reality, a return for the higher natural ability among physicians than among those in other professions. There are no data either to support or to refute this contention.

Because the practice of medicine is in part an art, it is difficult to measure accurately the quality of medical practice or to relate that quality to an examination score. Economics professor Leffler comments that, "As a result, medical students face uncertainty as to the correlation between their exam results and their skills. . . . Physicians [may] respond by over-investment in skills specialized to passing exams."[59] The skills to pass an examination are not necessarily the ones that are of the greatest importance in providing quality medical care.

The fact that the tuition for medical schools is far less than the actual resource cost[60] creates excess demand for medical education. Although state universities during the 1970s greatly increased tuition for their medical schools, students usually do not pay more than the full operating costs, or about 20 percent[61] of total costs. Taxpayers pay a large part of the costs of educating physicians.

A 1980 analysis states that the monopoly returns to practicing physicians are "negligible" and "evidence . . . is not compelling [that] medical schools conspire with organized medicine to restrain the number of graduates and thus the supply of medical practitioners."[62] The national and state licensing examinations also restrict the supply of physicians. The examinations are composed by physicians. Excess demand for a place in a medical school may exist because self-perceptions of ability may be too high, but the potentially high incomes also attract. Some persons are not accepted because their abilities are too low for acceptance. The mean Medical College Admission Test Score of applicants has steadily increased since 1958 in three areas: verbal, quantitative, and scientific ability. The average score on the general information test also has increased, but not steadily. Simultaneously, the overall Scholastic Aptitude Test scores for college entrance have been dropping. Thus, the quality of medical students has been maintained, possibly increased. The question whether the relatively high incomes of physicians is a result of higher natural ability or of artificially restrained supply, possibly resulting in higher quality, remains. The contention that physicians *knowingly* limit entry may be dismissed. The question remains, however, as to whether past actions of medical schools and licensing practices, with or without a conspiracy, have resulted in monopoly returns or economic rents to currently practicing physicians.

It is generally believed that students are unwilling to assume the full cost of a medical education. It has not been empirically tested whether the enrollment of students of high quality would be maintained if students were required to assume the full cost on a loan basis. Taxpayers in California, where there are five high quality University of California medical schools, subsidize all medical students attending those medical schools. However, their future earnings will place them in the upper 5 percent income bracket. The political argument for continuing this policy is that the individual whose parents have low income will be unable to attend medical school. This assumes that parents generally pay graduate school tuition, another assumption that has not been empirically tested. The primary cost of graduate education is not the cost of schooling but the earnings foregone or sacrificed. Few of the poor can attend medical school without full scholarships. Potential physicians of middle-income parents also face financial barriers. Higher tuition, but with generous loan and scholarship programs, is more desirable than heavy subsidization by all income groups of the state-supported medical schools. Continuing federal, per capita grants to medical schools need to be re-examined within the context of the increasing surplus of physicians.

As medical schools continued to expand under government grants, the role of licensure in controlling physician supply has expanded. Licensure rests on the assumption that it is the only way a level of quality acceptable to society can be maintained: "That society is a better judge than the individual concerning what is good for him."[63]

It is argued that the social costs of no licensure of physicians are higher than the private costs of higher doctor's bills. For example, unlicensed physicians could, by poor treatment, let an epidemic develop unchecked. While that may have been plausible before the use of powerful antibiotics, it seems an unlikely scenario in the United States of the 1980s. Supporters of state licensure maintain that it is preferable to national licensure because those states with higher levels of income and education "demand" a higher quality of services, including medical care. Residents of those states pay higher medical fees and have less opportunity to purchase less costly, possibly lower quality, medical care.

On the average, one-half of a licensed physician's bills for ambulatory care is paid by third parties, not the patient. Whether the other one-half of total billings paid out-of-pocket would, without licensure, on the average decline is unknown. Unlicensed health practitioners who are not reimbursed by third parties could become competitors to licensed health practitioners. Lonely and aged individuals who are chronically ill with an already diagnosed, incurable disease may prefer and be willing to pay out-of-pocket for more time of a less expensive health professional than a licensed physician. Many individuals are already paying for various forms of non-reimbursed "caring."

One facet of quality (and quality is part of the service being purchased) that the physician provides is confidentiality or privacy. There are some who argue that an unlicensed professional would not provide privacy to the same degree as the licensed lawyer and the licensed physician. However, this claim has not been tested.

If licensing boards perform well, they serve to maintain quality and to give quicker administrative redress. However, these boards also restrict entry into the health occupations and thus limit competition from others who could substitute services at lower prices. Licensing decreases the number of suppliers and results in higher prices to the consumer. This effect is sometimes delayed by "grandfathering" in workers who are already performing the newly licensed task.

In 1979, the Federal Trade Commission Chairman, Michael Pertschuk, maintained that "all too often licensing bears little relationship to quality."[64] Consumers generally accept without proof that any licensed practitioner is qualified. Certification that a course of study has been satisfactorily completed could replace licensing examinations and boards. Exceedingly capable physicians can differentiate themselves as more qualified than other physicians by taking specialty board examinations and writing and lecturing in their specialty. They do not need the protection of a license to assure an ample number of patients. It is the more numerous but less capable professionals and near-professionals who are so strongly in favor of licensing. An in-depth study of licensed clinical laboratory personnel found an "absence of any evidence that licensure increases the quality of laboratory tests and may increase costs."[65] Boards of Quality Assurance have rarely withdrawn physicians' licenses. Proof of lack of quality is as difficult to get as proof of quality.

Licensing boards have a negative power and usually their composition is such that a majority of their members come from the profession which they oversee. A licensing board does not assure that the licensed personnel will maintain a high level of quality. Several of the medical specialty boards have developed voluntary recertification examinations. Some states require practicing physicians to take courses to update their knowledge and skills in order to be relicensed.

Licensure, unlike certification, does not allow a non-licensed person who has completed required courses at accredited schools to perform licensed tasks and charge less than a licensed person. Non-licensed persons cannot practice; non-certified persons can. Leffler succinctly states the opinion of many economists: "Certification provides all the same information of licensure while offering a wider choice set."[66]

Lee Benham, also a professor of economics, explains the interrelationship of other forms of regulation as follows:

> The initial licensing process can be viewed as a technologic innovation which reduces the cost to the profession of obtaining additional controls. At the same time, the incentives to introduce additional controls are increased; thus, other controls are almost inevitable once control over entry is established. Establishment of jurisdictional lines becomes essential, for of what benefit is licensing if the non-licensed can practice? At the same time, there is pressure to expand jurisdictions and to sharply limit encroachment by others.[67]

If the licensing board is dominated by the group being licensed or by its competitors, the temptation is to restrict occupational entry. The greater the supply of a service, the lower the average income of the suppliers. An often-quoted, 1978 government study states that "the median income of selfemployed physicians ($63,000 in 1976) by 1975 already equaled four times the earnings of the census-defined, broad group of 'professional and technical workers.' But in 1939, their earnings were less than twice as great as the earnings of that group."[68] Physicians' appreciation of limited entry was illustrated by the standing ovation given by members of the Association of American Medical Colleges to former HEW Secretary Joseph Califano when he suggested that the medical schools "gradually reduce the size of their classes" over the next few years. The over-supply of physicians was threatening high incomes. Califano's simplistic explanation was that "every additional physician over the average career of 40 years adds $12 million in health care costs to the economy. By the year 2000, health care costs will reach $1000 billion—about 12% of the Gross National Product."[69]

It is the combination of guild-like associations (with the attendant mutual protection among physicians) and the uncertainty of specific treatments and their outcomes which make many physicians reluctant to fully inform the patient and to prepare him or her for participation in the clinical decision-making process that affects the patient. Medicine still depends on the placebo effect to mitigate or cure, which is another way of saying it depends on patient trust in the physician. Licensing is the traditional method used to create trust, but some signs in today's society show that this trust relationship is disintegrating. Some signs are an increase in malpractice suits, shopping around to select a physician, changing physicians, seeking a second medical opinion, and the excessive use of scientific tests and x-rays ordered by physicians. A large number of tests may protect physicians from malpractice suits but they may also relieve the physician's uncertainty about a diagnosis. The economic structure of group practice, especially the prepaid practice form, may undermine even more the trust relationship that in the past has cloaked the physician's uncertainty about diagnoses and health outcomes.[70]

The benefit to society from licensure is shrinking, yet the number of licensed health occupations is increasing. This is because licenses are issued in response to demands by persons who are acting in their own self-interest. Newly licensed occupations include jobs which consist mainly of quickly learned tasks that have no personal, professional trust component. For example, among the newer licensed occupations are nursing home administrators, dental hygienists, medical records administrators, medical technologists, and sanitary technicians. Licenses are sought as status symbols and as barriers to entry. Licenses are also believed to be a form of protection against legal prosecution. In reality, however, licensure does not provide this protection.

Replacement of licensure requirements by certification for many of the allied health occupations that are not truly professional would bypass the problems created by strict occupational licensure. Certification would permit more consumer choice because non-certified workers would charge less, although possibly provide a lower quality of care than their certified counterparts. Lower quality and lower priced services may be more appropriate for some consumers' or for some medical needs. National, rather than state, licensure examinations could reduce geographical barriers to entry into those occupations for which licensure is retained.

Self-Care: Supplement or Substitute?

In reaction to the high costs of medical care, some consumers are switching to physician substitutes. Among these substitutes are self-care books and non-traditional healers. Medical self-care books are not a new phenomenon. *Every Man His Own Doctor . . .* , by John Tennant, appeared in five editions between 1734 and 1737 and was reprinted in 1971.[71] What is new are the greater numbers, the greater sophistication, and the wider circulation of these books. Some of the most recent books are designed to help individuals evaluate their symptoms so that they may treat themselves when possible and rely less on medically trained personnel. These books may induce substitution. For example, a 1975 book, *How to Be Your Own Doctor (Sometimes)*, has been annotated as follows: "a guide to lay intervention in common illnesses, common injuries, most common emergencies, a drug index, treatment index, symptom-concept index, and testing index. A listing is included of self-help brochures, guides, pamphlets, and other materials useful in building self-help concepts, knowledge, and skills."[72]

The use of self-examination and self-care has been encouraged especially by feminists in the United States, who urge "increased knowledge of . . . anatomy, physiology, risk status for sex-related morbidities, and techniques of self-examination. The latter emphasis has moved self-care across the line from supplementation to substitutive behavior. . . . Self-examination of the vagina by speculum, however, a recent and unprecedented incursion into the professional domain, has caused widespread debate . . . challenging lay-professional jurisdictional taboos."[73] *Our Bodies, Ourselves: A Book by and for Women*, which had sold over one million copies by 1976 (its first publication was in 1971), stands as both an indictment of the male-dominated medical profession and a self-help book that encourages women to be questioning, assertive, and active participants in medical care decisions about themselves.

The women's health movement is part of the women's feminist movement of the 1970s. The women's health movement's complaints range from the general to the specific. A frequent and documented charge is that physicians are more likely to assume that vague complaints by women of fatigue or dizziness are purely emotional than if made by men. Medical textbooks and drug advertisements in medical journals may condition physicians to this view. Society still places males in the more dominant roles in most occupations and, because of this, it is not hard for the male physician to adopt a paternalistic and sometimes arrogant role. Many in the feminist health movement object specifically to the manner in which pelvic examinations are often conducted. The prestigious American College of Physicians published in their periodical, *Forum*, in 1980, a revealing article about women's attitudes towards the practice of medicine that includes the following:

> In the past, many practitioners did not see the patient until she was undressed, draped, and positioned on the table. Little verbal exchange took place except for short commands to the nurse and the final diagnosis and treatment instructions.[74]

Although this 1980 article in a journal published by the American College of Physicians speaks of this as past practice, it is still the practice in many physicians' offices. Additionally, many physicians never inform their patients, male or female, as to the results of tests when the findings do not call for medical treatment.

The titles of recent books illustrate an across-the-board dissatisfaction by some with the authoritative and sometimes arrogant control by the medical profession over areas of individuals' lives: *How to Choose and Use Your Doctor: Beyond the Medical Mystique*;[75] *Managing Your Doctor*;[76] and, *Talk Back to Your Doctor*.[77] Over one million copies of *Take Care of Yourself: A Consumer's Guide to Medical Care*, a decision-tree analysis approach, have been sold, mostly to insurance companies and Blue Cross and Blue Shield, who have distributed them to their policy-holders. This book has been so successful that a similar one was written about children's health for parents. Whether the use of decision-trees to evaluate complaints actually reduces the number of physician visits is unsure. Blue Cross and Blue Shield believe, however, that this approach does reduce physician visits. A recent academic article reports the reverse. The latter finding may be because the authors of *Take Care of Yourself*, Donald Vickery and James Fries, tend "to take a simplistic view of the doctor-patient relationship with a major cause of a poor relationship being identified as the recalcitrant patient."[78] Further refinement of decision-trees and some additional evaluations are needed.

The written word may be less forceful in alleviating anxiety because the readers cannot have their questions answered; "body language" does reinforce the written word. Moreover, persons who read several sources may encounter more unanswered questions than a simplified self-care book answers. Even when physicians appear to "manage" their patients successfully, many patients still do not fully comply with physicians' orders regarding diet, smoking, rest, exercise, and the intake of prescription drugs and alcohol. These are matters of life-style and thus habits which are difficult to change.

In addition to the flood of self-care health books, a great variety of medical devices are being sold directly to the consumers across the country. These include, in addition to the old-fashioned thermometer, dip-and-read tests, which indicate the amount of sugar in the urine; pregnancy test kits, which cost about $10; and sphygmomanometers, which measure blood pressure in arteries. Although tests to detect sugar in urine and blood pressure devices have long been available, the latter have only been marketed for home use during the past five years. Self-education permits persons with hypertension to monitor their own blood pressure. Most physicians argue that individuals should supplement physician care with these devices. Their use, however, could reduce the number of physician visits.

Pregnancy test kits that give reliable results are also relatively new. As with most laboratory tests, the results contain a few false negatives and a few false positives. Pregnancy kits, in cases with positive test results, rarely delay visits to a physician. When the results are negative, a pregnancy kit does substitute for a physician visit. Even more recent are self-care kits to detect breast cancer through heat-sensitive, specially prepared, paper-like strips that are simply placed on the breast.

Studies suggest that 70 percent of health care is not administered by professionals. Most mothers provide a wide variety of medical care within the home. In less developed countries, professional care is commonly given to adults by family members and religious leaders. Self-care or family care do not fall under the legal restraints of the various states' Medical Care Practice Acts.

A few physicians support their patients in increasing their self-help knowledge, but most physicians do not. A majority of physicians feel uncomfortable if the inherent uncertainties in the field of medicine are exposed. Others rationalize that, because most persons cannot understand medical problems, they are better off ignorant and submissive. Specialized self-help groups comprised of individuals with the same health problem are based on the belief that people can help each other to cope with their illness, whether it is obesity (Weight Watchers) or emphysema (Emphysema Anonymous). The functions of these self-help groups are usually complementary to physician services, but some are partially substitutes, as, for example, those that give supportive care to persons with chronic illness.

The scientific community recognizes the cost-savings potential of self-care as the following indicates:

> Organized self-care programs have proved especially effective among those suffering chronic illnesses, which represent a growing proportion of the diseases afflicting Americans. In a self-care program with hemophiliacs at the Tufts New England Medical Center, total costs per patient were lowered 45 percent. A diabetics' self-care program run by the University of Southern California reduced the number of patients experiencing diabetic coma by two-thirds and halved the number of emergency room visits. Hospitals and consumers saved $1.7 million over a 2-year period, a mere fraction of the overall savings that could be realized if self-care became the first line of medical defense nationwide.[79]

Some physicians actively oppose self-care concepts, especially when taught by clinics. Opposition has been expressed by naming the directors of holistic and wellness-oriented clinics as cultists at best and quacks at worst. Economists suspect that this opposition stems from the fact that these clinics attract patients who might otherwise seek traditional medical care. Some self-help clinics are run by well-trained physicians and offer viable self-care techniques: biofeedback, massage, and whirlpool baths to reduce stress; taking one's own blood pressure; and interpreting biochemical test results.

This type of medical care service recognizes that more consumers are seeking different methods to improve their own health. Such persons prefer to gain more control over their way of life by participating in the medical decisions that affect the quality of their lives. Holistic and well-care clinics emphasize health education as a form of cost containment and encourage fewer x-rays and tests.

Among groups that emphasize self-care and self-reliance by the consumer are the Swedish Medical Center in Denver and the Midpeninsula Health Service in Palo Alto. The latter has initiated a *Health Assessment Workbook* used by the consumer and a medical self-care course for adults. Such groups emphasize the more natural processes of healing and home care; they eschew expensive technological intervention and hospitalization. The approach may evolve into an effective cost-containment alternative which emphasizes "a partnership between patients and health professionals."[80] In cases of severe illness, limitations of this approach are obvious. Its use, moreover, requires an initial time commitment by health professionals if they are to educate consumers to rely more on themselves and less on professionals. Therefore, non-physician health professionals find a greater demand for their services in holistic medical practice than in other medical settings. These are pioneer efforts affecting only a small part of the total population.

Persons with equally severe diseases have different rates of medical care utilization. Behavior in response to like symptoms is extremely variable. However, it is more homogeneous in response to acute illness where the patient depends on medical personnel than it is in response to chronic and minor illnesses, where dependence is less. Psychological and socio-economic factors are more important in chronic, minor, and preventive medical care, where the patient may choose among options such as selfmedication, seeking professional help, or ignoring the problem. Not until 1938 did most drugs become prescription drugs, that is, non-attainable except under a physician's direction.

Non-prescription, or over-the-counter (OTC), drugs are often chosen without any advice, including that from a pharmacist. They are chosen primarily on the basis of past experience, advice from friends, or from information gleaned from advertisements and consumer magazines. In 1978, the sales of OTC drugs totalled about $4 billion.[81] In 1970, 22 percent of Americans used prescribed psychotropic drugs: sleeping pills, tranquilizers, and stimulants. About 12 percent bought non-prescription drugs of this nature. Psychologist Mitchell B. Balter, of the National Institute of Mental Health, comments that: "The people who go to a drugstore and buy over-the-counter psychotropic drugs are not, generally speaking, the same people who go to the doctor."[82] The buyers of street psychotropic drugs are a distinctive group, over half of whom are 18 to 29 years of age. The use of these drugs is more frequent among better educated persons. However, studies indicate that, for *all* types of OTC drugs, the same individuals will buy prescription and OTC drugs, and that the latter are often substitutes for the former.

The most popular non-prescription drugs are cough and cold remedies, then pain relievers and antacids. These OTC drugs are generally effective and many contain lesser amounts of the same ingredients that are in the prescription drugs. Labelling the packages of non-prescription drugs is crucial because they are sold in food stores and large drugstores where the consumer may not talk to a pharmacist. For this reason, informative advertising is also important. If OTC drugs are not advertised, it is very difficult for the consumer to learn what new drugs are available and how desirable they may be for him or her. Through experience with OTC drugs, the individual becomes his or her own best judge of their values because the individual knows best about his or her unique biological makeup, reactions, and tastes. Advertising saves the consumer time and money because it offers information, often in comparative terms that the consumer can understand.

Both the Food and Drug Administration (FDA) and the Federal Trade Commission (FTC) regulate OTC drug marketing, labelling, and advertising. Consumer satisfaction is reflected in the repeat purchases. If the major purpose of advertising is to inform the average consumer, it would be counterproductive to limit the terminology of advertising to the mandated FDA label. For instance, one mandated FDA label includes the term "hyperosmotic." It would be surprising if more than 5 percent of the population has heard that term before.

Consumers do gain knowledge from the competitive advertising of OTC drugs. For example, until recently aspirin was the primary OTC drug for pain of all types. Advertisements for Tylenol and Datril emphasize that their major competitor, aspirin, might cause stomach upsets. At the same time, the manufacturers of aspirin are pointing out, correctly, that Tylenol and Datril do not relieve inflammation associated with arthritis.

Without self-medication, minor illness would either go untreated, be treated with street drugs, or divert scarce medical resources from the treatment of more serious illnesses. A physician has written that "our entire health-care system would fall apart were it not for the opportunity of self-medication."[83]

HOW MANY HOSPITAL BEDS?

Forty percent of the nation's personal health care bill is for hospital care. There are two major types of hospitals: long-term (which are primarily psychiatric hospitals) and short-term (or general) acute care hospitals. The latter comprise nearly 90 percent of all the hospitals but provide only about three-fourths of all the beds. The non-federal, short-term, or community hospital is the one most commonly thought of as "the hospital." These are the hospitals that are the major providers of acute diagnostic and therapeutic services and have a rapid turnover of patients. About 94 percent of their revenues come from third party payers. Most long-term hospitals are government-owned.

Between 1960 and 1978, the number of all types of hospital services increased while the number of beds dropped by 18 percent, from 1.7 to 1.4 million. Long-term hospitals now have fewer beds because short-term general hospitals are providing care to many patients who would have been, prior to the development of new drugs, in long-term mental or tuberculosis institutions. In addition, many individuals who would previously have been hospitalized now live at home or in "half-way" mental care settings. Nursing homes also have expanded their role in caring for the elderly, long-term patients who do not need the facilities of an acute general hospital but who do need some nursing care.

Although there still may be shortages of beds in a few urban areas, the response to increases in demand for hospital beds in the 1960s and early 1970s has been more than adequate. By 1980, there was a surplus of over 100,000 beds. This is due in large measure to the Hill-Burton Act of 1946, which gave grants for the construction of public and non-profit voluntary hospitals, resulting in building too many small, rural hospitals. Under this Act, a total of $13 billion was spent between 1948 and 1971 for the construction of hospital facilities containing nearly one-half million inpatient beds. The Hill-Burton Act has since expired and its functions have been assumed by the regional planning bodies under the Health Resources Development Act of 1974.

The main purpose of the Hill-Burton Act was to improve access to medical care in the rural areas. Physicians and nurses were not attracted in sufficient numbers to run the new, relatively small, rural hospitals. Small hospitals are inefficient unless they provide a very limited range of services. During the 1970s, many small hospitals went out of business while others became part of a multi-hospital system that provides more cost-efficient purchasing, management, and capital planning. Air transport to move rural patients to larger hospitals for intensive and tertiary subspecialty care has become common practice.

Hospitals may also be classified by ownership into three types: government-owned, voluntary non-profit, and profit-making or proprietary. Of the 6,637 short-stay hospitals in 1977, 14 percent were profit-making, but these had only about 8 percent of the acute general hospital beds. By 1982, for-profit hospitals were one-third of all hospitals and about one-fifth of acute, general care hospitals. However, most of the large city hospitals are non-profit and many of these are losing money. Investor-owned corporations have increasingly been managing, under contract, some of the well-known county hospitals.

Non-profit hospitals often subsidize their more expensive cases by overcharging for the simpler, routine cases. Hospitals are reimbursed at less than claimed costs by Medicaid, sometimes as little as 60 percent, and by Medicare at 90 to 95 percent of costs. Accounting by hospitals does not follow the uniform practices of the Federal Accounting Standards Board (FASB) which govern corporate business. By including costs other than direct patient care costs, hospitals can receive more than 100 percent of actual costs under Medicare reimbursement. This is probably rare. Hospital charges to private patients are higher in order to make up for any shortfall stemming from government under-payments, especially of Medicaid patients. Thus, some in-hospital patients help pay for, or cross-subsidize, other patients.

Many of the large city hospitals are also teaching hospitals. These are being further squeezed by the decline in government funds for the training and education of new physicians. Their charges do not usually cover all the extra expenses involved in maintaining the range of training opportunities needed for a full residency teaching program. Logically, teaching hospitals could specialize and rotate interns among hospitals in a city area. The University of Washington has for some time coordinated intern programs among hospitals in Washington, Alaska, Montana, and Idaho (the "WAMI" program for rural western areas and especially for those states without medical schools). The Northeast and Midwest sectors of the United States could explore this approach as a means of integrating the for-profit hospitals into the training programs of the established non-profit hospitals that sometimes complain that the for-profit hospitals are more efficient because they escape the teaching costs. Although most city hospitals do not need to expand, some have dipped into their depreciation funds for needed renovation.

The inconsistency in government practices under its Medicare and Medicaid programs has worsened over time. The government reimburses hospitals below their full costs and, at the same time, approves Medicare payment for costly kidney and some heart transplants. The government has not recognized that taxpayers may not wish to pay for all the new and expensive medical techniques available for everyone who has a medical need and who wishes this type of care. Nor has government recognized the upward expansion of "need" in cases where disease is not clearly defined but is measured along a continuum where the division that separates those in need and those not in need of a procedure can readily be shifted.

Some large, non-profit hospitals claim that they are financially insolvent because they are saddled with a large percentage of Medicaid patients, other poor patients not covered by Medicaid, and patients with complex diseases requiring expensive treatment. Some large city hospitals, however, are managed successfully. Their success seems to be due to careful capital planning, computerized billing, and salary levels that attract highly qualified personnel.

An example of a currently (1980) successful, but previously insolvent, organization is the Baltimore City Hospitals System. In 1972, it was operating in the red. After considerable discussion with outside consultants, it was reorganized as a private non-civic institution. By 1979, it was operating in the black and had tripled its physicians' salaries. Now, the Baltimore City Hospitals System encompasses "three HMO-style operations, a malpractice self-insurance venture, a tax-exempt research and education foundation, a profit-making computerized billing and management consulting service for 17 medical groups, the nation's largest AMA-accredited jail medical service, and an informal 'think tank' of consultants to help other communities adapt to the Chesapeake Physicians, P.A. (CPPA) success story."[84]

Hospitals have in some ways benefited from Medicaid. Prior to Medicaid, a significant percentage of their revenues were uncollectable by default. Since then, Medicaid has reduced the level of defaults to almost zero. However, because some states define "poor" conservatively, there are people who are poor who are ineligible for Medicaid and they may incur uncollectible hospital bills.

Some large city hospitals in difficult financial circumstances have been taken over by for-profit management, for example, Cook County Hospital of Chicago by Hyatt Medical Management Services, Inc. Others are being managed by nearby university medical schools. Tulane University and Boston University medical schools are examples. Large city hospitals with many poor patients can offer medical schools what other hospitals cannot: an assured flow of patients willing to be "teaching" or "research" patients. In order to meet the public demands for cost-containment, some hospitals have banded together into multi-hospital systems to save on bulk purchases of drugs, blood, hospital linens, and malpractice insurance. Together they also use the type of capital planning routinely practiced by for-profit hospitals. Large urban hospitals are also exploring the relationship between specialization and cost-containment, and many consequently no longer believe that it is necessary for every hospital to have the latest expensive medical devices and diverse specialty medical teams. For-profit management firms have been making money from managing hospitals that previously were in the red.

Multi-hospital systems are competitive and appear to allocate scarce resources more efficiently and contain costs more effectively in areas where government regulations and imposed reimbursement controls have failed. Among the successful chains of smaller urban and rural nonprofit hospitals is the Intermountain Health Care, Inc. (IHC), system based in Salt Lake City, Utah. It has 30 hospital affiliates in 27 cities and towns in Utah, Nevada, Colorado, and Wyoming. A *Business Week* column states that the Intermountain hospital system's "patients pay 28 percent less per admission than the national average and 18 percent less than the regional average (and remained hospitalized for an average of 5.1 days, or 2.3 days less than the national average). And, IHC's $30 million in bonds carry an AA+ rating from Standard and Poor's. This means that the chain saves $1.6 million annually in interest charges over an AA rating and $3.8 million over an A rating."[85] Additionally, IHC carries its own malpractice insurance and workers' compensation up to the first $100,000 per occurrence and, through a multi-hospital Mutual Insurance, Ltd., obtains further coverage under an umbrella policy. IHC even processes the Blue Cross claims for many of its members and sends "a messenger to the Blue Cross Office in Salt Lake City each Friday so payments can be deposited in the bank to earn interest over the weekend."[86] Such hospital systems or chains enable some hospitals to specialize in cancer therapy, others in open heart surgery, and so on. Because transportation costs are minimal, the unoccupied beds in one hospital may be filled by overflow patients from nearby hospitals belonging to that chain.

The Associated Hospital System was formed recently (with only one full-time employee) as a network of hospital chains, and has given its members even greater purchasing power in negotiating volume buying for its members. DiPaolo writes that "AH's contracts average 10 percent to 15 percent better savings than contracts negotiated by individual member systems."[87] Although growth of profit-making hospitals is discouraged by the laws of some states, the number of their beds is growing. Some claim that for-profit hospitals generally handle less complex cases requiring less expensive equipment, and tend to specialize. Thus, they appear to skim off the more profitable type of hospital cases.[88] Economists see virtue, not fault, in specialization. Representative of the remarks that appear in business columns is the following: "Spearheaded by a dozen or so chains, investor-owned institutions now [1979] own and operate nearly 1000 of the 7000 hospitals in the United States and have 108,000 of the nation's 1.4 million beds."[89] Investor-owned chains point to their efficient management and to the fact that even some university hospitals, such as Tulane University Medical Center, use for-profit hospital management expertise. Although non-profit hospital chains could attain similar economies of scale, the for-profit hospitals have an advantage because they are less hesitant to fire the incompetent and to demand payment of unpaid bills.

There are about 400 hospital systems nationwide, including the for-profit hospitals. Nearly 15 percent of the non-profit hospitals are involved in multi-hospital systems. Ironically, the hospital chains seem to be achieving voluntarily what the 1974 Health Resources Planning and Development Act failed to do through government-mandated Professional Review Standards Organizations (PRSOs) and Health Systems Agencies (HSAs). Although that Act directs consideration of multi-hospital systems, it does not create incentives for their formation. Some HSAs have issued regulations that duplicate or conflict with state agency regulations. Moreover, Medicare's reimbursement regulations do not help achieve an economic climate favorable for rational hospital systems. Because Medicare regulations reimburse the depreciation, interest, and maintenance costs of unoccupied beds, the hospitals have kept open wings with very low occupancy rates. If the hospital closes the wing, the reimbursement ceases unless the unoccupied beds are deemed necessary as standby beds. In 1979, HEW proposed not to end reimbursement of unoccupied beds but rather to continue reimbursement for such beds even if located in an unoccupied hospital wing. This policy does not encourage a rational allocation of resources or a rational formation of hospital systems. Legislation to pay for converting unoccupied or unneeded acute care beds into beds suitable for long-term care has been suggested.

Hospitals are merging, sharing facilities, and specializing. Some unprofitable ones have been allowed to shut their doors. Duplication of facilities is being controlled not by government regulation but by economic responses from institutions to society's demands for greater containment of hospital care costs.

There are about twenty-five multi-hospital systems that own or manage over 50 percent of all the community hospitals in the United

States. Most of these conglomerates are non-profit; however, several hospital stocks are listed on the New York Stock Exchange and the American Stock Exchange. Those on the NYSE had an average increase in stock price of 45 percent between June and mid-November 1977.[90] The two largest chains are Humana and Hospital Corporation of America. In 1980, Humana had a 33.6 percent return on equity and a five-year average earnings per share of 34.4 percent while Hospital Corporation of America had 18.0 percent and 27.6 percent, respectively. These indicators of profitability were well above the comparative all-industry medians of 16.1 percent and 14.3 percent, respectively.[91]

Among the well-known hotel and motel chains, Hyatt Hotels and Ramada Inns have entered this area. From mid-1966 until 1972, Medicare assured hospitals an income to cover costs including interest payments, depreciation allowances, and a "reasonable return on equity." The latter incentive was eliminated in 1972, but by then the proprietary chains, many with motel experience, had entered the market and they managed the hotel-type hospital services more efficiently than did the non-profit hospitals. They continue to attract patients by offering better food, more attractive surroundings, and increasingly lower prices for quality that cannot be proved to be lower than in non-profit hospitals.

Most economists believe that specialization helps lower the cost in any industry. Specialization by both non-profit and for-profit hospitals is common. Specialization generally results in higher quality goods and services, and health care is no exception. It is logical that surgeons or surgical teams performing particular operations repeatedly will predicate better outcomes.[92]

The number of hospitals that are managed under contract by both profit and non-profit chains is increasing. Richard J. Kasten, of Ernst and Ernst, distinguishes the managerial philosophy of proprietary health care from that of non-profit health care as follows:

> The for-profit hospitals, particularly those that are investor owned, make decisions not only with regard to what will happen to the delivery of health care services, but what will happen financially. Generally, not-for-profit facilities make decisions primarily with patient care in mind; financial considerations play a secondary role.[93]

The greatest operating difference between the non-profit and the for-profit systems is that the latter employ a greater number of management specialists. Competition among hospital systems or chains is increasing. Many non-profit hospitals are managed by profit-making groups such as Humana, which bought American Medicorp, Inc., and Hospital Corporation of America, based in Nashville, Tennessee. Investor-owned hospitals can more easily raise, at lower interest rates, large amounts of capital to expand and update their facilities and they are more likely to use cost-benefit analysis in innovating managerial procedures. The non-profit chains are competing by reducing costs through centralized accounting and data processing, and by attaining capital through bond issues that carry the lower rates of the multi-hospital system's financial credit rating rather than that of a single, often financially struggling, hospital.

The "for-profits," with revenues of about $10 billion in 1978, are steadily increasing their share of the market over the "tax-exempts." The multi-national American Medical International, Inc. (AMI), owned 51 hospitals in 1971. AMI's United States hospitals earn less than its foreign ones, whose locations range from Britain and France to Australia and Venezuela. AMI manages 600 hospitals under contract. Although the company has kept its laboratory testing business, its major profits come from managing hospitals, with margins of 13 percent on its international business. Investment analysts agree that it "is operating in a 25 percent annual growth industry."[94] A case can be made that it is the multi-hospital *system*, whether profit or non-profit, which is raising the quality of care and at the same time increasing the efficiency of resource allocation.

It is ironic that the private sector is managing hospitals more successfully, even in some countries with some form of national health insurance, than a government-operated, government-owned institution. Although larger hospitals are more likely to be non-profit, the large, non-profit hospitals are increasingly being managed by profit-making corporations. This solution overcomes the "x-inefficiency" problem of large, non-profit institutions: that an individual decision-maker has less leverage and, therefore, less personal stake in the profits of the hospital where he or she works. Physicians, however, gain more prestige, services, and perquisites by working for a non-profit institution with tax-exempt status than for a for-profit hospital. In all countries, the hospital administrator is pressured by conflicting forces: by physicians and informed consumers to purchase new medical technology and by the consumers, the insurers, and the governments to operate at low costs. Attempts to reconcile these conflicts are increasing. New Jersey is using a system of uniform, statewide hospital rates to see whether cost containment can be achieved by pricing according to the illness treated rather than each service and each item consumed. If so, money "saved" could be used to purchase new technology or to contain price increases. Where government limits capital purchases, cost containment at least temporarily dominates decisions about the purchase of expensive, new technology. Benefits from that technology are often overlooked. The use of cost-benefit analysis would give more balance in the decision-making.

If a community attains additional hospital beds, the demand for those beds may increase and an equilibrium between supply and demand is often never reached. There are direct and indirect pressures on the boards of trustees, the physicians, and the staff to fill hospital beds in order to justify existing tax rates or new bond issues for hospital expansion. Incentives for providers and consumers to use in-hospital, rather than out-of-hospital, facilities are always present. It is more convenient for physicians to care for patients when they are under one roof. For the patient, it may be necessary to hire household help or home nursing care if he or she is an outpatient. Moreover, additional incentives for using in-hospital, instead of outpatient, facilities exist whenever third party payments cover only in-hospital care. Although outpatient care is being covered increasingly by major medical insurance contracts, limitations on reimbursement for out-of-hospital x-rays and tests in many Blue Cross and other insurance contracts still encourage hospitalization inappropriately. On the other hand, growth of prepaid group practice and other factors could lessen the demand for hospital beds.

Because the average cost of a one-day stay in the hospital is so high, about $300 a day in the United States in 1980, and because hospitalization accounts for the larger share of the total cost of personal health care, a sizable reduction in the average number of days of hospital care per person is the easiest route to cost containment. Geographical variations in the length of hospital stay by diagnosis, age, and sex are amazingly large in the United States. In 1978, the average hospital stay was 6.1 days in the West and 8.8 days in the Northeast. Through mandated review of hospital use, the government has attempted to reduce the total use of hospitals. But peer review of in-hospital care is costly. Forty-six million dollars were spent in 1977 to review the number of hospital days and attendant ancillary costs. Although the review claimed to have saved $50.5 million through lower bed utilization, only $5 million remain after subtracting the costs of the review and of maintaining the non-utilized beds.

Some increase in the bed occupancy rate of a hospital is to be expected whenever the percentage of aged persons in the bed population of that hospital increases. The elderly take longer to recover from illness than do the young, and they are more likely to require a second admission if prematurely discharged. Physicians try to avoid this eventuality by keeping them in the hospital for a longer period.

The occupancy rate in all non-federal, short-term general hospitals dropped slightly from 76 percent in 1965 (just prior to Medicare), peaked at 79 percent in 1969, and fell to 73 percent in 1978. Although the occupancy rate by the aged has been increasing since Medicare began and the percent of the aged in the population has increased, there has been some substitution of out-of-hospital care by younger persons. Another offsetting factor is the decline in the birthrate and the decline in the length of hospital stay per admission because of stricter peer review, improved drugs, and some more effective medical procedures. The greater use of surgicenters and out-of-hospital diagnostic laboratories also is reducing admissions per capita.

If HMOs such as Kaiser-Permanente continue to grow, they, too, will help decrease the use of hospitals. This is because physicians in HMOs have a monetary incentive to make lesser use of hospitals. Pressures by government, insurers, and fellow physicians on the hospitals with higher than average utilization rates are becoming effective. In pursuing its aim to contain costs by lowering utilization rates in the high-use states, the federal government is pursuing experimental reimbursement procedures.

Within the broader frame of world-wide practice, United States hospital usage is low. Among those European countries and other advanced nations for which the data are readily available, all except Australia have average rates well above the United States average of 7.6 days. However, economies of in-hospital costs within the United States may still be found. Incentives for such economies are greater in this country than abroad, where most hospitals are government-run, if not government-owned.

In the United Kingdom, strikes, that in 1973 forced 30,000 beds out of use, have helped maintain long hospital waiting lists. There has never been less than 400,000 persons on the waiting lists for a hospital bed since the National Health Service started, and there were as many as 600,000 individuals waiting in 1979.[95] Because the government pays for almost all health care in the United Kingdom, the financial incentives are to under-utilize hospitals, thus keeping costs within their budget of 5 percent to 6 percent of the GNP, compared to over 9 percent in the United States.

Although the United States has fewer hospital beds per 1,000 inhabitants than many European countries, the U.S. employs about 3.8 employees per bed (1978) and 3.5 (1975), compared with 1.0 in West Germany (1975) and 1.5 in the Netherlands (1975).[96]

Table 3. Hospital Days: United States and Europe

Country	Average Length of Stay (in days) Acute, General Hospitals
United States (1976)	7.7[b]
Australia (1977)	7.6[b]
Austria (1977)	14.5[a]
Belgium (1977)	12.6[a]
Canada (1975)	8.3[b]
Denmark (1975)	10.2[b]
England and Wales (1975)	10.1[b]
Finland (1977)	9.5[b]
France (1976)	13.2[b]
Italy (1977)	14.0[a]
Scotland (1976-78)	9.9[b]
Sweden (1977)	10.7[a]
Switzerland (1977)	14.3[a]
United Kingdom (1977)	12.4[a]
West Germany (prior to 1976)	16.7[a]
W. Germany (1976)	16.4[b]

[a] *Eurobook Health Handbook, 1978* (New York: Robert S. First, Inc., January 1978), pp. ix, xi.

[b] *Health, United States: 1980* (Washington, DC: Government Printing Office, 1980), p. 93.

CARE IN NURSING HOMES AND THE HOME

In the United States, the number of nursing home beds has been increasing steadily since 1963 in response to the rising demand by the typically mobile, nuclear, non-extended family units with no unemployed adult to take care of the ill and the aged. About 5 percent of the aged are in some type of institution, usually a nursing home. Medicare reimburses the costs of nursing-home care after hospitalization, which primarily substitutes for the more expensive hospital care. Medicaid, however, is the important government source of funds for nursing homes that provide all levels of care from custodial to skilled nursing care. By certifying standards of care and tying that certification to the cost-reimbursement under Medicare and Medicaid, government has tried to improve the quality of nursing homes.

Over 85 percent of persons living in nursing homes are 65 years or older, and 35 percent are 85 years or older. The latter group is increasing in numbers and are likely to be the sickest and poorest among the aged.

Recently, private health insurance has been increasing the coverage of expenses for nursing-home care and visiting nurse services. It is estimated that about one-half of nursing-home care expense and over two-thirds of the costs of visiting nurse care in the home are covered by private insurers. The trend is away from the use of expensive hospital care.

In 1967, Medicare began its coverage of post-hospital, skilled nursing home care. Medicare reimbursed the costs of only 6 million home health visits in 1972 as compared with 16 million in 1969.[97] By 1978, the number reimbursed was 17 million. Medicare pays "reasonable costs" directly to a participating nursing home for up to 100 days of care after hospitalization. Patients can be responsible for co-insurance amounts after 20 days of care. Medicare's requirement that skilled professional services be available on a continuing basis means that many nursing homes still do not satisfy the quality criterion in addition to the health and safety criteria. Many highly skilled nursing homes accepted under Medicaid are not reimbursed by Medicare. Skilled nursing homes have not been utilized to their maximum potential in substituting for hospital care of patients recovering from surgery or acute illness. In 1978, Medicare provided less than 2 percent of total nursing-home care costs because it reimburses nursing home care only "if it is required for convalescence and only if skilled-nursing care is provided."[98] Medicaid paid nearly 40 percent while about one-half of nursing-home care was paid for by private individuals.

Yet nursing home facilities have been increasing significantly. In 1977 there were 1.4 million beds in nursing-care homes compared with only 300,000 in 1963. Total expenditures for care in all types of nursing homes grew from $1.3 billion in 1965 to $17.8 billion in 1979.[99] However, there still are shortages, especially of low cost nursing homes of acceptable quality. A major problem is that "acceptable quality" nursing care is very difficult to provide at low cost and the financial resources of patients and their relatives are often insufficient to meet the bills. The average cost of one day's stay in a short-term community hospital was $173 in 1977 while the average of the daily charges by all types of nursing homes, using a thirty-day month, was only about $23 a day. At the larger, 200 or more beds, nursing homes, the average comparable daily charge was about $28.00.[100] With these low fees and continuing inflation, many nursing homes provide inadequate care, poor nutrition, unappetizing meals, and shabby physical surroundings. Medicaid reimbursement levels vary among the states, but are generally too low to support quality care. One commentator has written that "in 1973, in some states Medicaid actually reimbursed for skilled care less than what it would cost to rent a room in a third- or fourth-class hotel for a night."[101]

Of the $2.4 billion spent for nursing home care in fiscal year 1969, $1.8 billion, or 75 percent, was paid out of government monies but in 1976, out of $10.6 billion, the government paid $5.9 billion, or 56 percent. This decline in the government's share is a reversal of the usual expenditure patterns in health care markets and indicates substantial growth in private demand independent of government financing.[102]

Because the proportion of the aged in the population is increasing as medical science prolongs life and the birthrate falls, the number of available unemployed, able-bodied adults to care for the aged at home is decreasing. The demand to purchase custodial care and limited nursing-home care has risen sharply. More women are working, leaving few adults in the home to take care of even those aged persons who need only minimal help or care. A substantial number of the aged live alone. Contrary to popular belief, most persons 65 to 80 years are healthy enough to take care of their own needs.

In response to the increased demand for nursing-home beds, for-profit suppliers have rapidly entered the industry so that by 1976 they owned 75 percent of all the nursing homes and 68 percent of all the beds. Of a total of 1.4 million beds, only 0.2 million provide purely custodial care.[103] As is true in the case of hospitals, there is considerable variation by state in the number of nursing-home beds per 1,000 persons of age 65 or more. The rate is as low as 24 per 1,000 in Florida while Nebraska has 118.5. States with warmer climates generally have fewer beds. These are often the states to which retired people move. Older persons who move may be in better health than those who do not, and their lesser needs may contribute to fewer beds in those states.

Seventy-one percent of the nursing home residents are women, and 74 percent are 75 years or older. As the current near-aged persons retire, their social security benefits will be substantially higher. Those who are already 65 to 75 years old have much larger monthly benefits than those 75 years and older. It is the growth in social security benefits and of private pension plans, as well as that of Medicaid, that make nursing homes a profitable business.

The number of persons 65 years and older in nursing homes can be expected to increase. Because many of the aged today are more affluent than in the past, they refuse to give up their independence, hobbies, and friends, and also prefer not to live with their children. In 1976, 16 percent of those admitted to long-term care facilities were admitted on the grounds that the family was unable to care for the person.[104] In 1977, about one-fifth of the nursing home residents were mentally ill or senile, and about one-third had heart disease, hypertension, or other circulatory disorders. The data indicate that possibly one-fourth of elderly persons in nursing homes could live in a less institutionalized environment, but they have few alternatives.

The most viable alternative is the greater availability of helping services in the home. These include homemaker services, "meals on wheels," and visiting nurses and therapists. The for-profit, as well as the non-profit, organizations are expected to increase such services during the next decade. Among the large suppliers is the Upjohn Company. Business corporations are filling the gaps left by non-profit organizations. The Reagan Administration is on record as favoring the growth of home health care, a policy that goes hand-in-hand with the increase in the non-government provision of many of these services in the home.

Until July 1981, Medicare (under Part A) provided payment of reasonable costs for one hundred home health care visits per spell of illness if the patient is hospitalized during the year. The Omnibus Reconciliation Act of 1980 provides unlimited home health visits and eliminated the prior three-day hospitalization requirement. Under the supplementary medical care (Part B), unlimited home care visits are similarly reimbursed without the requirement of prior hospitalization and without payment, as previously required, of the $60 deductible. Annual costs have been less than a billion dollars under these programs. On July 1, 1979, new regulations had set limitations on the amounts paid. It is anticipated that expenditures for home health will increase substantially because not only is the prior hospitalization requirement lifted, but for-profit home health agencies may participate if a state's accreditation laws do not prevent.

Nearly 700,000 persons, or 26 of each 1,000 Medicare enrollees, used home care services in 1977. The average visit charge was $25 and the average annual total charges per person receiving the visits was $591, of which $527 was reimbursed.[105] About 90 percent of the users were aged; the remainder were permanently disabled or with end-stage renal disease. More health care in the home can be very cost-effective if it is a substitute for hospital or nursing home care. It is necessary to guard against excessive, additive use of home care.

It is less costly and more desirable to help people remain in their own homes as long as possible. Some societies other than the United States have government-financed programs of this nature, and the quality of life offered by multiple services coordinated to permit persons to live outside of institutions as long as possible is higher than that in institutions. There is, however, a large percentage of the institutionalized aged who, even with various types of home care, cannot manage on their own and must have some form of institutional care.

Retirement communities, a relatively recent development in the United States, may increase the percentage of the aged who, even with several chronic diseases, can manage outside of a nursing home and retain their independence to come and go as their health and inclination permit. Some of these special housing facilities consist of a single large building equipped as a hotel; in fact, many are refurbished hotels. Meals and cleaning services are provided, and physical therapy equipment is available. They also have on-call nurses. Because of the common dining and recreational facilities, the aged are aided in overcoming the loneliness about which many complain. However, when a person becomes permanently bedridden, even those retirement homes that have medical personnel can no longer serve as a substitute for the nursing home. If they do so, they become a nursing home.

It is important to recall that only 5 percent of the aged are in nursing homes and that only 20 percent of the aged believe that they are in poor health.

IV. ECONOMICS OF
MEDICAL MARKETS

The demand for medical care is not simple or unique. Medical care is not a single product supplied by one person or one organization. This might have been true when the United States was primarily an agricultural society that was characterized medically by the old-fashioned country doctor, few specialists, and less knowledge about disease and science. Over the past twenty years, the complexity of both demand and supply in the medical field has increased more than it had over the past one hundred years.

On the demand side, the financing of medical care has become so complex that an entire chapter (VII) of this book discusses in detail the development and pervasiveness of the third party umbrella. For analytical purposes, it is desirable to look at the medical care market as several highly fluid submarkets and consider them initially apart from the financing of the demand.

The same individual suppliers and consumers may behave differently and form different types of medical submarkets in varying medical situations. For example, the suppliers of emergency and non-emergency care are sometimes the same, but their reactions, and those of consumers, differ greatly under these two broad classifications. Four major types of health care can be distinguished: emergency, and the three non-emergency submarkets of minor, chronic. and preventive care. Even with these distinctions, the analytical problems of supply and demand may be obscured by the simplicity of the classification.

The focus here is on the *economics* of medical care, not because other factors are unimportant but because isolating economic factors, insofar as it is possible, is essential to an efficient or cost-effective allocation of medical resources. The discussion compares medical care markets to other existing service markets and not to an "ideal norm," which is unattainable within the complexity of our resources and needs in a modern, high technology society. As Harold Demsetz has said:

> [The] *nirvana* approach differs considerably from a *comparative institution* approach in which the relevant choice is between

alternative real institutional arrangements. In practice, those who adopt the *nirvana* viewpoint seek to discover discrepancies between the ideal and the real and if discrepancies are found, they deduce that the real is inefficient. Users of the comparative institution approach attempt to assess which alternative real institutional arrangement seems best able to cope with the economic problem; practitioners of this approach may use an ideal norm to provide standards from which divergences are assessed for all practical alternatives of interest and select as efficient that alternative which seems most likely to minimize the divergence.[1]

Most markets in the United States approach but do not achieve "Pareto optimality," an allocation of resources where no individual's position can be improved without hurting another individual's position. It is held here that medical care markets (except emergency care) differ from other markets only in degree, not in kind. There is included a brief theoretical discussion of the failures and success of insurance to improve the mechanisms of medical markets in approaching optimum welfare conditions for society. This sets a frame of reference for the empirical analysis of financing by third parties, insurers, and governments in Chapter VII.

Market decisions are preferable to government decisions because individuals are permitted to choose freely among alternatives. The responsibility for their decisions is theirs and is not spread through all of society or placed on a few bureaucrats or politicians. Informational feedback to suppliers is more rapid and specific through the marketplace than through election of persons to serve government. Allocation is determined by multiple decisions of all persons, "the invisible hand" theory. Therefore, government regulations based on a limited knowledge of individuals' preferences are not needed.

In the United States there are market prices for almost all medical services, including blood and other goods, although there are not for anatomical organs such as kidneys, hearts, and lungs. That blood is priced is abhorred by those whose value system rejects even thinking about pricing or setting a value on life. Lawyers Calabresi and Bobbitt write that

> any money market designed to allocate a scarce resource will result in a price being assigned to the resource. Even if the price accurately weighted wealth so that neither rich nor poor were advantaged, there remains the offense inherent in giving money values to sacred rights. . . . The more unintelligible the scheme (of allocation), the less obvious is the pricing of the sacred resource.[2]

An example of the less obvious pricing of a "sacred resource" is the "blood deductible" charge of "the first three pints of whole blood . . . furnished . . . and not replaced" required by HEW in the 1970s before permitting cost-reimbursement to skilled nursing homes for Medicare patients. The government's purpose was "to encourage voluntary blood replacement programs."[3] The patient was not responsible for supplying blood if the deductible has already been imposed in connection with the benefits for an immediately prior hospitalization.

The pricing of blood has become widely accepted, but the pricing of other organs of the body has been rejected as unethical even though public policy decisions on safety enforcement, the use of pesticides, the production of energy, or similar matters set an implicit price on life. Insurers and judicial decisions that award damages for disability incurred as a result of accidents also set an implicit price on life.

The external costs of moral injustice become known if, with an unequal distribution of incomes, a rich person can bid away an organ for transplantation or even more routine, but needed, medical care from a poor person. Thus societies, including the United States, have government provisions to finance medical care for the poor and also to finance the purchase of minimal food, shelter, and clothing for the poor. The latter are provided, however, through cash subsidies, not by direct payments (except in the case of food stamps) to providers. To permit the poor to receive cash and spend it in their own interest in lieu of paying the provider of medical care has been attacked on the grounds that the poor will not spend it on medical care even when needed. A voucher good only for the purchase of medical care would overcome this objection and would permit more competitive markets. It might also reduce the abuse and fraud by providers and consumers.

Many proponents of the thesis that medical care markets are unique, and thus *per se* require government intervention, tend to make their case on ethical and sociological grounds, not on economic grounds. For example, one author states: "I do not believe—either as a method of study or as a value judgment—that the economics of medical care can be considered apart from the ethical and sociological variables."[4] The literature of the medical care industry is rich in ethical and sociological studies that often are merely descriptive. The economic factors of costs and resource allocation to all of society's needs, the implications of consumer preferences, and the taxation of individual incomes tend to be overwhelmed by emotional portrayal of individuals in dire need of emergency medical care. Little, if any, recognition is given to the fact that the largest portion of medical care in the

Table 4. Disposition of Physician Office Visits
(1977)

Number of followups	11.2%
Return at specified time	60.8
Return if needed	22.6
Telephone followups planned	3.2
Referred to other MD	2.5
Return to referring MD	0.8
Admit to hospital	2.0
Other	1.3

Source: U.S. Department of Health, Education, and Welfare, "1977 Summary: National Ambulatory Medical Care Survey," *Advance Data*, No. 48 (April 13, 1979) (Washington, DC: Government Printing Office, 1979), p. 6. (The total does not add to 100 percent because of multiple outcomes of some visits.)

United States is not emergency care, but non-emergency care of chronic disease, acute and often minor illness, and preventive care is not acknowledged. Legislation for all medical care should not be based on conditions which exist only in the emergency medical care market and which are estimated to be, at most, 15 percent of all medical care.

In 1977, only 2 percent of all physician visits, numbering over half a billion, resulted in hospital admissions. The complete breakout of the disposition of the visits is shown in Table 4.

Not all persons who are hospitalized are in need of emergency care defined as life-saving care. Government data indicate that "childbirth was the major reason for hospitalization in non-federal, short-stay hospitals, accounting for 9 percent of all discharges in 1977."[5] Heart disease accounted for 8 percent; cancer, for 5 percent. Many of these were not emergency (life-or-death) admissions but others, such as the admission of some accident victims, were emergencies. Currently, only 15 to 30 percent of hospital emergency room visits are for urgent care,[6] and not all of these are emergencies in a life-or-death sense.

The major economic arguments which support the view that medical care is unique follow. Consumer ignorance, or lack of information, is greater than that of the provider's to a higher degree than in the markets of other professional services. There are greater consumer and provider uncertainty about the outcomes of medical interventions than about the benefits of other goods and services. There is an indivisibility in the supply of medical services, meaning that the consumption of small increments of medical care will not affect the outcomes, especially in medical emergencies. It is assumed that all consumers wish to avoid any risk of ill health and thus seek to purchase insurance to cover those risks of poor health which small expenditures might cover. It is claimed that health insurance is not available at reasonable cost because of "self-selection" among purchasers. Less healthy persons purchase more health insurance benefits while healthy persons purchase fewer benefits. This practice increases the prices of the more comprehensive health insurance purchased by individuals.

Unlike other forms of insurance where "moral hazard" (overuse induced by insurance) might occur, no remedies to penalize the cost impact of deliberate over-use of medical insurance are available. Examples include: the arsonist who has fire insurance is subject to prosecution, the survivors of a suicide do not benefit from life insurance, and persons who, based on their past driving records, are higher risks and pay higher automobile insurance rates. Similar restraints do not exist in the health care insurance markets because over-use with intent to defraud would be difficult to isolate.

The preceding arguments for the uniqueness of medical and health insurance markets are not entirely substantiated. For instance, it is wrong to say medical markets are unique because of a lack of information. Consumers of legal or architectural services, and even of automobile repair services, are also often more ignorant than the providers. Specialized information is the major component of all services. It is difficult to support the theory that consumer ignorance is unique to medical care. It may be that consumers are more ignorant about medical care, but that is a question of degree, not of kind, and also would be difficult to prove.

There may be more truth in the contention that medical care providers are more uncertain of the outcome of medical intervention than other service providers. However, other professionals are also uncertain of outcomes. For example, criminal lawyers cannot guarantee their clients that they will not be fined or jailed. It is possible that most consumers have greater uncertainty in the medical area than in the other professional areas because, until recently, physicians have cloaked their own uncertainty by fostering a "medical mystique" while no or little mystique is associated with the history and tradition of the other professions.

In all medical care markets except the emergency care submarket, substitutes for medical care exist. Therefore, opportunities for the consumption of incremental units of care exist, but not in as minute amounts as for most other goods and services.

The markets for medical care cannot be considered unique in an economic sense because consumers are ignorant, such care is a "necessity," or consumers cannot predict their own demands. Discontinuities of both supply and demand can be found in other markets, but to a lesser degree. Although the medical care market is not unique with respect to any one of these characteristics, it may be unique because of its special combination of these factors and their degrees of importance. Over-riding the economic characteristics are the lack of explicit prices of human life and vital organs that force the allocation of some resources outside the determination of the marketplace.

HEALTH INSURANCE AND "MORAL HAZARD"

There is little evidence that all consumers always wish to avoid incrementally small, possibly even some large, risks of ill health. Why else would people smoke cigarettes, ski fast, and drive recklessly?

It is true that a great deal of health insurance coverage (primarily for hospitalization) is first dollar expense coverage which gives this illusion. However, 75 percent of health insurance is bought by the employer, not by the individual. Labor unions have sought first dollar coverage, not necessarily the individual employee covered by health insurance. The employed individual must choose from among those financial arrangements which the employer has selected, and these may not be the ones that the consumer might have chosen in his or her own best interest. However, tax-free premium dollars received from the employer are worth more than wage dollars on which taxes are based and out of which insurance might be bought.

It is also true that health insurance to cover physician bills, whether or not as part of major medical insurance, has deductibles and other forms of consumer payments. Because insurance reimbursement is usually for "reasonable and customary" physician charges only, the out-of-pocket payments by consumers to physicians are often larger than the deductibles spelled out in the contracts and first dollar coverage is thus diluted.

People buy health insurance as they do other insurance: to reduce the risks of high, unpredictable expense. Health insurance has high administrative costs, but all insurance has administrative costs. To a degree, all forms of insurance have some self-selection and moral hazard components which add to costs. Health insurance differs from some forms of insurance not because of moral hazard, but because it cannot make whole the loss of a limb. But, neither can life insurance restore the loss of life. All insurance can do in these instances is restore some of the monetary loss which has occurred. In this sense, health insurance and life insurance markets are different from other insurance markets such as automobile, fire, and theft. In those instances, replacement of monetary loss enables the insured person to use the insurance money to become whole again. In the case of health insurance, "moral hazard" may exist because individuals may over-insure and then be less careful about their health. Preventive health care can substitute for purchase of health insurance.

Demand for medical care is to a degree a discretionary decision, and insurance may increase that demand. Martin Feldstein points out that "this destroys the optimality of complete insurance. The welfare loss due to the distortion of demand must be balanced against the welfare gain of risk spreading. The individual's optimal insurance policy therefore involves some degree of risk-sharing or 'co-insurance.'"[7] The latter statement is important in designing the forms of health insurance that most benefit society. If "excess" consumption of medical care were reduced by co-insurance or other direct payment by consumers, prices and utilization rates might fall. Value judgments are involved in weighing the loss to some poor persons who might not buy medical care when needed because of their out-of-pocket expenses against the gain to society from otherwise lower prices (and under present financial arrangements, lower taxes). The range of the more desirable co-insurance rates can be suggested from an examination of the available data about the effects of changes in co-insurance rates.

Moral hazard, it has been claimed, need not be "an inevitable consequence of market insurance."[8] Health insurance coverage paid for by an employer does not *per se* result in an increase of demand for medical care by the employee because health-insured persons also may practice self-imposed preventive care, as through more exercise and diet restraint, and these may act to reduce their demand for health care. This may offset the inducement to purchase more medical care because insurance reduces the net price at the time of consumption. Preventive health care may be complementary and not competitive with buying health insurance, as when persons pay for their own insurance. Economists Gary Becker and Isaac Ehrlich state that "moral hazard refers to an alleged deterrent effect of market insurance on self-protection" but also, "on the one hand, self-protection is discouraged because its marginal gain is reduced by the reduction of the difference between the incomes and thus the utilities in different states; on the other hand, it is encouraged if the price of market insurance is negatively related to the amount spent on protection."[9]

Further, Ehrlich and Becker state that, if market insurance is available at an actuarial, fair price, then it encourages individuals to spend for prevention amounts that maximize their expected incomes, and the optimal amount spent on prevention thus will be larger than the amount spent without market insurance.

To the degree that consumer health education regarding the value of better health from non-smoking, more exercise, and less food is successful, moral hazard may be decreased. Recent, improved mortality data and the continuing decline in physician visits per capita indicate that consumer health education may have offset to some degree the effect of insurance on utilization. However, there continues an impact on costs because of the "technological imperative" for some physicians to provide the latest, often the most expensive, diagnostic tests and treatment. Additionally, partly because of fear of malpractice suits and partly because of diagnostic uncertainty, some physicians request more, rather than fewer, routine tests.

In medical care submarkets where the potential of moral hazard on the part of the patient is greatest, insurance coverage is smallest. Relatively little private insurance covers drugs prescribed for out-of-hospital use. Only 8 percent of these costs are paid by private insurers, and only 25 percent by all third party payers. In contrast, 94 percent of hospital bills are paid by third parties.

Moral hazard is more relevant in some areas of health expenditures than in others. It is possible that only 40 percent (some believe only 20 percent) of demand for physician services is controlled by the consumer. Demand for a physician's services is complicated because, although individuals may initiate their own demand for a first visit, the number and timing of followup visits are determined by the physician. However, patients are not forced to follow these requests.

Consumers almost completely control their demand for out-of-hospital prescription drugs. Consumers do not always fill new prescriptions, and renewals and refills are primarily within their control. Some physicians may turn down consumers' requests for refills with suggestions of an office visit. If the price of drugs to consumers were reduced to zero by complete third party coverage, demand would increase considerably. Even with a $2 co-payment for each prescription, estimated 1983 costs under a national third party insurance program covering everyone would be $20 billion higher than if there were no program.[10]

Insurance coverage for drug expenditures is not as common as coverage for in-hospital anesthetic services. Once committed to surgery, an individual's choice of whether or not to have anesthetic services is unlikely to be influenced by who pays for them. Thus, Medicare pays for reasonable costs of anesthesia but does not pay for out-of-hospital drugs or for preventive physical examinations. Medicare also does not pay for eye refractions, immunizations, or routine dental care. In general, it excludes personal comfort items such as private duty nursing and plastic surgery which is not considered reconstructive.

There is no unique economic quality common to all types of medical care or health insurance. Rather, that uniqueness exists only in the emergency medical care market.

OVER- AND UNDER-UTILIZATION

It is difficult to define the desirable use of health services as distinguished from "over-use" or "under-use." To an economist, the concepts of over- and under-utilization are alien within the theoretical framework of economic demand in a free market, where the consumer pays directly for services rendered. In perfectly competitive markets, the price level "clears" the market. When a third party, not the consumer, pays the price for the service or when the price is pegged artificially below the equilibrium price, then the term over-utilization makes economic sense. However, there is then the concomitant problem: What is the standard or optimum against which over-utilization or under-utilization is measured?

Standard measures of utilization are particularly needed for hospital utilization because third party payments cover a greater portion of hospital bills (94 percent) than any other type of medical care. There is no restraint on hospital usage because the cost is not paid by the consumer. Despite the fact that physicians influence admissions and length of hospital stay, California data (see Chapter II, Table 1) support economic theory in that the longer the length-of-stay, the lesser the percentage of costs paid by the patient.

For some time hospital utilization review committees have, with varying degrees of success, set standards for the average number of hospital days medically needed for different diagnoses. In 1977, the average length of hospital stay in the West was 7.6 days and in the Northeast, 9.3 days.[11] Medicare has been paying for more than twice as many hospital days per 1,000 persons 65 years and over in some Professional Standards Review Organization (PSRO) areas than in others. The differences in average length-of-stay was greater than in hospital discharge rates. The latter varied from 257 per 1,000 Medicare enrollees in Hawaii to 468 in Texas' PSRO Area 1. The highest length-of-stay was 17.1 days in PSRO Area 13 in New York, and the lowest only 7.1 days in PSRO Area 11 in Central California.[12] The discharge rate explained only 9 percent of the overall variation in hospital days of care "whereas average length-of-stay explained 52 percent of the variation."[13] Although the percentage of those patients 75 years and over and other demographic and availability measures of substitute health resources in PSRO areas explain about three-fourths of the excess variation, the other fourth is unexplained and probably could be gradually eliminated by peer review if the West does not under-utilize hospital days. Increases in the number of skilled nursing homes would reduce the length of hospital stays.

Another type of hospital utilization control is pre-admission hospital screening. This was first tried in Sacramento County, California, under the Certified Hospital Admissions Program (CHAP), administered by the county medical society. CHAP's advance reviewer decides whether Medi-Cal (California's Medicaid) is liable for payment of the bill and, if so, for how long a stay. Reportedly, the initial results of such pre-admission screening for 73,000 Medi-Cal patients were "a dramatic drop in costs to the state and only isolated complaints from doctors."[14] The average hospital stay was reduced from about six days to four and one-half days per admission. In addition, because claims initially certified by CHAP were not subject to post-audit by Medi-Cal, there was, on net, an administrative saving. However, this technique has not been widely adopted.

A more recent approach to containing costs through controlled utilization rates is provider reimbursement of the average cost of each type of discharge diagnosis. This involves determination of the usual length-of-stay by geographic area and by diagnosis. Many PSROs do this and thus a "per case" average can be set. The third party reimburser uses the norms to decide reimbursement rates or the percentage of the claimed costs that will be paid. Non-reimbursement indirectly acts to reduce length-of-stay. An analysis of this approach by Blue Cross-Blue Shield in Pennsylvania found significant variation in effectiveness and significant reductions in only those hospitals with low occupancy rates. These presumably had allowed considerable slack to develop.[15] Assessment of the New Jersey experience with case reimbursement by 383 categories which take into account diagnoses and some demographic factors in setting prospective rates has not yet been made.

There is disagreement in the literature about whether states that have mandated hospital rate-setting have been successful in controlling the rate of increase in community hospital costs, rates and utilizations. Selected, six-state data (Connecticut, Maryland, Massachusetts, New Jersey, New York, and Washington) showed an annual rate of increase of 11.2 percent in 1976–78 while in all other states, five of which meet the criterion of having rate-setting programs but do not meet a compulsory compliance criterion, the increase was 14.3 percent.[16] Earlier studies do not support these rather restrictive data, and the hospital industry spokesmen argue that their "voluntary effort" (VE) has been successful in containing the rise in hospital costs. However, a nine-state survey that adds Colorado, Rhode Island, and Wisconsin to the six states listed above supports mandatory cost controls as being effective in 1977 and 1978.[17] A longer period than two or three years is needed to judge whether or not imposed capping of hospital costs can restrain hospital cost increases.

As a past member of the Phase II, Health Services Industry Committee (1971–74), I believe that some hospitals can deplete depreciation and other reserves for a few years. Other hospitals have "water" in their administrative costs. However, eventually quality will tend to fall if the total amount of reimbursed revenues of any enterprise are kept below actual expenses over a period of several years. In hospitals where government reimburses below expenses, the costs are passed on in higher charges to non-government reimbursed patients.

Whereas Medicare, Medicaid, and most Blues reimburse costs, others reimburse charges. The latter type of reimbursement has little if any influence on utilization rates and thus charges can remain constant while costs rise.

Third party payments that once concentrated almost entirely on hospitalization and surgical care now cover an increasing variety of ambulatory health care. As this expansion continues, effective utilization standards for newly covered types of care are being developed, but with varying degrees of success in implementation. Advance review along the lines of CHAP is potentially more cost-saving than *post facto* review. Advance review is a special form of prospective reimbursement that also appears applicable to areas of health care beyond the hospital setting. Prospective cost reimbursement involves negotiated rates for all hospital days during the ensuing year. Because it is based on costs of the previous year, it is often a lagged reimbursement that does not contain costs over the long run. Proponents claim that hospitals are not assured, under prospective reimbursement, that every cost that exceeds the standard guidelines will be reimbursed and that, therefore, the hospitals tend to curtail excessive expenditures. This argument assumes that without prospective reimbursement, hospitals tend to inflate costs. Thirty states have some form of this program, whether run by the state or by Blue Cross or hospital associations that have vested interests. A recent preliminary analysis, published in the federal government's *Health Care Financing Review*, "suggests that mandatory programs have a significantly higher probability of influencing hospital behavior than do voluntary programs."[18]

The terms "under-use" and "under-utilization" generally refer to medical needs left unfulfilled. A lack of money, education, or transportation may act as barriers to the transformation of needs into effective demands. The concept of under-utilization seems to beg the question of what implicit standard is used. There is also no precise standard from which to measure over-utilization. Many articles have been written about over-utilization of surgery for elective operations in the fee-for-service sector in the United States. The concept of over-utilization used is a relative one that compares surgical rates across states and with those in other countries. Little research has been done on whether there might be under-utilization in prepaid group practice where salaried surgeons have an economic incentive not to operate because the group as a whole thereby saves money. Such savings are then available for bonuses to employees and partners, including member physicians. Prepaid group practice reverses the incentives of fee-for-service practice. There is a lack of definitive standards from which under- or over-utilization can be fairly judged. During the 1970s, a series of costly regulations under Regional Health Planning and Health Systems Agencies have developed. These govern hospital expansion and the purchase of new medical technology. The regulations are claimed to rest on hard data about medical needs, but the guidelines are often criticized as arbitrary and the decisions to use them as political.

Professor Blomqvist, the author of Table 5, writes that "low-mortality diseases . . . account for 35.5 percent of all episodes in Canada but only for 25.6 percent of those in the U.K." and concludes that the data "*are* consistent with the idea that a larger proportion of resources in Canada are spent on treating disease associated with temporary disability and pain only and hence that the U.K. system is relatively less effective in eliminating those than it is in reducing mortality."[19] It would be interesting to compute a similar table comparing large HMOs with fee-for-service medical care delivery in the same area.

To what extent under- or over-utilization occurs in the treatment of minor and chronic diseases is difficult to determine. The quantity of treatment needed depends not only on the specific health problem but also on its severity, the general health of the persons afflicted, and their responses to both the disease and its treatment. Thus, the av-

Table 5. Hospitalization Episodes per Death by Selected Disease Categories, Mid-1970s

Disease Category	United Kingdom	Canada
Tuberculosis	13.5	12.5
Malignant neoplasms	2.5	4.0
Benign neoplasms	89.3	277.0
Endocrine, metabolic	12.4	18.5
Nervous system	13.1	28.4
Cardiovascular system	1.6	4.5
Respiratory system	5.2	43.9
Digestive system	33.4	73.5
Genitourinary system	10.1	79.4
Childbirth	#	#
Musculoskeletal system	66.7	277.0
Fractures, injuries	30.2	35.3

(# not computed because of the very small number of maternal deaths in either country.)
Source: Ake Blomqvist, *The Health Care Business* (British Columbia, Canada: The Fraser Institute, 1979), p. 121.

erage number of physician office visits may be determined for the treatment of the usual course of a particular disease. But a *specific* deviation from the average of all patients in a given geographical area is not proof of either under- or over-utilization. Many medical groups that have subscribers paying a set monthly charge regardless of use have developed medical review criteria for common diagnoses which spell out for each diagnosis the desirable frequency of visits, whether referral to a specialist may be needed, kinds and number of laboratory tests and x-rays, type and amount of therapy indicated, and the expected duration of the disease.

The average number of procedures may be determined for the treatment of the usual course of a particular disease. Sizable deviation from the area average for many diagnoses by one physician's profile of patients does raise questions unless the physician has a very unique case mix. Records of physicians' treatments of patients are being developed and compared with the averages of those of all physicians in their medical group or in their area. These physician profiles are used to monitor the quality of care, a concept which encompasses under-utilization as well as over-utilization. These techniques are commonly used for cost containment by state-administered Medicaid and federal Medicare programs which reimburse providers.

In the case of minor health problems, effective utilization control is difficult because it is almost wholly within the control of a would-be patient to initiate the first visit to a physician for a new health problem. Determination of the number of followup office visits is influenced by the physician although the patient, by not complying with the physician's request for return visits (or delaying them), may exert considerable control over use. The patient also may seek the services of more than one physician for any health problem, except possibly in an extreme emergency where physical limitation may prevent seeking additional sources of medical help.

Over-use in emergency situations and for acute diseases is possible because of the provider's actions. For example, physicians may prescribe more tests and x-rays than are needed to make a diagnosis or prescribe too long a hospital stay. However, in emergencies, medical procedures often take place in an institutional setting—a hospital or clinic and/or under group practice—and are therefore more susceptible to standardization imposed by the organization involved. Because utilization of such care is primarily within the physician's initiative, it usually is subject to peer review. For these reasons there is a presumption that over-utilization in the cases of emergencies or acute diseases can be controlled. The problem of claimed over-utilization of non-emergency surgical procedures in the United States under fee-for-service practice is discussed in the next chapter.

In general, salaried medical practice in institutions and/or groups affords more opportunity for controlling utilization costs than do solo practice arrangements. Economic rewards to physicians in a group are dependent more on other physicians in the group than on all the physicians practicing in a community. The fact that group organizations of salaried personnel with per capita fee arrangements permit more control does not mean that these organizations are necessarily more efficient. Indeed, the Veterans' Administration hospital system, with its salaried personnel and annual budgeted costs, is sometimes criticized for inefficiency, poor quality care, and relatively high costs.

V. SUBMARKETS OF
MEDICAL CARE

Care for a medical emergency is a high-cost necessity that is unpredictable. It is often accompanied by consumer ignorance about the quantity and quality of care needed. Emergency care is indivisible because the hospital room, surgical services, in-hospital physician services, drugs and nursing care, and tests and x-rays are a package that the patient must accept or reject as an entity. Unlike many other necessities, small increments of effective emergency medical care are difficult if not impossible to purchase and, even if they were available, their use would be ineffective in most cases. The extreme emergency of a life-saving operation may not occur often for an individual, but when it does, the individual must buy the whole package or none at all.

The emergency medical care submarket is not typical of all, or even of the majority, of the medical care submarkets. The combination of the demand and the supply factors that characterize it is unique. Physicians influence the demand for emergency medical care more than other types of medical care. In emergencies, patients may be unconscious, they may be too ill to make a rational choice, or they may not want to be involved in making a medical decision which may affect them drastically. Moreover, consumer ignorance of the risks and benefits from alternative medical procedures may he greater in emergency than in some non-emergency situations. The length of time required to explain adequately each treatment option may, in the physician's opinion, create too great a delay in the implementation of care.

However, if the definition of emergency is not strictly defined as an immediate, life-threatening situation, then patients can be involved in choosing among options. For example, patients with breast cancer should be informed about the risks and benefits of all the alternative therapeutic options and then give their consent for the option chosen. This mode of practice is required in California in cases of suspected breast cancer.

A consent form for surgery is a legal document designed to protect the patient, physicians, nurses, and the hospital. The form indicates the medical or surgical procedures to be performed and the probability of potential risks and benefits to the patient. Practicing physicians as well as their patients are often ignorant of the available hard data about the efficacy and risks and costs of alternative options of medical procedures. This is because of the rapidity of change in medical technology and the flood of literature. In some instances, there are no hard data available.

The American College of Physicians has, through its Medical Necessity Project, evaluated some sixty diagnostic tests and procedures with recommendations to third parties whether or not to reimburse for the procedures. Blue Shield reported probable savings of $860,000 if, in 1975–78, they had discontinued routine reimbursement for phonocardiograms.[1] The College's new Clinical Efficacy Assessment Project has released judgments on the efficacy of eight fairly expensive procedures and has avoided the more controversial part of their earlier project by not specifying reimbursement or non-reimbursement. The new (1978) National Center for Health Care Technology has been doing similar assessments for the Medicare and Medicaid programs. The decision whether or not to reimburse remains with the latter programs after the assessment is made.

Some well-informed patients, depending on their physical condition and the suspected diagnosis, may insist on non-invasive, but expensive, computerized scans (or ultrasound) to be used where practicable rather than the invasive, less expensive arteriography that involves a much higher risk. Knowledgeable patients with cancer are increasingly exploring their options among treatments, about which there is often no hard scientific data to support one over another. Cornelius Ryan's taped diary account of such a search, which became a book written by his wife, A Private Battle, is illustrative of how much the intelligent lay person can understand.[2] Patients know their preferences in respect to the potential tradeoffs between length of life and quality of life, and their preferences need to be recognized in clinical decisions.

Because third parties usually pay most of the bill, differences in the monetary costs are not usually considered by the patient. However, where one's own health is concerned, the patient may be very willing to spend large sums. There is a growing body of literature which argues that, because it is the physician who actually orders the expensive procedures, it is the physician who must consider the societal costs of the use of the expensive medical technology.[3] The physician, however, is the patient's agent, not society's budget-keeper. In an emergency situation, few persons may accept that societal costs should over-ride the best interests of the patient. The patient's best interests, however, are not always clear. For example, is it in the patient's best interest to use expensive medical care to prolong life when there is no possibility of the patient regaining consciousness? Today, the courts have become involved in answering this question that previously lay entirely within the physician's realm. Also, third parties in the name of cost containment are affecting clinical decision-making through denying reimbursement. Because government is an important third party payer, this has become a public policy matter. Reimbursement can be denied on the basis that a test is not needed, a medical procedure is not effective, or that a medical procedure still lies in the realm of experimental—not therapeutic—medicine.

Physicians differ in how much information they discuss with their patients. Traditions, beliefs, professional training, and uncertainties as well as referral patterns influence physician behavior about their involvement of the patient in clinical decision-making. A patient's financial arrangements for medical care and level of education may affect the quality of the voluntary informed consent obtained and the treatment options available.

The proportion of the total medical care that is emergency care is difficult to judge. One indication is hospital inpatient and outpatient emergency care costs. Hospital costs represent about 40 percent of all United States expenditures for health today. But some inpatient and many outpatient hospital services do not constitute emergency care. In recent years there has been a tremendous increase in the use of hospital emergency departments by patients seeking other than emergency care. Such patients are using the hospital as "their doctor." This practice unnecessarily depletes more expensive resources and is a factor in rising medical costs. However, consumers in some geographical areas have no choice if they believe that it is a necessity to purchase medical care on a Sunday or during evening hours.

Another indicator of what proportion of medical care is emergency care is the share of physicians' time devoted to emergencies. A 1976 United States study states:

> In view of the great absolute increase in the use of emergency medical services during recent years, it is of interest that they account for only 2 percent of all visits to physicians. It is a very visible 2 percent, however, since the hospitals bear the entire

brunt of this pressure and a large proportion of patients in emergency departments are not there for true emergency reasons.[4]

Of all visits to office-based internists in 1975, 28.6 percent are estimated to have been for a "serious or very serious problem."[5]

In many countries, including the United States, one hospital in an urban area may specialize in handling automobile accident victims and another the treatment of badly burned individuals. Other trauma specialties are spinal cord injuries, critical newborns, and cardiac patients who require surgery. Emergency medicine has recently become a new board specialty.

Federal funding of regional emergency medical systems for ambulances, helicopters, radio networking, and extension of the 911 emergency number continue through 1982. The original Emergency Medical Sources Systems Act of 1973 had envisioned about 300 regional systems. At the end of 1979, about fifty regional programs have been developed and are operating. Training of ambulance and fire department personnel in emergency medical techniques to stabilize the patient during transportation is an important part of an emergency system.

The demand for emergency care differs from the demand for non-emergency care. In economic terms, the demand for emergency care is highly inelastic or insensitive to price. An increase in price does not appreciably diminish demand for emergency medical care. On the other hand, the same consumers may shop around for non-emergency care. The price has a considerable effect on the amount of care that they demand if they do not have health insurance that covers a large part of the costs. When all the expenses are covered, consumers may use their time to shop for quality. Recent studies indicate that consumers are beginning to shop for non-emergency medical care as they do for other non-medical services.[6] The demand for non-emergency care is affected by price in terms of time, that is "waiting," as well as by price in monetary units.

The suppliers of medical care respond in one way to emergencies and in another to non-emergencies. For example, physicians in many countries traditionally have given emergency medical care on a charitable basis far more routinely than non-emergency medical care. This is partly because of the church-financed, and more recently government-financed, hospital-based structure of emergency care. Because historically the poor have been understandably reluctant to seek other than emergency medical care, the development of "two streams of medicine" by income levels was not challenged earlier. Today, many individuals define emergency care very broadly, and many also believe that there is a right to all medical care, not only emergency medical care.

In the United States, the financing of emergency medical care has developed differently from the financing of non-emergency care. The priority of an emergency is unchallenged. For the poor, emergency hospital care often has been wholly or partially supplied by the church, wealthy donors, governments at the local and county levels, and individual physicians. Similarly, private health insurance developed primarily and most extensively to cover in-hospital costs, which are those most akin to the medical care costs of emergencies.

In general, emergency cases take precedence over other types of medical problems because of the obvious urgency of the symptoms. Nowhere is this more clearly evident than in the case of accidents, the fourth leading cause of death in the United States—after heart attack, cancer, and stroke. Accidents create demand for substantial amounts of emergency medical care. Prevention of accidents would reduce that demand. In 1960, the death rate per 100,000 population for all accidents was 52.3; in 1976, about 46.9. However, the absolute number of accidents rose during the same period. About one-half of all accidents in the United States involve motor vehicles.

Although there was a sharp reduction from 1968 to 1975 in age-adjusted deaths due to motor vehicle accidents, from 28.4 to 21.3 per 100,000 persons, that rate rose slightly to 22.4 in 1977[7] despite the 55-miles-per-hour speed limit that became effective nationwide in 1974. The rise could reflect the increase in the number of younger drivers, who have a higher accident rate than older drivers, and the fact that more miles per capita were being driven. Although, as of this writing, there are no data available for 1979 or later, the motor vehicle accident rate probably has fallen again because the rising cost of gasoline will have induced a reduction in miles driven per capita.

For all other accidents, the age-adjusted monthly rate also declined from 26.7 per 100,000 population in 1968 to 21.9 in 1977. Part of the decline reflects the decrease in work-related accidents, which are about one-third of non-automobile-related accidents. Major factors in improved work safety are improved design of manufacturing equipment and safer industrial plant lay-outs. Evidence, however, indicates that other variables are also involved in the increase in occupational and home safety. Worker and consumer safety education programs have increased in number and effectiveness.

Governments world-wide have concentrated policy to reduce medical emergencies on the prevention of motor vehicle collisions. However, studies indicate that driver safety education about the dangers of driving while drunk and the recall of drivers' licenses based on a point system tied to the number of individual traffic violation tickets issued have not had unqualified success in any country. Even the much-touted strict laws in Scandinavia, which sentence violators to institutions for weekend "rehabilitation" and also revoke the driving licenses of persons found drunk while driving, have not been as successful as is widely reported in the United States. One expert has labelled this misconception the "Scandinavian Myth."[8]

Within the United States there is conflicting evidence as to whether the 1968 federal standards for improved motor vehicle design reduced deaths from motor vehicle accidents. Economist Sam Peltzman, after an intriguing analysis of the effect of the several government-mandated changes in automobile design, concludes that they did not reduce the anticipated highway death rate. He interprets the data as follows: "Drivers have offset this [greater product safety] by taking greater accident risk" and market forces had already set in motion "a long-term decline in the highway death rate" so that the response "has been to have more severe accidents while continuing to have fewer accidents."[9]

Among important variables in his analysis are the low use of seat belts, a shift to a younger driving age population, an increase in vehicle speed (analysis is prior to the 55 MPH speed limit set in 1974), and a 63 percent increase in drunk-driving arrests per 1,000 drivers from 1965 to 1971. On the other hand, a government report[10] argues that the required higher safety standards reduced the death rate from what it otherwise would have been. All agree that higher speeds cause more traffic fatalities and thus the 55-miles-per-hour speed limit, when enforced, has been effective, as has been better road engineering. The policy dilemma is illustrated by the following quotations:

Speeding is commonly a response to the pressures of society and to the self-imposed pressures of people's life style. But it also provides excitement, and the sense of power and freedom. No road safety campaign could do much about any of these motivations. Moreover, speeding is encouraged by better roads, whose benefits may then be partly cancelled out. Traffic engineering can help to reduce the hazards, offering better and certainly more immediate prospects of road safety than attempts to change behaviour.[11]

Subjective factors, largely social and cultural in character, are of decisive importance in road accidents. Unconscious impulses and 'exasperated individualism . . . ' lead to irrational behaviour at the wheel, whereas driving objectively requires a high degree of civic consciousness and awareness of the rights of others. Such awareness is hampered by the fact that drivers transfer to their cars the sense of safety they have within their homes and thus feel separated from the world and from the other drivers all around them. Ultimately, the causes of car accidents can be traced back to failure to come to terms with the process of cultural transformation inherent in industrialization and to the persistence of traditional, anachronistic cultural values.[12]

Both active intervention to reduce automobile accidents and passive control through making driving more safe seem to have had little effect.

However, passive intervention has had greater success than the conventional safety education programs in preventing fatal accidents from other causes. For example, industrial presses that shut off when a human hand crosses a safety line beyond which the operator's hands could become caught in the press have eliminated one type of accident. The design change has been far more effective than trying to educate people not to put their hands under dangerous parts of machines.

Because accidents are the number one cause of death for persons one to thirty-eight years, it is important that efforts to find effective means to educate for safety continue. Safety at the workplace has been under state laws, and recently also under the federal regulations of the Occupational Safety and Health Act (OSHA). Integration of the existing state and federal regulations to eliminate conflicts is beginning to occur. This could result in individuals being more willing to conform to a single standard, not conflicting ones.

NON-EMERGENCY CARE

Non-emergency care may be divided roughly into three types: (1) care of minor health problems, (2) continuum of care required for chronic disease, and (3) preventive health care. The first two are the more traditional areas of medical care.

Among the submarkets of non-emergency medical care, changes in prices charged and differences in the amount of time needed to obtain and receive care create varied responses in demand. Prior to the general pervasiveness of the third party umbrella, consumers' income levels also affected the size and urgency of their demands for all kinds of medical care services other than emergency. For those health services for which there is little third party coverage, the income effect remains strong. In 1978, for example, 37 percent of persons with less than $7,000 annual income had a dental visit as compared with 67 percent of those with a $25,000 or more family income. However, in 1978, some 73 percent of persons with less than $7,000 family annual income had a physician visit as compared with 78 percent of those with a family income of $25,000 or more.[13]

Evidence points to the probability that as individuals' incomes increase, they will spend more for all types of medical care than they did previously. For some types of medical care, notably dental care, people may increase their expenditures by a greater percentage than the increase in their income, thus making dental care, especially orthodontal care, a "luxury" or "superior" good or service.

The overall amount spent for medical care is increasing faster than the rise in national income. This is caused by four factors: (1) an increasing proportion of aged persons in our society, who consume more medical care per capita than younger persons, (2) a faster rise in medical care prices than the general inflation rate, (3) a shift in tastes or consumer preferences in favor of medical care over other goods, and (4) a stable out-of-pocket price of medical care as a result of the increase in the percentage paid by third parties.

The recent shift in consumer preferences may push more items of medical care into the luxury or superior good category. Preventive care, now rarely reimbursed by governments and insurers, is probably being purchased as a luxury good. Conclusive data to prove this are difficult to find. The investment of personal time in the consumption of medical care can be added to waiting and travel times to derive a "time price" of medical care. The time price acts to conceal price and income effects. Moreover, it is difficult to delineate the effectiveness of some preventive medical care procedures such as the annual physical and some specific tests.

The increase in expenditures on prescription drugs has been noticeably less than for medical care services and may reflect not only the usual difference that prices of goods do not rise as fast as do prices of services, but also that the large pharmaceutical companies were more affected by price controls (1971–74) and competitive market forces than physicians and hospitals. Third party coverage of out-of-hospital, prescription drugs expense is comparatively very low.

The overall out-of-pocket cost of all medical care to the consumer, corrected for inflation at the time of consumption, has been stable for the past ten years at 2.6 percent of GNP. The percentage of costs paid by third parties (private insurers and government) has so increased that the net price of medical care is very low compared with those of other goods, making medical care a relative "bargain." By 1975, out-of-pocket spending by all families (two or more persons) was $93 for hospital and $201 for physician services as compared with only $72 and $164, respectively, in the higher value dollars of 1970. These are increases of 25 and 23 percent over five years—far less than the rise in cost-of-living during the same period.

Recent studies of demand indicate that time price and money price affect the number of physician visits. Waiting, transportation time, and the loss of time spent by the consumer in the consumption of any medical procedure are all time costs. In recent years, time price has been rising faster than the out-of-pocket money price for medical care. This is especially true for mothers who enter the labor force while they have young children. Forty-three percent of mothers with children under six years and 53 percent with children under eighteen years are working. However, time costs are also high for the self-employed, blue-collar workers who lose wages when not at work, and for many others. Because until very recently productivity per capita has been increasing, every worker's time costs have increased. Thus, it is not surprising that studies which estimate demand in relation only to the money price find that the elasticity (sensitivity) of demand to changes in price is less than one. If the time price were included, more elastic demand curves would result, thus indicating considerable sensitivity to both time and money spent in getting medical care. The decline in the number of physician visits per capita despite increasing third party coverage and higher real incomes has not been by chance.

A complicating statistical factor in analyzing income effects is that income is positively correlated with education. For example, in 1978 the mean annual earnings for persons 14 years and older with only eight years of schooling was $11,425; one to three years of high school, $13,697; four years of high school, $17,648; and four years or more of college, $27,236. The comparable medians (the median is an average which deletes the effect of extremes) were: $8,752, $11,205, $15,884, and $23,295, respectively.[14]

To what degree expenditures on non-emergency medical care by higher income groups is a function of income level and to what degree a function of education is not precisely known. There are Australian data which do correct for all variables except education, and show that the more years of schooling, the less physician visits per capita. It may be that the more educated in advanced industrial societies are increasingly aware of the limitations of medicine and also that their time costs are higher than those of less educated persons.

Persons of higher socio-economic status are more likely to use internists than general practitioners, be operated on by established surgeons rather than residents, and see private physicians rather than use clinics. This raises the questions of whether they are purchasing a higher quality of medical care, albeit at higher prices, and of how extensively their higher expenditures are subsidized out of taxation revenues, as when they are covered by Medicare, or if they work for an employer who expenses health insurance premiums paid on behalf of his employees. About $14 billion in 1979 were paid by employers as health insurance premiums. Most economists argue that these dollars would have been paid out as wages and salaries if they had not been earmarked otherwise. Persons with higher incomes pay more income tax, but the tax subsidies for medical care premiums are not related to personal income. On the other hand, the tax-financed British National Health Service (NHS) has not been able to equalize the quality of care among that country's socio-economic classes nor decrease that country's geographical inequalities.

Some persons question the ethics of having two or more levels of medical care quality. Variation in levels of quality will always exist because some physicians and hospitals are better trained and equipped than others. What disturbs people is how the higher quality medical care is allocated. In some countries with national health care systems, bribery or under-the-counter payments enable the better informed, and those with better political connections, to obtain higher quality care. In all countries, those with more education tend to receive better quality care because they can articulate more accurately their needs and better understand the medical options. In all countries, those who live in rural areas receive poorer medical care. In the United States, persons in those metropolitan areas with teaching hospitals have access to high quality care regardless of income, and especially if they need emergency care or have a rare disease. This is a matter of physical access; the barrier is not financial. In the United States and the United Kingdom, persons with higher socio-economic status generally obtain higher quality medical care.

It is generally accepted world-wide that sustaining a continuum of different levels of medical care is empirically unavoidable and ethically defensible. Resources are limited, and it is impossible to define precisely "medical need." The arguments are summarized as follows: medical care that may be considered needed by a patient may not be considered medically necessary by a physician. If all medical care is virtually free, "needed" medical care becomes a very expansive term. Without a money price, demands for health care grow far faster than demand for other goods and services. Resources then are diverted away from satisfying nutritional, housing, and other needs that might improve health more than additional units of medical care. Rapid innovation of high cost, supportive medical technology makes it impossible for countries to provide the latest, most costly, diagnostic and therapeutic procedures to all individuals who believe that they need them without exorbitant levels of taxation, resulting in undue sacrifice of other worthwhile social goals. If the federal government becomes the payer of last resort for treatment of all diseases, as it already is for persons with kidney failure in the United States, then the high total costs of all organ transplants and many other medical procedures will become so great that other expenditures that might yield greater total health benefits will probably never occur. Because of this possible outcome, the use of cost-benefit analysis has evolved as the basis of administrative, allocative rules governing the delivery of medical care in some countries and is evolving as such in the United States today.

Medicaid, the government's program that pays the medical bills for the poor, has reversed the earlier (pre-1966) direct relationship between low income and few physician visits. Today, among individuals in the lowest income category, physician visits per capita are higher than in the middle and high income group. In 1977, per capita physician office visits, excluding inpatient hospital visits, were: 5.8 for family incomes less than $5,000, 4.9 for family incomes $5,000 to $10,000, 4.7 for family incomes $10,000 to $15,000, and also 4.7 for those in the income class $15,000 to $25,000. Visits per capita were only 4.8 for those with incomes of $25,000 or more. A breakdown of telephone visits indicates that those with incomes under $5,000 had more telephone communication with physicians (0.60 per capita) than those in income groups up to $15,000, and nearly as many as in the higher income groups (0.64 and 0.65).[15] This is surprising to those who hypothesized only a few years ago that the poor did not use the telephone for medical care advice and information as often as persons with higher incomes and higher education.

Minor Illness

The data for separating minor from more serious illness can only be collected and analyzed *post facto*. A provider of medical care may be able to label a health problem as minor only after he or she has talked with or examined the consumer. Consumers also cannot always distinguish between minor and more important health problems. The use of self-care books may decrease the number of instances in which consumers misjudge a health discomfort as not serious and also reduce physician visits for treatment of minor illnesses.

In formulating national health policy, it is necessary to consider how best to allocate scarce medical resources so that "minor" health problems do not draw large quantities of medical resources away from the care of acute and chronic disease, as well as preventive health procedures. The data limitations which make it difficult to develop policy do not, however, hinder the theoretical analyses that underlie the formation of national policy. There is no easy way to isolate and then not reimburse medical care for minor diseases.

In non-emergency care markets, demand is more responsive to changes in price than in emergency markets. Therefore, use of consumer co-payments, whether an amount such as $2 or $4 paid at the time of a physician's office visit, a $100 or larger deductible, or a required cost-corridor of 20 percent, will restrain the use of medical care resources. However, there are differences in the effects of deductibles and cost-corridors that discriminate in the use of medical care between minor and chronic illness. In cases of minor illnesses, the deductible is not likely to be reached and thus is effective in restraining demand in minor illness. In cases of chronic illnesses, the patient expects medical costs to be substantially higher than the deductible because of anticipated, repeated visits to the physician and, therefore, the patient "would be likely to immediately act as if insurance were paying for services."[16] Thus, a $5 out-of-pocket payment for each physician visit would affect demand for ambulatory care of chronic illness more than a deductible with no cost-corridor, and would also simultaneously reduce demand for care of minor illnesses. Many of the new, prepaid group practices have an out-of-pocket payment for each physician visit.

During the 1970s, health insurers developed increasingly sophisticated restraints on consumer use and also introduced incentives for providers to reduce the number of referrals and the use of tests and x-rays. Control over provider-induced utilization has been through reimbursement rules. Insurers commonly reimburse only a percentage of billed charges and may not reimburse some charges at all, such as those for the routine battery of tests upon hospital admission.

From the consumer's point of view, it is often difficult in the initial phases of an illness to separate a minor from a more serious illness. The point at which a minor disease presages a more serious problem and treatment becomes preventive care is not clear. Many consumers do not elect to be patients until pain or discomfort impedes their normal functioning. Many diseases may not seem serious enough, initially, to seek medical care. This is one of the major reasons for periodic physical examinations. On the other hand, some consumers seek medical care for very minor health problems, the progress and outcome of which the physician cannot change. Apparently the number of self-limiting illnesses for which a physician can do nothing and from which one eventually recovers, such as a cold, is far higher than many people realize. Suspicion of over-utilization of medical care for minor health problems is greater when the consumer does not pay directly for his own medical care. It is, however, very difficult even to guess how much over-utilization of this type occurs.

Chronic Disease[17]

Chronic diseases are those that typically have a slow beginning, can be present for many years before clinical symptoms appear, and may be alleviated for long periods of time but are usually without permanent cure. Treatment of such diseases is primarily designed to alleviate symptoms and to provide supportive therapy and/or psychological comfort. Treatment may or may not prolong life; it often improves the quality of life.

In 1976, chronic diseases limited the normal activities of 30 million persons in the United States. All diseases lasting over a three-month period are considered chronic. While 28 percent of persons with chronic disease worked outside the home, 33 percent were homemakers, and some were students. Only 25 percent were unable to carry on their major activities. Persons with disabling chronic diseases usually retire earlier than others. Because our population is aging, the incidence of chronic disease and resulting disabilities is increasing. Some believe that this trend has been offset by increasingly healthier people and an average later age of onset of chronic disease. In 1976, 80 percent of all deaths, as compared with 46 percent in 1901, were attributed to chronic diseases.

Empirical data on the nature of consumer demand for care of chronic illnesses indicate that the persons whose activities are limited by chronic diseases have the highest utilization rate of acute general hospital days. In 1977, hospital days of care for chronic diseases were 59 percent as compared with 41 percent for the treatment of acute conditions. In 1975, of all the physician visits for the diagnosis and treatment of either chronic or acute diseases, 52 percent were for diagnosis and treatment of chronic disease, 45 percent for acute disease, and 3 percent for patients having both chronic and acute diseases. The bulk of demand for care of chronic diseases is in the following major diagnostic categories: tuberculosis; neoplasms (cancer); endocrine; nutritional and metabolic diseases; diseases of the blood; mental disorders; nervous system and sense organ disorders; circulatory and genitourinary system; musculoskeletal system and connective tissue diseases (such as arthritis); and congenital anomalies. Consumer demand for care of chronic diseases responds to changes in money price, time price, and level of income.

There are considerable data on the incidence of chronic diseases in the United States by income groups. It is clear that, in general, the lower the income, the greater the incidence of chronic health conditions. This is not surprising. Persons who develop chronic disease early in life may on the average earn less than those free of disease. Lower income often means poorer diet and housing and lower resistance to disease.

Work limitation is a function of both the severity of the disease and the physical demands of a person's work. Disability data on chronic diseases indicate that individuals with higher incomes are more likely to be working than persons with the same health status but with low incomes. Persons in higher income brackets are less likely to do hard physical labor and are more likely to have better medical care.

Analysis of the demand for treatment of chronic diseases by income groups suggests two hypotheses: (1) the higher one's income, the greater one's demand for medical care to alleviate chronic illnesses, and (2) the lower the money price, the greater the demand for such medical care. The higher one's earned income, the greater the monetary value of controlling impairment because of the disease and also the greater is the availability of means to pay for the care. Social security provides high monthly cash benefits to the permanently disabled as well as payment of their medical bills. The Medicare coverage that began in 1973 has probably increased the demand for medical care by a limited but increasing number of the chronically ill. In 1981, almost three million persons were receiving permanent disability, Medicare benefits either as workers or dependents of workers. The social security-required medical prognosis in early 1981 was a projected one year of disability as compared to the initial requirement of "a medically determinable physical or mental impairment which can be expected to result in death or to be of long-continued and indefinite duration."

An increase in time costs may have little effect on the demand of persons who do not work because of disease or disability. Alternative uses of their time are fewer and the value of their time is probably less for most than that of those who are working. For a select group, older persons who state that they have "nothing to do that makes a day worthwhile," it is a viable hypothesis that they may regard a physician visit as a social event. Some, while waiting in the office to see a physician, appear to enjoy swapping tales with other patients. Some, however, appear to dislike waiting and others seem indifferent.

Most of the data about chronic disease are from individuals' self-perceptions of their illnesses. A Stanford University Business School study suggests that "if perception of ill health, regardless of the diagnostic realities, motivates individuals to seek care, then such a measure will be a good predictor of utilization."[18] It is, however, in cases of chronic disease where the return visit rate may be influenced more by physicians than by patients.

The strength of physician-induced demand can be observed when patients with chronic diseases have remissions. These patients then believe that, because they have no symptoms, they have no medical need to see a doctor and do not make a "return visit" after the time interval that is suggested. Some specialists respond by refusing to give appointments or creating unreasonable delays in appointments to patients who do not keep their physician-imposed schedule of return visits. This mode of practice is rationalized on the basis that return visits are, in most cases, eventually necessary and closer scheduling may be preventive. Closer scheduling is more common in chronic disease management in geographic areas where an over-supply of physicians exists than where there is a shortage of physicians.

A study of eight internists in group practice found that "an internist can make himself inaccessible to many of his patients who have new problems or the exacerbation of old problems simply because he recycles patients more frequently than is necessary."[19] In that group "only one-third of physician 1's patients were given a return appointment, but almost two-thirds of physician 5's patients were to return at a definite date and time."[20] It does not appear from the analysis of the patients in this study that the case mix of physician 5 explains this differential.

Figure 3. Rate Per 100 Population of Physician Visits for Diagnosis and Treatment, According to Condition Causing Visit and Age, 1975

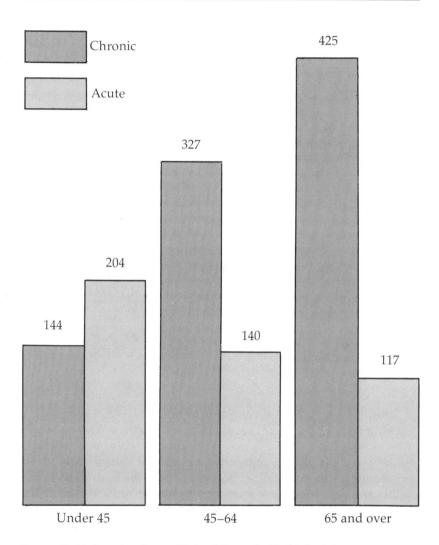

Source: Health Interview Survey, National Center for Health Statistics

An economist views a mode of practice which "recycles patients" more frequently than medically necessary as an income-maximizing technique. This mode of medical practice invites such criticism as that by Ivan Illyich: "the medicalization of society is turning everyone into a life-long patient."[21]

Preventive Health Care

Not all individuals value equally the advantages of preventing potential ill health of unknown probability and time. Some individuals are by nature greater risk-takers than others. They get a thrill from fast driving or skiing, enjoy a fast-paced life-style, and consider excitement an increment out-weighing any anticipated increase in loss of health in the future. Their estimate of the probability of loss in their health resulting from these activities is lower than estimates by more cautious individuals.

Economists know little about the demand curve with respect to money price for preventive health services.[22] If the out-of-pocket price for preventive health care falls, more will be demanded but how much more is unknown. There is no rigid relationship between a fall in the money price of preventive health care and its effect on demand. Preventive medical care services are more generally encouraged by physicians in areas where there are enough physicians to handle existing symptomatic care. Not all medical procedures labelled as "preventive" have been proved to be effective in improving health. The over-use of some helps to maintain physician income in physician surplus areas. Only relatively wealthy societies provide much preventive health care.

Substitute goods for preventive medical care exist. Examples are life preservers in boats and seat belts in automobiles. The outcomes from expenditures on these may be compared with outcomes from dollars spent on proven preventive medical measures, such as immunizations. In industrialized societies where the traditional public health measures to assure safe drinking water and effective waste disposal treatment are in place, the average gains to health per dollar spent by the individual on non-medical items are often greater than if spent on individual preventive medical procedures. Many consumers prefer non-medical preventive substitutes because they can control their use.

The degree and certainty of the benefit that an individual receives from different preventive medical procedures varies widely. The benefits derived from vaccination and immunization against such diseases as polio and diphtheria are proven while the benefits from a comprehensive, time-consuming physical examination for young adults are not.

Some preventive medical procedures carry a risk. The most notorious was the immunization shot used against the predicted swine flu epidemic of 1976. The federal government's vaccination program, planned for 200 million injections, apparently induced several cases of the Guillain-Barre syndrome, a rare neurological disease about which little is known. By September 1979, nearly 4,000 claims for damages of about $3.4 billion had been filed.[23] Because the disease occurs without flu injections, proof that a specific case of Guillain-Barre syndrome was indeed caused by the flu injection is needed in order to collect damages from the government. It is noteworthy that the insurance companies with whom pharmaceutical manufacturers primarily deal would not underwrite the risk of adverse effects from distribution of the planned 200 million dosages. The incident has "seriously crippled influenza immunization policy and has raised new questions about legal liability for government-sponsored preventive health efforts."[24]

There is no consensus, either among physicians or informed consumers, about the effectiveness of different preventive health measures. Many consumers have no knowledge of the various kinds of preventive health services offered or whether they are cost-effective.

The 1973 *Health Interview Survey* collected, for the first time, information on preventive care, defined to include the electrocardiogram, glaucoma test, chest x-ray, eye examination, breast examination, pap smear, and routine physical. The results are given in Tables 6 and 7.

A comparison of Tables 6 and 7 implies that a good deal of formal preventive care is given during a visit for diagnosis and treatment. None of the totals of the physician visits for preventive-type care ("general checkup, immunization & vaccine") reported by even those persons at high income and education levels approaches the levels of consumption of preventive medical tests suggested by Table 6.[25] One would anticipate similar under-reporting of the provision of preventive care for the lower income levels.

A 1977 survey, also part of the ongoing national *Health Interview Survey*, states that 18.3 percent of all physician office visits were in the "diagnostic, screening and preventive module," as apart from the "symptoms, disease, treatment," and other non-preventive modules. Because private insurance usually does not pay for preventive visits, physicians are less likely, in borderline cases, to check "pre-

Table 6. Percent of Persons Using Selected Preventive
Care Services: United States, 1973

Type of Care	Never Had Care	Had Care in Past Year
Electrocardiogram (40 yrs & over)	60.4%	24.5%
Glaucoma Test (40 yrs & over)	53.7	23.4
Chest X-ray (17 yrs & over)	80.1	31.2
Eye Examination (3 yrs & over)	87.7	41.3
Breast Examination (females, 17 yrs & over)	76.3	48.0
Pap Smear (females, 17 yrs & over)	75.2	45.9
Routine Physical (under 17 yrs)	86.2	50.1

Source: United States Public Health Service, "Current Estimates from the *Health Interview Survey, U.S. 1973*," Series 10, No. 95, Errata Data Sheet for Table D, p. 6.

ventive" rather than "diagnostic" as the reason for a physician visit
or prescribed medical procedures. The percent of the population that
reports having a general checkup is considerably higher than physicians report. In 1979, the government survey reports that "59 percent of men and 70 percent of women had had physical examinations
(although the completeness of these examinations is not known)
within the 2 years prior to the survey."[26] The higher the income and
educational level, the more likely an individual was to have had a
general physical.[27]

Only 18 percent of office visits in 1977 were classified by physicians
as "serious or very serious." The national *Health Interview Survey*
comments that of the 51 percent of "not serious" visits, 31 percent
were evaluated as "slightly serious," and "a large proportion . . .
were for routine prenatal care, immunizations, routine eye examinations, periodic checkups and other types of preventive health
care."[28]

Over ten years ago, I wrote that "it is recognized today that the
individual's state of health or illness is a continuum, ranging from
optimum adaptation to environment and no disease to maladaptation
with various levels of disease. This concept puts stress on prevention
and early detection of disease—as well as on the care of symptoms
and, if possible, rehabilitation."[29]

Recently, screening for early, symptomatic disease followed by
health education has been proposed as a method of delaying symptomatic disease, increasing the quality of life, and even prolonging
life. Screening for a specific disease among older persons may be

Table 7. Physician Visits* by Type of Service, 1975

	Visits	Diagnosis and Treatment	Pre- and Post-natal Care	General Checkup	Immuni- zation & Vaccine	Other
All Persons	100%	84.9%	3.1%	8.4%	2.1%	2.8%
Families with incomes $25,000 or more	100	83.0	1.8	11.2	1.9	3.3
Families with 13 years of education or more	100	81.8	3.4	10.4	2.5	3.3

*Excludes Alaska, Hawaii, and specialists in anesthesiology, pathology, and radiology. Source: United States Public Health Service, "Physician Visits . . . , 1975," Series 10, No. 128, p 34.

cost-effective if the disease is relatively common, if it can be treated effectively, and if patients cooperate with the treatment. Screening infants at birth for hypothyroidism at an incremental cost of $1 per infant is cost-effective because medical treatment is virtually assured to prevent otherwise ensuing, irreversible mental retardation that may result in life-long custodial care or at best, a much less productive person than might otherwise have been.

But screening for many other specific diseases has not been cost-effective even when directed at targeted populations believed to be most at risk. This is because all diseases cannot be treated effectively, followup medical care cannot be always assured, and there are often a large number of "false positives," indicating that persons have a disease when in fact they do not. The latter creates anxiety and the need for retesting. The anxiety costs from false positives can transform an otherwise positive benefit into a negative benefit. Sometimes when followup care is given, the life-time costs are higher than they would have been without early screening and the benefits from improvement in morbidity and mortality may or may not offset these higher costs.

The technique of screening for prevention may be oversold. For example, the pap smear is used to detect cervical cancer, a disease of relatively low incidence. Those most at risk (women with multiple sexual partners) are not usually screened, and no decline in deaths from cervical cancer in the non-targeted population which has been screened can be documented.[30] The pap smear generally detects a precursor to a type of cancer that takes at least fifteen years to develop. Screening for cervical cancer has also turned up many "false negatives." These give a false belief to persons who have been screened that they are well. On the other hand, some researchers maintain that *annual* screening for cervical cancer "can reduce the incidence and mortality rates of invasive cervical cancer."[31] Recent recommendations by knowledgeable individuals are for older women who have had two consecutive normal pap smears to then have one once every three years. Also recommended is an endometrial biopsy every five years.

Screening targeted population groups for genetic disease has had some success. For example, tests are made to detect the probability of Tay-Sachs disease occurring in future births to women at risk. This is a severely disabling disease for which there is no cure and which leads to early death of the child. The direct costs of caring for such infants are high and the psychic costs to parents who know that they can do nothing to halt the child's deterioration and death are immeasurable. As indicated earlier, amniocentesis for genetic screening raises difficult ethical questions. Perfecting of this technique is, however, permitting successful treatment of some infants prior to birth, thus increasing chances for healthier babies.

The largest HMO, Kaiser-Permanente, has decreased the frequency of its earlier annual multiphasic health checkups of non-symptomatic persons because they were not, except among "45–54 year-old male participants after five-seven years," cost-effective over the long run as measured by the number of days of work lost due to disability and chronic illness.[32]

Some believe that there should be mass screening to detect, in their early stages, specific asymptomatic diseases such as hypertension. However, "there is no hard evidence that any therapy will change the natural history of the disease"[33] and adherence to prescribed therapy is low. There is also some evidence that asymptomatic persons labeled as hypertensive have a diminished feeling of well-being and may stay home from work more often as a result.[34] Government policy to encourage mass screening for hypertension seems unwise given the information available at the beginning of the 1980s. The well-known physician and writer Lewis Thomas acknowledges that "medicine has not become very skilled at disease prevention . . . because the needed information is still lacking."[35] Ignorance acts as a bar to effective demand for preventive medical care. Third party coverage, whether by government or private insurers, is rare. A complication in the demand for preventive health services is that many individuals fear the results of a test designed not to lead to a cure of a known symptom but to look for unknown, existing ill health.

Preventive medical procedures can be carried to extremes. At the end of 1980, some physicians were advocating "preventive mastectomies" for high risk women who have benign, fibroid tumors of the breast! A hysterectomy is routinely performed by some surgeons as a preventive measure without first performing an endometrial biopsy, an in-office procedure if done by a skilled physician.

Individuals' educational levels may affect their demand for preventive health services more than for other medical care submarkets. Evidence to support this has been reported in several studies. A Group Health Insurance, Inc., study of its prepaid group plan subscribers (including dependents), who paid no co-insurance or deductibles, found that preventive health service visits were lowest among blue-collar workers.[36] Blue-collar workers' time costs are higher than other employees because they usually have to sacrifice hourly pay to consume health services. This, in addition to their level of education, affects their demand. The study also noted that blue-collar workers used all other types of health services equally. Medicare, probably because it pays for persons 65 years and over, does not cover preventive services. However, as life expectancy at age 65 is 79 years for men and 83.4 years for women, there is no reason except budget restraints for continuing, in 1982, this money-saving policy. Screening for glaucoma and other clearly cost-effective procedures should be encouraged. Medicaid, if fully implemented, would provide for the screening of most children in poor families. It is cost-effective to detect and correct vision, hearing, and other health problems of children prior to their entrance to public school, although not if the only outcome measure used is level of health. Often overlooked benefits are the greater ease of teaching a child who can see the blackboard and has normal hearing and the second-ary effect that his or her schoolmates will also have a better learning environment.

Some of the studies on preventive care of children have a self-selection bias that results in showing that "pediatric care has little impact on children's health" and "that this . . . extends to health problems that are capable of being affected by pediatric care and by family decisions."[37] Analysis indicates that needed corrective action was not always taken and where it was that the non-health benefits that are difficult to quantify were not always considered. A general policy conclusion that preventive medical care procedures other than immunizations are not effective for children can be questioned with "not effective" for society or "not effective" in any respect to children? The wearing of corrective eyeglasses does not improve uncorrected vision or technically one's health, but it does have benefits. It may improve one's health by reducing eye strain, which causes headaches or nausea.

Some argue that consumer health education can be used to change life-styles so that mortality and morbidity outcomes would improve. There is increasing evidence to support this. Mortality from heart disease, the leading cause of death in the United States, has declined over 20 percent since the mid-1960s, while in Sweden and the Iron Curtain countries there has been an upturn in heart disease deaths for males.

It is not clear what part of the decline in the United States can be attributed to a change in life-style, more exercise, less smoking, lower weight, less consumption of high cholesterol foods, or possibly less economic or job-related stress because both spouses work. Not all of the decline can be attributed to better medical care immediately after a heart attack, though better medical care obviously has contributed to the decline. Among suggestive data is an earlier decline in terminal myocardial infarctions in California than in the rest of the nation. Exercise and biofeedback relaxation techniques are identified with the California life-style.

Although the number of fatal heart attacks has declined, there is no definitive data over a given period of time on the incidence of non-fatal heart attacks. If these have declined as well, it would be clear that the individual's way of life plays the more important role in decreasing the incidence of cardiovascular disease. If non-fatal heart attacks have increased, the role of better medical care would be the more important factor in explaining the recent decline in mortality due to heart attacks.

A 1978 conference on "The Decline in Coronary Heart Disease" noted that, although "the worldwide experience has shown an unchanged or increasing death rate from coronary heart disease (except for Australia, Belgium, Canada, and perhaps for England, Finland, Israel, and Japan)," the United States' decline began in the mid-1960s, and since 1968 "has been seen in men and women, whites and blacks, and for all adult ages."[38] Unfortunately, the conference did not clarify what proportion of the decline is due to preventive measures and what proportion is due to coronary heart disease care once ischemic heart disease is diagnosed.

Among the diverse facts are: the first coronary care unit in the United States began in 1963, and 70 percent of coronary heart disease deaths occur out-of-hospital. There are only sparse data on the number of non-fatal heart attacks. The precise role of reduced fat intake in reducing mortality is unknown. Some physicians believe that high salt levels in the diet of many Americans is more conducive to early heart attack than a high fat diet. It is widely acknowledged that cigarette smoking increases the risk of heart attack. The studies of the San Francisco longshoremen and Harvard University's 17,000 alumni over a 20-year period indicate that men who engage in vigorous physical activity are much less at risk than sedentary men.[39] These studies support the personal philosophy of the twenty-sixth president of the United States, Theodore Roosevelt, who overcame the ill health of his youth through outdoor sports and the pursuit of "the strenuous life." However, there is some evidence that early self-selection by hardier individuals to pursue a vigorous life probably accounts for some of the observed differences in risk of heart attack between those who work or play strenuously and those who do not.

Further, the Harvard "alumni data show no difference in risk of sudden death with high or low activity index or by level of strenuous sports play."[40] This weakens but does not destroy the thesis that strenuous, habitual exercise protects against heart attacks.

Michael Grossman hypothesizes that individuals in higher income brackets who live luxuriously are less likely to pursue preventive health measures and more likely to depreciate their health from this standard of living.[41] Whereas this might have been true some years ago, today many of the wealthy are slim, watch their diet, enjoy expensive but physically demanding exercise, visit health spas, and vacation more than the non-wealthy. The higher the income, the more likely an individual exercises. On the other hand, the more wealthy may consume more alcohol and saturated fats. However, a recent study indicates that some alcohol intake may be good for one's health. The relationship between heart disease and low dietary fat intake has not been proven. Sidney Abraham and Margaret D. Carroll, in their paper at the 1978 conference on "The Decline in Coronary Heart Disease," state that "since the atherosclerotic process is long term, it is questionable to relate recent dietary habits to the risk of coronary artery disease."[42] The time costs for wealthy persons are usually very high and thus many of the rich forego those forms of preventive medical care which are most time-consuming.

Consumers cannot control the time costs of medical care except by changing providers. This creates discontinuities and possibly a decline in the quality of medical care. A portion of the time costs are not a result of waiting, but the time spent in consuming medical care. As third party payments increase, time costs become more important than money costs. Thus, the income elasticity for consumption of preventive medical care is probably lower than the total price (time cost plus money cost) elasticity.

Among the few available studies on the response to increasing time costs are three analyses of pediatric care. A summary of these concludes that "the number of visits fall as the time cost of a visit rises, . . . that time and transportation costs are significant rationing mechanisms in the pediatric care market."[43] Preventive health care for children has not become continuously more popular. In the 1920s, almost every public school had a school nurse but, today, only 30,000 school nurses are employed by about 89,000 schools. About $1 billion is spent annually on school health activities[44] but relatively few dollars are used for public preventive care programs. If children are screened for illness, followup to assure that medical care is provided is not always available. Most public schools still provide some health education, first aid, and minimal hearing and vision testing. In Colorado, where child health associates or general nurse practitioners have been trained, and, in several other states that have received special private grant money to provide primary medical care at the school site, preventive health programs for children are extensive.[45] In Cambridge, Massachusetts, "comprehensive health care from birth through high school" is available through its public school system. In Cambridge, "immunization levels have reached 98 percent (compared to a national average of about 60 percent)" in 1978.[46] A major federal effort to increase childhood immunization has resulted in 91 percent of the 24 million children in kindergarten through the eighth grade being immunized, by 1980, against measles, polio, diphtheria, pertussis, and tetanus.[47] Smallpox has been eradicated.

Children in schools and adults at work are, in a sense, captive populations. Screening, immunization, and health education programs may thus be more efficient when directed to individuals in these settings. Waiting and transportation time is saved if individuals can obtain care on the job.

Insurers and employers have economic incentives to encourage individuals insured or employed by them to consume preventive medical care if it is effective and contains long-run, total medical care costs. However, insurers generally do not cover the costs of preventive medical care, implying that they do not believe in its cost-effectiveness and/or the demand for preventive care would greatly increase if covered by health insurance. Most health insurance is group insurance derived from employment. It is possible that the anticipated mobility of employees is judged to be great enough to offset anticipated cost containment benefits. The potential cost-effectiveness of formalized preventive care, including consumer health education, may be higher than is generally recognized. Previously, preventive medicine was facilitated by the stable relationship between the general practitioner and the patient, a characteristic of a more rural and less mobile society.

As I have written several years ago,

> the frequent contact between patients and physicians tended to provide a "listening post" for early detection of disease— although even then, this ideal situation was probably not common. Today, increased mobility of patients and greater specialization of medicine mean less physician-patient contact

on a continuing basis. As a substitute, physicians advise annual physicals, but their advice is not always followed even by middle income and wealthier families.[48]

Very few large companies provide comprehensive medical care to their employees. The Gillette Company, at its two Boston locations, does include "periodic examinations, conducted at no cost to the employee and on company time . . . every two years for those under age 35 and every year after that age. The rationale for the preventive survey is based on . . . the earlier a disease is detected, the easier it is to cure or control."[49] Because the company has specialists under part-time contracts, its medical clinics practice peer review, and its physicians emphasize ambulatory over hospital care, Gillette realizes many of the same types of cost savings as HMOs. Additionally, the time costs for transportation and waiting are extremely low. The number of outside referrals is controlled because specialists on the staff have developed on-going relationships with their patients.[50] Each employee chooses a physician to act as his or her primary care physician. The physicians are board-certified in their specialties and are also medical school faculty members with on-going teaching responsibilities. A general nurse practitioner acts as liaison to the patient in the home or hospital. Ninety-five percent of the company's employees in the Boston area used these services in 1979 as did members of their families who pay additionally. Gillette carries Blue Cross, Blue Shield, and major medical insurance for its employees and their dependents. The medical records are confidential and are not available to management.

The director of the Gillette clinics believes that the employees return to work sooner than when they use private physicians, who "often have a tendency to be excessively conservative in letting people return to work."[51] This is a unique system of medical care delivery that cannot be copied easily by other companies. Its success depends on the employee's faith in the medical director and trust that his or her health records will remain private.

However, the belief that consumer health education pays off in a benefit-cost sense is growing among employers and insurers. Many large companies have in-house education programs to persuade employees to change health-related habits such as smoking, nutrition, and exercise. The provision of physical facilities at work sites for employees to exercise is becoming more common. Extensive physical therapy facilities are available in some factories for employee use. A few companies even use money payments to reward non-smokers.

Blue Shield of New Jersey provides "stop smoking clinics without charge to subscriber groups . . . because a healthier lifestyle is a key factor in controlling increasing health care costs."[52]

Funds for the prevention of illness may also be spent at the macroeconomic level to improve the environment and to encourage medical research. Although judicial relief for ill health resulting from environmental causes such as water and air polluted by industrial wastes and chemical spills is available, it is difficult to recover. Involuntary risks such as from polluted air are ethically different from voluntary risks. Increasingly, known risks associated with working in some industries are being discovered. Individuals holding such jobs are legally taking a voluntary risk. Ill persons in this category appear to have, until recently, better legal redress under the Workmen's Compensation Act than by general civil actions. It is difficult to prove that environmental work hazards are the cause of ill health. Because these are class action cases, the total awards often involving long-term disability can be very large and push some business firms towards bankruptcy, with resulting unemployment. Prevention of environment-related disease continues to have a higher priority than compensating persons who may have been harmed. In fiscal year 1979, the federal government spent $7.4 billion for pollution control and business firms about $14 billion.

The costs of environmental air and water cleanup programs to business firms have largely been passed along to consumers through higher prices. The use of scarce resources for cleaning up the environment means that there are less resources available for other uses, including preventive medical care, consumer health education, and medical research. Benefits per dollar spent on pollution control are probably still higher than an additional dollar spent on direct medical care. To plan additional governmental expenditures, it is wise to compare the marginal benefits resulting from different types of expenditures with their marginal costs. This means a comparison of the incremental increases in benefits resulting from an incremental increase in spending a given amount of dollars. Where the return in benefits is greatest, the expenditures are preferable. This is a very naive, idealized account of a primarily political process, the actual construction of the U.S. budget. My only defense is that the same rationalization is made by others. This is an ideal, not an actuality. However, it is also how decisions already made for political reasons are sometimes defended. This is so even though actual estimates of anticipated benefits, marginal or otherwise, are only often informed guesses.

Marginal benefits will approach zero the closer a goal of perfection, such as absolutely pure air or pure water, is reached. However, it is not necessary to purify all water to the same degree. Water that is used for cooling systems and many other industrial uses need not be as pure as water for drinking.

Policy-makers compare the incremental benefit resulting from an additional increment being spent across competing uses, not the average benefits. However, it is interesting that the total costs of air pollution control in the United States were about $21 billion in 1979 and that "annual benefits realized in 1978 from measured improvements in air quality since 1970 could be reasonably valued at $21.4 billion, [of which] $17 billion represented reductions in mortality and morbidity."[53]

The 1979 report of the Council on Environmental Quality maintains that the "combined data from twenty-five major metropolitan areas show that the number of unhealthful days declined by 15 percent between 1974 and 1977 while the number of very unhealthful days declined 32 percent."[54] Although water quality did not improve in the years 1975 through 1978, it did not become worse.[55] It is possible that the marginal benefit from additional resources would not have exceeded the marginal cost in those years. The area of greatest concern in environmental health is the increasing exposure to toxic substances from nuclear, industrial, and municipal waste dumps.

Money for medical research, that may also be classified under prevention, has been declining relative to expenditures for all health care. The federal government funds about two-thirds of all health research. The outlays have not kept up with the inflation since 1974. Government expenditures on health research have declined as government expenditures on energy research have increased. In fiscal year 1979, the federal government spent nearly $4 billion on health research. One billion dollars is scheduled for cancer research alone in fiscal 1980, more dollars than will be spent for research in all areas of environmental health and far more than the $96 million spent by the government on children's health care in 1977, some of which was not preventive in nature.[56]

The amount spent on cancer research appears out-of-line when compared with research monies for other specific diseases but it is acceptable because of the high incidence of a dreaded, often fatal disease. As persons are kept alive because of successful treatment and/or prevention of other diseases, more persons incur cancer. People are cured for one type of cancer possibly only to incur another type of cancer induced by the treatment for the first form of cancer.

The federal government funds two-thirds of all biomedical research, only some of which is conducted in government laboratories while most is performed under contract in university facilities. Private industry conducts and pays for the remaining one-third. Both government and industry are decreasing their expenditures on basic research. Industry has been hampered by excessive government regulation of basic and applied research. Pharmaceutical companies cite the increasing number of years it takes to develop a new drug and meet the federal requirements necessary to get permission to market. Some estimate that it averages ten years after filing a patent before approval is granted, thus effectively reducing the value of a 17-year patent by more than one-half.

Despite the well-publicized Monsanto-Harvard research partnership,[57] there has been a decline in earlier, more extensive linkages between industry and academia. University research equipment and facilities are falling behind industry's. DNA research may revitalize industry and university linkages for research. Government is concerned about the decline of industrial research and development (R&D) across all industries. A *Science* magazine editorial states that "as a percentage of economic output, R&D in the United States fell 20 percent between 1968 and 1978 but rose by 16 percent in West Germany and by 20 percent in Japan."[58] The preferred remedy lies in tax incentives and less regulation rather than in more government spending on research. If U.S. industry makes larger profits, the percent spent on research may remain the same but the dollar amount would grow.

Basic research is done primarily in universities, but companies also do basic research prior to developing new technologies leading to new products. This is especially true in the pharmaceutical industry. Regular interaction between academia and industry occurs often. University-based industrial associate programs are common in engineering and chemistry. Examples are the Massachusetts Institute of Technology program in biology and biochemistry and the Monsanto-Harvard twelve-year contract covering cooperative basic research.

Recent discoveries in biomedical research, such as recombinant DNA techniques, indicate that an explosion in benefits from basic biological research is not far off. The costs of producing human insulin to replace animal insulin for the treatment of diabetes should be lower if gene-splicing or recombinant DNA techniques are used. The price of the pituitary gland hormone, which promotes growth, should be greatly lowered. New antibiotics and cheaper antiviral interferon, that might be an improved treatment for cancer, also appear to be medical research areas of great potential.[59] To remove government funds from biomedical research in order to support delivery of more of the existing medical care techniques defeats long-range cost containment via prevention.

In fiscal year 1979, the federal government spent on medical research nearly $4 billion,[60] primarily conducted by the eleven research groups in the National Institutes of Health (NIH) and the National Library of Medicine. By allocating one-fourth of the health research monies to cancer disease, the federal government leaves the other National Institutes of Health (such as the Heart, Lung, and Blood Institute; the General Medical Sciences Institute; the Arthritis, Metabolism, and Digestive Diseases Institute; the Allergy and Infectious Diseases Institute; the Neurologic and Communicative Disorders and Strokes Institute; and others) with lesser shares. These other diseases are not unimportant causes of death. Heart disease and stroke are the first and third causes of death, respectively, in the United States.

The overall costs of cancer are not greater than the overall costs of cardiovascular disease or of accidents, but are similar to the costs of mental disorders and respiratory and digestive diseases.[61] Although these costs include the direct and indirect costs, they do not include declines in the quality of life and the toll of pain and suffering. In fiscal year 1981, the National Cancer Institute was earmarked to receive nearly one-third of NIH's total $3.5 billion budget.

In allocating research monies among the NIH, politics is a very visible factor. Each of the Institutes defends its own budget before congressional committees. Because of this, and the fact that a considerable part of their budgets are for continuing support of research, it is difficult (even if Congress wished) to cut their appropriations while reordering research priorities in line with long range, national health goals.

Secretary of HEW (now HHS) Patricia Harris approved, in October 1978, a plan that "emphasizes basic research, both clinical and applied, though technology transfer and training are also included."[62] This broad plan of national health research policy can be criticized for its lack of explicit direction. Because of several Congressmen's complaints about lack of payoff from basic research, such ambiguity is understandable. On the other hand, the DNA breakthrough is dramatically indicative of how advancement in medical treatment depends on basic research.

Although the Office of Management and Budget in recent years has substantially cut federal research monies, in the final analysis Congress makes this important public policy decision. The Health Science Promotion Act, which was sponsored jointly by Senators Kennedy and Schweiker, would have established a twenty-six-member commission to review the annual science research budgets within a framework of five-year goals. Some long-range planning is needed, but this is expensive and not necessarily the best way to accomplish the goal of better targeted basic research.

VI. ORGANIZATION
OF DELIVERY

An often-made criticism of the way medical care is delivered in the United States is that it is a "non-system." If a "system" requires centralized organization or control, then medical care is indeed a "non-system." However, there are systems, such as the capitalist system, where the direction of the parts, here the allocation of resources, is provided through a decentralized mechanism. Medical care delivery in the United States fits this model more closely than that of a non-system.

Is it possible to devise a system of medical care delivery that permits freedom of choice by consumers and providers, yields a distribution that is equitable, and maximizes "health?" Other countries have failed to attain this nirvana and regrettably the mix of public and private medical care system of the United States also has failed. Thus, the relevant question is whether a government-planned, total system yields better results than the U.S. mixed government and private system. Further, how can the preferable system be improved?

The submarkets of the medical care industry are not models of perfect competition. Yet their numbers of suppliers have grown in response to higher prices and greater profits, although perhaps not as freely as they would have if restrictions such as licensure and accreditation did not exist. Although the ignorance of some buyers about what a medical service is worth may be greater in medical care markets than other markets, this is not true for all buyers and all kinds of medical services. Buyers and suppliers of medical care do interact to negotiate prices, but not to the extent as in many other markets. Buyers find it difficult to judge quality and are reluctant to discuss prices with physicians. The individual buyer's incentive to negotiate has been weakened by the extent of third party payments for services. However, these third parties, governments, insurance companies, and industrial companies, which pay private health insurance premiums for their workers, have become more active in price negotiations.

The capitalist market system that operates through competition does not work perfectly in the medical care industry or in most other industries. There are two general approaches to government policy on health care: (1) to make the decentralized system we have work better by improving competition and resource allocation within the industry in part by providing the consumer and third party payers with more information, or (2) to impose a central control authority over the industry.[1] The latter would go beyond the existing governmental financing of care but would not necessarily involve the actual provision of care. However, it would mean adding to the already extensive, costly regulations over the industry.

A brief description of the present organization of the delivery of care in the United States follows. Demand for medical care is usually channeled through a physician. The physician may be in solo practice, in group practice, employed by a hospital to work in its emergency room, or employed by an outpatient clinic. In some cases, the patient may see first a general nurse practitioner or other health personnel. In some prepaid groups or health maintenance organizations (HMOs) the patient may first fill in a self-health history form and/or complete an automated multi-test series. Subsequent care may be provided by a physician, a nurse, and/or a medical technician under the MD's direct supervision.

In the United States, a primary care physician may refer a patient to a specialist or the patient may initiate his or her own referral to a specialist. In countries with national health insurance, self-referral to a specialist is not allowed because it means higher costs than if visits to specialists are controlled by the primary care physician, who acts as "gatekeeper." Similarly, most HMOs do not pay for their enrollees' self-referrals and their designated primary care physicians are gatekeepers, who guard access to the more expensive specialist care.

In many instances a would-be patient in the United States cannot obtain initial medical care from a nurse or other medical technician. Exceptions, as noted, occur in some HMOs and in facilities where automated multiphasic screening is offered by medical technicians for "checkups," whether directly to the consumer or in accordance with a physician's request.

There are over 400,000 professionally active physicians in the United States, of whom about 350,000 list "patient care" as their primary activity. Physicians represent less than one-twelfth of the nearly 7 million workers in the health field. The total number of health workers increased nearly 60 percent from 4.3 million in 1970 to 6.7 million in 1978. Among the 7 million are some 3,000 anthropologists, medical sociologists, and health economists who have little to do with the provision of primary health care. Other workers, for example

2.5 million nurses with varying levels of training and 117,000 dentists, are directly involved in the day-to-day procedures of health care. By 1990, there will be nearly 570,000 physicians in the United States.[2]

Advances in medical technology with concomitant dilution of the more complex functions into a larger number of very specialized tasks have created many new health occupations. This is beginning to narrow the gaps in the vertical manpower ladder in the health industry.

PHYSICIAN REIMBURSEMENT

A physician's compensation may be in the form of (1) a fee for each service rendered, (2) an annual prepaid, per capita charge to a patient, usually in a group setting, (3) a salary, (4) a percentage or set share of the income of a group or corporation of physicians, and (5) very rarely, except for obstetricians, payment "by the case." That a physician customarily charges a given fee does not mean that he or she will always be paid that sum. Under Medicaid and Medicare, physicians may receive less than they charge from the third party payer and the patient combined. Medicaid pays about 60 percent of charges in California and the patient does not pay the remainder. Medicare reimburses 80 to 95 percent of charges, but the patient is billed for the remainder. Third parties use fee screens, "usual, customary, and reasonable" charge guidelines (UCR), which recognize 290 geographical area differentials and several hundred procedures in about 30 specialties. Some third party payers have a dollar fee schedule. When the physician's charges exceed the reimbursement amount, the patient is billed for the remainder, except under Medicaid. The patient may protest an insurer's UCR determination of the percent of a bill that the insurer will reimburse and force the bill into arbitration by medical peer review. Although the patient is the final payer, the patient is not involved in the settlement between the physician and the insurer. This practice may contain costs or at least create a lag in the rise in costs, but it also can foster collusion between providers and insurers and hide information that would facilitate more competitive markets. There are few if any other items than medical care which individuals buy, the price of which the individual does not usually know until after the purchase is completed, and in some instances, not even then.

Many employers do not even inform their employees that the insurer pays a UCR charge determined by the insurer. Rather, the employer uses the euphemism of "covered expenses" and does not spell out its true meaning. In a high cost area such as California, the gap between an actual charge and the reimbursed UCR is significant. Employers should spell out the fee screen levels under the different financial arrangements offered so that employees can make an intelligent choice among the health insurance plans that are offered.

Physicians who are paid a fee for each service they perform may work alone, in "solo, fee-for-service" (FFS) practice, or with other physicians in a group. Although most groups with FFS reimbursement do not accept prepaid enrollees, a few do. They are called Independent Practice Associations (IPAs). In 1975, about four-fifths of all physicians were solo, FFS physicians, and about one-fifth worked in 8,500 group practices.

The proportion of all practicing physicians who have incorporated had increased to one-third in 1972,[3] to 50 percent in 1979,[4] and I estimate that by the early 1980s that proportion will increase to two-thirds. In most states, a corporation is a legal form of medical practice. Incorporation limits the physician's personal liability and permits the lower corporate tax rate as compared to the personal income tax rate on physicians' incomes. Although self-employed individuals may, as of 1980, set aside up to $7,500 of untaxed income annually to be received upon retirement as a pension, there is no limit on the amount which a corporation may set aside for this purpose. The higher the personal income tax rate, the greater the incentive for self-employed persons with high earned incomes to incorporate.

In 1972, incorporated physicians saw "11 percent more patients than self-employed men do [sic] in the same median 60-hour week and get almost 50 percent more for doing it—$62,500 median per year total compensation including salary, bonuses, and retirement set-asides."[5] An AMA sample survey reports that incorporated physicians averaged $77,100 net income in 1978 as compared to $54,400 for non-incorporated physicians.[6]

Almost all physicians have admitting privileges in at least one hospital although many non-surgical, primary care physicians may use their admitting privileges rarely. The hospital is the major work setting for surgeons and many medical specialists. About one-third of all physicians engaged in patient care are hospital-based and, of these, over 61,000 are involved in training new physicians. Full-time hospital staff physicians number over 25,000. Radiologists and pathologists are the specialists most likely to be hospital-based.

The organization and operation of hospitals have been studied in depth, and only a brief sketch follows. Trustees of hospitals can be compared with directors of corporations because they bear the final responsibility for the hospital's activities. In non-profit hospitals, trustees raise money in addition to taking the final responsibility for the hospital's practices. The hospital administrator is increasingly not a physician. The chief of its medical staff is chosen by the physicians who work in the hospital. Administrators must operate within budget, and help to restrain costs. On the other hand, physicians tend to order equipment with lesser regard for the budget, and exert an upward force on expenditures. Physicians recognize that specialized, high technology equipment attracts patients and tends to increase physician income.

The concept of a closed hospital staff is under attack because it denies some physicians opportunities to work and limits competition. A hospital's insistence that it pass judgment on staff physicians may act against the public's interest. It is understandable that physicians prefer to work with colleagues of their choice and that some hospitals have higher physician standards than others. However, examinations and licensure laws guard entry to the medical profession. It is also understandable that bed shortages in a given geographical area encourage closed staffs: hospital managements have only a given number of beds and, therefore, can accommodate the needs of only a given number of physicians. In such areas, the preferred solution may be to increase the supply of beds. However, there are very few areas which in 1980 have too few beds, but an increasing number of areas have a surplus of physicians. Thus, hospital beds can appear to be in short supply when they are not. The teaching hospitals of medical schools are most likely to have closed hospital staffs. Their administrators argue that the staff competency and the training needs of teaching hospitals have to take precedence.

Because all hospitals have the final responsibility for the quality of the medical care given in the hospital, minimal staff standards are expected. However, questions of antitrust law may be involved in specific cases of a hospital denying a physician staff privileges. There is legal protection against "unreasonable, arbitrary, capricious, or discriminatory denial . . . in public hospitals" and this "is now fully recognized in private hospitals as well, with judicial recognition of the fact that private hospitals serve particular communities under public charter and operate increasingly with public money."[7] Nonprofit hospitals usually do not pay local property taxes. Further, "a requirement that staff members be 'temperamentally and psychologically suited for cooperative staff hospital functions' has been rejected."[8] If a hospital has a closed staff and no other hospital with facilities relevant to a specific specialty is in reasonable proximity to the non-staff specialist, he or she may question whether the hospital has a local monopoly. The legal charge would be interference with the right of a physician to pursue his chosen occupation. Among technological services which may be in limited supply are neurology, cardiology, nuclear medicine, and nephrology. There is a delicate balance between maintenance of quality and denial of a physician's opportunity to follow his chosen profession. Open staffs would permit more competition.

Because of the growth of Medicaid, there are fewer low income patients willing to be "cases" for training medical students. It is becoming more difficult to train physicians as HMOs and Professional Standards Review Organizations (PSROs) cut the utilization of hospital patient days and simultaneously do not reimburse for training costs that are clearly not treatment costs. Equity considerations support the position that training costs should not be met by those already sick; rather, by the fortunate well or, preferably, by the future physicians who will eventually earn relatively high incomes out of which they can repay loans. If taxpayers foot the bill, the arguments *pro* and *con* will depend on what taxes will be increased and on whom they will fall. The U.S. price controls of 1971–74 forced some large hospitals to begin keeping their accounts in accordance with the usual practices of other businesses. To the degree that normal accounting practices are followed, charges to a consumer can be related to that consumer's consumption of goods and services. It then becomes more obvious that the charges include training costs.

It is difficult to isolate the substantial intern training costs normally interwoven with patient care costs. The intern performs work of considerable economic value; in fact, some believe more than he or she is paid in dollars and training. Because of the difficulty in measuring the intern's output, it is impossible to estimate the proportion of intern training costs reflected in patients' hospital bills.

A related problem is who should pay for the training services of attending physicians. Medicare payments for the services of "supervisory physicians" in teaching hospitals were $100 million or more annually in 1970.[9] The general public may be willing to bear training costs directly, either out of general tax funds or as a per capita assessment. Society is already bearing some of these costs indirectly— through Medicare reimbursement. Medicare, until late 1980, also paid more of a hospital's malpractice insurance than the actual malpractice costs reflected in claims by Medicare patients. The latter rarely file suit, but hospital administrators assert that the total premiums depend on the total number of patients. The 1980 rule squeezes further those hospitals with a high Medicare patient load.

Established hospital beds, whether occupied or not, require continuing financial support. Tension among local hospital administrators and physicians is being created by arguments over who is to pay for an increasing number of empty standby beds and which beds are to be phased out. The National Institute of Medicine estimates that in 1980 there were 100,000 excess hospital beds. The gap between Medicare and private patient charges is widening. Apparently a subsidy to a hospital by the ill private patient is considered warranted when government is the third party payer. In California, the administrative costs of their non-profit hospitals is about 20 percent, but a for-profit hospital management firm's contract costs are often as low as 10 percent. A fairly uncommon source of savings among non-profit hospitals that is usual when under business management is the scheduling of admissions to even out demands on hospital beds over the week. Not all physicians can admit on Mondays. This different scheduling alone is sufficient to make some physicians on non-profit hospital staffs oppose the for-profits.

ALL GROUP PRACTICE

About one-fifth of all physicians who provide patient care are members of a group practice. Group practice is a formal organization that usually is either a partnership of three or more physicians or a corporation employing three or more full-time physicians. In a group practice, nurses, laboratory technicians, secretaries, and other personnel usually work for the group as a unit. The group may own and share expensive laboratories and medical equipment.

Before the Fall of 1969, the Internal Revenue Service did not permit professionals to incorporate. Prior to that date, group practices were, therefore, usually partnerships. Under this financial arrangement, each partner is liable for the debts of other partners. Thus, group practice did not grow substantially until the 1970s. From 1969 to 1975, the number of medical groups in the United States increased by 33 percent and the number of physicians in group practice by 67 percent. By 1975 there were 8,483 medical groups involving 66,842 physicians.[10] Of these groups, 35 percent were multispecialty, 54 percent were single specialty, and 11 percent were general practice. The multispecialty groups were larger and employed 59 percent of all physicians in group practice. Of the other group physicians, 35 percent practiced in single specialty and 6 percent in general practice.[11]

In 1975, some 27 percent of group practices were partnerships, 61 percent were corporations, 10 percent were "associations, foundations, or other," and 1.6 percent were "single owner groups in which the owner employed the other physicians in the group."[12] Medical corporations grew during a ten-year period from 8 percent of groups in 1965 to 61 percent in 1975 (covering 57 percent of group physicians). The tremendous growth in the limited liability, incorporated form of group practice explains in part the great increase in malpractice suits and the size of awards in recent years. It is easier for an individual to envision taking a "corporation" or even a non-incorporated large group practice to court rather than the family doctor. The annual growth rate of the number of groups decreased from 1969 to 1975 while the average group size increased, further weakening the patient-physician relationship. The growing complexity of medical technology that enlarges the potential for harm and almost has eliminated a one-to-one physician/patient relationship in cases of serious illness also contributes to the growth in the number of malpractice awards.

Eighty-three percent of groups pay physicians a share of net income. The revenues of most multispecialty groups include physicians' fees received (or, alternatively, a prepaid monthly set charge per enrollee), charges for x-rays, laboratory tests, and physical therapy procedures. The individual physician's share of net income is determined by the number and kinds of medical services he or she provides, specialty status, length of time with the group, and in prepaid group practice by various formulae designed to contain costs for the group as a whole. These formulae often reflect for each physician the level of utilization by his or her patients of all the health services provided by the group.

Group practice permits physicians to share overhead costs, to schedule time off for vacations and educational purposes, and also to discuss puzzling medical problems informally with colleagues. Group practice is especially helpful to young physicians who may not have personal credit lines large enough to permit them to purchase needed capital equipment while building a practice. Under group practice, a new physician will start out with a sizeable flow of patients.

What are the economies of scale derived from group practice? Savings in the overhead costs of office space and expensive equipment, shared clerical and paramedical staff services, and volume purchasing are evident in different degrees in all groups. Large groups, especially those with several clinic buildings, benefit from computerized billing and record-keeping, centralized purchasing and capital planning, and use of specialized, central management staff. Furthermore, in large groups expensive equipment and specialized personnel are less likely to be idle during working hours. When groups are growing in size there are discontinuities in adjustment: crowded schedules for physicians and lengthy waits for their patients until a new physician is hired. It is not economical for the group to pay physicians who have less than a full schedule. Thus, the group will not hire an additional physician until it is reasonable to assume that he will be carrying close to a full load. Similar discontinuities of production occur in the purchase of expensive, specialized machinery.

One study estimates that there are increasing returns to scale for single-specialty groups that hire up to ten physicians. However, this is too small a number for the efficient operation of multispecialty groups.[13] Other analyses suggest that sharing overhead costs and revenues in group practices may reduce, however, the physician's incentive for efficiency (the result of the 'x' inefficiency factor that is due to the larger an organization, the lesser the impact of a single member's actions) and offset potential gains in productivity resulting from economies of scale. Net income to a physician in a group is affected by the mode of medical practice of other physicians in the group as well as by his or her own efforts. Because the total net income is shared under different formulae by all the physicians, any one physician's actions have less effect on his income than if he practiced alone.

To the author's knowledge, no study has been made of what is the optimum size of a multispecialty group in an urban area of a given population. Thus, the group size with the lowest average cost per unit of output is unknown. Groups with lower average unit costs may tolerate longer periods of tight scheduling than some less "efficient" groups. One by-product of tight scheduling that results in lower costs is reduction in patient demand. The patient who feels that he needs immediate attention may not wait for an appointment but, rather, seek care outside of the group practice. When the cost of hiring an additional physician is less to the group than the loss of income which occurs, an additional physician is hired. This trade-off at the margin is more complicated in prepaid group practice. One director of a medical group stated that "there is a crucial size to a medical group (approximately 100 physicians) beyond which a patient is in danger of losing personal care."[14]

The cost-effective sharing of expensive x-ray equipment and laboratory functions among physicians in a group is a logical development. It is not necessary, however, to have an organized group in order for physicians to benefit from the efficient use of expensive medical devices. Laboratories and medical devices of all kinds are owned by persons other than physicians. In many cities, physicians in centrally located medical buildings send patients to laboratories owned by other individuals or organizations. It is more convenient for patients if ancillary services are available in the building where their physicians are. Therefore, medical buildings rent space in the same building to solo practitioners, physical therapists, independent laboratories, pharmacists, and other medical providers.

There are two kinds of waiting: (1) waiting in offices and examination rooms, which is usually a "loss" to the consumer because it reduces the consumer's productivity, income, and leisure time, and (2) waiting for an appointment, which may or may not reduce the consumer's productivity. Waiting for an appointment results in a loss of income when an untreated illness prevents the consumer from working. Both types of waiting may cause some persons to seek services elsewhere. Many employed people do not have sick leave and are not paid unless working. Untreated illness may reduce productivity on a job but not income from employment. This may occur when an individual has sick leave or continues to work although sick. Untreated illness may create increased anxiety costs stemming from the uncertainty and fear of the would-be patient. In 1976, the average waiting time for an appointment was 6.9 days with solo practice physicians and 17.7 days with groups having 26 or more physicians.[15] It is usually the consumer who pays most of the cost of waiting, not the employer or the third party payer. However, insofar as the employers' costs are higher due to the employees' absences from work to obtain medical care, employers pay indirectly for waiting. Employer costs may be greater when employees obtain medical treatment from groups than from non-group practices. One large multi-national company providing in-house, complete medical care to 95 percent of its employees in some of its geographical locations claims that its additional costs over the costs of more traditional insurance packages are more than offset by reductions in absenteeism. Time otherwise spent traveling to, from, and waiting for medical care from providers not on the premises are avoided and the company's employees return to work sooner than those in similar health who are treated by outside physicians.

Studies show that the utilization rates of tests and x-rays are rising because of the advent of "defensive medicine" as well as the growth of group practice. The diagnostic procedures are used defensively to reduce physician vulnerability to malpractice suits. A physician who was Assistant Secretary for Health during the Nixon Administration testified that "putting a national price tag on the unnecessary defensive medicine is speculative, but the true figure including excess radiology, excess pathology, and unnecessary hospital stays may exceed three billion dollars."[16] The American Medical Association (AMA) reports that 36 percent of surveyed physicians, in 1976–77, "responded defensively" to the malpractice situation "by ordering more tests and procedures for their patients than they might have considered previously."[17]

It is also claimed that the number of tests and x-rays, as well as their prices, are greater in like situations when physician-owned rather than independent facilities are used. However, until recently it was unusual for physicians to know the costs of the procedures that they order. The higher the volume of tests, the lower the unit cost. Thus, solo practitioners tend to use independent or commercial laboratories while large multispecialty groups run their own laboratories and x-ray departments. Commercial laboratories must conform to state laws and the 1977 federal legislation which sets uniform standards for quality control, maintenance of records, and evidence of proficiency of personnel. However, laboratories in physicians' offices are generally exempt. Hospitals also have in-house clinical laboratories, usually under the direction of a pathologist, while commercial laboratories may have non-physician directors.

A comparison of solo and group practice notes that

> . . . gross revenues derived specifically from the sale of
> laboratory and x-ray services amounted to less than 5 percent of
> total internist billings in the solo practices; in the largest multi-
> specialty groups, revenues from laboratory and x-ray services
> approached 40 percent of the total billings of the internists. As
> size increased, even within single-specialty internist group
> practices, there was a distinct and steady increase in the
> proportion of laboratory and x-ray billings to total billings—again
> attributable to the ability of the larger practices to diversify and
> profit from their offerings of services . . . [and] higher earnings
> appear to reflect the fact that different services are being sold in
> the various forms of practice. These additional services contribute
> to the gross revenue of the practice, but they do not meet our
> technical concept of greater production of services rendered by the
> physician.

. . . it is to be expected that the presence of these ancillary facilities within a group practice— coupled with their use positively affecting the physician's income—may, at the margin, result in higher usage than where these incentives do not exist.[18]

Revenues from in-hospital and in-house group practice tests have the same relationship to health providers' revenues as alcoholic drinks do to hotel revenues. However, often overlooked in the claim of over-testing, especially by group practices that use multi-testing to screen who needs to see a physician, is that automation permits a panel of twenty tests to be done for the previous cost of one manual test. Automation has made, within reasonable limits, the costs of an additional common test very low, possibly even zero.[19] Thus there is economic justification for their use to allocate the physician's time. In addition, the gain in certainty of diagnosis has become increasingly worthwhile to obtain. The low costs of most additional tests should be added to the other causes of ordering large numbers of tests: the economic gains from in-house testing, the insured consumer's insensitivity to their costs, and the physician's greater protection from malpractice suits. Additionally, large, multispecialty groups may attract a large number of both healthy patients who want a complete physical and patients whose illnesses are difficult to diagnose. In both of these circumstances, more tests are likely to be prescribed than would be the case if an average population were served.

More traditionally, physicians who believe that their greater allegiance is to their patients, not to cost containment for society, will order more x-rays and tests to resolve a doubtful diagnosis. That physicians, in the conduct of their clinical practices, owe their allegiance to their patients, not to the amorphous body, society, is being currently contested. Some physicians state that "students and house officers must be encouraged to recognize and accept a measure of ambiguity and uncertainty in clinical decision-making and to adopt probability theory to clinical decision-making under conditions of high uncertainty. Perhaps in this way the driving power of technologic imperative can be blunted."[20] In essence, this suggests a cost-benefit analysis of individual clinical decisions.

The rising use of all kinds of medical technology in treatment, especially of terminal patients, may be more easily attacked than the increasing use of CAT scanners and ultrasound in diagnosis. To deny more definitive testing in diagnosis without involving the patient in that decision seems unethical on the surface. Use of sophisticated technology and repeating the more usual tests, however, do not always increase reliability; scientific data about the efficacy of even common treatments are not always available and an informed patient may not want all that medical technology can offer either for diagnosis or treatment. Uncertainty is possibly the most difficult condition under which to live. The costs, including risks, may not always be considered by the patient to be worth the gain. The giving of truly informed consent about highly complex options, often for which reliable data about their efficacy are not available, requires more of the art than the science of medicine.

Geographical differentials and city size are important determinants of fees. A 1978 federal government study by Zachary Dyckman states that "real physician fees are approximately 20 percent higher in the West than in the North Central region and about 10 percent higher than in the Northeast and East."[21] This is after correcting for differences in the cost-of-living, supply of hospital beds, number of physicians, and other factors. Earnings of physicians that encompass more than fees are highest in the South, followed by the North Central region, West, and Northeast. The Dyckman study concludes that "there is no simple relationship between regional fee and earnings patterns. While fee levels are obviously relevant to a determination of earnings levels, so are relative physician supply, productivity, insurance coverage, and other factors."[22]

The average income of physicians in group practice is higher than those in solo practice, and the latter have average longer work hours. Groups have a higher concentration of board-certified specialists and this in part accounts for their higher incomes. Specialists charge more than general practitioners for similar services. There are also more older, semi-retired doctors in solo than in group practice. In 1976, the larger the number of physicians in the group, the fewer patient visits the average physician had per week. In a 2-man group, the average number of visits per physician was 146.5 in a week while in a group with at least 26 physicians, the average was 110.3 visits per physician in a week. This number compares with 123.5 for solo practitioners.[23] The data for only general practitioners are more extreme: solo, 161 patient visits per physician per week; 2-man group, 207; and 26- and larger groups, 127. The measure of average number of weeks practiced per year was also less for physicians working in groups of more than 25 physicians. However, the total number of hours practiced per week was slightly higher in large groups than by solo physicians, though considerably lower than in small, 2- and 3-man groups.[24]

Large groups generally give their physicians more time off for continuing education and to take short courses, and some groups even give several months of educational, sabbatical leaves. It has been charged that physicians in large groups work less hard for higher incomes than do solo physicians. Large groups claim that their quality of care is higher because of more effective peer review, and some claim that they are more efficient in the use of non-physician health manpower.

Mortality and morbidity data indicate that the quality of medical care, whether provided by solo or group physicians, has improved over the past forty years. The improvement stems in part from new and effective drugs, medical devices, and surgical procedures. That some new diagnostic and treatment procedures may have been ineffective or indeed a few harmful does not reverse the overall impact. Cost-benefit analyses are increasingly being developed to assess new surgical procedures and drugs.

A path-breaking study of the American College of Surgeons and the American Surgical Association has an estimate

of the economic benefits of surgical research for the year 1970 . . . [which] showed that the 16 surgical advances we considered produced, collectively, a 60-fold return on the investment in research and resulted in a net saving of $2.8 billion for the year. Since [the] analysis was concerned with only one year and the benefits from reduction in mortality and morbidity accrue over many years, it is clear that the actual economic benefits are substantially greater than those estimated. Although the methods for performing benefit-cost analyses in the health field are imprecise, the economic benefits from surgical research have clearly been enormous.[25]

There are some who might criticize the size of these savings because of the assumptions about the efficacy of the procedure, the assumptions involved in deriving the valuations placed on the quality of life-years saved, and on the reduction of bed-disability days. However, the magnitude of the economic benefit is too great to deny that a benefit exists. The results of the increasing use of quality-adjusted life years (QUALY) where no monetary value is derived from payment for one's work in risk-benefit analyses also support that over many years medical care outcomes from all factors have improved. However, there is some disturbing evidence of declines from specific factors. Los Angeles County had a significantly lower death rate in January and February 1976 when surgery dropped by 40 percent because of a physicians' slowdown to protest the level of malpractice premiums. This implies a lower level of quality than physicians generally are willing to admit. How unique this incidence is and whether it would be duplicated elsewhere in similar circumstances is difficult to judge.

New drugs and better management of cardiovascular disease account, in part, for the striking decline in the age-adjusted mortality rates from heart disease and stroke. From 1970 to 1977, the number of cerebrovascular, age-adjusted deaths decreased from 48 to 27 per 100,000 population. "Improved management and rehabilitation of the stroke victim and effective hypertension therapy"[26] are considered to be major causative factors. New antihypertensive drugs yield a high net economic benefit to some individuals. Antibiotic drugs and polio vaccines are older examples of medical treatments whose benefits clearly outweigh their costs.

Providers' qualifications, the type and number of diagnostic procedures used, and health outcomes—life or death—sick or well—are the usual proxies to measure the quality of care. There are no clearcut, readily available measures of the quality of medical care, and consumers rarely have adequate information to judge the level of care that they are receiving. This is often true in other service markets. However, consumer feedback and final outcomes are more quickly realized in other markets and are less drastic. Consumers of medical care make judgments whether they are well informed or not. The patient's last resort is to sue health providers. Although an increase in malpractice suits and size of awards during the 1970s occurred in several professional areas other than medical in the United States, their growth in the medical sector outstripped these. Technological advance has widened the potential of medical malpractice.

Medical malpractice can be simply defined as injury to a patient resulting from negligence. In 1974, the legal definition of "negligence" was broadened to include sins of omission as well as commission and the comparative standards of quality used were extended beyond the local customary standards. Whereas it had always been difficult to get one physician to testify against a fellow physician, the door was thus opened for a physician who lived where local standards were higher to testify about another physician who was not a significant source of referrals. The level of malpractice suits has levelled off. It may be that the effect of these legal interpretations is a one-time occurrence. However, it is estimated that less than 20 percent of all patients who suffer an injury due to negligence file a claim.[27] Thus, it is likely that the level of malpractice suits will again rise. Insurance companies believe that about 46 percent of all claims are meritorious. Nuisance suits are usually not successful. There is no assurance, however, that successful claims are against only incompetent physicians or that all incompetent physicians are sued. It is often outstanding physicians who get the riskiest cases and who thus are more likely to face a malpractice claim.

It is of interest that "a physician in non-solo practice has a 2.8 percent higher probability of a malpractice claim than a solo practice physician."[28] Without experience-rated premiums, a relatively few physicians can be expected to be involved in a high percentage of the successful claims. A study over a four-year period of 8,000 physicians in the Los Angeles area showed that 0.6 percent of physicians accounted for 30 percent of all the claims paid by the insurance plan.[29] Space limitations prevent an in-depth discussion of malpractice and its intricate relationship to the quality of care.

The availability of automated, multiphasic testing centers to all physicians in a community means that productivity gains stemming from greater use of allied health workers is no longer necessarily limited to group practice. Such centers have multiplied rapidly. Some are open to patients with referrals from any physician and some to individuals without referral who may or may not specify a physician to whom the test results are to be sent. In these centers, most diagnostic measurements—from ocular tension and vital capacity to even height and weight—are made electronically and the data are fed into an on-line computer. The George Washington University Center employs "medical hostesses" with no prior health training who take x-rays, draw blood, and perform pap smears, "tasks that in many other centers must be performed by technicians, registered nurses, or doctors."[30]

It is possible that solo practitioners, by making use of competitive laboratories and automated multiphasic test centers, can provide care just as efficiently, or even more efficiently, as group physicians with their own testing facilities. The group's specialized equipment often has more unused capacity than a commercial laboratory servicing a larger number of physicians.

What is the optimal size, multispecialty group? Are groups necessarily more efficient, do they better utilize paramedical personnel, and do they deliver equal or higher quality medical care for the same cost as do solo practitioners? These are questions that need analysis. However, such studies face a major obstacle at the outset. The term "physician productivity" is usually loosely defined as the number of patients a physician sees per hour. Although different weights may be used for different types of visits (history, diagnostic, followup, etc.), there remains a vital factor that cannot be quantified: quality. Paradoxically, low quality often results simultaneously with a high number of patient visits per hour, the data measure that indicates high productivity. High quality care is often associated with fewer visits per physician-hour because of the longer duration of time that the physician sees the patient. Fewer visits per hour also means lower physician productivity. Kaiser-Permanente (K-P) has been criticized because it sets a one-half hour maximum even for an initial, comprehensive physician office visit. A few solo practitioners set aside up to two hours for such a visit made by an older person, and one hour appears to be a fairly common time allotment for initial comprehensive physician visits. A K-P patient before seeing a physician takes an automated examination and fills in a questionnaire about his or her health history. Does this permit equal quality with less physician time? It is difficult to compare the implied quality of a one-hour and a one-half hour physician visit because of other variables as the differing ability of physicians and the differences in levels of health among the patients of different physicians.

The 1974 California Relative Value Schedule (CRVS) sets 17.5 units for an "initial comprehensive history and examination, including initiation of diagnostic and treatment program and preparation of records."[31] The CRVS values at 16 units "detention, prolonged, with patient requiring attention beyond usual service, per hour" and 20 units for a "specialist 'standby' for Caesarean or complicated delivery requiring services of additional physician, per hour."[32] CRVS units of 8.7 are listed for an office visit described as "established patient, extended re-examination and/or re-evaluation." Under "psychiatric services," the ratios of CRVS units in terms of only time can be examined. Here 16 units are listed for "45-50 minutes, 9.7 for 25 minutes, and 6.4 for 15 minutes."[33] Readers must make their own judgments about the relationship between the length of a physician visit and quality of care. This is not to imply that all physicians are of equal quality. One-half hour of a superior physician's time may be worth more than an hour of a less able physician's.

HEALTH MAINTENANCE ORGANIZATIONS (HMOs)
OR PREPAID GROUP PRACTICE

It is important to distinguish among three types of groups: (1) groups that pay physicians fees for their services and charge consumers fees for services, (2) groups that pay physicians "fee-for-service" (FFS) but whose subscribers prepay a per capita amount determined annually, and (3) groups whose physicians are salaried and whose subscribers prepay a per capita amount determined annually. The latter two types are sometimes referred to as "closed panels" because their enrollees cannot use, unless they pay them, physicians who are either not part of the group or to whom a group physician has not referred them. Many prepaid groups have bonuses and/or penalties that reward physicians whose primary care patients use fewer services than the average of the group.

Prepaid groups do not pay for self-referrals, referrals initiated by the patient and not by the group primary care physician. Such groups may employ a majority of all physicians in a community, making this restriction of little practical importance. Most new groups have strict referral controls because the group may not have a full complement of specialists and the potential drain on their funds from self-referrals may be substantial.

The first category, groups that do not receive prepayment, has already been discussed. These physician groups share facilities and equipment, overhead costs, and ancillary staff costs and substitute their services for one another's services within the group, but they bill patients on a fee-for-service basis at the time when their services are rendered. This form of practice is a natural evolution from the solo, fee-for-service practice. The Mayo group is a well-known, early example. Many groups of this nature are single specialty, not multispecialty practices.

Prepaid groups or Health Maintenance Organizations (HMOs), categories (2) and (3) above, are defined to include Independent Practice Associations (IPAs). IPAs pay physicians on a fee-for-service basis while other HMOs pay salaries. Most if not all HMOs pay bonuses and/or use financial penalties. The effects of these financial incentives differ between salaried physicians and fee-for-service physicians in group practice as is explained later in the analysis. Some IPAs have joined under a contractual arrangement to provide prepaid medical care at their different locations but have one central point of financial accountability. Many such networks have Blue Cross involvement.

Prepaid group practice in the United States is a miniscule part of all group practice which has grown rapidly. Although by 1969 there were over 6,000 group practices, employing 18 percent of active non-federal physicians, only 85 of the 6,000 groups had more than half of their business in prepayment plans. By 1975, there were almost 8,500 groups employing 24 percent of all active, nonfederal physicians, but only 142 groups earned 50 percent or more of their gross income from prepaid practice.

HMOs are a special hybrid form serving as both insurers (because they bear a large degree of financial risk) and as medical organizations delivering medical care. Most HMOs usually have lower per capita costs than the average of those persons using fee-for-service (FFS) practice for various reasons. Their enrollees who are workers are pre-screened because they hold a job and probably enjoy a higher level of health than non-workers. Although there is no reason to believe that their dependents are also healthier than the average, the lower average age of the HMO population implies a relatively healthy population. Workers with young children usually choose an HMO, if available, because most other third party insurance does not pay for well-baby care or other preventive medical care of children that is out-of-hospital. Most of the lower costs of HMOS derive from their lower use of hospital days, which may be in part due to their healthier membership, but also HMOs emphasize the use of the least costly resources appropriate to a given medical problem. Their hospitals are managed in respect to scheduling of admissions more like a for-profit than the traditional, non-profit hospital.

It is also claimed that HMOs provide more preventive care than do non-HMO physicians. This claim has been challenged on the grounds that HMO enrollees often see several different physicians over time because "their physician" is unavailable and thus the continuum of care is not maintained except through impersonal, written records. Some HMOs may have lower per capita costs because their enrollees may use outside services for which the HMO does not pay and because some HMOs may make more intensive use of physician assistants and general nurse practitioners and use other cost-saving devices. An analysis of the federal government's 1975 ongoing national *Health Interview Survey* recall data covering 8,449 persons in Northern California by a physician in Kaiser-Permanente's administrative offices concludes that there is no proof that self-selection by the more healthy has helped to contain costs in HMOs. Rather, Mark Blumberg stresses that, in his opinion, it is the fact that FFS physicians over-utilize in response to monetary incentives.[34] Several economists, however, believe that self-selection by the healthy does account in large measure for the lower per-patient costs among HMO enrollees.

Subscribers to HMOs pay a given amount per month, determined a year ahead, for medical care. The amount is determined per capita, not per service. The physician may be paid a salary, usually with a bonus. The lower the costs of tests, x-rays, hospital days, and physician visits charged to the primary care physician's patients, the higher the bonus.

Many IPAs, which are HMOs whose physicians are paid fees for services, use a negative, not a positive, financial incentive to induce physicians to order only the tests and x-rays medically needed. HMOs do not pay for a specialty referral to a specialist outside the HMO. Most IPAs also have rules that minimize the number of referrals to specialists even within the IPA. If IPA patients are a small percentage of a physician's total workload, a small penalty payback of fees to an IPA, as well as persuasive peer review, may have little effect on the physician's mode of practice. This can be overcome by varying the percent of charges at risk with the number of IPA patients the physician has. If the physician's IPA patients comprise less than 20 percent of his or her practice, the percent of the physician's IPA fee at risk should be higher than if they comprise 50 percent. Persuasion through peer review with informational feedback of medical charges of specialists and hospitals in the area to the primary care IPA physicians is becoming more common. These do not usually work to contain costs unless the bonus or the penalty is large enough to make it worthwhile for the primary care physicians to keep up to date on costs. Quality maintenance under this system is difficult to monitor, especially when high cost procedures may increase the patient's comfort but not length of life and also when the patient does not have, nor seek, the knowledge about the risks and benefits of alternative procedures and treatment.

Meaningful comparisons, even without consideration of quality, of competing HMOs' charges and corresponding benefit packages with competitors' charges and benefit packages are rare. This is because of the great diversity of the benefit packages and the high number of variables involved.

Legislation

President Nixon's 1971 health message to Congress defined HMOs as a single organization providing a comprehensive range of medical services "for a fixed contract fee which is paid in advance by all subscribers," a definition which could have included some people served by the neighborhood clinics or the community health comprehensive centers originally funded by the Office of Economic Opportunity and subsequently transferred to the Department of Health, Education, and Welfare. Under the Partnership for Health Program (PL 89-749), many prepaid groups organized by private institutions such as the Harvard Community Health Plan, Inc., received federal grant monies.[35]

In 1973, federal loans were authorized to HMOs providing a very broad range of benefits. To be a "non-profit" HMO does not necessarily mean that its managers are receiving a competitive salary and that the total costs, which in the health sector as in the defense industry are reimbursed, have no surplus in them. Cost overruns have been common in both areas. The major argument against for-profit HMOs also exists against non-profits. Both have strong incentives to minimize the average cost per enrollee. It is often assumed that persons working for non-profit organizations will be more altruistic than those working in for-profit organizations. Government regulation and self-imposed peer review to protect quality was anticipated to become common. To remove the financial risk for either profit or non-profit would result in higher prices and costs although it probably would be less inflationary among the "for profits" who would continue to compete.

A comparison of the two-year period, 1973 and 1974, of the per capita charges by profit and non-profit HMOs in California is enlightening. As indicated in Table 8, by the end of the two-year period, the non-profits were charging more per capita than the for-profits. Yet the 1974 *Annual Report to the Governor and Legislature on Prepaid Health Plans* (PHPs) states on page 21 that the "for-profit PHPs . . . provide significantly more physician services than do non-profit PHPs. Nonprofit PHPs, however, provide significantly more consultative services and prescription drugs than do for-profit PHPs. Both types of PHPs provide comparable levels of nursing home care, vision care services, and obstetric care." The change in the political administration of California meant that the proposed analysis of the demographic data to assess these differences was never made. Government and private analyses of the experiment find that there was a stronger link between the length of time an organization existed and the quality of care than between whether the PHP was for-profit or non-profit and the quality of care.

The California legislative audit committee found duplicate payments because persons used county facilities for health services that

Table 8. Prepaid Health Plan Charges for Medi-Cal Subscribers in California, 1973 and 1974

Date	Monthly Composite For-Profit	Per Capita Charge for All Aid Categories Non-Profit
July 1973		
First year	$26.78	$23.45
Second year	28.30	27.49
September 1973		
First year	25.80	23.70
Second year	29.43	29.41
December 1973		
First year	25.08	24.96
Second year	29.09	29.53
March 1974		
First year	26.21	26.12
Second year	29.30	29.90

Source: "Annual Report to the Governor and Legislature on Prepaid Health Plans," California Health and Welfare Agency, Department of Health (Sacramento, California: June 1974), pp. 25-28. (Mimeo)

the PHP was paid to provide. If there had been a longer period and stricter controls, it seems likely that this problem would have been overcome. The protests about poor quality care centered around deceptive enrollment practices and non-provision of promised, twenty-four-hour emergency care.

In 1976, the federal HMO Act was amended to give a more competitive edge to prepaid group practice. To qualify for federal funds, an HMO with fewer than 50,000 members or one which had been in existence for less than five years would no longer be required to maintain open enrollment. Thus, those persons with chronic illness or permanent injury who represent an economic drain to prepaid organizations could be excluded from new HMOs. The required benefit package was decreased by exclusion of preventive dental care for children although certain other preventive services were added. Additionally, the ban on the HMO's use of part-time physicians for the care of their enrolled population was lifted.

The amendments decreased the range of mandatory benefits, but the requirements that an HMO, to qualify for federal support, have community-rated charges and be a non-profit organization were retained. Most commercial insurers set premium levels in accordance with the claims experience of a group (i.e., of employees) in the previous year. This practice is experience-rating. Many Blue Cross and Blue Shield plans set premium levels in accordance with the claims experience of a geographical community during the past year. This practice is community-rating.

In 1978, Congress authorized continuing three-year support via grants and loans for the expansion and creation of HMOs. The legislation also states that HMOs are required to reimburse their members for the purchase of care from another provider, but only in cases of an emergency. In 1979 Congress, under PL 96-79, exempted HMOs from the certificate-of-need requirements, which state that all hospitals and physicians must give the appropriate Health Systems Agency (HSA) thirty-day notice prior to the purchase of diagnostic and therapeutic equipment costing $150,000 or more even if the equipment is not intended for inpatient hospital use.

The federal law requires companies to offer their employees the choice of an HMO if twenty-five or more employees live in an HMO service area and they request that option. Thus, more employers are offering the option of HMOs in addition to private health insurance options that usually include community-rated, Blue Cross and Blue Shield plans. Where there are no HMOs in a geographic area, some employers have become involved in starting one. New HMOs are also being organized by large commercial insurance companies such as Prudential, and especially by the service-oriented Blues. Because the Blues have had longer and closer relationships with providers than the commercials, they have in general found it easier to develop such plans. Competition in physician-surplus areas and the attractiveness of federal dollars stimulate established multispecialty groups, hospitals, and some medical schools also to organize an HMO.

Under the Carter Administration, the federal government developed a ten-year program of sustained HMO support to be followed during the 1980s. It was aimed at twenty metropolitan areas[36] with high health care costs and is based on the assumption that HMOs will, through competition, contain costs in areas where they are located. Noticeably missing from the government's target areas are Los Angeles and San Francisco, two high-cost cities. In both cities, HMOs are already firmly established. Why medical costs have been and remain high in these cities is not explained. In 1979, there were 217

HMOs in the United States enrolling about 8 million persons, still less than 5 percent of the population. In 1979, Utah passed a law instructing certificate-of-need agencies to foster competition and the expression of consumer choice. With the subsequent powerful position of that state's senator, Orrin Hatch, federal legislation to encourage competition through giving HMOs an even more favorable environment than now exists appears plausible. The 1979 legislation had exempted HMOs with 50,000 members from certificate-of-need legislation and also those smaller HMOs that had given certain tangible evidence of reaching that membership goal.

The federal authorization of $164 million in grants to HMOs over three years expired in September 1981. Because of the size of the budget deficit in 1981 and the number of recent defaults on loans to HMOs, new lines of government credit and outright grants probably will not be made under the Reagan Administration. Anticipated is a phasing out by 1984 of federal loans concomitant with a reduction in the mandated minimum benefits requirements. The Reagan Administration's February 1981 "Economic Recovery Program" states that "defaults on unsecured loans for HMO operating deficits and required interest subsidy payments will exhaust the $116 million HMO loan revolving fund by the end of the year 1981 and will require substantial future spending even without awarding any new loans."[37]

Competition

The largest HMO, Kaiser-Permanente Foundation, is concentrated in the Far West with "substantial market penetration in Seattle, Portland, San Francisco, Los Angeles, and Honolulu." It is claimed that many HMOs in these cities have "brought about a positive response from the predominant fee-for-service sector."[38] But surgical fees corrected for differences in cost-of-living are, among comparable urban populations, the highest in the Los Angeles area and relatively high in the New York City area.[39] About 20 percent of the California population are enrolled in HMOs. Portland, Oregon, also has had substantial prepaid group penetration for a number of years. Yet, its basic per-day charge in hospitals is one of the highest in the country, and the average covered charges reimbursed per hospital day has increased for the aged under Medicare by 94 percent from 1973 to 1977 while nationwide the increase has been 77.5 percent. California's rate of increase during that period was also high, 87 percent. Although the average length of hospital stay is less in California and

Oregon than the national average, the rate of increase of total hospital reimbursements, 1973–77, was greater in these states than in the country as a whole.

The effect of HMOs on medical charges in both the northern and southern California areas is difficult to detect. From 1971 through 1979, prices of medical care items in the San Francisco-Oakland area rose 94 percent while prices of all items in the Consumer Price Index (CPI) in that area increased 79 percent. In the Los Angeles-Long Beach-Anaheim area, medical care prices rose 95 percent, and all items 80 percent. These are significant differentials. In one year, April 1979–April 1980, the U.S. average medical care price index increase was 11.4 percent; in the San Francisco area, 13.0 percent; in the Los Angeles area, 15.7 percent; and in Portland, Oregon, where about one-fourth of the population is enrolled in HMOs, 14 percent.

Among the areas where HMO enrollment is significant (Hawaii is not included in the analysis because of the many factors unique to that state which affect pricing and the level of use of medical care), only in the Minneapolis-St. Paul area have medical care prices not risen faster than consumer prices in the same area. From 1970 to 1980, however, the differentials even there have not been large. The CPI national average increase was 103.5 percent; Minneapolis-St. Paul, 110.9 percent; and medical care prices in the latter area, 105.6 percent. However, although HMOs may have not always contained prices, most are (through reduction in hospital days used) containing costs for the HMO. In effect, this permits HMOs to charge lower premiums or prepaid fees per capita. At the same time, the existence of strong HMOs in many areas may have resulted in insurers offering more comprehensive benefits and, in addition, providers outside the HMO charging higher prices. Prices higher than otherwise would exist can force up insurance premiums. Thus, insurers are very interested in establishing their own HMOs or at least getting management and/or consulting fees from other HMOs. Blue Cross, because it provides service benefits, may be better able than commercial insurers to do this.

The large prepaid group, Health Insurance Plan (HIP), has been located in New York City for over twenty years. The Blue Cross and Blue Shield of Greater New York HMO, although it began operation in December 1973, had only about 28,000 enrollment in June 30, 1980. There is a need to test whether or not HMOs, by competition, lower the non-HMO physicians' average fees and patients' medical care costs in a given geographical area. More data is also needed to establish clearly the degree to which HMOs substitute more office visits for in-hospital patient care and the resulting effects on costs, prices, and quality.

A comparison between patients enrolled in a new prepaid group with the traditional fee-for-service population of the salaried physician Marshfield Clinic in Wisconsin indicates that the new prepayment arrangement resulted in more ambulatory care and in-hospital discharges. Self-selection, a short observation time, and several unknowns do not permit this study to give a clear answer.[40]

Harold Luft's comprehensive summary of many studies of HMOs neither supports nor denies the contention that, because HMO subscribers are workers, the enrollees are younger and are likely to be healthier than the adult population as a whole and thus use less resources. Luft does point out that hospital admissions are lower in HMOs for both surgical and medical cases and hypothesizes that "better health or greater aversion to hospital admissions among HMO enrollees"[41] may, as well self-selection among providers, contribute to lower hospital utilization rates by HMO enrollees.

In dual-choice situations, persons with chronic disease may be more likely to select prepaid group practice than FFS. Similarly, young people who anticipate having children tend to enroll in HMOs, where maternity and pediatric care coverage is more comprehensive because ambulatory visits are not usually covered by insurance companies.

There is some recent evidence that healthier persons, even among the older Medicare population, have self-selected into prepaid groups. A study of Medicare enrollees of the Group Health Cooperative of Puget Sound (GHC) in Washington indicates that prior to enrollment they "used inpatient services 52 to 62 percent less than a comparable population."[42] The authors of the study write that there are two possible explanations: only low-risk people were attracted to GHC, or GHC encouraged low-risk persons to join and discouraged high-risk persons. Earlier the same article states, "Poor health risks were offered only the low option although the majority of the better risks choose the high option."[43] Can one infer from this that high-risk persons were thus discouraged from joining?

In support of the Kaiser Foundation Health Plan and HMOs in general, Mark Blumberg[44] compares HMO members' use rates with those who have private health coverage in eight California metropolitan areas. He defines, as does the government survey data that he is analyzing, a physician visit in the Kaiser Plan as those conducted "by a nurse or other person acting under a physician's supervision."

Because the data are recall data, it does not seem very likely that all persons covered by private health insurance would consider these "physician visits." The Kaiser enrollees in the study have a higher number of visits, 4.15 per year as compared to 4.05 for those covered by private health insurance. Very relevant to this analysis is that the Blues in Northern California pay 90 percent of a subscriber's office visit, thus lessening the financial advantage of joining a prepaid group, even if the worker has dependents. This benefit of the Blues appears to be a competitive response to Kaiser's market penetration. If the Blues increase benefits for the same premium, it is equivalent to a lower premium or price for the same benefits. Because prices of medical care and health insurance are increasing, it is impossible to prove or disprove precisely if and to what degree Kaiser has affected pricing in these markets.

To receive a federal loan, an HMO must meet the federal requirement that its per capita charges are community-rated. Competition within a geographic area forces HMOs to meet the premium rates offered by insurers and the rates of other HMOs. The consumer who makes the choice pays, on the average, only about 15 percent of the premiums and charges; his or her employer pays the remainder. If the consumer paid a greater percentage of the cost, and if the per capita fee of the HMOs were experience-rated, then the choice of provider would be more closely related to the level of actual costs. Competition could then force down HMO rates and resulting insurance premiums.

HMOs serve primarily working people. Healthy work forces can, under other financial arrangements, attain lower experience-rated charges than the average for the whole population. If the government requires community-rating, then less healthy populations such as enrolled Medicare patients may benefit from lower average subscriber charges than otherwise would exist. Community-rated charges for benefits average the costs of low and high utilizers of medical care. This benefits the government-paid programs of Medicare and Medicaid but hurts private incentives for prevention, health education, and self-care practice programs in most employee groups. Because Medicare since the end of 1979 requires individuals to pay Medicare deductibles and co-payments and reimburses HMOs at about 80 to 90 percent of their regular charges, only a few HMOs enroll Medicare beneficiaries and less than two percent of the aged are enrolled in HMOs.[45]

Hospital utilization under HMOs is less than under private health insurance. Until there is some means of measuring the optimum number of hospital days for a patient of a given age, sex, and severity of disease, it is difficult to state whether or not persons enrolled in HMOs under-utilize and privately insured persons who use fee-for-service physicians over-utilize hospital days. Similarly, it is difficult to judge whether or not surgical rates that govern, to a large extent, use of hospital days are optimum or not. Elective surgery rates have increased 24 percent from 1971 through 1977.

The number of IPAs has been increasing in response to government legislation, competition, and, in some areas, surplus physicians. In these areas, many physicians belong to several groups in addition to maintaining a solo fee-for-service practice. Such areas include Boston, Massachusetts; Rochester, New York; Minneapolis and St. Paul, Minnesota; and Palo Alto, California.

In Palo Alto, physicians who are listed as specialists may have specialist status for FFS and prepaid group practice and yet at the same time be listed as primary care physicians in one or more IPAs. Under "TakeCare," an IPA started in 1980 by an established multi-specialty fee-for-service group of about 130 physicians, primary care physicians forfeit a percentage of the cost of a specialist referral within the group and also the costs of tests and x-rays which they order. Under "Lifeguard," another 1980 IPA primarily promoted by local medical societies, the same physicians are not so penalized. Moreover, the physicians may offer their services to non-members of any IPA. Because these physicians are offering the same service at different prices, the economist describes their behavior as price discrimination. If the physicians were providing different qualities of care at different prices to differently financed consumers, it would not be price discrimination. However, if the quality does differ with the price and this is not known, that practice appears to conflict with proclaimed medical ethics. Lower quality services are usually sold at lower prices, not at the same price as higher quality services. Price is broadly defined to include time costs. If longer periods of waiting were paired with lower money prices, price discrimination could be obviated.

Two HMOs in Washington, DC were widely recognized at the end of 1979 to be using waiting for appointments (1 to 12 weeks) as a method for keeping down costs. Long waits encourage self-referrals to medical care provided by physicians who do not belong to the prepaid group. Published comments about this practice of structuring demand raise problems of quality. Waiting for a medical appointment can heighten the patient's anxiety and worsen his or her physical condition. Women who believe that they are pregnant may use self-care pregnancy kits, pay to see a physician outside of the prepaid group, or wait. Pregnant women who elect to wait for many weeks have fewer options once they know that they are pregnant. They probably also have less confidence in medical providers when they eventually do see a physician. The latter effect may, in the long run, be the most pernicious. Many severely ill people who wait also may reduce their treatment options. Some prepaid groups have reduced waiting for appointments by using for initial visits nurse practitioners, who determine those who need to see a physician soon. Would-be patients, rather than waiting to see a physician of the group, may elect to use and pay for services from physicians who are not members of the group. The costs of outside providers should be considered part of the health care costs of HMO enrollees when HMO costs are compared with fee-for-service costs.

Some Selected HMOs

Large companies attempt to present capsule comparisons of the various options available to their employees. However, such comparisons rarely (Lockheed Missiles and Space Company, Inc., is one exception) point out that reimbursement by insurers is generally a percentage of the "usual, customary and reasonable" (UCR) fee and that therefore the employee will often have to pay physicians more than anticipated. "Holes" in the HMO coverage blanket are often glossed over. Careful perusal by the reader of newspaper advertisements will reveal the use of carefully worded language, making it easy to overlook actual restrictions by almost all the plans. Some employers send summary sheets issued by each plan to their employees, and a few companies write up comparisons of benefits and costs. For example, the Lockheed Missiles and Space Division summary for "Lifeguard," an IPA headquartered in San Jose, California, does not state that for reimbursement, pre-admission certification for all hospital admissions is required. Yet the plan's description of that program in part includes the following:

> . . . all hospital confinements must be C.H.A.P. [Certified Hospital Admissions Program] certified.

> . . . pre-admission certification is required for elective (medically necessary nonemergency) admissions. Emergency admissions require that C.H.A.P. be notified after the admission has occurred so the member's condition may be monitored and the confinement certified.

Nurse Coordinators and Physician Advisors administer C.H.A.P. Based on your physician's diagnosis, an evaluation of the medical necessity of hospitalization is made before and during your confinement. A specific number of days is then assigned and certified.

. . . If hospitalized out of the area, C.H.A.P. will keep in touch with the hospital for evaluation of your progress.[46]

In a Harvard Community Health Plan advertisement, "Harvard" is used twelve times. Harvard professors and staff have a different health plan than the "Harvard Community Health Plan." The implication is clear. A "TakeCare" advertisement, a new, federally approved HMO in Palo Alto, California, has (in bold type) "Personalized Group Health Care Goes Worldwide" and follows with: "TakeCare offers quick, convenient health [care] on a worldwide basis. Wherever you go, TakeCare goes with [sic] to provide emergency private physician and hospital care when necessary."[47] Even with the third sentence's limiting words of "emergency" and "when necessary," the promises are somewhat exaggerated. A common Blue Shield advertisement depends primarily on the emotional appeal of a sick child and implies that only through Blue Shield can you obtain care from "the best doctors." None of the above referred-to advertisements mentions prices or costs. Competition is achieved only by attempting to differentiate the product.

The growth in HMO enrollment from 2 to 12 percent or more of the Minneapolis-St. Paul population during the 1970s is often cited as an example of how HMOs can create a competitive climate to control costs. The seven HMOs in that area have financial arrangements with physicians and hospitals and, unlike in other areas, appear to compete on the basis of monthly family charges and the corresponding benefits offered. Because only one of the HMOs is federally qualified, individuals older than 65 years are not enrolled because Medicare will not reimburse non-qualified HMOs. Their costs have been contained by low surgical rates, low but stable hospital utilization rates, reliance on various kinds of physician assistants, and a relatively young employed population. However, there does seem to be a spill-over. Credit is usually given to the employers in the area who more actively supported the HMOs than to employers in other areas. Medical care prices in the Twin Cities rose only 92 percent from 1971 to 1980 compared with 106 percent nationwide;[48] but, hospital use rose.

The monthly charges above the employer's costs to a Honeywell employee in Minneapolis-St. Paul for family coverage in April 1978 varied from $14.35 for Blue Cross-Blue Shield coverage and $13 for the Physicians Health Plan to only $5 for the MedCenter plan.[49] Three of the other HMOs would cost an employee $8 monthly. Over one-half of Honeywell's employees selected the highest premium HMO, Physicians Health Plan. The non-monetary factors apparently outweighed the costs. The items of greatest importance were geographic location as well as the previous relationships with and the reported quality of the physicians in the plan. Location reflects a "time price," and the individual physicians in the plan represent a quality factor.

Similar reasons of location and physician choice were given by Stanford University employees who selected, for June 1973–June 1974, the Palo Alto Medical Clinic (PAMC) prepaid plan rather than the alternative Kaiser plan. However, those who chose the Kaiser plan stated that the higher out-of-pocket costs under the PAMC plan that has a 25 percent cost corridor of all charges were a significant factor.[50]

An initial decline and then levelling off of subscriber loss is typical of prepaid group plans. Nineteen percent of the members of all HMOs in the Twin Cities terminated their membership in 1974 and 12 percent in 1978.[51] This is a close parallel to the retention experience of the Kaiser Health Foundation Plan in Portland, Oregon, where about 19 percent of its subscribers left during the first six months and almost one-third after the first year.

In Rochester, New York, young, highly mobile individuals enrolled in prepaid group practice. Many younger persons were married with dependent children and thus, for them, a prepaid group was a better buy. Costs of office visits for children's health care are rarely covered other than by HMOs. A survey made in 1973 in that city indicates that costs also dominated the decision by those who did not join prepaid groups: "Two-thirds of the non-joiners gave high cost as a reason for not joining."[52] A mixture of non-economic reasons, "greater access, availability, comprehensiveness," and the promise of 24-hour availability (which is important to parents who travel) dominated the choices for joining the new prepaid groups in Rochester. Usually young, single persons, who are on the average healthier people, do not join prepaid groups. They prefer the lower price premium commercial insurance for which they may or may not pay, with the freedom it gives them in selection of physicians when they are traveling.

The number of referrals per enrollee in the Twin Cities' various plans increased slightly from 1974 to 1976. However, the "average cost of a referral visit decreased from $53.62 to $49.78. This lower cost per referral could reflect either an increase in cost consciousness in the selection of referral physicians or a decrease in the seriousness of the medical condition of the average referral patient."[53] The drop in the referral costs is startling because price controls ended in the health services industry in April 1974 and marked the beginning of a substantial catch-up rise in medical care prices during the years given. HMOs compete in the Twin Cities by varying the benefits. All the plans now give complete coverage for maternity expenses and some have Saturday morning clinic hours. Advertisements placed in local newspapers cover services, benefits, and location, but not prices. Consumers are interested in both convenience and costs because, in the Twin Cities, many employers pay only the lowest of the charges by the plans that are offered.

Advertisements by HMOs are increasing nationwide in response to the increased supply of physicians and the Supreme Court's ruling that professionals may advertise. Individual physicians are reluctant to advertise prices, and HMOs appeal to employers who pay most of the costs and who budget their costs at least one year ahead. HMOs want healthy persons as enrollees. Employed persons have been, to a degree, pre-screened as healthy enough to work on a steady basis. HMOs advertise, as do insurers, in order to increase their business. It is surprising more HMOs do not point out that commercial insurers usually pay only a portion of physicians' fees, and that in many instances the consumers will pay more out-of-pocket costs than they anticipate.

Established HMOs have established name recognition, which acts to assure a degree of quality. New HMOs, by advertising, may acquire tradename recognition and the preceding advertisements illustrate this point. Television advertisements by HMOs are also becoming more common.

Kaiser-Permanente (K-P) has attained wide name recognition. In 1979, K-P had 3.7 million enrolled members and employed 3,900 clinical physicians in California, Colorado, Hawaii, Ohio, Oregon, and Washington. K-P, with Prudential Insurance Company, has opened a new HMO to serve the Dallas-Fort Worth, Texas, area. K-P enrolls almost one-half of all HMO members nationwide.

K-P has 1.1 physicians per 1,000 enrollees as compared with 1.8 physicians per 1,000 nationwide. In 1980, K-P plans to hire about 240 additional full-time physicians and for each of these, "8 to 9 new employees in the various allied health care occupations and professions."[54]

By keeping K-P's ratio of hospital beds to enrollees substantially lower than the national standard, the potential savings of the Kaiser system are substantial. K-P's ratio, in 1970, was 1.8 hospital beds per 1,000 members, and below that in the late 1970s as compared with over four acute care beds per 1,000 in the U.S. as a whole. K-P estimates an annual utilization rate of 525 days per 1,000 and an occupancy rate of 80 percent in K-P hospitals.[55] Community hospital beds per 1,000 in the United States in 1977 were 4.6 and in California, 3.9; occupancy rates were 73.3 percent and 65.8 percent, respectively. As Table 9 indicates, the actual K-P bed ratio in 1978 and 1979 was below 1.8 per 1,000 population, and occupancy rates close to 100 percent have been reported in scattered instances.

K-P received, in 1979, $1.3 billion in revenues: 80.1 percent from members' dues, 5.3 percent in supplemental charges to members, 10.4 percent from Medicare, and 4.2 percent from non-plan patients and other sources. Whereas its medical services accounted for about 50 percent of expenses, hospital services accounted for only one-third. Kaiser Foundation Health Plan, Inc., its subsidiaries, and Kaiser Foundation Hospitals keep their cash balances low and finance expansion from earnings. A Kaiser Foundation publication states that "start-up costs and allocated amounts of mortgage interest incurred during the construction period for new facilities and major additions to existing facilities are deferred and amortized over periods of three to five years."[56] Cash balances, including short-term investments, were about $6.5 million (December 21, 1979) while K-P's physicians' retirement fund was $175 million (benefits of $1.2 million paid in 1979). The reserve fund for self-insured losses was $32 million. K-P's total reserves were several million dollars greater than the total long-term debt of $144 million. Examination of the financial statements indicates that the "K-P Health Plan" components are highly successful businesses with considerable growth potential. K-P has built successfully upon its initial advantage of captive subscribers, employees who worked and lived where no other medical facilities existed. Newer HMOs have been trying to compete during a highly inflationary period but, with few exceptions, have failed to establish their names as trademarks of quality. The size of Kaiser permits planning on a regional scale with known revenues a year ahead.

The Kaiser system uses nurse practitioners more extensively than most other practices. The ratio of K-P's outpatient visits to hospital admissions as early as 1969 was 45 to 1 compared with much lower ratios nationwide. K-P's hospital occupancy rates have occasionally been reported at 100 percent or more.[57] Because K-P owns most of the hospitals that it uses, it can maximize revenues over total costs

Table 9. Kaiser-Permanente Medical Care Program:
Hospital Beds per 1,000 Population

	Licensed Beds		Staffed & Ready For Occupancy[a]	
	1978	1979	1978	1979
Ohio	1.67	1.63	1.35	1.29
Hawaii	1.54	1.50	1.39	1.34
So. Cal.	1.68	1.76	1.30	1.44
Oregon	1.72	1.64	1.31	1.33
No. Cal	1.85	1.72	1.41	1.35
COMBINED	N/A	N/A	1.36	1.39

[a]Telephone conversation, Medical Economics Office, Oakland, California, May 6, 1980. *Definition:* Number of available beds regularly staffed and otherwise ready for occupancy by inpatients exclusive of newborn beds (bassinets), recovery and labor room beds, supplemental and other non-Kaiser Foundation Hospital beds, and beds staffed intermittently under overflow conditions. Source: Computed from 1978 and 1979 *Kaiser Foundation Medical Care Program Annual Reports.*

by substituting ambulatory for the more expensive hospital care when assessed as appropriate.

Obviously many persons are satisfied with the medical care provided by K-P programs. Complaints about Kaiser are the same as those about other HMOs. The following quotations are taken from a 1971 pamphlet published by the Kaiser Foundation and, therefore, might be under-statements. "Waiting times for appointments commonly run from three to six weeks and, in one large Permanente group, as high as 55 days." "Patients have been 'left hanging' [on the telephone] for as much as 30 minutes."[58] Additionally, newspaper articles indicate that the waiting problem for some other HMOs is probably worse, not better. Nearly 4 million persons receive medical care from Kaiser and, although it is obviously not everyone's choice, neither is the higher cost, lower waiting time, and higher resource utilizing fee-for-service system.

IPAs avoid the large start-up costs of the closed panels, such as K-P, because they use existing facilities. Most IPAs integrate physician services for a patient through one primary care physician. IPA's rapid growth in the 1970s has paralleled the growth of a surplus of physicians. IPAs are a competitive answer by FFS physicians to the established closed-panel HMOs. Some patients of FFS physicians may prefer budgeted prepayment of medical bills rather than un-foreseen, erratic payment when illness occurs. IPAs may deflect these patients away from salaried physician, prepaid groups.

Discussion in academic and government circles tends to assume that physicians in prepaid group practice usually respond to long-run, not short-run monetary incentives. Thus, it is also assumed that physicians in HMOs commonly emphasize preventive care, early diagnosis, and periodic physical examinations so that per-patient long-run costs will be lower and the quality of care higher than under other forms of practice. A recent comprehensive review found that comparisons where third parties reimburse for preventive visits yield little or no HMO effect and that "studies comparing HMO enrollees with people having conventional coverage for preventive services typically produce ambiguous results. The HMOs provide more preventive care of some types and less of others."[59] This may in part reflect uncertainty about the effectiveness of periodic checkups and other services to improve long-run health.

In any given prepaid group practice, it may be that at all times the combined effect of anticipated long-run monetary gain and altruism act in combination to yield the highest quality care and outweigh in choice of treatment any effect of an anticipated *short-run* net gain. But the structure of a prepaid group is such that it creates the potential for those suppliers with high valuations of present versus future income to select, consciously or unconsciously, courses of action which net more in the short run than in the long run. A geographically mobile, subscriber group would reinforce an emphasis on the short run. In periods when labor costs are rising rapidly, the government, a large buyer, is exerting pressure to hold prices down, but the temptation for HMOs to restrain short-run costs by cutting quality will increase.

It is doubtful whether the federal government should continue loans to new HMOs that apparently are not economically competitive or otherwise they could borrow private funds. If federal loans and underwriting of prepaid group practices were continued, it should be accompanied by measures that protect the quality of care given to the consumer and also give protection against default on the loans. These assurances would be difficult to obtain. If the government grants low interest loans to prepaid groups and guarantees payment of annual per capita fees for those defined as poor, new suppliers will be attracted into prepaid group practice. Such suppliers may not be so altruistic as the original pioneers who had an interest in proving the superiority of this organizational form. This was the experience in California during the period 1972–74 when the newer prepaid groups abused their Medi-Cal contracts as compared to the older, established groups. Although that time period was too short to reveal whether the established groups under the stress of competition may have also succumbed to short-run gains, the potential for them to do so is there.

The federal government, by mandating an artificially larger package of minimum benefits than is common, has forced the newer and smaller HMOs to be priced out of the market. Thus, numerous defaults have occurred. Economically viable HMOs will continue to develop and grow if government support and government-imposed standards of benefits and pricing are removed.

Cost Containment in HMOs

The economic climate of the 1970s discouraged the growth of HMOs. In any inflationary period,

> a prepaid group has the disadvantage of a fixed monthly income, whereas a fee-for-service group [without prepayment] has a steadily increasing income resulting from an increasing number of services sold in response to rising demand and at higher prices. Thus, one would expect prepaid groups to increase during deflation and fee-for-service groups to increase during inflation.[60]

The recent inflationary climate discourages the formation of HMOs, whether they pay physicians on a fee or on a salary and bonus basis. Per capita prepayment is not in itself a cost containment method but creates a lag in adjustment of per capita charges to changes in utilization of services and in costs of providing services.

In prepaid groups, individual per capita charges are not related to individual utilization. But neither is the per capita annual premium under group health insurance, which comprises most health insurance in the United States.

Data indicate that established HMOs' average per capita charges are usually less than FFS charges computed for comparable populations. In cases where HMOs own their own hospitals, per capita costs are even lower than where the HMO arranges hospitalization. The major savings of HMOs derive from the fewer hospital days used per enrollee. Surgicenters are utilized for minor surgery, review over hospital admissions is stricter, and the average length-of-stay is shorter than under FFS. HMOs also have lower surgical rates than non-group FFS. These observations raise again the question of whether the quality of medical care in HMOs is equal or less than that in other forms of medical practice. A 1980 review of the evidence states that the "available data suggest that outcomes in HMOs are much the same as, or somewhat better than, those in conventional practice" and "there is no evidence that HMOs achieve their utilization and cost savings by offering substantially lower quality care than the fee-for-service system . . . there is some suggestion of higher quality."[61]

The above carefully worded generalization appears true, but the great diversity of HMOs and their relative short history make it unclear what is the value of the generalization as applied to a particular HMO. There are high-quality and low-quality HMOs, large HMOs and small HMOs, and salaried-physician HMOs and FFS-physician HMOs. The basic question that needs answering is whether the structure of HMOs creates a tendency for a greater number of lower-quality systems of medical care delivery to develop than under alternative financial arrangements.

California has relatively greater experience with HMOs than other states. Under Governor Reagan, a determined effort was made to use prepaid group practice to provide medical care for those on welfare. In 1974, fifty-four HMOs covered 250,000 welfare recipients, or about 10 percent of all of California's 2.5 million cash welfare recipients, and about one-fourth of the potential enrollment based on geographic availability.[62] This represented very rapid growth. Medi-Cal (California's Medicaid) was and is big business. The program paid out $1,278 million in fiscal year 1974 and covered, in addition to the usual hospital and physician services, prescribed drugs, dental care, eyeglasses, physical therapy, and services of optometrists, podiatrists and chiropractors, as well as other items. In 1974, the California legislature restricted individuals not enrolled in prepaid plans to two services per month unless they had prior authorization for provider reimbursement. Legislation also required those persons with some non-welfare income to pay $1 for each physician visit and 50 cents for each prescription filled. The requirement of copayments ended in July 1973 but the "prior authorization" requirement, that was with good reason hated by FFS physicians, remained. Eligibility for a state contract to provide prepaid services was contingent on the cost per enrollee being less than in the FFS sector, that the contracting plan seek enrollees from a given geographical area, and that it not refuse membership to anyone who was eligible. The method of projecting actuarial rates was not initially specified although the data and calculations used had to be made public.

In order to promote competition, two or more HMOs could seek enrollment in the same area. In San Diego, seven contracts were in force covering almost an identical geographic area. Profit and non-profit HMOs and their subcontractors, such as dentists and clinical laboratories, were acceptable. Quality level was to be maintained by open enrollment periods. Voluntary disenrollment rate per 100 employees per month dropped from 3.56 per 100 enrollees in May 1973 to 1.20 in March 1974. Involuntary disenrollment rate per 100 was about 3 per month, stemming from persons losing Medi-Cal eligibility. Charges of poor quality, misrepresentation, and lack of availability of promised services persisted into 1975. Stricter regulation with ceilings on administrative costs and consumer participation were legislated in 1976. In 1977, the numbers of Medi-Cal eligibles enrolled in a prepaid health plan had dropped by one-half to 120,000.[63] Meanwhile, about fifteen other states had contracted with HMOs to provide health care to Medicaid recipients. Today, HHS continues to encourage such arrangements for Medicare and Medicaid patients, and in 1980 federal legislation has been introduced to widen the use of HMOs in government reimbursement programs.

In 1980, fewer physicians than previously accepted new Medi-Cal patients because of low fees, excessive paperwork, and bureaucratic meddling. Medi-Cal reimburses general practitioners and specialists alike while Medicare reimburses the latter at a higher level. In 1978, Medi-Cal payments were about 60 percent of billed charges and for surgery, below 50 percent.

The California experience indicates that the major problem in the use of HMOs for extensive use among the poor (often the non-working and non-educated population) is the inherent conflict between cost containment and quality maintenance. The arguments about whether HMOs have higher or lower quality as compared to the FFS sector are largely theoretical. HMOs usually have more board-certified physicians and effective in-house peer review. On the other hand, the monetary incentive is for HMOs to skimp on the quantity of services, including the number of hours that they are available, an aspect of care easily judged by anyone. Higher income and more educated persons tend to use medical care less than low income and less educated persons. The low income individuals who are in Medi-Cal's population are likely to be sicker than higher income people and have a high demand for medical care. There is some evidence that persons in the United States and Australia who have more education *per se* have a low level of demand for medical care. They may be healthier or have lower expectations and substitute self-care, including preventive care to a greater degree than those with less education. There is also no clear-cut agreement whether or not an HMO's savings result in part from healthier enrollees (healthier because they are employed) and providers that are less prone to use hospitals, or because FFS over-utilizes surgery and hospital days.

HMOs may contain costs by selecting physicians who prefer a mode of practice that uses relatively fewer tests and x-rays in diagnosis and treatment and who also hospitalize patients less. In large, salaried HMOs that own laboratories, part of the physicians' incomes may derive from group-owned laboratories. Salaried group practices can more effectively influence their physicians' mode of practice because these doctors see only group enrollees, and informed peer pressure is generally in the direction of restraint. Salaried HMOs are effective in containing costs because the income generated by the HMO represents almost all of the physicians' earned incomes while in a fee-for-service HMO, physicians derive only a small part of their total income from the IPA. A 5 to 7 percent penalty reduction in IPA fees because of non-conformance means little to physicians whose practice is predominantly made up of patients who do not belong to the IPA and from whom the collection rate averages about 93 percent.

That salaried HMOs and some IPAs find it necessary to contain medical care costs through various economic incentives and peer review implies that there is a tendency without such pressure to have higher referral rates and higher use of procedures. Some physicians believe that the quality of medical care is improved or at least not impaired by induced cutbacks. Others argue that there is little or no over-utilization of surgery, tests, and x-rays in the FFS sector. Although most studies of large HMOs show lower surgical rates than in FFS, at least one prepaid group practice studied over a three-year period had no significant measurable difference from a control group in the FFS sector in its use of surgical care, including non-urgent surgery. The 1975 paper authored by four physicians and published in *Surgery* reporting the following data is usually ignored. "Indeed, surgical admissions rates were slightly higher for Medical Care Group enrollees than controls, and ambulatory surgery was used only modestly."[64] The surgical admission rates were relative to the U.S. average low in both the group and the control. The physician authors believe that no impact occurred from the new method of medical care organization and payment, prepayment, because the quality of care practiced in the area (St. Louis, Missouri) was already high and excess surgery did not exist. If this were true and the observation could be repeated, it indicates that HMOs can induce only a one-time saving and that only if the quality of existing care in the comparative FFS sector is low. The recent increases in some types of elective, non-emergency surgery have been too high. Most notable is the increase in the Caesarean rate, but that increase cannot be attributed solely to responses to the financial incentives of the FFS sector. Technical reasons, for example, fetal monitoring gives earlier warning of problems, contribute to the rapid increase in Caesarean deliveries. Data are needed to sort out the importance of different factors.

Medical, technological advances have been dramatic and, although all new procedures do not improve mortality outcomes, many improve the quality of life. An increasingly better educated public might demand more of the latter. It is this type of operation that HMOs may do less frequently.

If society as well as an HMO is to attain savings, it is necessary that the group's subscribers do not obtain additional medical care from outside physicians. Out-of-plan use of medical care by prepaid group subscribers may be fairly substantial. In 1972, almost one-third of New York City's Health Insurance Plan (HIP) Medicare enrollees had out-of-plan physician services reimbursed by the government.[65] About one-fourth of East Baltimore Medical Plan's Medicaid enrollees, 814 individuals, voluntarily left that plan between November 1971 and September 1973.[66] Data are scarce in this area. Interviews of persons who leave an HMO are needed to find out what percentage might have moved away (possibly low in Medicare and Medicaid populations), traveled extensively, disliked long waits, were dissatisfied with the perceived quality of the medical care because they did not see a physician, did not like their physician, did not select a particular physician, found diagnosis or treatment decisions unacceptable, or did not wish to use the specialists to whom they were referred. Only some of the reasons for discontinuing enrollment in an HMO have quality implications.

When referral by an HMO physician is made to a specialist outside the HMO, the HMO pays the bill. Tertiary care specialists cannot be efficiently utilized even on a part-time basis by any but the largest HMOs, and even they must negotiate a contract for care as needed with some tertiary care specialists. The degree of an IPA's potential financial exposure to costs from outside physicians is higher, the smaller the HMO.

In most instances, self-referrals are paid by the subscribers or by third parties on their behalf, such as the Social Security Administration for Medicare patients. The New York HIP study found that "out-of-plan users tend to be more seriously ill than those receiving all their services within the plan" and they are also more likely to be hospitalized.[67]

The authors of the HIP study appear most concerned about the implications of self-referrals if HMOs were to become the major source of medical care in the United States. The study does not explore why patients initiate referrals. Rather, the extent of out-of-plan use becomes an argument for even more comprehensive and widespread HMOs under an integrated national health insurance program with limits on enrollment transfers. It seems unwise to recommend a national health insurance program in which HMOs are, or because of financial arrangements will become, the dominant mode of delivery until it is known why people leave HMOs. Although many large HMOs have more board-certified specialists than FFS, this is no guarantee that their quality of care is higher in practice than the FFS sector, but neither can one prove that it is generally less.

Strict control over referrals is the basic element of cost containment by HMOs. Control over referrals to specialists within the group permits the HMO to limit effectively its utilization of hospital days. Patients enter hospitals primarily as a result of a specialist's decision, not a primary care physician's. Most of the 10 to 40 percent savings documented for salaried HMOs are because fewer hospital days are used by their members. Whether these savings for the HMO are also cost-saving for society depends on whether or not outside physicians are used. If their enrollees do see specialists outside the group and are hospitalized as a result, then not all the savings attained by the HMO are savings for society.

IPAs vary in their degree of utilization controls over the use of referrals to other physicians within and outside the IPA. A few IPAs have had no effective controls. The Health Alliance of Northern California (HANC) was forced into receivership in 1978 primarily because it paid for patient referrals to physicians outside of the IPA. A Superior Court of California, in its 1978 receivership ruling of Health Alliance of Northern California, Inc., states:

> Since members could not receive immediate medical attention at HANC's existing clinics, they were permitted to visit independent physicians who, not being under contract with HANC, naturally charged HANC their usual medical fees. Those fees usually exceed the cost otherwise sustained by HANC in providing equivalent medical services within HANC's own clinic. Even more seriously, HANC's staff in many instances lost control of the referral process; in other words, the members may have gone to independent physicians without prior approval and referral by

HANC. Apart from imposing a heavy financial burden on HANC, these referrals also created potential liability for the members, in the event that HANC did not pay the bills rendered by those physicians when due.[68]

Most IPAs and all salaried HMOs do not pay for self-referrals made by their subscribers to outside physicians. If a salaried HMO does not have on staff the appropriate specialist, a referral is made by the primary care physician to an outside specialist at the HMO's expense. The specialist may be under a contract that fixes the level of payments negotiated with the HMO. The United Healthcare Plan, organized in 1975 by Safeco Insurance Company in Seattle, Washington, is an open-panel IPA of 610 primary care physicians exercising tighter control over hospital use and referrals to specialists than is customary even in most closed panels. Primary care physicians, including pediatricians and internists, are rewarded one-half of any surplus in the account of any of their patients, and penalized 5 percent of the capitation fee and 10 percent of a FFS if there is a deficit. Unlike many IPAs, "accounts and incentives exist for each primary care physician, the physician's accountability is not shared by other physicians, even among partners in a group practice."[69] Thus, there is no sharing of a physician's savings as exists in the usual IPA. The primary care physician is paid to manage the total medical care needs for the patient. More medical care problems under this plan than is usual are managed initially by primary care physicians, thus reducing referrals to specialists. Professional fees are redistributed from specialists to primary care physicians.

It is unknown to what degree this may or may not reduce the quality of care. However, it is unlikely that the majority of patients of this IPA fully understand its cost containment system and its potential impact. The plan is not old enough to observe consumer reactions to the quality of care. No physicians have, as of June 1979, left the plan. There is in-house review to find any substandard care. Six physicians have been put on probation as of the beginning of 1980. The quality within this IPA might even be higher than otherwise because no tests and x-rays are duplicated and the continuity of care is greater. Use of specialists *per se* does not always translate into better health outcomes. An eminent rheumatologist has written that "a literature search fails to reveal unequivocal evidence that the outcome for an arthritic is better on the average when he or she is treated by a rheumatologist rather than a general practitioner or internist."[70]

The IPA-type of primary care network is spreading because an IPA needs no new capital and the primary care physician controls costs through referrals that directly affect hospital utilization. In addition, insurance companies and Blue Cross/Blue Shield are helping to underwrite some of the IPA's risk. Because this type of plan is usually offered "to an employer only after at least 60 percent of the primary care physicians in the area are participating in the plan, most patients can continue to receive care from their physicians when they join the plan. They also have a much wider selection of specialists and hospitals than in the closed-panel HMO."[71] United Healthcare in Seattle, Washington, used only 293 bed-days per 1,000 enrollees in 1978 as compared with 350 bed-days used under its competitor's plans and 479 bed-days used under Blue Cross. Age-adjusted data correcting for the relatively high enrollment of younger persons in United Healthcare yield 310 bed-days per 1,000 enrollees. The plan provided medical care to 38,000 persons with 750 participating physicians and has spread into northern California and Utah and to the state of Washington. Through control over referrals to specialists, primary care physicians can reduce the number of hospital days used by IPA enrollees below the number used in the more traditional HMOs.

CONSUMER CHOICE

Employers, not consumers, usually pay health insurance premiums or per capita fees to HMOs. It is the consumer, however, who selects a fee-for-service physician or an HMO according to anticipated health needs in the coming year. Because of the dual nature of HMOs, employers are becoming increasingly involved in their employees' selection of medical care providers as well as health insurers. Because of the rapidly rising costs to employers, their interest in the health care sector has greatly expanded. In part, large comporations are playing active consumer roles in order to contain these costs, but the choice of provider is made by the employee.

Subscriber fees to HMOs are continually increasing, as are health insurance premiums, thus making the fringe benefit of health insurance a substantial cost of doing business. Annual charges of HMOs and health insurance premiums appear to rise more than the general inflation. The executive of a large company testified before the Senate in 1979: "Expenses for prepayment and administration" of health care rose from $10.93 per capita in 1970 to $44.94 in 1978, a four-fold increase.[72]

Young, healthy, unmarried individuals are less likely, if they pay the bill, to select an HMO that has relatively high monthly charges albeit larger benefits than a less costly commercial insurance plan, which offers fewer benefits. If the company pays the worker's premium or HMO charge, the single employee has no incentive to choose the less costly plan. Companies may pay 100 percent of charges for the employee and usually varying amounts from 0 to 100 percent of charges for the employee's dependents. Some HMOs make it more advantageous for a two-worker family to belong than a single-worker family with a dependent spouse. The Harvard Community Health Plan charged, for example in 1980, $50 per month for a single employee and $125 per month, or $1,750 annually, for a family of two or more, based on the actuarial assumption that a family has one and a fraction children. However, members of two-worker families can enroll separately for a total monthly charge of $100. This distinction in monthly charge can imply that workers are more healthy or at least use less medical care, possibly because of higher time costs than non-workers. It may, on the other hand, reflect that most non-working wives in that plan have eligible children at home. It is interesting that Senator Kennedy's national health insurance proposals in recent years, and Alain Enthoven's consumer choice health plan, would not because of potential duplicate coverage permit husband and wife to choose different health care financial arrangements.

Most firms pay the premiums or monthly HMO charge only for their employees, not their dependents. Thus, the employer is more interested in comparative rates for one person rather than those for a family. The employee with dependents who chooses this common financial arrangement is, however, more interested in how much extra he or she will have to pay in order to cover their dependents. Table 10, which shows 1981 rates under various health plans offered by Stanford University, California, is structured to show how financial interests of the employee and the employer may differ under different employee arrangements. Stanford pays $68.16, an amount that covers more than any of the charges for the employee, and contributes towards the charges of a dependent. (Left out of the analysis for simplicity is the fact that Stanford University pays $6.41 for each employee's major medical expense coverage plus part of a dependent's major medical cost if any amount above the $68.16 remains.) In all instances, the employee pays nothing for his or her own coverage. The highest monthly charge among the three HMOs and one insurer is for an employee alone, $61.05. The lowest is $38.16.

Employers, depending on the characteristics of their labor force, can minimize their total premium but under differing arrangements. Under the existing financial arrangements of Stanford University for

Table 10. Stanford University Health Plans, 1981 (per month)

| | Employee Pays | | | Employer Pays | |
	Own	Own +1	Own +2 or More	Employee	Employee +1
Kaiser	$0	$ 8.16	$41.82	$38.16	$68.16
Blue Cross	0	9.89	35.12	41.18	68.16
TakeCare	0	37.66	65.64	51.84	68.16
Bay Pacific	0	39.08	60.52	61.05	68.16

Source: Data from Stanford University, January 1981, are used for Table 10 because they are readily available to the author. Existence of a Major Medical Plan is ignored for simplicity.

employees without dependents, the benefit package and mode of delivery of care, not the costs, solely influence employee choice. Single employees may choose the higher-cost plans. The employer, however, would prefer them to choose the lower-cost plans. The employee with dependents has to ask whether the additional costs to him or her of especially the two more expensive plans are worth his or her perception of additional benefits.

A labor force with a low percentage of employees with dependents will have under this arrangement much the same consumer choice inducements that is proposed in some congressional bills: that the employer pay only a fixed amount that in practice would be presumably related to the lowest premium for the single employee.

The two columns of Table 11 represent what would occur if Stanford University paid as those congressional bills suggest. Costs to employees without dependents would increase sufficiently under the higher-cost plans to present them with the same type of choice as is now presented to employees with dependents. Costs to all employees would increase and the employer would benefit from a reduction of costs. This outcome may account in part for industry's support of this financing option. If the proposal were tied to mandate use of the employer's "savings" to purchase catastrophic health insurance for employees' dependents where not previously purchased, it might be more acceptable. Union acceptability will depend on whether the savings are used for higher wages to make up employees' losses of after-income tax premium dollars that the company payments of premiums afforded. I do not believe that these proposals will be politically acceptable to the many companies where $2,000 or more are paid annually in health insurance premiums. The existing industrial financial arrangements are so diverse that it is not easy to plan how to move from these policies to new ones.

Because employers pay 85 percent of health insurance premiums, consumers are not concerned with total medical costs. Consumers respond primarily to their out-of-pocket costs at the time of consumption, which may be nil. Convenience and perceived quality dominate individual decisions: During what hours are services available? How long are waits for appointments? What is the level of quality of the physicians, including referred-to specialists? Who provide the services? The answers to these questions strongly affect consumer behavior.

For consumers who place a high value on their time, waiting in an office or examination room acts as a barrier to medical care. This type of waiting usually is a loss of time that cannot be productively used

Table 11. Effect of Pending Congressional Bills, 1981
(Employer Pays Costs of Lowest Charge Covering Employee Only)

	Employee Pays	Employer Pays
Kaiser	$ 0	$38.16
Blue Cross	3.02	38.16
TakeCare	13.68	38.16
Bay Pacific	22.89	38.16

Source: Data from Stanford University, January 1981, are used for Table 11 because they are readily available to the author. Existence of a Major Medical Plan is ignored for simplicity.

in paid or unpaid work or constructive leisure. Rationing medical care on a "first come, first served" basis or by waiting does not guarantee that medical resources will be distributed according to medical need. Married women who have children and who work outside the home place a relatively high value on their time. Children of married women who work see physicians less frequently than of mothers who do not work outside the home. Self-employed individuals, professionals, and the blue-collar workers who lose wages when not at work place a higher value on their time than do most older, retired persons.

Prepaid group practice does not replace fee-for-service practice in the eyes of all consumers. Prepaid group practices that use multiphasic screening to separate the sick from the worried-well do not usually provide for the latter to see a physician. Some prepaid groups use non-physicians for 25 percent or more of ambulatory visits. Forty percent of visits in the Harvard Community Health Plan are handled by nurse practitioners, not physicians.[73] Although this is cost-effective, it may sacrifice satisfactory patient/physician relationships. Limited surveys indicate that many consumers are happy, and some even happier, seeing trained health personnel other than physicians, especially for routine care during pregnancy and for pediatric care. In those cases a patient/nurse practitioner (or physician assistant) serves as a substitute. Pediatric care is rarely covered by commercial and Blue Cross/Blue Shield insurance. As long as no serious illness develops, this may be a welcome tradeoff. Pediatricians in FFS practice are experiencing a decline in the demand for their services, partly because of the decline in the birthrate but also because of the growth of HMOs. Office hours more convenient for working mothers is one method being used by FFS pediatricians to hold their patients.

Since 1960 federal government employees in the Washington, DC area have had the option of choosing a large prepaid group (the Group Health Association, organized in 1937) to provide medical care to them and their families. Of the nearly 15 percent of federal employees who live in the Washington, DC area, about 20 percent belong to the Group Health Association or other prepaid groups in or around Washington. Nationwide, there are at least seven individual and nineteen group practice plans available to federal employees.

In 1975, only 7.2 percent of all federal employees, most of whom live outside of the Washington, DC area, were subscribers to HMOs. Although a few governmental bodies such as the Armed Services and the State Department have complete medical care facilities, most do not. The government, as well as other employers, prefer that their employees enroll in HMOs because medical care costs can be more easily budgeted for the year ahead. This makes planning easier.

Because the government is a large buyer of medical insurance, it may be able to negotiate lower per capita costs with an HMO than insurance companies could offer for a comparable benefit package. Most insurance companies, including Blue Cross and Blue Shield, are larger than HMOs, with the possible exception of Kaiser-Permanente. Contracts offered by insurers do not cover all hospital and physician care costs. In addition, the Blues and other insurers have several options with lower premiums for smaller benefits. The Blues low-cost option in northern California reimbursed, in 1980, just $50 of charges for laboratory tests and x-rays per illness.

Insurers are helping physicians organize prepaid groups, are underwriting some of the expenses, and are lending physicians marketing and management expertise. In June 1980, Blue Cross and Blue Shield plans operated thirty-three various forms of HMOs and provided services to them and to twelve additional plans. These include a network model that contractually links several IPAs to a central point of accountability.

Large companies such as General Motors, that pay $1.3 billion annually in medical care premiums, encourage employees to become board members of hospitals, insurance companies, and Blue Cross and Blue Shield. In the New York City-Connecticut area, the Fairfield/Westchester Business Group on Health has been formed to represent twenty-one major companies, whose combined direct health care costs are $2.2 billion. In order to contain costs, they have met with HMOs. All the provider representatives developed their own PSRO and HSA committees and work with their established counterparts. Their members are on HMO Boards, and some are actively promoting new HMOs. This 1979–80 start among large business corporations may be the beginning of their negotiating and monitoring prices for medical care in the same hard-nosed fashion as they do for other goods and services. General Motors holds seminars for their employees who are interested in serving on boards of health providers in order "to help them become expert at asking what and why."

After 25 years' experience with HMOs, the Vice-Chairman of General Motors states, "It seems to us that group practice is not for everyone [and] we hope that it will grow and become an economical alternative to the traditional health care delivery system."[74] If it does, business will benefit.

The consumer, less informed than those medically trained, must make some kind of judgment about quality. The consumer also must anticipate medical needs a year ahead in order to select that unique package of medical benefits which, related to the cost, appears most economically advantageous to him or her. This is difficult because the benefit packages and the out-of-pocket costs to consumers differ. One plan may charge a co-payment fee of $5 for each office visit and another 25 percent of the total charge for each office visit. The combinations are myriad.

Employees who choose from an array of plans offered by their employer try, during the annual open or "switch-over" period, to maximize their benefits. For example, older persons under a limited Blue Cross/Blue Shield plan that pays only $50 annually for x-rays and tests may switch to a prepaid plan for the year in which they plan a comprehensive physical examination. If individuals know that incentives for the physicians are structured to discourage use of tests and x-rays in one prepaid plan and not in another, their logical choice may favor the latter. The word "may" is used because it is difficult to know whether tests and x-rays are or are not over-prescribed and thus restraint could conceivably improve the quality of their care. Fewer tests and x-rays would also save consumers the often sizeable amount of time necessary to consume these medical resources.

Enrollees who plan to have a baby may switch to a salaried group practice, such as Kaiser-Permanente, where medical costs of pregnancy are fully reimbursed and there is no limit on pediatrician visits. Maximization by the consumer in this fashion can be documented by the past behavior of federal civil servants who have a choice of financial arrangements.

The complexity of choice can be likened to that which faces the uninformed consumer wishing to purchase stereo equipment.[75] Without knowledge of electronics and with only average appreciation of the different qualities of tone, the consumer will find it difficult to assemble the various components, each of which has its own specific quality, into an integrated system that best fits his or her musical preferences.

Although one-third of subscribers leave some prepaid plans in their first year of enrollment, the reason they leave is not known. Interviews with persons switching out of plans are needed, but are costly. The Kaiser Foundation has recently reported on a survey conducted in 1975 among enrollees in their established HMO in Portland, Oregon. K-P mailed questionnaires to a random sample of subscribers who left the plan in 1975 and to a matching group enrolled for three months or longer. A 29 percent response rate, or 1,404 replies from former subscribers were received. Twenty-eight percent of those terminating apparently had moved away and 40 percent had changed jobs. Of the remaining, only 8 percent were classified as dissatisfied, but some of the other response classifications such as "cost factors" and "for other group insurance" probably encompassed some measure of dissatisfaction. Even so, these numbers seem small when compared to the total membership. What is more interesting about the survey is that among those who terminated and also those who remained, the largest number of specific complaints was about the "Length of time between calling and date of appointment," 42 percent of replies by current subscribers and also 42 percent by former subscribers. The second highest area of complaint was "amount of time spent on telephone with appointment or message center," 31 percent for current and 30 percent of former subscribers.[76] Waiting of different types appears to be a characteristic of prepaid groups.

SUMMARY

The primary public policy question is whether HMOs actually contain costs for society as a whole without sacrifice of quality of care. The great diversity among HMOs makes it difficult to generalize. Moreover, it is nearly impossible for a consumer to compare rationally three or more diverse combinations of financial arrangements, each with variable charges and benefits. Consumer ignorance of the financial arrangements of physicians in HMOs, including the new IPAs, can be lessened. Newspaper and television advertisements describe benefits, and employers can give information about total and employee out-of-pocket charges. If, in the surplus physician areas, physicians are charging different customers different prices for their services, price discrimination is occurring. It can be argued that price discrimination in favor of the poor has always existed in medical care and continues under the various government programs. Do physicians vary the type and/or quality of their services in relationship to the price charged? If they do, price discrimination does not exist because different services are being rendered for different prices. But, is that medically ethical? Consumers should not remain ignorant about existing and potential cross subsidies. If open panel IPAs are controlled by Blue Shield or other physician organizations including the IPA and the control is over more than 50 percent of the local supply of physicians and physician visits, then an antitrust problem may exist because there is an apparent physician monopoly.

Medical care prices in the Los Angeles and San Francisco areas are among the highest in the nation despite the comparatively high penetration of the markets by prepaid group practices in those areas. Prices can be kept low if quality is sacrificed. Input control, sometimes process control, is the rule for quality control in ambulatory medical care. Tissue audit is a common form of quality control of outcomes in surgical care. All physicians do not agree on what are quality norms of procedures and outcomes. This is because the natural course of many diseases is unknown, the efficacy of many medical procedures is unknown, and also because there are confounding variables in addition to medical care that affect health outcomes.

Less than 5 percent of the population are enrolled in HMOs, indicating that the quality problem may be greater than usually is accepted. Faced with a newly developing type of supplier market, labelled competitive by the proponents of HMOs and favored by the Carter Administration's 10-year federal government program of loans and grants to new HMOs in targeted high-cost areas and anticipated 1982 legislation to promote competition, consumers are expected to find quality care at competitively restrained prices. I am not convinced, but legislative bills to induce HMO growth will be introduced in the 1982 Congress.

VII. THIRD PARTY PAYMENTS

Payments for medical care by other than the patient account for about two-thirds of the total medical care expenditures in the United States. Because these other payers are neither medical care providers nor consumers, they are called "third parties." Third parties include governments and private insurers. Third parties have a vested interest in the success of their organizations, an interest that does not necessarily correspond with the needs of the consumer or health care providers. These vested interests are pursued differently by different institutions. Government agencies usually try to enhance their importance and political influence. For example, some government employees may wish to expand the number of personnel under their control and thus increase their civil service grade. The non-profit Blue Cross and Blue Shield associations strive for the success of their member hospitals and member physicians, respectively. Commercial insurers, as for-profit companies, strive to generate a surplus in order to pay dividends to their shareholders.

The justification for the government to be a third party payer rests on the political consensus that inability to pay should not affect access to medical care of an acceptable quality. Thus, in 1966 Congress initiated its own third party payment programs: Medicaid for the poor and Medicare for the aged.

Private health insurance was first offered in the United States in 1847 by the Massachusetts Health Insurance Company of Boston. The growth of the industry during and after World War II was spectacular. By 1960, slightly over 70 percent of the civilian population had some form of private health insurance and by 1967, about 83 percent.[1] As government insurance coverage grew, private health insurance growth lost its momentum. In 1977, 80 percent of those under age 65 and 62 percent of those 65 years and over had some form of private hospitalization insurance.[2] Many believe that the early extensive private health insurance coverage in the United States is the major reason why the federal government never legislated compulsory national health insurance. Although private health insurance has been attacked because it does not cover all medical care expenses, it very early covered those areas where large, unpredictable medical expenses are greatest: hospitalization and surgical care. Most people are adverse to bearing the risk of unexpected large expenditures and, as a result, insurance has evolved to protect against the expenses of fire and automobile accidents as well as medical care expense. Health insurance, like all insurance, transforms large, unpredictable expenses into smaller, budgetable premium expense. By using the euphemism "health" rather than "medical," the insurance industry conveys a positive image that the purchased insurance might offer protection against illness itself and not just medical bills.

Although in 1967 about 83 percent of the civilian population had some form of private health insurance, by 1980 the percentage had fallen to 77 percent. The continuing decline reflects the fact that Medicare, with substantial government third party protection, covers about 25 million aged persons, or roughly 11 percent of the total population. However, Medicare pays less than one-half of all health expenses of the aged. There are also several other government programs that pay for the medical care expenses of individuals. These include: Medicaid and Supplemental Security Income for the poor, for which about 24 million people are eligible; the Veterans' Administration military medical care program for civilian dependents (CHAMPUS), covering about 12 million persons; and, Medicare's permanent disability program with its specific disease programs for black lung disease treatment, kidney dialysis and transplantation, covering in total about 3 million persons. Thus, in all, about 60 million persons (excluding four million for duplication) are subsidized by government health programs. Additionally, Workmen's Compensation pays for the work-related medical expenses of nearly 70 million persons.

Some of the aged under Medicare also have private health insurance protection. The latter is often referred to as "Medigap" insurance and has proved to be very profitable, but it, like Medicare, does not usually cover nursing-facility or home care, which is for a small percent of the aged a heavy burden.

The mid-1981 "$31 million marketing war for 1,750,000 retirees' health insurance policies between Prudential Insurance Company of America and Colonial Penn Group, Inc."[3] indicates the size of this market. Although millions were spent on advertising, the benefit packages offered were also increased with Prudential's totalling 80 percent of all premiums and Colonial Penn's 75 percent.

Whether or not medical care markets are unique has been discussed in Chapter V. The question of whether the health insurance market is unique remains to be analyzed here. The arguments in support of the uniqueness in the medical care markets emphasize the unusual degree of uncertainty about the outcomes of medical interventions. Whether or not medical treatment will be effective is a unique risk. The individual's uncertainty as to whether one will become seriously ill or not is, however, similar to uncertainty in other insurance markets. Insurance can reduce the impact of large expenses of the latter type of uncertainty, thus increasing the welfare of the person with health insurance coverage. However, insurance cannot reduce the effect of the former type of uncertainty: the possibility of failure to benefit from the medical care that one receives. It is not feasible to provide "ideal insurance." The concept of ideal insurance as applied to medical care markets has been explained as follows:

> [Ideal] insurance will necessarily involve insurance against a failure to benefit from medical care, whether through recovery, relief of pain, or arrest of further deterioration. One form would be a system in which the payment to the physician is made in accordance with the degree of benefit.

> Under ideal insurance the patient would actually have no concern with the informational inequality between himself and the physician, since he would only be paying by results anyway, and his utility position would in fact be thoroughly guaranteed.[4]

The concept of ideal insurance for medical care is, in essence, an esoteric intellectual exercise. The very nature of illness, the fact that everyone dies eventually, and the difficulty of proving the degree of benefit resulting from medical care makes the concept an arbitrary value judgment. A more realistic view of insurance is that it is purchased to lessen the economic impact of events which cannot be predicted: loss of life, loss from fire, or hospitalization. In all these instances, insurance benefit money does not necessarily restore one's previous level of well-being. If only the automobile is damaged in an accident, complete restoration is possible. This is not the case, however, if an individual is badly hurt. Health insurance, by reducing the uncertainty of economic loss, increases the welfare of the insured. When an insured loss occurs, money is paid to the insured on the assumption that the receipt of the money *per se* benefits the insured. However, insurance does not guarantee that the insured will benefit from spending the money received.

With these concepts as a frame of reference, data on the size, composition, and growth of third party payers are presented. The federal government's Medicare program for persons sixty-five years and older, the federal and state governments' Medicaid program for the poor, and the several private insurance options are examined within the context of how best to restrain the cost impact of third party payments on medical care prices without sacrificing the equality of access to some minimal level of medical care that the political consensus deems "necessary."

WHO ARE THE UNINSURED?

After correcting for those persons who have more than one type of coverage (about one-fourth of the population), the estimates of those who do not have any health insurance coverage in the United States range from 5 percent to 13 percent of the population. A recent reworking of the Congressional Budget Office's estimate of 5 percent for 1978 yielded an intermediate estimate of 8 percent, or 14.5 million persons, who do not have medical expense coverage.[5] The government's ongoing *Health Interview Survey*, however, estimated that 11 percent of the civilian, non-institutionalized (primarily those not in nursing homes) population were in this category in 1976. Part of the difference between the low and the high estimates is because the *Health Interview Survey* covers only non-institutionalized individuals while the government programs, Medicare/Medicaid and the Veterans' Administration, include and pay for persons who are in institutions. LuAnn Aday and Ronald Andersen of the University of Chicago estimated that, in 1976, 12 percent of persons under sixty-five years of age did not have third party coverage. This number agrees with the *Health Interview Survey* data.

It is difficult to predict whether the percentage of uninsured will fall or rise less in the early 1980s. Employment and unemployment are both growing. As more women work, more have private health insurance derived from their own jobs. If unemployment grows, private health insurance coverage will tend to decrease. The newly unemployed persons whose employment-related coverage will expire will not necessarily be eligible for Medicaid. Illegal immigrants are increasing in the United States and these persons probably will add to the percentage of the uninsured. On the other hand, employers are increasingly paying for health insurance protection of their employees' dependents. The early outcome from all these factors is uncertain but, by the end of this decade, the percentage of the population without any health expense coverage should be lower.

Data identifying the uninsured are necessary for the formulation of national health policy. Fifty-five percent of the uninsured are not in the labor force.[6] As already implied, many of these are the dependents of those covered workers who waived dependency coverage rather than pay the premiums that their employers do not pay for dependents. Others without insurance are members of the labor force who are unemployed and whose health insurance coverage has run out.

Employed persons who are not insured are primarily migrant, rural workers, and part-time and intermittent workers in retail trade, personal services, and construction. Also, many of the self-employed in small business are unwilling to pay the higher individual premium rates for health insurance coverage. Non-group coverage has high premiums because of adverse self-selection. Persons who are often ill are more likely not to join an employed group but may purchase health insurance because of anticipated high medical bills. Additionally, some very small businesses do not provide coverage to their employees because their premium rates are higher than those for large businesses. This is because the insurer believes that the adverse selection effect may prevail in very small group employee situations.

Because some states have stricter income and asset entitlement rules for Medicaid benefits than other states, there are some persons with low incomes who are not eligible in their state of residence who would be eligible in another state. Arizona is the only state without a Medicaid program. Arizona has a program of medical care for the poor which is supported entirely from state revenues.

Estimates of those who do not have "adequate" health insurance protection are higher than the estimates of uncovered individuals. The precise percentage is dependent on the definition of "adequate." A concept of adequate coverage follows.

WHAT IS ADEQUATE MEDICAL EXPENSE PROTECTION?

The net price to consumers of about three-fourths of their medical care purchases is less than the true resource cost of the medical care, so they may feel that they "need" medical care items for which they would not be willing to pay the full resource price. At the same time, there is usually no agreement among knowledgeable medical care providers as to which components of medical care are medically needed, desirable even if not needed, or even neither needed nor desirable. What is optimum medical care and what is adequate medical care are difficult to define for insurance purposes.

Medical care is a personal service that is an art as well as a science. What is optimum care for one person might not be optimum for another person with precisely the same health problems and genetic endowment. Personal preferences evolve so that the imposition of preconceived medical needs, even if developed by expert panels, will not satisfy everyone's self-conception of his or her own needs. Thus, when third parties impose their criteria of medical need in order to contain costs through denial of reimbursement, some consumers and providers will protest that the criteria adopted limit the use of needed care just as can higher prices. Denial of reimbursement by some government and private plans may be imposed unless the covered person received prior authorization of hospital days. Some states limit the number of medical services per month per person that Medicaid will pay for. Medicare does not pay for heart transplantation.

An attempt to define a standard of adequate medical expense protection has been made by a six-member panel primarily of academics and providers who were apparently selected by a large pharmaceutical company. Their findings are reproduced in Table 12. The percent of the total population that receives this standard of adequate expense protection varies by benefit from 96 percent for inpatient laboratory and x-ray services and 91 percent for hospital inpatient admission, including psychiatric care to 40 percent for physician office and home visits.[7] Nearly 90 percent of the population has catastrophic expense coverage under combinations of private health insurance, Medicare, and Medicaid. Although Medicaid more than meets the above standard of adequacy, Medicare is not so generous for out-of-hospital care.

MEDICARE

Health is accepted as a major concern of the federal government. About 43 percent, or nearly $110 billion of the nation's personal health care bill, is financed under government programs. The largest of these are Medicare for the elderly and Medicaid for public assistance recipients and the indigent.

Medicare was designed for the largest group in society without employer-paid health insurance coverage, the aged. Today, many

Table 12. Consensus: A Standard of Adequate Health Expense Protection

Benefits:	*Protection:*

An adequate benefit package must include protection against the expense of the following services:
 	
  physician services
  laboratory and x-ray services
  prenatal care
  inpatient psychiatric care
  outpatient services
  nursing home care
	At least 80 percent of the expense of covered services must be borne by the third party entity, with the exception that patient cost sharing for inpatient psychiatric care may be required in excess of 20 percent of expenses.
	At least $250,000 of catastrophic expense protection must be provided by the third party entity, and the sum total of patient cost sharing must not exceed 10 to 30 percent of income

Source: Stephen G. Sudovar and Patrice Hirsch Feinstein, *National Health Insurance Issues: The Adequacy of Coverage* (Washington, DC: Roche Laboratories, December 1979), p. 11.

NOTE: The panel members were a dean of a graduate school in social welfare, past deputy assistant secretary of health, business school professor of health care economics, hospital administrator, actuary and life insurance company administrator, professor of economics, and physician.

companies have plans that allow employees to convert coverage upon retirement. Usually they receive the same benefits, but at age 65 the plan is integrated with Medicare by dovetailing private with Medicare benefits, thus reducing private insurance benefits and premiums after age 65. Some large employers continue to pay their long-term employees' health insurance premiums after their retirement.

Medicare also covers the permanently disabled. In 1979, Medicare paid out under Part A (hospitalization) $21.7 billion, and under Part B (physicians' services) payments were $8.3 billion. These amounts were 18 percent higher than in the previous year. In fiscal year 1982, Medicare expenditures are expected to reach $47.1 billion.

Although Medicare absorbs two-thirds of federal expenditures on health, it pays for less than one-half of the health bills of the aged. The Medicare program was, however, initially thought of as a financing mechanism that would pay almost all of the medical care bills of the aged. In 1977, Medicare paid only 41 percent of the aged's medical bills. A recent description of Medicare published in the government's *Social Security Bulletin* explains that, "the Medicare program does not attempt to provide total coverage for all medical care costs for the aged. It is patterned after private health insurance coverage with emphasis on coverage of hospital care and physicians' services. Thus, 74 percent of hospital care expenses and 56 percent of the expenses of physicians' services are paid by Medicare."[8]

In 1957, the Social Security Administration divided medical care into two categories: "currently insurable" and "potentially insurable." The definition of currently insurable included "total expenditures for services of physicians, dentists, and hospitals."[9] HEW criticized private health insurers because they paid only 74 percent of hospital expenses and 32 percent of all physician services, although the insurers were covering a much higher percentage of surgeons' bills. In 1967, the goal of government health planners was as follows: "Health insurance should be covering somewhere in the neighborhood of 90 percent of all consumer expenditures for health care."[10] Experience has taught that this is not a feasible goal. In 1965, 33 percent of all consumer expenditures for health care were paid by private health insurers, including 71 percent of hospital care expense and 32 percent of physician services.[11] These percentages are close to those of Medicare's percentage payments in 1977: 44 percent, 74 percent, and 56 percent, respectively.

In 1981, the deductible under the hospitalization part of Medicare was $204 (up from $180 in 1980), with no additional payment required from the patient until after 60 days of hospitalization. The deductible is equal to the average cost of one hospital day and helps to contain hospital expense reimbursement costs. Medicare (Part A) does not pay for hospital days beyond the length of stay authorized by a utilization review committee, the added price of a private room when supplied for other than medical reasons, services of hospital-based physicians such as radiologists and anesthesiologists (who are paid under Part B), and pure comfort items such as rentals of television sets. About 63 percent of the aged have supplemental health insurance coverage, Blue Cross or other private health insurance. Because of the growth of these policies, Congress passed, in June 1980, a "Medigap" law, under which "the Department of Health and Human Services would certify Medicare supplemental health insurance policies which meet certain minimum standards; . . . require the Secretary to make information available to persons entitled to Medicare to help them evaluate such policies; . . . [and] provide increased penalties for insurers and their agents for misrepresentation."[12]

The source of Medicare, Part A, hospitalization program funds is primarily a 2.6 percent payroll tax, divided equally between employers and their employees, for 1981 through 1984. Federal employees and many state and local government workers do not pay this tax. Everybody is eligible for Medicare, Part A, at age 65 but all do not apply. A small but increasing number do not meet the "fully insured" status or forty quarters of coverage under social security first required in 1979. General revenues provided 6.1 percent of the cost of Part A in 1977.[13]

In 1981, the monthly premium will rise to $11.00 from $9.60 for Medicare, Part B, the physician services program. Although the government implies that the monthly premium is sufficient to support its payments of the physician bills, general revenues, not the so-called premium payments, are the main source of the funds. In 1977, premium payments by the aged met 26 percent of the bills while general revenues paid 68 percent. The Part B, premium rate, increases with the increase in the cash benefits. The annual premium payment of $132 for physician services under Medicare, Part B, is (in 1981–82) a great bargain as anyone who pays their own physician bills can attest. Yet the government continues to project the myth that Part B premiums do pay for the physician bills of the aged. This is despite the publication of data indicating that the monthly actuarial rate for the aged is $22.60 and for the disabled, $36.60, which are buried on page 139 of *Health Care Financing Review* (Winter 1981). There are few in the general public who are aware that some part of the general tax revenues support Medicare expenses and few young persons who do not believe that Medicare pays most of the aged's medical bills.

The 1980 trustees' report on Medicare, Part B's trust fund, estimated that "allowable fees for physician services will increase an average of 7.9 percent in the 12-month period ending June 30, 1980 [and] 10.9 percent, 1981."[14] However, *all* medical care fees actually rose by 11.1 percent in the fiscal year ending June 30, 1980. Thus, Medicare will apparently reimburse a smaller percentage of the bills charged than estimated for that year.

Because Medicare is such a large program, its method of payment has affected the methods of payment throughout the medical care industry. Medicare initially reimbursed hospitals for the costs of care plus 2 percent. The 2 percent, a profit add-on, was eliminated in 1969. Whenever there is cost reimbursement for a product or a service, there is no incentive for the provider to contain the costs except for the potential loss of future purchases. The latter acts as a restraint among competitive suppliers. Most hospitals do not compete for patients on the basis of price. This is true for the non-profit hospitals as well as the for-profit hospitals.

The problem of cost restraint under cost reimbursement is even greater in the hospital sector than in other sectors of industry because many hospitals do not keep strict financial accounts. The recorded charges may not represent the actual costs of the items for which the patients are billed. Many university hospitals, for example, have financed their more expensive operations, not by charging the true resource prices for these operations but by inflating the "cost-based" bills for minor operations. There are also cross-billings or cross-subsidies between different classes of customers defined by who actually pays their bills.

In June 1980, the Massachusetts Rate Setting Commission proposed regulations "to prevent hospitals from passing on to those charge-paying customers a number of costs that other payment schemes refuse to reimburse. The most important of these are government-assessed penalties for low occupancy rates and inefficient operation. This would have limited their freedom to shift revenues from 'profit-making' to deficit departments or to build surpluses."[15] The newspaper account continues with an example of "large inequities in payment for the same service is at Ludlow Hospital where a self-paying patient, or one insured by Aetna, would be assessed about $441 per day . . . while a Blue Cross patient would pay, through his insurance, $274 a day—a 167 percent difference."[16] Precise Medicare and Medicaid rates were not given in the newspaper articles quoted but the example suffices to indicate that in 1980, cost reimbursement of hospitals is still not related to actual cost, and that Medicare's and Medicaid's lower reimbursement rates result in the commercially insured patient paying twice: when they are hospitalized and through taxes to support these programs.

The 1971–74 federal price controls imposed by the Health Services Industry Committee (HSIC) required the large hospitals and those seeking exceptions to increase prices or wage rates above the limits to use normal accounting procedures. Subsequently, some states, among them California and New York, demanded the same standardized accounting procedures from hospitals requesting Medicaid reimbursement. The federal government's 1977 Medicare-Medicaid Anti-Fraud and Abuse Amendments also require uniform cost accounting by hospitals seeking reimbursement. In 1977, HEW issued guidelines in the form of "System for Hospital Uniform Reporting" (SHUR), but non-compliance and protests about the complexity of SHUR, which had a 606-page instruction manual, led to the publication of a simplified form in 1980. The American Hospital Association (AHA) still protests "the continued linkage of reporting and reimbursement. . . . Clearly, the flexibility and accuracy of the Medicare cost reporting system is not compatible with the standardization and rigidity of any uniform reporting system."[17] The federal government's Health Care Financing Administration (HCFA) estimates that only 21 percent of the country's hospitals have uniform reporting systems.[18]

The U.S. Comptroller General stated during testimony in March 1980 that "hospital managers nationwide have not generally implemented many of the management techniques that could significantly restrain hospital increases."[19] Among those techniques, Comptroller Staats noted, were patient pre-admission testing, admission scheduling, and checking the more significant price differentials among the suppliers of items purchased.[20]

The states also are not requiring uniform data from HMOs. In California there are three state agencies, each requiring a different set of data from the HMOs under their supervision. The Department of Insurance handles the Blue Cross-affiliated HMOs, the Department of Health services those HMOs that have Medi-Cal contracts, and the Department of Corporations supervises plans registered under the Knox-Keene Act. The federal requirements may also differ, and one HMO may have to report data to two or more agencies. Uniform reporting requirements for HMOs as well as hospitals and insurers can reduce costs and are important to the maintenance of competitive markets; without, information that permits purchasers to compare providers is difficult to construct.

Uniform reporting in accordance with the National Center for Higher Education Management Systems methods has been required for many years by universities applying for grants from HEW. A uniform method permits quick comparison of similar institutions and easy identification of those that are out-of-line. Both colleges and hospitals provide services that are difficult to measure in terms of quality. It may be easier, however, to measure the quality of different surgical procedures by mortality rates (corrected for differences in patient age, sex, severity of disease, etc.) than outcomes from a four-year college education. In the latter case, there are differences in the capabilities of students, but biological inheritances also differ and although many variables other than education affect an individual's earning power and satisfaction with life, other factors than medical care also affect health outcomes.

During the four-year period between eighteen and twenty-two years, a tremendous amount of personal growth takes place with or without a college education. There is rarely such a long period between a medical procedure and its effect on health. However, the course of a disease is unaffected by medical intervention in about 80 percent of cases. Both education and medical care are services the output of which are hard to evaluate. For entitlement to federal government grant monies, uniform accounting by universities is required. A similar development in hospital accounting can be expected.

There are some who believe that, if cost-reimbursement is conducted on a prospective rather than a retrospective basis, hospital costs will be better contained. Blue Cross maintains that prospective reimbursement induces hospitals to live within a fixed annual budget because they are penalized for any year in which they exceed the negotiated amount. Others comment that all this method does is create a one-year lag in the costs catching up with the increase. Not all of the nearly 30 states that have prospective payment programs have an agency or commission that can change rates; many are purely advisory.

Two components are involved when reimbursing costs: the price and the number of units sold at that price. This means that, even if the price is controlled, the costs can continue to increase because there is no ceiling on the number of units sold or used. When the patient is in the hospital, it is the physician who decides the number of units used. Price control alone will not contain hospital costs. The Carter Administration, therefore, repeatedly requested that Congress pass a cost containment bill in order to confine government's liabilities under the Medicare and Medicaid programs. Congress is not expected to pass a hospital cost containment bill in the near future. Price control and cost caps are not compatible with deregulation and more competition. To require hospitals that have over a given number of beds to comply, as do other businesses, with the Federal Accounting Standards Board's (FASB) requirements is more compatible. FASB is developing special rules for all non-profit institutions, and hospitals can be expected eventually to conform.

The Reagan Administration is anticipated to increase the climate of competition in the health care sector but how successful this will be, especially in the area of hospital care, remains to be seen. In 1972, Congress authorized Medicare to enter into contracts with qualified

HMOs. As of December 31, 1979, only 42,000 Medicare patients were enrolled under 31 HMO contracts. During 1979, HHS' Health Care Financing Administration informed nearly 4 million Medicare beneficiaries of available HMO services in their immediate area. Continuance of this information program, plus permitting a Medicare beneficiary to share in the anticipated savings from prepayment above the costs of using the fee-for-service sector, are believed by many to be sufficient to induce greater enrollment in HMOs by Medicare beneficiaries. The latter inducement in the Stockman-Gephardt bill of the 1980 Congress (HR 850) that was not passed is expected to be repeated in the 1982 bills.

If more persons covered by Medicare enroll in HMOs as a result of financial inducements and mailings targeted towards newly enrolled Medicare beneficiaries who, when they were working, may have used HMOs, the probability of the success of this program might greatly increase. However, less than 5 percent of the population are enrolled in HMOs. HMOs do have a special appeal to those who dislike the complexity of billing that Medicare combined with insurance presents. Many of the aged may fit into this category, but at the same time the aged are more at-risk to incurring diseases that need tertiary care specialists. HMO arrangements for the latter, unless it is a very large HMO, may be unsatisfactory to the patient because the selection of specialists in an HMO is limited. It would cost the HMO money to refer enrollees to specialists outside the group; therefore, some HMOs have contracts with outside specialists. If the enrollee is dissatisfied with the HMO-supplied specialist and self-refers to a specialist outside the HMO, the enrollee pays.

Persons over 64 years usually do not have children whose ambulatory health care bills are not covered by private health insurance coverage but are covered by HMOs, and thus the aged do not gain the major monetary benefit of HMO enrollment that younger persons do. Blue Cross is experimenting with separate prepaid hospital enrollment. However, the primary financial problem of the aged is financing of nursing-home care or its equivalent, not the expenses of being in an acute, general care hospital. Medicare acts as catastrophic insurance for hospital expense for the aged.

There have been experiments in which hospital costs are reimbursed in accordance with a differential diagnosis of a disease: by age and sex, by given geographical area, and a hospital class defined by size and type. Such a cost containment program "by diagnosis" has to have the cooperation of hospitals, physicians, and private insurers as well as the government. The results do not yet indicate whether it is or is not a feasible method to contain costs. It creates additional administrative costs of implementing and monitoring and is also open to the charge of indirectly interfering with medical practice by hampering innovations in medical treatment.

Medicare, a large payer of physicians' bills, $28 billion in 1979, has helped to increase the level of physicians' fees. Over recent years, a decreasing proportion of physicians accept the "customary, prevailing, and reasonable fee" or the assigned fee of Medicare as the total fee for their services. More than one-half of physicians are in effect paid by two or more parties: Medicare, the private insurers, and the patient. Medicare defines its assigned fee as "the lowest of either the actual charge or the physicians' fiftieth percentile charge, or the prevailing charge set in the seventy-fifth percentile."[21]

In 1971, 54 percent of physicians accepted Medicare's assigned fees as their total fees, but in 1978 less than 50 percent of physicians accepted a Medicare fee as their total fee.[22] In other words, aged patients are responsible for paying at least one-half of their physician bills. Acceptance of Medicare-assigned fees varies by physician specialty. The lowest acceptance rate in billing the aged was among ophthalmologists, 44 percent billing at Medicare fees; the highest among podiatrists, 62 percent of whom billed at Medicare fees. The rate of acceptance in internal medicine, which is the largest specialty, is 48 percent.[23] However, in billing the disabled, about 60 percent of physicians have consistently accepted Medicare rates as full payment.

There are even wider discrepancies in acceptance of assigned fees among physicians by geographical area. Nearly 80 percent of physicians in the state of Maine accept Medicare reimbursement as total payment; in Oregon only 18 percent do. Yet Portland, the largest city in that state, has a relatively high percentage of its population enrolled in HMOs. Competition does not seem to contain physician costs in Oregon. When physicians do not accept the fees assigned by Medicare, the patients are liable for that amount charged above the assigned fee. The Medicare fee level sets a floor for private fees. Whatever rate Medicare pays, private patients are usually charged this, and often more to make up for what might be termed a shortfall. An analysis of fees of 152 physicians reimbursed by Blue Shield of Florida found that 22 percent of their actual charges in 1979 were greater for private patients than Medicare patients and, generally, that "physicians were allowed over 10 percent more by private plans than by Medicare in 82 percent of cases" surveyed.[24] To cap Medicare fees would be helpful in containing the costs of Medicare, but it would not result in containing the total costs of the nation's total expenditures on medical care or on medical care for the aged alone. Insofar as Medicare patients pay higher time costs, especially in waiting in physician offices, these should be added to their money costs in order to obtain their true costs of medical care.

Medicare, because it finances nursing-home care only after the patient has been in a hospital for three consecutive days, pays for only 3 percent of the total nursing home care bill in the United States. The nursing home population in absolute numbers is increasing. In 1979, Medicare paid out more for home health care than for nursing care in institutions. The expense of long-term nursing care of the aged falls primarily on Medicaid, which is financed from general revenues and on private individuals that pay 49 percent and 47 percent of the bills, respectively. If Medicare pays for the very high-cost procedures, such as heart transplantation for a few, it has less money to pay for the more routine care for the many aged.

MEDICAID

Medicaid (Title 19, Social Security Act) is a federal/state program that in some states pays for a wider range of health care than private insurance offers for persons "whose incomes and resources are insufficient to meet the costs of necessary medical services" (Section 1901). It has become the most important source of medical funding for the aged who are institutionalized as well as the non-institutionalized aged who are poor. It also covers many poor who are not aged and who receive cash welfare benefits under Aid to Families With Dependent Children (AFDC), the Supplemental Security Income (SSI) program for the blind, disabled, and the near-poor or medically indigent. The extent to which the latter group is covered differs by states.

In 1978, 23 million persons received Medicaid and its costs were about $18 billion. In 1980, the annual cost was about $20 billion. When unemployment grows, Medicaid costs increase. In 1980, payments were higher because of the higher prices and the increase in the number of those covered. The Reagan Administration has proposed a 5 percent cap on the 1981–82 increase in Medicaid expenditures. The cap can be considered realistic if the inflation rate is decreased and the numbers who receive Medicaid are restricted to those actually in need. Fourteen percent of California residents receive Medi-Cal (California's Medicaid); that is about one of every seven persons in a state that has the fifth highest per capita income.

During 1973–74, the last years of Ronald Reagan's governorship of California, 11 percent of California's population was eligible for Medi-Cal.

What percentage of the poor and the medically indigent are not eligible for Medicaid nationwide and what percentage of those receiving benefits are not poor have been matters of considerable discussion. Both sets of data are important for government policy-makers. In 1970, about 60 percent of the poverty population were actual Medicaid recipients. A Congressional report explained that "the range, however, . . . was extreme, with Medicaid recipients totaling less than 20 percent of the poverty population in eight states (Alabama, Arkansas, Mississippi, South Carolina, South Dakota, Tennessee, Texas, and Wyoming) and a number that is more than 100 percent of the poverty population in two states (California and New York)."[25] One-third of the total U.S. Medicaid bill is spent in New York and California; two-thirds in only ten states.

Obviously, the states differ in eligibility requirements and in services provided. To attain federal sharing of the costs, the state must provide the following services: inpatient hospital, outpatient hospital, laboratory and x-rays, skilled nursing facility for individuals 21 years and older, health care in the home, physician care, family planning, and early and periodic diagnostic screening and treatment services for individuals under 21 years of age. In addition, states may provide a number of other services, and large states such as California and New York do.

In fact, California and some other states provide more services under Medicaid than it is possible for the non-poor to purchase, either under a prepaid group health plan or by a combination of various health insurance plans. In the 1970s, California provided the following services: clinic services, prescription drugs, dental services, prosthetic devices, eyeglasses, physical therapy, screening for preventive and rehabilitative medicine, emergency hospital, skilled nursing facility for patients under 21 years of age, services of optometrists, podiatrists, and chiropractors, institutional care for mental disease and tuberculosis for patients 65 years or older, care in psychiatric hospitals for patients under 21 years of age, and institutional care in intermediate care facilities. The only one of the optional services that some other states provide and California does not is private duty nursing.

Individual states may set numerical limits on access to services. California for several years has limited individuals to a total of two outpatient services per month unless prior approval is obtained. Colorado, Louisiana, Ohio, Massachusetts, and other states limit services to one or even less a month unless a special exception is made. Many states require prior authorization for in-hospital and nursing care services.

In fiscal year 1978, Medicaid spent more money on nursing home and intermediate care facilities than it did on hospital care. Each of these amounts was more than three times the amount that was spent on physician services. Preventive services do not rank high among Medicaid's spending categories. Whenever funds are short, medical care of symptoms takes precedence over the less urgent, preventive care and consumer health education. Yet, for long-run cost containment, these have importance.

In September 1977, Medicaid spent 32 percent of its monies for inpatient hospital care, 39 percent on nursing home and intermediate care facilities, 9 percent for physicians' services, 6 percent for drugs, 2.5 percent for dental care, and 11.4 percent for lab tests, x-rays, home health care, family planning, and outpatient hospital services.[26]

Medicaid was initially enacted in order to provide medical care for the poor and for those who are considered to be medically indigent: persons who can meet everyday bills as long as they are healthy but cannot when they become ill, either because they are not covered by adequate health insurance or they do not receive their paychecks. For example, blue-collar workers and temporary and intermittent workers may not have sick leave, and costs of a lengthy illness are difficult to pay from unemployment compensation benefits.

Only five states (California, Hawaii, New Jersey, New York, and Rhode Island) have temporary disability insurance plans. These require the worker and employer to pay a tax or a compulsory private premium to support a cash sickness benefit program. Nine out of ten wage and salary workers in these states receive a wage-replacement benefit when they are sick. Sixty-four percent of 80 million wage and salary workers nationwide were, in 1977, under some formal, employment-related plan: either insured for a cash benefit or entitled to sick leave pay. However, on an overall basis, private industry's sickness cash benefits covered only one-fourth of lost wages while government employees had benefits that were four-fifths, or 80 percent.[27] The reason for the large difference that favors government workers is that sick leave pay, which is 100 percent of salary, is more common in government than in private industry. Additionally, private cash benefit plans usually require a waiting period of three to seven days before any benefit is paid.

The number of persons who receive Medicaid has been increasing annually. Although most of the growth in Medicaid costs is the result of a higher number of beneficiaries and the inflation, the 1972 reassignment of payments for intermediate care nursing homes from the states' cash assistance programs to Medicaid was also a major factor during the early 1970s.

Supplemental Security Income (SSI) became effective in January 1974, and although it was initially thought that this new cash assistance program with its more liberal eligibility rules than existed under the prior categorical grants would result in doubling the number of Medicaid recipients, it did not. Receipt of cash assistance benefits under the replaced federal/state categorical grants for the aged, blind, and disabled had meant automatic eligibility for Medicaid. Policymakers decided, however, that receipt of the new SSI benefits would not automatically guarantee eligibility for Medicaid. Moreover, some states that use a stricter definition of disability than SSI were allowed to keep their more restrictive 1972 standards. Thus, the number actually receiving Medicaid payments for their health care bills grew by only 30 percent, from a monthly average of 2.5 million in 1971 to 3.3 million in 1975.[28]

In 1971, Medicaid payments averaged $331 per recipient and almost one-half billion dollars monthly. By 1979, the payment per capita averaged $947 and the total monthly bill was about $1.8 billion.[29] In 1979, total public, Medicare, and Medicaid expenditures per capita were $406, or 7 times higher than in 1965. Public health expenditures have increased 1.6 times the rate of private expenditures. The proposed 5 percent cap on increases in Medicaid spending during fiscal year 1982 will help to push up medical care prices in the private care sector to an estimated annual rise of 15 percent. California's Medi-Cal costs were $4 billion in 1980, with about one-half of the bill paid by the federal government.

Despite the 1971–74 dismal experience with using HMOs for Medi-Cal eligible persons, California seems to be reviving this approach. The 1974 *Annual Report to the Government and Legislature on Prepaid Health Plans* stressed that the "for-profit PHPs . . . provide significantly more physician services than do non-profit PHPs. Nonprofit PHPs, however, provide significantly more consultative services and prescription drugs than do for-profit PHPs."[30] The stress on physician services under the for-profits suits the prevailing views on national health policy in the 1980s more than does the greater use of specialists and drugs under the non-profit HMOs. As discussed earlier (Chapter VI), it was not the distinction between for-profit and non-profit but rather, the older, more experienced HMO versus the newer and sometimes fraud-ridden HMO that was important in the failure of Medi-Cal's experiment to encourage HMO usage by Medi-Cal's enrollees.

New experimentation, possibly with the active participation of the established Kaiser plans in the design stage and with some commitment by HMOs to accept Medicaid enrollees in return for their existing protection from the certificate-of-need laws, might be worked out.

Both Medicare and Medicaid have been subject to considerable criticism because of the fraud and abuse found among some of the providers as well as among the recipients of care. Fraud against the government is the illegal act of taking money or in-kind benefits to which one is not entitled either as a provider or a beneficiary. Abuse is more difficult to define because it is not illegal *per se*, but some forms of it tread close to the line. For example, physician "gang visits" to patients in nursing homes where multiple billings are made for one or two minutes with each patient may be an abuse. To charge for a visit that did not take place is fraud. On the consumer side, it is an abuse to knowingly seek medical treatment for non-existent health reasons, but it is a fraud to have Medicaid pay for one's physician's visits when one's income is above the eligibility level of income as defined by the state in which one lives.

The amount of fraud existing under Medicare and Medicaid has been one of the major arguments against a national health insurance program. Congressional proponents of such a program constantly face the attack that, if Medicaid and Medicare programs are abused, multiples of this fraud and abuse would exist under national health insurance. Federal programs alone were being exploited in the latter part of the 1970s by about one billion dollars yearly, and additional millions were being bilked out of state funds under store-front operations, or "Medicaid mills." The fraud is usually judged to have been greater among institutional than non-institutional providers. Fraud and abuse is a nationwide problem that diverts scarce resources to non-productive uses away from the improvement of health. On October 25, 1977, President Carter signed into law a bill that increased the penalties for persons

> . . . who are convicted of false claims, kickbacks— changing these from misdemeanors to felonies—and also prohibiting those who are convicted of this crime from delivering any services in the future.
>
> This legislation also permits—in fact, requires—the Department of HEW to set up both simplified and also standardized forms for reporting the delivery of services in the health care field and also the charging for those services . . . [and] requires that anyone

who owns as much as 5 percent in a health provider company or hospital or health care center must reveal their identity to the public.[32]

During 1979, there was relatively little newspaper coverage of the activities which this legislation aimed to eliminate. However, some states, such as Pennsylvania, continue (as of Spring 1980) to use manual, not automated, review systems. In the first two months of 1979, Pennsylvania "recouped about $446,000 through provider and prepayment claims adjustments" from automated review of only 5 percent sample of claims.[33] California's investigative staff in the Department of Health Services had 112 persons in 1978 and these were cut to 40 at the end of October 1979. The Attorney General's Office in California had a Medi-Cal fraud unit of 56 people in 1979.[34] The states are increasingly adopting computerized claims processing and retrieval. In Spring 1980, FBI testimony left no doubt that substantial amounts of fraud still occur in Medicaid and Medicare. A 1981 estimate of $4 billion of probable potential annual fraud, including $1.2 billion "eligibility error," is about 5 percent of a total federal health bill that in fiscal year 1982 will be over $90 billion. Some believe that fraud and abuse together account for 10 percent of the total expenditures. However, the amount of dollars involved in potential "abuse" is very difficult to guess and readers are left to make their own judgments.

BLUE CROSS AND BLUE SHIELD

The most important insurer acting as a fiscal intermediary for the Medicare program is the national Blue Cross and Blue Shield plan that merged into one in 1978. Their associated state plans cover hospital and physician bills, respectively. In the United States, there are 70 Blue Cross and 70 Blue Shield plans, each affiliated with the national association. Prior to 1978, Blue Cross and Blue Shield plans in some states competed with each other by each offering both medical and hospital coverage. However, "more commonly . . . the two types of plans do not compete and their coverages are frequently marketed together."[35] Thirty Blue Shield plans administer payments of 55 percent of the total physician bills under Medicare, Part B. In 1977, 83.5 million people were in Blue Cross and 71 million in Blue Shield.[36]

Blue Cross and Blue Shield differ from the for-profit indemnity insurers in that they usually pay the providers directly and their benefits are "in-kind," such as thirty semi-private hospital days. Cash indemnity plans pay cash benefits to the consumers; for example, $100 for each of thirty hospital days. Most, but not all, benefits of the Blues are expressed in units of service and not in cash amounts. Blue Cross will pay the hospital, but indemnity plans send a check to the covered person. The Blues vary in how they pay non-institutional providers, such as physicians. "Over insurance" occurs when individuals plan to receive more than their medical expenses by obtaining coverage under several plans.

Under both types of insurance the consumer usually pays a portion of the bill. This may be a co-insurance amount (for example, 20 percent of amounts above a deductible of $100 or more) or a copayment charge at the time of consumption of a nominal amount from $1 to $5 for a physician office visit. The 80 percent paid by the insurer (a common percentage) is often applied, not to the total amount of a physician's bill but to an amount reduced in accordance with a fee screen or determination of a "usual, customary, reasonable" (UCR) fee. If the consumer had absolute knowledge of what medical care expenses he or she might incur and also what percentage would be reimbursed, the consumer would rationally continue to choose medical care up to the point where its benefits to him or her are judged to be worth only the out-of-pocket dollar cost, and not the total costs of the resources. Often the consumer over-estimates the percentage that will be reimbursed. Because the consumer equates expected benefits with expected out-of-pocket costs, there is a welfare loss, or waste or misuse, of society's resources under health insurance.[37] Consumers purchase more medical care than that for which they, as uninsured individuals, would be willing to pay.

The advantage of insurance is that it reduces the economic risk to the insured. Society has to weigh the reduction of individual risk against the more efficient use of scarce resources. Theoretically, the higher the co-insurance payments, the lower the efficiency loss and the less the inflation. On the other hand, co-insurance payments can become so high that they defeat the purpose of insurance: to reduce the economic risk of catastrophic expenses. If an insurer's fee screen cuts the reimbursable fee on a physician's bill by one-half and only 80 percent of that is reimbursed, then the consumer may question if the actual 40 percent reimbursement is worth the premium. Given the information and opportunity, a consumer may opt for other choices: no insurance and thus no premium and a higher disposable income, usually elected with a sizable deductible catastrophic coverage; or an HMO that may have much smaller copayments. However, because the payer of insurance premiums is usually the employer, not the employee, and because HMOs are not available in all areas of the country, most people do not have the option of making this informed choice. Moreover, an increase in wages in lieu of and equal to the premiums' cost would be subject to income tax and, in many instances, the social security tax. Thus, non-premium wage dollars, even if partly used to purchase catastrophic coverage, are worth less than employer-paid premium dollars. Because of this disincentive and the high costs of obtaining information about medical markets and prices, consumers of health care do little comparison shopping unless they perceive themselves to be seriously ill. At this point, most consumers search for quality, not price. A lack of information about price and quality makes the medical care and health insurance markets non-competitive.

The effect of indemnity benefit insurance as compared to service benefit insurance is as follows: "*Prices are lower under indemnity benefits than under coinsured service benefits at any given output. . . .* Blue Cross insurers have traditionally been controlled by medical care providers, and it is these insurers that use service benefits predominantly. This type of benefit may have been chosen to maximize the income of providers. It should be noted that the result obtained above holds only when an element of monopoly exists in the medical care market."[38] Because service benefits under the Blues pay a higher percentage of the bill and thus most of the higher fees of providers, the inflationary push against prices is greater under the Blues than under indemnity insurance. When some providers know that their patients are insured, they may exercise less restraint on covered costs by suggesting return office visits more often, by recommending in-hospital rather than outpatient care, and may prescribe more tests and x-rays.

Although comprehensive Blue Shield plans comparable to the catastrophic expense plans of indemnity insurers reimburse expenses for each subscriber, the individual benefit items are expensed in terms of service units. Thirty-one percent of Blue Shield subscribers are under the lower, premium rated contracts that have fee schedules with less financial protection than the Blues' UCR reimbursement contracts. Persons covered are often ignorant of whether their contract is on a fee schedule or UCR reimbursement basis. The latter has a built-in inflationary factor in the same fashion as does Medicare's payment of prevailing fees that are usually interpreted as "reasonable and customary" charges. Those fees below "usual, customary, reasonable" are moved up. In an inflationary economy, service benefits for hospital expense have less risk to the consumer.

By the mid-1970s, forty-seven states had passed special enabling acts to prohibit entry of new Blue Cross-type organizations while, in 20 states, Blue Cross plans were exempt from state income taxes. Blue Cross is viewed in some states as a business (not a non-profit association) because it charges a fee, all its customers are not subsidized low income persons, and it competes with commercial insurers. However, all individual Blue Cross plans and the national Blue Cross Association are exempt from the federal income tax because they are held to be non-profit organizations. Most are also exempt from local property taxes. The Blues and HMOs also enjoy preferential treatment in comparison with the commercial insurers that in many states pay taxes on insurance sales or premiums.

State insurance commissions regulate premiums of all commercial insurers, although they regulate Blue Cross rates only in those states where it has a large share of the insured population. In states with strong insurance commissioners, requests for rate increases in recent years have been drastically trimmed. Blue Cross is a dominant supplier, often the largest firm in a geographic area, and has the largest share of the area's hospital insurance market. Thus, it has been able to negotiate discounts from the hospitals. The Blue Cross discount varies by states. Traveler's Insurance Company sued Blue Cross of western Pennsylvania on the grounds that it had a discount as high as 14 to 15 percent against which Traveler's could not compete. Traveler's lost the case. It has been stated that Blue Cross' "discount can range as high as 30 percent in some areas."[39] Blue Cross states that it should get a substantial discount because the hospitals can save by processing several of its claims together. Commercial insurers point out that they, too, may have several patients whom they cover in one hospital at a particular time.

With these tax advantages and sizeable hospital discounts, Blue Cross should be able to compete more successfully than private insurers, even driving them out of business. This has not occurred. At the beginning of 1978, commercial insurance companies had 118 million enrollees as compared to the Blues' 85 million.[40] Blue Cross, however, paid out a larger share of hospital expenditures in 1977 (47 percent) than either insurance companies, which paid out 46 percent, or independent plans, which covered 7 percent.[41] This reflects self-selection of healthier persons who prefer the lower premium, commercial plans that do not reimburse as high a percentage of hospital costs as does Blue Cross.

Some critics claim that Blue Cross is not, in essence, a non-profit organization because it has salaries that are too high, "plush office space, extensive travel budgets, and other executive perquisites draining off what might otherwise be profit."[42] Charges of managerial slack are also made. The same charges can be made against many other non-profit organizations and especially some of the non-profit hospitals that are largely paid on a cost-reimbursement basis. During the 1970s, Blue Cross had a low operating expenses-to-premiums ratio, just over 5 percent, while Blue Shield's was about 11 percent. Commercial companies, in part because they must pay additional taxes, had a higher ratio of 19 to 21 percent.

Non-profit organizations by their very nature have to replace the goal of maximizing profits with other goals, such as maximization of enrollment or enhancement of status. Blue Cross' greatest growth was during the 1940s when it penetrated about 60 percent of the hospital insurance market. During the mid-1950s and early 1960s, Blue Cross enrollment dropped while commercial insurers increased their enrollment. By 1979, commercial insurers covered about 60 percent of the market, Blue Cross had dropped to about 35 percent, while HMOs covered the remainder. A new surge of life was given to the National Blue Cross Plan when Medicare and Medicaid selected it to act as the primary fiscal intermediary that then subcontracted to its state plans. Their state plans handle most of the administration of the government's programs.

Blue Cross initially community-rated its plans; that is, the premiums were based on the average of the actuarial experiences of all employee groups of different companies in an area. In contrast, commercial insurers have always experience-rated their plans so that each company's actuarial experience sets the premium for that company. Thus, Blue Cross has gradually lost ground to the commercial insurers that offer lower rates to those companies with a relatively younger labor force with lower health expenses. By 1980, most Blue Cross plans for employee groups had become experience-rated while its individual policies are still community-rated.

Throughout the history of the Blue Cross, its association with the American Hospital Association (AHA) has been very close. At the national level, there have been periods of interlocking directorships between Blue Cross and Blue Shield. Special discounts from hospitals and the limitation of entry via state enabling laws have resulted in Blue Cross domination of the service form of hospital insurance. Within this context, Blue Cross is a monopoly. The 300 indemnity insurers have no protection against entry.

In recent years, Blue Cross has responded to government persuasion to appoint more public members to its various boards of directors. By 1978, 59 percent of its total board members were "not at-interest." The remaining members were 17 percent physicians, 16 percent hospital administrators, and 8 percent hospital trustees.[43]

Blue Shield was organized originally by physicians in order to provide a means for patients to spread their physician bills over a series of payments. It also acts to insure against non-payment of physician bills. The *Blue Cross/Blue Shield Fact Book, 1978* reports that "the first Blue Shield Plan-type group was founded in California by the California Medical Association (CMA) in 1939."[44] The 69 Blue Shield plans of 1979 covered slightly over one-third of the United States population.

Blue Shield has agreements with its physician members about reimbursement of their fees. Forty-six percent of Blue Shield contracts with employers pay physicians on an UCR basis, 31 percent in accordance with a fee schedule, while the remaining 23 percent have various arrangements under the supplemental benefit packages that dovetail with the Medicare benefit package.[45] In 1977, the market shares of Blue Shield plans ranged from 7 percent to almost 88 percent in different areas of the country. A Federal Trade Commission's staff report states: "In that year, 56 of the 70 plans covered 25 percent or more of the people living in their service areas. . . . Where Blue Shield Plans have substantial market shares, their reimbursement levels set the going rate for fees in the community, . . . some view this sort of 'price leadership' to be one of their functions."[46] Others view this as a form of price-fixing. The Blue Shield committees that set these charges are usually composed solely of physicians. About 80 percent of Blue Shield's business comes from group plans. The premiums under these plans that reflect the negotiated UCR and fee screens are essentially less controlled than are the indemnity insurance premiums by the state regulations. The prices paid to physicians and most hospitals are negotiated under the Blues by at-interest parties. To control the premiums after the prices on what they are based have been set—in what some Federal Trade Commission (FTC) reports term a monopoly fashion—is not effective.

The FTC also claims that the AMA's and CMA's "relative value schedules" create a price schedule that in turn sets a minimum level for prices for all physicians. Physicians under the UCR system rarely allow their fees to remain below the UCR level so the lower fees rise. Consequently, fees increase continually because, as physicians with low fees raise their fees, the average for the geographic area, and thus the UCR screen, moves up. During price controls in the health sector in the early 1950s, the federal government's criteria for physicians' fees were "usual and prevailing" fees. The author's experience as an economist on the Wage Stabilization Board (WSB) in the 1950s was that these criteria also automatically acted to increase fees for the same reason. A common in-house reference to the WSB was "Wage Stimulation Board." The use of UCR fee schedules and screens eliminate what little price competition there may have already been among physician fees. As the lower charges all move up, the higher charges are raised in order to maintain their customary price differentials. Physicians may test the system by increasing fees. Repeatedly updating the date to which the "single screen" applies means that physicians' prices rise continuously.

The use of the word "reasonable" in UCR means that in the opinion of the peer review physician committee, it is reasonable for a particular physician in a particular case to charge more than the usual and customary fee. The case may be unusually complex and the physician unusually skilled. Most Blue Shield plans use a ninetieth percentile screen while Medicare uses a seventy-fifty percentile screen to determine their maximum "reasonable" fee.

The Blues service-type contract with employers has developed in such a fashion that more health care and/or a possibly higher quality at a higher price is purchased than would be if indemnity insurance alone existed. The practices of Blue Shield, Medicare, and use of the physician associations' "relative value studies" have resulted in rigid fee differentials. These differentials favor surgeons and other specialists who use tests, x-rays, and increasingly more complex medical procedures over those physicians whose prime input is their professional advice and time. Thus, the use of all types of medical technology has increased and contributes to the increase in the costs of medical care.

Some state that the Blues is a quasi-government agency that provides a needed service. The organization's supporters point to recent cost containment efforts by the various state plans of the Blues. Forty-five plans reimburse for pre-admission testing, some reimburse second opinions for surgery, and a few cover hospices and home care expenses for the terminally ill. These policies reduce the use of hospital days. After several years of bad publicity resulting from state insurance commissioners' publicized reviews of rate increase requests, Blue Cross is emphasizing consumer health education through its *Consumer Bulletin*, first issued in 1976. The Blues, in response to competition from HMOs, are also involved in jointly running HMOs, advising other HMOs, and in a few cities are expanding benefit packages.

Whether or not Blue Cross and Blue Shield act as a monopoly was still being debated in 1979. A monopoly is usually considered to be an organization which controls more than one-half of a market. In areas where more than one-half of physicians belong to the Blue Shield Plan, Blue Shield can act as a monopolist. In some areas, 80 percent or more of physicians belong. A monopoly position, however, depends on what percentage of the physicians' billings go through Blue Shield, not necessarily the percentage of physicians that belong to Blue Shield.

Many of the new, physician-sponsored IPAs (see Chapter VI, Section C) may, where a high percentage of area physicians belong, also be monopolies. This possibility has not escaped the notice of analysts and antitrust lawyers. However, because many of these IPAs are new and have a small enrollment, it is unlikely that 51 percent or more of the physicians' billings are under an IPA's billings. Many physicians are frequently selling the same services to patients and/or the third party paying for their care at several different prices to: Medicaid, Medicare, Blue Shield, commercial insurers, and different HMOs. Government regulation has supported this. Some physicians could be receiving the same price for different sets of services, which may or may not represent lower quality. A situation where physicians receive the same price for different qualities of service also permits physicians to act as price-discriminating monopolists (intended as a descriptive, not a pejorative, term). The opportunity to do this exists because government and other third party payers have created a reimbursement structure that encourages price discrimination.

The general consensus among economists is that Blue Shield acts as a price-setting monopoly. After several days of testimony, the House Subcommittee on Oversight and Investigation found that Blue Shield permits physicians "to affect their reimbursement" and prevents subscribers from having "an effective voice in determining the type of providers able to be reimbursed, the scope, and the cost of health care coverage."[47] The antitrust lawyers of the FTC point out that the opportunity for Blue Shield to act as a price-setting monopoly exists, whether or not it is used.

An unofficial (that is not adopted by the FTC) FTC staff report on "Medical Participation in Control of Blue Shield and Other Open-Panel Medical Prepayment Plans" goes further. Its seven authors with three senior staff approvals "found that medical participation in the control of many Blue Shield plans is sufficiently great that physicians and physician organizations are able to control or influence economically significant decisions made by the plans. These decisions concern how much to pay physicians, whether or not to pay non-physician health professionals who compete with the physicians, what cost containment mechanisms to employ, and other matters that affect competition in the professional health services sector of the nation's economy."[48]

The public does not usually think of medical providers as in business or acting as monopolists. Rather, "the medical profession . . . has benefitted from a widespread cultural acceptance of its own self-description as a group of people who serve the public interest."[49] Many physicians believe that because, as individuals, they do perform in their patients' best medical interests, this also means that they are acting in the public's economic interest. The two are not the same. Continuing price increases of medical care above the general inflation rate is gradually changing the public's perception. It is not unexpected that medical care prices have been rising rapidly. Physicians are like other people in that they respond to higher earnings. They, too, have families to support, loans to repay, and children whom they wish to send to college. General inflation encourages any supplier to increase prices if possible.

It has been stated that "public dissatisfaction with the industry's economic performance created a political opportunity that the FTC could not have been expected to resist."[50] In 1979 and 1980, legislative bills were introduced in both the Senate and the House to promote competition in the health care industry. In 1982, the new Secretary of HHS, Richard S. Schweiker, can be expected to push for the proposals that, when Senator, he supported in his Health Care Reform Act of 1979 and 1980. The stage for more competition among providers of health care had been set in the mid-1970s.

In 1975, in the landmark Goldfarb case, the Supreme Court ruled that lawyers were not exempt from the antitrust act. This ruling is considered applicable to physicians. Initially, the FTC forced the medical professional associations to eliminate restrictions on physician advertising. However, individual physicians have not advertised. It is an unusual physician who would risk the loss of referrals by his colleagues and the probable ostracism he or she might incur by advertising. However, group practices, and especially HMOs, are advertising in newspapers, radio, and television, but they are not advertising their prices.

The FTC also investigated whether the use of the relative value studies (RVS) fee schedules are a form of fixing prices. Although there is not agreement, some lawyers believe that the RVS schedules are price-fixing but that "the antitrust enforcers were right but for wrong, or at least incomplete, reasons."[51] They argue that Blue Shield and IPAs are a form of "joint selling agencies through which competing doctors indirectly fix prices and determine their own incomes."[52] However, the FTC has jurisdiction over a non-profit organization only if that organization functions for the profit of its members. This may not be always easy to prove in the medical care sector. It is puzzling to a lay person that the review of physicians' fees is "peer review" with government encouragement, that is, review by other physicians who *per se* are "at-interest." On the surface, this is not in accord with antitrust actions to encourage competition in other sectors of the economy. Large companies that purchase medical care for their employees and pay out billions of dollars annually in premium fees are beginning to become involved in "peer review" in some Connecticut and New York areas.

FTC's staff investigated Blue Shield in some detail and concluded that it is a monopoly. A physician's source of power in dealing with any insurer is the ultimate one of denial of services to patients covered by that third party. Some physicians, for example, refuse to take patients paid for by Medicaid. The FTC has proposed a regulation to prohibit a physician majority on the board of directors of any Blue Cross/Blue Shield Plan and also on the price-setting committees. While the actual regulation was held up, the Blues added public members to their boards but not to their price-setting committees. Among other indirect responses of the Blues to the monopoly charge are providing more information to consumers, using incentives through reimbursement coverage to contain costs in the medical care and health insurance markets, and promoting HMOs.

In the early part of 1980, Congress cut off the FTC's appropriations for a short period of time in an apparent congressional signal that the commission had gone too far in some of its regulatory actions. This dampened the FTC's zeal. However, Blue Cross and Blue Shield remain vulnerable.

Many Blue Shield plans do not reimburse clinical psychologists, psychiatric social workers, optometrists, and certified nurse anesthetists even though the state law where the service is rendered may permit independent practice by these generally certified or licensed personnel. Some Blue Shield plans will reimburse persons in these and similar categories if the services are rendered under the direct supervision of a physician. Some Blue Shield plans even deny reimbursements to non-specialty physicians for performing specific procedures that a medical specialist might provide. A common example is Blue Shield's refusal to reimburse for anesthesia administered by an obstetrician during delivery of a baby. Blue Shield will pay an anesthesiologist, but not an obstetrician, for this service. This practice is analogous to some trade union make-work laws that require unneeded, trained persons to continue to be paid when innovations have made their services unnecessary. The usual reasoning that the retention of an extra worker is necessary to maintain quality is the same.

Blue Shield points out that many persons find their plans an attractive alternative to commercial insurance, and in this sense have promoted price competition within the health insurance market. This is, of course, true. Whether the Blues have promoted price competition in the medical care market is, however, difficult to say because of the secrecy that surrounds their financial arrangements with physicians. Some physicians still regard themselves as above public discussion of monetary matters such as their fees and charges for x-rays, tests, and hospital days. Because physicians' and patients' assessments of values from medical intervention may differ, failure to discuss these differences also hampers rational choices. Whereas in the past most other professionals displayed a similar reluctance to advertise or even discuss monetary matters, today physicians' attitudes are out-of-step with those of other professionals. Some physicians, and more nurses, have recently unionized. Although strikes in the health sector are rare, they are growing in number. Large group practices that hire physicians and large hospitals are especially vulnerable.

The decision about who is qualified to deliver care is a public policy question that is governed by state certification and licensing laws. Refusal to reimburse approved providers by private insurers can effectively negate state laws. Public policy can thus be made by non-accountable, at-interest groups rather than by elected policy-makers.[53] How politics affects national health policy can be documented by watching what happens over the next few years to the FTC and its suggested proposals to promote competition in the health sector.

The questions of whether monopoly power exists and is increasing in the medical care market are important because higher prices result under monopoly than otherwise would occur. Traditional economic theory does not explain satisfactorily why the more physicians practicing in an area, the higher their prices. San Francisco, with a highly mobile population, has one physician for every 161 persons; Marin County has one physician for every 284 persons.[54] This compares with the national average of one physician for about 500 persons. The specific areas cited have high medical care prices despite their extremely generous supply of physicians and an HMO coverage of nearly 20 percent of their population. There is a "target income" theory which posits that physicians target an income goal. When there are more physicians in an area, the demand for each physician's services decreases. The physician then increases prices to compensate for potential loss of revenue.

There is also the possibility that, as the number of physicians increase in a geographic area where the local residents have high mobility, new residents "will tend to have less accurate information about the price and quality of any provider."[55] These consumers will be less sensitive to changes in medical prices because they lack knowledge to compare prices. Empirical testing of this theory using primary physician fees in 100 large metropolitan areas found that a lessened information flow explained the higher medical fees better than did the "target income" theory coupled with provider-induced demand. Theories to explain physician pricings are difficult to substantiate empirically because of the many variables involved for which there are no data.

A major requirement of any competitive market is information, which is often lacking in medical care markets. A unique new health resource center, Planetree, has been started in San Francisco. It is both a free library and bookstore that acts as a reference guide to all possible treatment options and plans "to develop a comprehensive listing that includes the credentials, services, and fees of physicians and other health care practitioners in every shade of orthodoxy from which patients can select their own preferred provider. The list will be supplemented by a Planetree brochure called 'How to Choose a Doctor,' prepared with the help of a 'Physicians' Exchange' that now includes many leading medical specialists."[56]

Some claim that HMOs have had a direct competitive effect on medical care costs, and Hawaii and northern California are often used as examples. It is claimed that Blue Cross has responded to the HMO coverage of 20 percent of the population in northern California by improving its utilization review procedures, increasing benefits, and by starting rival HMOs.[57] The Blues did increase benefits in some contracts to cover 90 percent of UCR charges for physician office visits for employees, although not for their dependents. Blue Cross continued, in its less costly plans, the less-visible $50 per year limitation on reimbursement of outpatient x-rays and tests in some of its northern California contracts until 1981. The charge for a front and side chest x-ray in the Palo Alto, northern California, area is $45 to $50. Blue Cross/Blue Shield coverage was made more competitive with HMO coverage when the $50 was increased to $300. Whether HMO growth in the area can be considered the sole causative factor is unknown.

The primary advantage of the Blues is that third party coverage is retained irrespective of the individual's choice of physician and what geographical part of the nation that individual is in when becoming ill. Blue Shield and medical societies have been starting their own HMOs, often with sizeable copayments for each office visit. Competition appears to center on the premiums of insurers and the per capita charges of HMOs that the employer pays, not on the medical charges which, at least in part, the consumer pays. However, the premiums and per capita rates reflect, but with a lag, the medical charges and utilization rates. The actual out-of-pocket charges for which the consumer is liable are generally not well known. Probably among the best known are the non-reimbursed expenses of pregnancy and well-baby care. Informed consumers switch coverage in "open season" in anticipation of their health needs in the year ahead.

It has always been difficult to obtain financial information about the Blue Cross plans. "The Blue Cross Association and published materials do not provide even basic information on the practices of various plans with respect to reimbursement of hospitals, claims review, determination of subscriber rates, governance, or state and federal regulation."[58] Although that statement is made in a 1974 book, the acting insurance commissioner of Michigan ruled on March 30, 1979, that "Blue Cross and Blue Shield of Michigan must make public financial documents it wants to keep secret, . . . rate-making [method of setting premiums from given prices] documents. . . . The information includes the formula the Blues use for setting rates, the difference between doctors' charges for medical treatment and the Blues payments to them, and studies showing price trends."[59]

Government programs and the Blues have helped hospitals and physicians by eliminating almost all bad debts. Although Medicaid does not reimburse anywhere near the incurred costs of hospital patients, what it does reimburse is far more than many poor patients paid in the days of charity care prior to Medicaid. Moreover, most hospitals make up losses under Medicaid by charging other patients more. Many hospitals have thus been able to operate with less risk of loss than other businesses have but with concomitantly less chance of a sizeable excess of revenues over costs. About three-fourths of hospitals set their costs in accordance with the anticipated percentage of costs that they expect will be reimbursed. Sylvia Law (1974) writes:

> Reasonable cost reimbursement had, and has, little to do with
> reasonableness. The method as utilized by Blue Cross simply
> meant that an average daily cost of hospital care was determined
> by dividing the hospital's total allowable expenses by the total
> number of patient days. An adjustment was then made for
> private, semi-private and ward service, with semi-private costs at

100 percent, private at 115 percent, and ward at 90 percent. These figures were recognized to be essentially arbitrary. No effort was made to determine whether total hospital costs or any component thereof were reasonable according to some market or other standard. Rather, Blue Cross use of the concept focused solely on what costs were "allowable." Even the standards governing what was "allowable" were rather limited and arbitrary.[60]

Some claim that Blue Cross and the hospitals have manipulated hospital charges so that those procedures commonly used by the aged are more expensive than their actual costs indicate. If this is so, Medicare reimburses some hospital costs for the aged at inflated amounts as compared to costs for younger age groups. It is impossible to judge whether this practice exists without an examination of thousands of pages of accounting data. There are also claims that some physicians charge their Medicare patients more than patients not under Medicare. The reluctance to disclose payment schedules makes it difficult to judge the extent of this practice. However, the General Accounting Office (GAO) (1979) found that in Florida 22 percent of physicians' charges were lower under Medicare than their charges to private patients.

Medical advertisements are almost always by insurers, not by providers except for a few HMOs, and then in their capacity as insurers not providers. The advertisements are aimed at employers, not consumers. The few exceptions are some advertisements by weight, smoking, and stress control clinics. The large employer is just beginning to act as a prudent consumer in seeking information about these markets.

Further research and analysis are needed to explain the degree of monopoly in the health sector and its impact on fee structures. Antitrust action can forestall more, and replace some, government regulation.

COMMERCIAL INSURANCE COMPANIES

Private commercial health insurance coverage continues to grow, reaching about 55 percent of the hospital insurance market, or nearly 118 million people in 1977. Commercial insurers have been selling more plans dovetailed to Medicare benefits for the aged than do Blue Cross and Blue Shield. In 1977, insurance companies covered 68 million persons as compared to 39 million by the Blues under group supplementary policies. However, from 1976 to 1977, Blue Shield's market share among persons under 65 years has been dropping even more rapidly, by 22 percent, than among the aged, by 14 percent. The Blues had a 29 percent decline in coverage for physician visits.[61] It is, however, in the area of major medical and/or catastrophic expense insurance where commercial insurers have made their most rapid gains. In 1965, 60 million persons were covered by major medical plans of the commercial insurers and, in 1976, 105 million. Blue Cross/Blue Shield's coverage under their comparable plans grew from about 15 million to about 42 million persons over the same period.[62]

By 1977, 75 percent of the population (162 million) had major medical expense coverage under all types of private insurers. This percentage includes the 12 million individuals covered by HMOs and the self-insured plans.[63] The total number of persons with catastrophic expense protection is over 200 million in the United States. This figure includes approximately 45 million people with Medicare and Medicaid protection. Thus, nearly 90 percent of the population have the type of health insurance that most economists consider preferable: catastrophic expense rather than comprehensive, first dollar coverage.

It is the unpredictable large expense against which purchase of health insurance should be made, not the predictable and often planned small expenses such as drugs, routine dental care, and the average number (four to five annually) of physician office visits. The costs of administering the coverage of small, frequent expenses are high. First dollar coverage of all health expenses under a fee-for-service and hospital cost reimbursement system without regulation of those fees and costs leads to spiralling inflation.

There are varying ways a government can provide for 100 percent coverage of its population for major medical or catastrophic health expenses only. The United States, however, is the only country where private markets have even approached an 80 percent coverage of the population for major medical expenses. The private insurance companies believe that, by use of deductibles and co-insurance, they have held down the demand for medical care and thus the amount insurance companies pay out. This has been contested. A 1979 Canadian study argues for first dollar coverage. It states that deductibles, co-payments, and other forms of

> direct charges will benefit providers, private insurance
> companies, and the provincial government. Direct charges in
> most forms (particularly the ones most frequently recommended)
> will serve as an injection of additional funds into the sector and

thus as a source of increases in provider incomes. Furthermore, exposure to any significant direct charge is likely to lead consumers to seek supplementary private insurance coverage. Finally, direct charges provide a means of keeping the lid on health care expenditures in government budgets while allowing total (public plus private) expenditures to rise.[64]

The authors state further that there is little evidence that payments by consumers act to deter unnecessary or marginal care and that empirical evidence that demonstrates co-insurance is effective is still lacking. They also write:

It is well known that gentle massaging of relatively straightforward economic models can yield predictions of an inverse impact of direct charges on total health care expenditures. Furthermore, with the assumption that patients are fully informed consumers, those same models will also tell us that the least efficacious services will be those first deterred. But demand theory applied in this manner is devoid of any consideration of need, agency relationships, and the reasons for their importance in this market.[65]

The last sentence of the above quotation implies that the authors' value judgments may be influencing their assessment of the effect of copayments.

By concentrating on Canada, where fees and a budget for health are negotiated by the government as compared with the United States where they are not, these critics have conveniently ignored the experiences of private insurers in the United States and the governments of other countries where copayments or user charges help to contain their health expenditures.

The British National Health Service (NHS) has contained costs primarily through use of budgets that do not permit spending substantial amounts on the construction of new hospitals and equipment. The NHS mandates that a patient have a referral from the less expensive general practitioner in order to see a specialist. The U.K., however, has also manipulated user charges or copayments to control costs for prescription drugs, eyeglasses, and dental care.

Sweden has used copayments to deter physician office visits. HMOs within the United States have also found that small copayment charges restrain office visits for minor illness with no countervailing increase in utilization. Large, salaried HMOs that own their own hospitals are in many ways comparable to a national health system even though taxes are not their revenue source. HMOs use copayments—$2, $4, and some even $5 per physician visit—primarily to restrain demand. HMOs also have the same referral rules as the NHS.

The critical Canadian study quoted above accepts that a system of direct charges by providers to patients for a portion of the costs would effectively restrain demand if the "charging behaviour . . . is truly independent, open, and advertised" and "there is an absence of provider collusion."[66] These are the conditions which the recommendations made at the end of this book are intended to create.

U.S. insurance companies have over the years used deductibles, co-insurance, and various forms of copayments in attempts to restrain the demand for medical care. Economists have analyzed the effects of these financial devices tailored to restrain demand. In recent years, however, time costs have so increased as to blur the effect of requiring direct money payments by consumers, at least in cases of minor ailments.

The continued use of large deductibles, $300 to $1,000, under private major medical plans, and especially the common cost corridor that requires the consumer to pay 20 to 25 percent of expenses over the deductible, indicates that there is a discretionary element in consumer demand for medical care in even serious cases. Medicare is also formulated on this principle. The facts, however, do not refute the contention that a major beneficiary from two payers, the patient and the third party, is the provider of the medical care. If the patient is not involved in deciding whether it is worthwhile to spend even a small percent of the resource cost for medical care, then without a budgeting system there are no limits on the consumers' demands unless the provider exercises limits. A provider who is paid a fee-for-service and also lives in an area where the ratio of physicians to the population is high is more likely to encourage greater use of medical care.

Direct charges to the consumers of medical care should be retained even though their precise effect with rising time costs is hard to estimate. As more information develops about how consumers through personal living habits can contain, within limits, their long-run medical expenses, the argument for direct user charges is strengthened. However, some of those who are most ill cannot affect their health by improvement in their personal living habits. Others who are ill are also poor. These are not sufficient reasons to eliminate all forms of cost-sharing since there is an existing, effective national program to pay medical care expenses of the poor. If there were no Medicaid program, equity arguments might suffice to eliminate out-of-pocket payments. However, to do so under existing government financial arrangements would make the medical care system and the allocation of resources less responsive to the desires of all consumers.

VIII. NATIONAL LEVELS OF HEALTH

EXPENDITURES ON HEALTH AND
LEVELS OF HEALTH

The United States is not unique in its expenditures on health. They have been increasing in all the industrialized countries of the world since 1960. The United States is the only one of these countries, however, that does not have a comprehensive national health insurance program.

In most countries, health care costs are rising faster than their general inflation rate. By 1990, even without legislative changes or further expansion of government health programs in the United States, the percentage of the gross national product (GNP) being spent on health will have doubled to 12 percent as compared to 6 percent in 1965.

Some industrialized countries spend more on health care than the United States while others spend less. Among nine industrialized countries, three expended a higher percentage of the GNP on health care in 1975 than the United States while five spent less: West Germany spent 9.7 percent, Sweden, 8.7 percent, the Netherlands, 8.6 percent, United States, 8.4 percent, France, 8.1 percent, Canada, 7.1 percent, Australia, 7.0 percent, Finland, 6.8 percent, and the United Kingdom, 5.6 percent.[1] The U.S. is only an 0.3 percentage point above the median of 8.1 percent.

The U.K., however, stands apart because its expenditures are the lowest, 5.6 percent of its GNP. This is 2.5 percentage points below the median point while the highest is only 1.6 percentage points above the median. The U.K. has a deliberate, centralized national policy to limit monies used for new hospitals and high-technology medical care.

The percentage increase in real (adjusted for price inflation) health costs over the 16-year period 1960–76 was greatest in the Netherlands and West Germany, each at 10 percent annually, while it was lowest in the U.K. at 5 percent and next lowest in the United States at 6.5 percent.

To determine any precise relationship between expenditures for all types of medical care with the level of a nation's health is impossible.

The primary determinant of the average level of personal health in a nation is its real national income per capita. The higher that is, the higher the quality and quantity of food per capita, the level of public sanitation, and the many other goods and services that affect health. In addition, genetic endowment, climate, environmental factors, and life-style, in the sense of physical activity and access to high-speed automobiles, also affect a nation's overall level of health. In the developing countries, expenditures per capita on personal health care are less than in the industrialized countries, but this differential alone does not account for the fact that at birth their babies have an average life expectancy "of 20 years less than those born in the industrialized world"[2] and that early deaths are more prevalent.

Medical resources differ among countries usually labelled as industrialized. For example, among 18 industrialized countries in 1977, Finland had the fewest physicians per capita, one for every 1,570 people. Sweden had one for every 1,150, and the U.K. had one for every 1,100. Yet Sweden has the lowest infant mortality rate in the world. For comparison, there was one physician for every 550 persons in Austria, one for every 670 in Western Germany, and one for every 760 in the U.S. Low infant mortality rates are associated with high numbers of nurses and midwives per capita and a low number of physicians. The quality and quantity of diet of the mothers is a very significant factor in the births of healthy babies.

The health of the people living in the United States has been improving, as are health levels in other countries. For example, in 1978, infant mortality fell to 13.6 deaths per 1,000 live births, a 53.4 percent decrease since 1950. By the end of 1980, the rate had reached an all-time U.S. low of 12.5 deaths per 1,000 live births. Between 1960 and 1977, the difference in infant mortality rates for non-whites and whites was nearly cut in half and by 1978, the 1960 seven-year greater life expectancy of white infants had been reduced to 4.8 years.

A new baby born in this country in 1979 can expect to live 73.8 years on the average while a baby born in 1900 could expect to live only 47.3 years. The life expectancy for female infants is about eight years greater than that for males. However, the male-female differential in life expectancy shrinks to about four years by age 65 and the white and non-white differential disappears.

Over a period of only ten years, 1968–78, age-adjusted deaths due to heart disease decreased in the United States by 23 percent.[3] Are the gains in life expectancy and other advances the result of greater medical outlays and concomitant better medical care or because of changes in environment, nutrition, housing, and other factors derived from a higher per capita real income, changes in personal life-style or, as most likely, a combination of all these and other factors not enumerated?

Despite large health care expenditures, the United States still lags behind some industrialized countries in some measures of health outcomes. Likewise, some industrialized countries lag behind the United States in other areas. Yet the United States has had remarkable gains since 1970 with an age-adjusted rate decline in mortality by 17.8 percent and a life expectancy gain at birth of three years by 1980, from 70.9 to 73.8 years. Most of this gain is after age 65. Persons surviving to this age will live on the average until 81.7 years. This accounts for the great concern about the support of the increasing numbers of retired persons 65 years and over as the number of productive workers in the low birthrate period of the 1960s and 1970s become the mainstay of the labor force. Although in 1980 only 5 percent of the aged were institutionalized, this percentage will increase if our health care financing arrangements are not changed to encourage more home health care, including hospices for the terminally ill as well as the less dramatic provision for home-maker services and nursing care. In 1980, the aged were 11 percent of the population. This percentage may, depending on biological advances, creep up even faster than the current prediction of 19 percent of the population by the year 2050.

Overall comparisons of levels of health across nations' boundaries are difficult to make. Expenditures on medical care are not the sole, or even always the major, determinant of health outcomes. Liberalization of the abortion laws and financing under Medicaid abortions for the poor may have affected substantially the infant mortality rate. Two economists write that between 1964 and 1977 in the United States "the reduction in the white neonatal (within the first four weeks after birth) mortality rate due to abortion ranges from 1.5 to 1.7 deaths per thousand births. The comparable figures for non-whites is . . . 2.5 deaths per thousand births."[4] Unmarried teen-agers who become pregnant often eat very little in order to hide the pregnancy. This practice results in low birth weight (under 5.5 pounds) babies. Such babies are at much higher risk than larger babies. Pregnant women who do not want to bear a child sometimes attempt self-induced abortion. It is possible that this practice is more common among the poor who may not be able to afford or may not wish to pay the clinic charge of $150 to $200. Many authorities object to general revenue financing of abortions because it compels some people to support through taxes a procedure that their moral convictions abhor. Others argue against other tax-supported actions as being against their moral convictions.

One study is not usually accepted as incontrovertible evidence of biological facts. An additional study that clearly establishes whether the liberalization of abortions has decreased the infant and maternal mortality rates is needed. It is quite clear that the number of legalized abortions has doubled from 1973 to 1978 to about 1.2 million annually.[5] Many argue that each abortion is a "death." It is not the economist's expertise that can decide the emotional matter of abortions. The economist supplies only the available data because the judgment that an abortion is a death permits no compromise — and, also because of the legal and moral issues involved, no attempt is made to discuss the full range of options. The rate of abortions in the United States is much higher than in the United Kingdom, France, and the Netherlands, is about the same as in Sweden, and is lower than in Japan. It is important to recognize that infant mortality rates in the United States are still higher than in many other industrialized countries despite the historically rapid increase in the number of women receiving early prenatal care, substantially improving nutrition, and the recent gains in the level of real per capita income. Other industrialized nations are sharing in these same gains.

Some persons have attributed the failure of the United States to keep up with some of the industrialized countries in mortality, age-adjusted outcomes solely to the fact that there is no national governmental system of health care in the United States. Senator Edward Kennedy introduced his proposed Health Security Act of 1975 into the 94th Congress with the following statement:

The know-how exists to create a better organized system of health care in America. Other nations have in fact gone ahead of us in this regard. The United States is the only major industrial nation in the world without a system of national health insurance or a national health service. While none of these systems seems suited to America's values and society, they have, in fact, succeeded in moving their nations ahead of our country in many important areas.

In infant mortality, among the major industrial nations of the world, the United States today trails behind 19 other countries, including all of the Scandinavian nations, most of the British Commonwealth, Japan, and East Germany. Half of these nations were behind us in the early 1950's. . . .

Tragically, the infant mortality rate for nonwhites in the United States is nearly twice the rate for whites. And nearly five times as many nonwhite mothers die in childbirth as whites—shameful evidence of the ineffective prenatal and postnatal care our minority groups receive.

The story told by other health indicators is equally dismal. The United States trails 27 other nations in life expectancy for males at age 45, and 11 other nations in life expectancy for females.[6]

Leaving aside the question of whether age-adjusted, mortality outcomes are good measures of a nation's level of health, some of the data cited in the above 1975 quotation are out-of-date and current data do not support all the claims.

In 1978, the U.S. infant mortality rate of 13.8 per 1,000 live births did not trail that of the U.K. or Western Germany, and both of those countries have nationalized systems of medical care. In the U.S., the "infant mortality rate for all other infants exceeded that of white infants by over 75 percent in 1978 compared with more than 90 percent in 1958." More can be done but the improvement is substantial, and among non-whites as well as whites. The narrowing of the black/white differential has been despite the much higher percentage of teen-age mothers among Blacks than whites with the accompanying higher health risk derived from poorer nutrition. By 1981, the infant mortality rate was 12.5 per 1,000 births.[7]

The United States has also made significant progress in lowering maternal mortality rates and increasing life expectancy at birth during the past decade for both whites and non-whites. The maternal mortality rate had decreased from 24.5 per 100,000 live births in 1968 to only 7.8 (provisional rate) in 1979, an impressive accomplishment.

The U.K. has had a notably slower rate of progress than the U.S. A 1980 U.K. report, *Inequalities in Health*, documents the persistence of "inequalities in health between the different social classes in Britain . . . through 30 years of a national health service," and these include especially infant mortality outcomes.[8] If life expectancy at 65 years were used for comparison, a far more commonly used figure than 45 years, then the U.S. compares favorably. "Women at 65 years of age in the United States could expect to live as long or longer than women in all other selected [for comparison by HEW, 12] developed countries. Life expectancy for men at 65 years of age also compared more favorably with other countries than did life expectancy at birth."[9] Male life expectancy at 65 years in the United States exceeded that in the Netherlands, England and Wales, East and West Germany, Italy, France, and Australia. Thus, in 1976, among 13 comparative nations, the U.S. trailed only five: Canada, Sweden, Switzerland,

Israel, and Japan.[10] It can be argued that higher life expectancy rates at later ages reflect better medical care more than do higher life expectancies at younger ages.

Health status may be assessed in a variety of ways. The traditional way is to analyze age-adjusted, statistical data on mortality, life expectancy, and morbidity or illness. There are limitations in using only mortality data as the indicator of health status. The limitations have been well expressed in the government publication *Health: United States, 1978.*

> No one measure accurately reflects the health of the American people and, in fact, a determination of how healthy Americans really are depends to a large extent on how health is defined. With more people living longer than ever before, measures of health other than death are necessary to characterize the disease and disability patterns of an aging population.[11]

Similarly, there are limitations in using only disease incidence as the indicator of health status, as the same government publication quoted just above indicates.

> Estimates of disease incidence may rise artificially as diagnostic procedures and reporting practices improve. Also, with increased accessibility to medical care, the measures of health status currently used may indicate an artificial "worsening" of health rather than an improvement. For example, as more people receive medical care it is likely that more people will be diagnosed, thereby increasing the number of conditions reported in health surveys.[12]

A major problem in using vital statistics to make international comparisons of health arises from differences in reporting and compiling the statistics, especially in the timing of recording births and deaths.

There are other factors, cultural and socio-economic, in addition to purely administrative differences that affect mortality rates. There is a wide range among countries in the percentage of births to women under 20 years. In the United States, 18 percent of births in 1976 were to women under 20 years, the second highest percent of teen-age mothers among thirteen (selected by HEW) countries. In Sweden, which has the most favorable infant mortality rate, only 7 percent of their births in 1976 were to women under 20 years. In the United States, teen-age births were 16 percent of all white births but 31 percent of all black births.[13] It is known that teen-age pregnancies have greater health risks to both the infant and mother and that this factor, therefore, contributes to the higher infant and maternity mortality rates among Blacks.

Comparable data on the incidence and duration of disease in different countries are difficult or impossible to obtain. Mortality data, however, tell us nothing about the percentage of the population that is well or about the quality of care received by the chronically ill. Nor does a low mortality rate necessarily reflect accessible, high-quality medical care.

The measure of illness most often used in the United States is the number of bed-disability days. Comparable data are not available in other countries. Hospital days per capita are sometimes used to assess changes in the level of health of a group of people. It is not possible to make meaningful international comparisons, nor even among the fifty states, by using self-reported at-home or recorded hospital bed-days data because the modes of medical practice, climate, and other factors differ.

Even if mortality and morbidity data were comparable across nations, it is impossible to ascribe what part of the differences are due to differences in levels of medical care. Climate, per capita real income, occupational distribution, the level of technology and education, racial composition, housing, diet, air quality, pace of life, and many other factors affect a nation's level of health. For example, the high incidence of lung cancer in the United States is more the result of intensive cigarette-smoking per capita than because of deficiencies in the medical care system. France, a country where consumption of alcohol has long been a way of life, has one of the highest death rates from cirrhosis of the liver in the world. England, renowned for its fogs and its coal dust, has unusually high death rates from bronchitis and respiratory cancer.

Another major health problem in the United States is obesity, a condition associated less with poor medical care than with poor nutrition, lack of exercise, and eating habits that involve desirable cultural/social activities. Thirty-five percent of women aged forty-five to sixty-four with incomes below the poverty level and 29 percent of those with incomes above are estimated to be obese. For men, the comparable figures are reversed: 5 percent and 13 percent.[14] Although exercise as a way of life has been increasing in the United States, it still is not popular among all groups. Gallup polls report that 24 percent of Americans exercised daily in 1961; 47 percent claimed to do so in 1977.[15] Recent large immigrations of Vietnamese and Spanish-speaking peoples, who each have distinctive food habits, may affect overall U.S. measures of health status in the future.

The following observation, made in 1960, is still true:

> When communicable diseases were the chief causes of death, measuring medical achievement was relatively easy—through determination of the death rate by age, sex, and cause. . . . As the death rate has been cut in half, the leading causes of death of fifty years ago have been replaced by heart disease, cancer, and accidents. . . . In fact, if the leading causes of death in an area *are* heart disease and cancer, one can be assured that the area has kept abreast of modern medicine and its application. Other measures of effectiveness are infant mortality rates by cause and maternal mortality.[16]

Crude versus Age-Adjusted Death Rates

The crude death rate is the number of deaths reported for a calendar year per 1,000 persons at the mid-point of that year. Crude death rates are not adjusted for age and sex differences among populations and thus are of limited use in making international comparisons of health or in assessing a change in health status of a given population over time. Age-adjusted death rates, by contrast, take into account changes in the age composition of a population. Thus, in the United States, the crude death rate increased 0.5 percent between 1977 and 1978 but the age-adjusted death rate decreased by 1.1 percent.[17] The crude death rate will continue to rise as the proportion of elderly in our population increases, but the age-adjusted rate will decline because of advances in medical technology.

Age-adjusted death rates vary by sex, race, educational level, geographical region, and many other characteristics. Although the gap between the age-adjusted death rates for whites and non-whites in the United States has narrowed, there remains a 35 percent differential. Death rates for each age group under 85 years were higher for non-whites than for whites in 1978.[18] The difference is due primarily to the relatively high death rates among Blacks and native Indians. The age-adjusted death rate of Orientals (Japanese and Chinese) who live in the United States is substantially lower than the rate for whites.[19]

The U.S. age-adjusted death rate declined 18.6 percent between 1968 and 1978 from 743.8 per 100,000 population to 605.5.[20] The estimated 1979 rate is 587.4, reflecting a continued downward trend. Among twelve industrialized countries, four (Mexico, West Germany, Italy, and Australia) had a higher age-adjusted death rate than that of the United States in 1974.[21]

Life Expectancy at Birth and at Age 65

Expectation of life at birth and other ages provides another measure of the health status of a population. Average life expectancy at birth in the United States in 1979 was 73.8 years as compared with 47.3 years in 1900. Although the difference in life expectancy at birth between whites and non-whites had narrowed to five years, life expectancy at age 65 was 16 years for both groups.[22] These data reflect enormous gains.

A comparison of life expectancies at birth in 1977 among seventeen countries show Austria, East and West Germany, Ireland, Italy, and New Zealand having lower life expectancies at birth for men than in the United States. For women, England and Wales, France, and Israel, in addition to the six already mentioned countries, also have much lower life expectancies than the United States.[23]

In life expectancy at 65 years, the United States compares even more favorably. This outcome reflects a greater use of medical resources to maintain older lives in the United States than in many of the countries that have national health insurance systems. None of the twelve countries for which data in 1976 are given by HEW in *Health: United States, 1978* had greater life expectancies than the United States for women who had survived to 65 years, and Canadian women alone have the same life expectancy as their American counterparts. American men at age 65 could expect to live 13.7 additional years in 1976. Only five of the countries had longer life expectancies for men at 65 years and in no case was the difference significantly longer, with 0.3 years for Japanese males being the greatest.[24]

The United States has a far larger and more racially heterogeneous population than most other countries. The shorter life expectancy at birth for Blacks in the United States lowers the average life expectancy while the longer life expectancy of the much smaller number of Orientals who live in the United States hardly affects the over-all figures. To what degree, if any, genetic differences among races affect life expectancy rates when all other factors are held constant is unknown.

Differentials in life expectancy at birth and at older ages are greater among the states of the United States than among the twelve or seventeen industrialized nations that HHS now uses for international comparisons. In 1975, life expectancy at birth for white males and females was the highest in the West North-Central states and lowest in the East South-Central states.

Infant and Maternal Mortality

About 85 percent of over three million pregnancies annually result in healthy new-born babies in the United States. One percent result in fetal death, and about 1 percent in death during the first month of life, seven percent are low-weight babies at high risk, while 4 to 5 percent have a significant birth defect or genetic disorder.[25] There is a minimum rate of infant deaths below which no country is likely to fall. However, the United States has further to go than some other countries.

By 1977, among seventeen industrialized countries, only seven (Canada, Austria, German Federal Republic, Ireland, Italy, Israel, and New Zealand) had higher infant mortality rates than the United States.[26] However, there has been a continuous downward trend in the U.S. infant mortality rate since 1977 from 14.1 to 12.5 births per 1,000 in 1980. International comparisons that are available only for earlier years understate the greater relative advance in the United States in the past few years. The United States, through prenatal detection of disease, better health habits of pregnant women, and fewer teen-age mothers could approach the lower rates of more homogeneous populations that range from 8 deaths per 1,000 in Sweden to 10.65 in Norway.

The greatest gain would be from reducing the number of low-weight births that are associated with teen-age mothers. Fifteen percent of babies born to girls under age 15 have low birth weights, twice the percentage for all babies born. Among these very young mothers, 21 percent had no prenatal care until after six months of pregnancy compared to only 6 percent without prenatal care among all mothers.[27] However, numerically the number of births among those under fifteen years is a very small part of all births, as are births to women 15 to 19 years old: In 1977, 1.2 births among 1,000 females 10–14 years and 53.7 births among those 15–19 years. How best to reduce pregnancies among children—females under 15 years of age—is not known. Education within the home and the schools have both failed. Since 1960, live births to children 10–14 years have increased from 0.8 to 1.2 births per 1,000 teen-agers in that age group in 1977 while the rate for those 15 to 19 years has dropped from 79.4 to 44.6 per 1,000.[28]

Obviously, comparisons within the United States can be made in many ways. Rural mortality rates are generally higher than urban mortality rates and black mortality rates are higher than whites'. However, there are no individual states that have infant mortality rates as low as those for Sweden and Norway. The higher infant mortality rates among Blacks reflects nutritional patterns, the poor housing of low income groups, the low educational levels of the mothers, the greater percentage of births among teen-agers, as well as the somewhat later use of medical care during pregnancy. Low birth-weight babies are more common among low income groups in all nations, irrespective of race.

Because the average birth weight of black infants of high socio-economic status are comparable to the average birth weight of white infants, it is clear that socio-economic status rather than racial identity is the chief determinant of birth weight and thus probability of survival. Regression analyses are needed to establish the relative importance of diet, sanitation, geographical location, education of the mother, accessibility of medical care, smoking, alcohol, drug abuse, and other factors that influence infant mortality rates.[29] Increase in real income per capita, more than any other factor, would reduce the infant mortality rate.

The more liberal abortion laws of the 1970s may have contributed to the decline in infant mortality during the past decade. Hawaii, in 1970, became the first state to permit abortion, in essence on request. In that state, low-birth-weight babies declined from 8.0 percent in 1966–69 to 7.1 percent in 1971–74. Infant deaths during the first four weeks after birth (neonatal) fell from 14.7 per 1,000 to 12.1 per 1,000.[30]

Decreases in neonatal and postnatal mortality (the postnatal period is 28 days to 1 year) were observed in Oregon after passage of its liberal abortion law.[31] It is, however, impossible to say how much of the decrease in infant mortality in either case was due to liberalized abortion and how much to other variables. Adolescents are 30 times more likely to bear a low-weight infant than women 20–24 years of age. Nineteen percent of all births in the United States in 1975 were to teen-age mothers compared to 17 percent in 1968.[32] Also, unmarried women are less likely than married women to receive early prenatal care and more likely to give birth to a low birth-weight infant.

Bearing a child out-of-wedlock is increasingly concentrated among teen-age mothers, from 44 percent of such births in 1965 to 52 percent in 1975. Only 40 percent, as compared with 76 percent, of all unmarried mothers had completed high school. Fetal deaths per 1,000 live births was 15.9 for illegitimate and 10.2 for legitimate births in 1975. The fetal death rates for babies of unmarried women has dropped from 17.4 per 1,000 in 1960.[33] In 1976, the rate of illegitimate births among non-white mothers was 78.1, and among white mothers, 12.7. Both births and fetal deaths of babies of unmarried mothers are under-reported.

Low birth weight is the single most important cause of neonatal mortality and accounts for 65 to 75 percent of all neonatal deaths.[34] Infants weighing less than 5.5 pounds at birth are twenty times more likely to die, often from infection, within the first year than other infants. In the United States in 1976, approximately 7 percent of all newborns weighed less than 5.5 pounds.[35] In Sweden, only 4 percent of newborns weighed less than 5.5 pounds.

The decline in infant mortality in the United States has been sharpest for American Indians, which is not surprising because they have had the poorest rate initially. In 1950, the rate for Indians was more than three times the rate for white infants and nearly twice the rate for black infants. But by 1977, the Indian infant mortality rate was 34 percent lower than for black infants and 26 percent higher than that for white infants. The Japanese and Chinese historically have had the lowest infant mortality rates in the United States. Hawaii, whose population is predominantly Oriental with smaller populations of Caucasians and Polynesians, usually has the lowest infant mortality rates in the nation. Utah, a state with a homogeneous population, many of whom follow strict religious dietary rules, also has a low infant mortality rate. States such as Maine and New Hampshire that have cold climates and also have homogeneous populations have in recent years been experiencing very low infant mortality rates. Wyoming, in 1978, with 9.2 deaths per 1,000 live births, had the lowest infant mortality rate in the country, and Idaho with a 9.6 rate was a close second.

In 1978, three-fourths of all pregnant women in the United States had received prenatal care by the end of the first trimester of their pregnancies whereas, in 1970, a little more than two-thirds did. Only 5 percent of pregnant women in 1978 received prenatal care as late as the last trimester of pregnancy while 1.4 percent received no prenatal care.[36]

Early prenatal care reduces the likelihood of a pregnant woman giving birth to a low birth-weight baby because the major potential health problems of the mother that increase the risk to the baby, for example, diabetes and toxemia, can be detected early and treated. It is possible, however, that women who obtain early prenatal care are a self-selected group with a low risk of having a low birth-weight infant. Also, it is questionable whether women who have given birth before without encountering medical problems are likely to benefit as much from early prenatal care as women who are pregnant for the first time.

There is evidence that early prenatal care can lower infant mortality and morbidity among low income groups. Younger women and women over 35 years are less likely to receive early prenatal care than women 20–34 years of age, but for different reasons. Many unmarried teen-agers try to ignore their pregnancies as long as possible. Older women are more likely to have already given birth and thus are knowledgeable about the personal living habits of diet, exercise, and rest that are necessary to help ensure a healthy baby. Women who have had a child also know what to expect as the pregnancy progresses.

Increasingly, high-risk infants are being saved and infant illnesses reduced by innovations in medical technology. However, even "the right kind of clinical intervention, in high risk situations . . . can probably reduce infant mortality [only] by about one-third. That leaves two-thirds of the cases. Their outcome is related to socio-economic factors, not medical factors."[37]

The maternal mortality rate is the number of maternal deaths divided by the number of live births. The figure is not a true rate because in the population at risk the mother is not included in the denominator. A major statistical limitation is that women may die during or immediately after delivery from causes unrelated to childbirth, yet these deaths may be included in the maternal mortality rate. There are also the usual problems in comparing data across national boundaries. Thus, the statistical data on maternal mortality are limited to a brief paragraph below.

The maternal mortality rate declined 90 percent in the United States between 1936 and 1975. The provisional maternal mortality rate of 7.8 deaths per 100,000 live births in 1979 is less than one-third the 24.5 rate in 1968.[38] The maternal mortality rate in 1977 among non-whites was three times that of whites. The decrease in the rate between World War II and 1963–65 was about the same for whites and non-whites: 88 percent and 82 percent, respectively. However, Asian-Americans living on the Pacific Coast have the lowest maternal mortality rate in the United States. There are considerable geographical differentials that reflect differences in the racial composition of the areas, as well as other factors.

The use of blood and blood substitutes for treatment of hemorrhages, the use of sulfonamides and antibiotics to control infections, and intensified hospital review of the causes of death were among medical developments that contributed to the earlier period of improvements. However, it is the increase in use of prenatal care and even possibly the change in the legal climate toward abortion that primarily account for the remarkable drop during the past few years. The median number of checkups made during pregnancy by white women is 11.2; among non-whites, 9.4. Abortions accounted for only 6.7 percent of all United States maternal mortality in 1975 compared with 23 percent in 1963–65.[39]

OTHER INDICATORS OF NATIONAL LEVELS OF HEALTH

Despite the problems involved in sole reliance on mortality data to compare national levels of health, mortality data are the most comparable measures available and are used. There are no other measures to assess national levels that are used by even a small number of countries. The United States studies continuing statistical trends in morbidity rates (national *Health Interview Survey*) on varying issues. In 1976, a sample of the U.S. civilian, non-institutionalized population was asked to assess their own health status in comparison to that of others of their age. Forty-eight percent considered themselves to be in "excellent" health and 40 percent in "good" health. For those under seventeen years, "self-assessment" indicated that 95 percent believed that they were in "excellent" or "good" health; 91 percent of those 17–44 years, 78 percent of those 45–64 years, and 68 percent of those 65 years and over. Of the total population, only 3 percent believed their health was "poor" while nine percent of those 65 years and over placed themselves in this category.[40] Older persons are understandably less likely than younger persons to perceive themselves to be in excellent or good health. An individual's self-perception of health status is not always accurate. Consistency of responses is notably low, and many illnesses have no overt symptoms, especially in the early stages. Hypertension is such a disease.

The proportion of persons in the same survey who assessed themselves to be in excellent or good health increased with higher family incomes. Seventy-four percent of those with a family income less than $5,000 considered themselves in excellent or good health; 84

percent with an income $5,000–$9,000; 90 percent with an income $10,000–$14,000; and, 93 percent with an income of at least $15,000 (1976 dollars). There is a circular effect involved. Those who are less well usually earn less money and may have poorer nutrition and housing as well as less education—all factors that contribute to illness. Levels of income and education are closely correlated. Studies indicate that the higher the education level of the mother, the healthier the family.

The time lost from work because of illness is another measure of the level of health. Data on hours worked are more accurate than days worked because many persons, such as professionals, who are not paid an hourly rate, are likely to come in late and/or leave early when ill rather than miss a whole day of work. In May 1978, "managers and administrators, except farm" had an average of 1.4 percent of total work time lost because of illness and injury. This was the lowest absentee rate due to illness among all occupations. The average was 2.3 in the United States.[41]

The relationship between absence from work and severity and type of illness obviously differs among different persons, depending on the individual worker's circumstances. Size of earnings, how well a person likes the paid work, whether sick leave is paid or unpaid, whether the worker has high opportunity costs of unpaid time, how the homemaker values her share of household labor, how pleasant remaining at home might be, and other independent variables affect the decision of whether or not to work. In cases of asymptomatic disease such as hypertension, there is some evidence that merely labelling a person ill will decrease his or her work hours.[42] There are few, if any, studies that use regression analysis or similar quantitative techniques to explore to what degree variables in addition to health status influence working hours of individuals.

If there has been a decline in the "work ethic" in the United States, then sickness may be used as an excuse for absence from work when no sickness exists. However, data from the Bureau of Labor Statistics (BLS) for full-time, non-farm wage and salary workers show no increase from 1973 through 1978 in the percentage of scheduled weekly hours lost for any reason. Total time as a percentage of scheduled work hours was 3.5 percent in 1973 and in 1978; and, for those weekly hours lost because of illness and injury, 2.5 percent in 1973 and 2.3 percent in 1978.

Because there is no national sickness benefits program in the United States, it is reasonable to expect that a stronger work ethic exists in the United States than in other countries that do have such a program. In 1972 and 1973, "in West Germany, 11 percent of scheduled work-time was lost; in Holland, 10 percent; and in Italy, 15 percent, as compared with 3.5 percent in the United States. Nonetheless, paid sick leave accounted for about 1 percent of total compensation paid by U.S. employers in 1976, a cost equivalent to six cents for every hour paid."[43]

THE LEADING CAUSES OF DEATH IN THE UNITED STATES

The four leading causes of death in the United States today are heart disease, cancer, stroke, and accidents, together accounting for four out of five deaths each year.

Heart Disease and Strokes

Heart disease accounted for about two of five deaths in 1980. Women, until menopause, have about one-third the rate of heart disease of men; thereafter, the female rate increases and approaches the male rate by age 70, equalling it by age 85. The 1979 Surgeon General's *Report on Health Promotion and Disease* stresses that

> Heart disease not only produces fatal heart attacks; it is also the greatest cause of permanent disability claims among workers under 65, and responsible for more days of hospitalization than any other single disorder. And it is the principal cause of limited activity for some 2.5 million Americans under age 65.[44]

Thus, although a "cure" for heart disease in its various forms may not always extend days of life, it may greatly improve quality of life.

The age-adjusted death rate due to stroke declined between 1968 and 1978, as did that for all types of heart disease. The rate for strokes declined by 38 percent and the rate for heart disease, 23 percent. Improvement in rehabilitation of stroke victims has greatly increased their quality of life.

There are many risk factors that are commonly associated with both heart disease and stroke, but agreement on the degree of their importance does not exist. A measure of incipient problems is "high blood pressure," or hypertension, often defined as systolic pressure exceeding 160 when the heart contracts and diastolic pressure of 95 when the heart relaxes, or a reading of 160/95. Some define mild hypertension as readings higher than 140/90 and believe that treatment of mild hypertension is warranted. Individuals usually have different levels of blood pressure in a single day. However, the Framingham, Massachusetts, study in the 1970s found that men aged 45–64 with mild hypertension had two to three times the coronary heart disease rate of those with systolic pressures under 140 during that period.[45]

Among the predisposing factors in heart disease is smoking. Although there are few who dispute that smoking is deleterious to one's health, it is difficult to measure the precise cause and effect relationship because other factors that simultaneously affect risk to heart disease are occurring. The relative amounts of low density and high density lipoproteins are confounding variables in determining whether or not the single measure of a high cholesterol level is an important factor in the development of cardiovascular disease. Low density lipoproteins (LDL) have been found to accelerate atherosclerosis (cholesterol deposition in artery walls) while high density lipoproteins (HDL) retard it.

It is similarly difficult to assess the impact of changes in national diet and life-style. An accelerated decline in mortality due to coronary heart disease has been simultaneous with a change in consumption of tobacco, high cholesterol foods, and increased exercise.

Although the consumption of saturated fats, especially eggs and homogenized milk, has decreased in recent years while the consumption of polyunsaturated fats has increased, overall meat consumption and the total fat intake have increased. A 1978 national conference on the reasons for the decline in deaths from heart disease was held in Washington, DC by the National Institutes of Health. The summary of the proceedings states:

> The net effect on blood cholesterol levels cannot be determined accurately but it appears that there may have been an overall reduction in blood cholesterol levels of up to 5 percent. This change is consistent with the overall effect of the observed dietary changes. Depending on the assumptions that are made, such a change could translate into about a 5 percent or greater decrease in coronary heart disease deaths in middle-aged men.[46]

Since publication of the proceedings of a conference held in the Fall of 1978, the National Academy of Sciences has issued a report that maintains that there is no proof that high cholesterol counts *per se* increase the risk of heart attacks. Moreover, evidence is beginning to accumulate that indicates low cholesterol counts less than 190 milligrams per 100 milliliters of serum are associated with cancer among males. Because diet does not lower cholesterol concentration by more than 15 percent, those with high cholesterol (250 mg or more) may benefit through diet by lowering their risk to heart disease without increasing their risk to cancer.

The incidence of heart disease and strokes is also affected by the co-existence of other diseases. Diabetics are more prone to athero-sclerotic disease, hypertension, and obesity than non-diabetics and are twice as likely to suffer a heart attack and twice as likely to suffer a stroke than non-diabetics.[47] It is not clear whether risk factors such as lack of exercise and excessive stress independently increase the danger of heart disease or stroke, or merely are associated with other major risk factors. For example, lack of exercise is associated with excess weight, elevated blood cholesterol and sugar, and high blood pressure—all of which independently increase the likelihood of car-diovascular disease. Similarly, although it is believed that a genetic predisposition to heart disease or strokes exists, this is difficult to prove because families frequently have common habits as well as genetic make-ups.

The reasons for the striking 20 percent decline in deaths due to cardiovascular disease (heart disease and strokes) in the United States since 1968 continue to be debated. Undoubtedly many developments in the areas of medical care such as specialized coronary care units, new drugs, and preventive health behavior have played a role. Fre-quently cited are a per capita reduction in smoking and the nicotine content of marketed cigarettes. The proportion of heavy smokers (those who smoke at least two packs a day), however, has remained the same.[48]

The effectiveness of many of the numerous new forms of medical intervention in the treatment of heart attacks and stroke remains con-troversial. The effectiveness of coronary bypass operations to prolong life is not universally agreed upon although there is agreement that decreasing the pain of angina improves the quality of life. A newly developed brain artery bypass operation is a controversial method of preventing stroke. New drugs especially have proven effective in treating hypertension and lowering the risk to heart attack. The beta blockers aid some victims of cardiovascular disease, and CAT (com-puterized axial tomography) and PETT (positron emission transverse tomography) scanners and ultrasonic arteriography have improved diagnoses.[49]

Although fatal heart attacks have declined, there is no definitive, long-run data on the incidence of non-fatal heart attacks. If these also have declined, it would indicate that the individual's way of life, through prevention, plays a more important role in decreasing mortality from cardiovascular disease than the increased promptness of good medical treatment after a heart attack has occurred. If non-fatal heart attacks have increased, the role of quicker and better medical care would be the more important health factor than education and prevention in explaining the recent decline in mortality due to heart attack.[50]

Regular exercise that increases cardiovascular fitness such as swimming, bicycling, jogging, and walking is claimed by many to reduce risk to heart attack. However, it is probable that less than 50 percent of adults exercise regularly. A 1979 survey found that only 36 percent of those who interviewed exercised regularly. There is a recent trend among healthy retirees, often in their early sixties, to exercise more because they have the time and they enjoy it. Among younger people, jogging, skiing, tennis, swimming, and bicycling is also increasing. Walking, which is more of a European pastime, is being promoted by health educators as a preventive measure that may also contribute to lower mortality rates for cardiovascular disease.

The role of drugs in the improved treatment of hypertension to decrease mortality from hypertensive heart disease and stroke is difficult to assess. Because the decline in mortality has been greatest among women, especially black women, and because this is the group which is thought to have benefited most from the improved treatment, it is tempting to claim a cause and effect relationship. The proceedings of the 1978 conference on heart disease, however, emphasizes that "mortality from hypertensive heart disease and stroke began to decline some years before effective medical therapy for hypertension was available and during a time when coronary heart disease mortality was increasing."[51] But, two-thirds of the thirty-year decline of all cardiovascular mortality has been in the last ten years, the period of the 1970s. New drugs and surgical procedures may have been more effective in increasing the quality of life of heart disease patients than increasing their longevity. A Kaiser-Permanente study of mortality from heart disease in Northern California (1971–77) suggests

> that most of the downward trend in national mortality rates in the past seven years [1971–77] is due to decreasing occurrence of clinical CHD [coronary heart disease] rather than more effective hospital treatment. The latter may certainly be a factor, however, as may an improvement in outpatient care. . . . [It] cannot be attributed to coronary bypass surgery.[52]

Part of the decline in deaths from cardiovascular disease stems from the use of the new drugs. Alprenolol, that has been proven in Sweden to reduce mortality in patients who survive a heart attack, has not been approved (as of this writing) in the United States.[53] Other drugs useful in the treatment of heart disease are available only abroad, but approval to market some is anticipated.

Coronary bypass surgery, by reducing pain, improves the quality of life of many persons with heart disease who are thus able to lead more active lives than without the surgery. However, drugs have provided the most effective treatment resulting in greater life expectancy. "Since 1963 most new antihypertensive drugs have been marketed first outside the United States."[54] There have been long delays in approving the new beta blockers, a class of drugs that block the action of adrenaline-like compounds in body tissues. All effective drugs have risks. Those who are seriously ill should be informed about the known probability of risks and benefits and be involved in making the decision whether they will or will not have surgery but also whether they will or will not take a powerful drug. Exceptions to such a general rule are desired by most physicians to permit them not to inform mentally ill patients, but exceptions are also desired by many physicians who express concern over creating undue anxiety among their patients. It may be that patients are, however, more willing to undergo such anxiety in order to have more control over their own actions. Research is needed to assess how best to inform patients when the data about risks and benefits of medical intervention are known.

The Food and Drug Administration (FDA) has a negative mandate: to protect the public from harm. A positive mandate, to protect the public's health, would force greater recognition of favorable experiences with new drugs abroad. No drug to the author's knowledge has been approved by the FDA solely on the basis of foreign, controlled, clinical trials and experience.

There is a loss of benefits to ill persons who do not have access to all proven effective drugs that have relatively low risk. High risks may become comparatively low risks when an ill person faces, without access to the new drug, a high probability of death or great disability.

Cardiovascular disease develops over a long period of time, may be asymptomatic even when diagnosed, and is not susceptible to immediate improvement. Only about 50 percent of diagnosed mild hypertensives continue to take the appropriate drugs, which may have side effects more noticeable than the symptoms of the disease.

Merely labelling a person as ill with hypertension may decrease the number of hours that he or she works.[55]

Although mortality from all cardiovascular disease has been declining in the United States, the world-wide experience has shown an unchanged or increasing death rate from coronary heart disease except for "Australia, Belgium, Canada, and perhaps for England, Finland, Israel, and Japan."[56]

Cancer

In the United States, cancer accounts for about one-fifth of all deaths and it is the second leading cause of death. In 1968, the age-adjusted death rate from cancer was 129.2 per 100,000 population; in 1978, it was 133.8 per 100,000. Mortality from all cancers except lung cancer has declined slightly, between 0.4 to 0.6 percent annually since 1950. The decline has occurred despite the many popular media articles that attribute increasing pollution of the environment for much of the existing cancer. The etiology of cancer is still being researched. Some believe that concomitant risk factors interact to create population subsets that have greater risks to some forms of cancer. If only one risk factor is present, the exposed population may have very low risk. For example, recent studies indicate that women who take estrogen and smoke cigarettes have increased risk to stroke while women who do consume estrogen but do not smoke do not increase their risk. Most cancers have a long gestation period (20–30 years) but some are prevalent among children, e.g., leukemia. In fact, cancer is the second leading cause of death among children aged 1–14 years. Although precipitating causes for some kinds of cancer are known, the roles of such factors as heredity, diet, tension, environmental carcinogens, and emotional distress in predisposing individuals to the disease are unknown. It is likely that most cases of cancer are caused by a combination of factors.

The age-adjusted death rate of lung cancer is increasing. The 1979 Surgeon General's report estimates that cigarette smoking was the major cause of 80 percent of the deaths from lung cancer in 1977.[57] That report states that smoking cigarettes increases not only the risk of lung cancer (ten-fold) but also cancer of the oral cavity (three- to five-fold), cancer of the larynx (three-fold), and cancer of the urinary bladder (two-fold). Some smokers compensate for a lower level of nicotine per cigarette marketed in 1980 either by inhaling more or smoking more cigarettes. It is not known whether smoking the filtered or low tar and nicotine cigarettes reduces the risk of cancer.[58]

The presence of other risk factors in addition to cigarette smoking can increase the risk of cancer many-fold. For example, when cigarette smoking at a given level is combined with daily exposure to asbestos, the risk of lung cancer is increased ninety times.

Workers in certain occupations have a higher risk of cancer than the population at large. Space limitations prohibit an in-depth discussion of this important topic. Some claim that specific chemicals in the environment are the major causes of cancer. If this premise is accepted, and it is not accepted by all scientists, can prevention best be attained through regulation of industry and the toxic substances in the environment or through individuals practicing restraint in their personal habits of smoking and protecting themselves against air pollutants by wearing gauze masks? It is a combination of prudent regulation and individual self-protection that would probably result in the greatest net benefit in the prevention of cancer.

Most age-adjusted cancer death rates by type of cancer show very little change (except for the rise in lung cancer) from 1950 to 1977. However, some have decreased; for example, among women, cancers of the bladder, colon, liver, and stomach. As is true of cardiovascular disease, it is difficult to determine whether heredity or shared environmental or behavioral characteristics are responsible for the unusually high incidence within a particular family of some forms of cancer.

The modern American diet includes an increasingly large proportion of processed food that contain preservatives, flavor and color enhancers, and spoilage retardants. While some of these additives may help prevent cancer by inhibiting the natural carcinogen mold, aflatoxin found in peanuts and corn, others may promote cancer. Among the risk factors believed to increase the risk to cancer are high-level alcohol consumption, radiation, excessive exposure to sunlight, frequent high altitude air travel, water and air pollutants, and predisposing genetic conditions.

Patterns of cancer incidence vary by sex, race, and geographical area. Cancer of the lung, intestines, bladder, and stomach are more prevalent among men in the United States than among women. The age-adjusted death rate from cancer was 21 percent higher for nonwhites than whites in 1975.[59] Incidence and death rates vary by type of cancer. The American Cancer Society states that "most of the differences in black and white cancer rates were (1937–1973) attributed to environmental and social factors rather than to inherent biological characteristics."[60]

Cancer mortality rates for 1974 among selected industrialized countries of Western Europe, Canada, Australia, Israel, Japan, and Mexico are available from the World Health Organization and have been publicized by the United States. In four of the countries (Mexico, Sweden, Israel, and Japan), the death rate for males was lower than in the United States, and in five countries (Mexico, Japan, Australia, France, and Italy) the rate for females was lower.[61] These differences may be the result of differences in diet or environment. For example, the rates of breast and colon/rectum cancers are lower in Japan, where consumption of beef and fat is lower and consumption of salt and pickled foods is higher than in the United States. On the other hand, the rate of stomach cancer—possibly reflecting a higher consumption of smoked fish—is greater in Japan. Because Japanese immigrants to the United States tend to have higher rates of breast and colon/rectum cancer and lower rates of stomach cancer than people in Japan, it seems that these differences are not entirely genetic.

Other explanations may account for international variations in cancer death rates. One country's relatively high mortality rate may result more from a severe incidence of the disease and another's from inferior medical care once the disease is diagnosed. An older population *per se* would be expected to suffer a greater rate of cancer because it takes many years for most cancers to develop and thus its incidence increases with age.

Accidents and Violence

Accidents and violence account for one in ten deaths in the United States. Automobile accidents have already been discussed under emergency medical care markets in Chapter V and they account for almost one-half of all accidental deaths. Teen-agers who combine alcohol and drugs with driving are especially at risk.

Because deaths from accidents and violence occur most frequently among the young, they cause a greater loss of potential years of life than do deaths from disease. As in the case of death rates from accidents, death rates from homicide and suicide are affected primarily by factors other than the availability and quality of medical care. Because these deaths are also included in national mortality rates, the use of the latter data is weakened as indicators of a country's quantity and quality of medical care.

Accidents are the leading cause of death among children one to four years. Nearly one-half of such deaths occur as a result of an automobile accident. Deaths from fire, drowning, and poisoning are other major categories. The latter have declined with use of child-proof caps on drug containers and some household cleaners. In many cases of accidents, death does not occur but the person's quality of life is sharply lowered.

In the United States, suicide and homicide together account for about the same number of deaths as accidents other than motor vehicle accidents. Men are much more likely than women and non-whites much more likely than whites to die a violent death. There are significantly fewer murders of older persons than younger persons. Suicide rates are higher for whites than for other races and are approximately the same for all age groups. Suicide ranked ninth as a cause of death in the United States in 1978 and homicide ranked twelfth. Both the suicide and homicide rates began a general upward trend in the early 1960s.

NUTRITION AND HEALTH

In the United States, over-eating and quality of the diet are greater problems of nutrition than too low a level of caloric intake. This is not to say that there may be a very small percentage of the total population who, for reasons other than dieting or ill health that inhibit eating, do not have a large enough caloric intake for normal activity. Even among the very poor, however, it is improbable that this is likely. It is more likely that the very poor cannot afford (and may not be aware of the need for) consumption of the more expensive, high protein foods. Even the eleven-billion-dollar food stamp program of the 1980s could not correct faulty diet habits such as eating too many sweets and using too much salt.

Americans have become increasingly aware that they may over-eat. Over the past 80 years, "the mean body weight of the total U.S. population has steadily increased. For people 20–74 years of age, 14 percent of men and 24 percent of women are significantly over-weight, that is, they are more than 120 percent of desirable weight for their height and sex."[62] The roles of nutrition and vitamins in the prevention and treatment of disease are still not fully understood.

The already developed and still developing countries have different food consumption patterns. Different cultures and religious taboos also affect diet patterns. Generally, as countries become wealthier, their consumption of animal products increases. In the United States, the average person consumes more than 2,000 pounds of grains per year but only 150 pounds are eaten directly while the rest, more than 90 percent of the total, is fed to animals.[63] Raising animals for consumption is an inefficient use of grain because it takes roughly five pounds of grain to produce one pound of meat. The world food shortage could be greatly decreased if persons in the industrialized countries ate less meat.

There is a growing gap between per capita food production in the developed and the developing countries. Globally, most of the 500 to 800 million malnourished people are living in the developing countries of Latin America, Africa, and Asia.

Malnutrition increases susceptibility to common childhood illnesses because it depletes nutritional reserves and the result too often is a downward spiral ending with death. The infant mortality rate in Zambia and Bolivia is about 250 per 1,000 live births, 140 in India and Pakistan, and 95 in Brazil.[64] Few industrialized countries have an infant mortality rate in excess of 20. In a study of thirteen cities and five rural South American areas, malnutrition was found to be an associated cause of death in 30 to 60 percent of all deaths of children under five years of age.[65]

In the United States, malnutrition as a cause of children's death has been virtually eliminated. The school lunch program was started in 1946. In 1980, 27 million elementary and secondary school students shared in that federal $3.4 billion federal subsidy. That the family of four upper income limits in 1980 were over $15,630 annually indicates that this program has not evolved to be directed solely towards the poor. Among other federal food programs are the Child Nutrition Program, the Special Milk Program, and the Womens, Infants, and Children (WIC) Program. These total about $2.5 billion annually. They are specially targeted to low income mothers and children. Cash monthly benefits to the poor began in 1974 under the Supplemental Social Security Income (SSI) program. The food stamp program was not established on a nationwide basis until 1964 at an annual cost of $31 million. Not until after 1970 were the costs over one billion and by 1980, ten billion dollars.

The greater malnutrition of children of low income parents results in part from the ignorance of the poorly educated mother as well as from the lack of income. Thus, education about good nutrition is important. Although nutrient deficiencies are rarely so severe in the United States that they cause death, they can increase the number of stillbirths and births of children with birth defects, stunt growth, impede learning, and increase susceptibility to illness.

In the United States, breast-feeding has been gaining in popularity in the 1970s because the nutritional superiority of mother's milk over substitutes is becoming increasingly clear. Between 1973 and 1975, the proportion of babies who were breast-fed for two months or more increased from 24.7 percent to 34.5 percent. Infants of mothers with more than a high school education are more than twice as likely to be breast-fed than infants of mothers with a high school education or less.[66]

The effect of the Reagan Administration's 1981 cuts on subsidizing food for the poor is expected to be slight because of the already mentioned relatively high income level of the cut-offs. Under the Carter budget, the federal government would have been spending, in fiscal year 1982, $12.2 billion annually on food stamps. In February 1981, the Reagan Administration proposed to limit the eligibility for food stamps to only lower income persons, for example, to families of four with less than $11,000 annual income.[67] This and other reforms are expected to reduce expenditures as inflation progresses in fiscal year 1982 by over $2 billion annually.[68]

In March 1981, milk supports were not increased as scheduled by the Carter Administration and thus the price of milk, a staple food, was not increased. The over-all outcome of federal expenditure cutbacks in food subsidies is not clear. State and local governments can assess area needs for school lunch programs more easily than the federal government. The latter can finance more easily basic research about the relationship between nutrition and disease.

The impact of diet on health in industrialized nations is more through the quality than the quantity of intake. It is not the greater sum spent above a certain level, but the knowledgeable spending for nutritious food that makes individuals less susceptible to disease and premature death.

There is ample room to reduce the major causes of death and disease in the United States, the societal costs of which are enormous both in terms of loss of real goods and services that might have been produced by the well and alive as well as in terms of the costs of individual suffering. Attempts to quantify these losses are now being made, but the measures are relatively crude. However, the tentative results indicate that prevention of one-fifth of the preventable (with today's technology) diseases and premature deaths would yield greater gain than an increased use of scarce resources for curing already existing disease. Estimates do not always take into account that, even when premature lives are saved, there are some who will die from other, non-preventable causes. However, as the percentage of aged in the population increases from 11 percent to 19 percent of the population in 2050 or earlier, the total costs of each further gain in life expectancy of the aged will be substantial. Only a reduction in deaths from accidents and violence, not from heart disease and cancer, will increase the labor force substantially and permit those who are saved from early death to live free of disability and the need for large quantities of medical care. Increasing life expectancy at older ages will place a greater burden on working younger persons in our society. The allocation of resources to yield the greatest improvement in the nation's health is discussed in Chapter IX.

The greatest gains in improving the health of Americans will be a result of changes in life-style rather than a result of increasingly large expenditures on medical care. The Greek axiom "nothing to excess" and the old-fashioned precepts—eating moderately, eating regularly, eating breakfast, smoking no cigarettes, drinking alcohol moderately, exercising at least moderately, sleeping seven to eight hours per night, and having friends—are increasingly being proven as very important for maintenance of good health.

REASONS FOR THE DECLINE IN U.S. MORTALITY RATE

Major gains in life expectancy in the United States in the early 1900s, as in the developing countries today, were from improved public sanitation. In the 1940s, major gains came from the development of antibiotics and vaccines. Thus, during the first half of this century, infectious and parasitic diseases were dramatically decreased, especially at younger ages.

Since 1950, the major causes of death—heart disease, cancer, stroke, and accidents—have been less successfully fought. However, heart disease mortality has been declining fairly steadily, although more so for women than for men. Future gains in life expectancy probably will depend more on factors other than medical care.

Gains in life expectancy at birth today would be small even if significant reductions were achieved in mortality from the three leading causes of death: cardiovascular disease, malignant neoplasms (cancer), and motor vehicle accidents. A 1978 article clarifies that "the number of years gained by a new-born child with a 30 percent reduction in major cardiovascular diseases would be 1.98 years, for malignant neoplasms, 0.71 years, and for motor vehicle accidents,

0.21 years. Application of the same reduction to the working ages (15 to 70 years) results in a gain of 0.43, 0.26, and 0.14 years, respectively, for the three leading causes of death."[69]

A Canadian government report[70] proposes that all causes of death and disease have four contributing elements: inadequacies in the organization of the health care system, life-styles, environmental hazards, and biological or genetic inheritance. Analysis of the twenty leading causes of death in the United States in 1976 under these categories suggests that half of the U.S. mortality in that year was due to a life-style harmful to health, 20 percent to environmental factors, 20 percent to human biological factors, and only 10 percent to inadequacies in the health care system.[71] More resources spent on consumer education might well improve levels of health more than resources spent on medical care.

The chief health hazards today, unlike a century ago, are degenerative diseases, not infectious diseases. The most effective defense against many of these degenerative diseases is a healthy life-style, e.g., nutritious diet, regular exercise, proper sleep, and no smoking rather than an improved health care system. The 1979 Surgeon General's report sums up the case for spending more dollars on prevention:

> Prevention is an idea whose idea has come. We have the scientific knowledge to begin to formulate recommendations for improved health. And, although the degenerative diseases differ from their infectious disease predecessors in having more—and more complex—causes, it is now clear that many are preventable. . . .
>
> Currently only four percent of the Federal health dollar is specifically identified for prevention related activities. Yet, it is clear that improvements in the health status of our citizens will not be made predominantly through the treatment of disease but rather through its prevention.[72]

The national health policy should promote more consumer health education but also greater support of basic research in the biological, chemical, and applied medical sciences, as well as the development of improved methods to communicate knowledge to the consumer. A recent article in *Business Week* comments: "Most doctors agree that a greater emphasis on preventive medicine would be an important first step toward decreasing the need for expensive treatment."[73] Many economists are becoming increasingly concerned about how the monetary costs of caring for an increasingly aging population will be met.

IX. ALLOCATION OF
MEDICAL CARE

Individuals with the same or similar states of health make different value judgments about their health care needs. Only in emergency situations can medical "need" come close to being unambiguously defined. Individuals subjectively define their medical needs in a manner that has little to do with any empirical standard that the word "need" usually implies. Medical need, as perceived by individuals, is really discretionary and would not always create effective demand if people were expected to pay the costs out-of-pocket.

The net prices consumers pay for physician care and hospital services are far less than the true resource costs. However, the prices paid by third parties may be higher or lower than the real resource costs. Consumers tend to assess their medical needs without considering the full price of medical care and they seek more medical care than if they had to pay the full price. Self-perceived medical needs act to demand more medical care than individuals are personally willing to finance. When the total of self-perceived "needs" overwhelms medical resources, prices rise above the resources costs and an artificial shortage arises. Because the resource prices do not apply, they cannot clear the market. Constraints, medical customary practice, waiting, and government rules evolve to allocate medical care effectively.

Several studies have been made that attempt to analyze why, among persons with apparently similar levels of health, some seek medical care while others self-treat almost exclusively. Although the out-of-pocket prices influence the decisions to seek medical care, the British data, covering a country with no out-of-pocket prices for physician visits, exhibit greater amounts of self-reported sickness in the households of partially skilled and unskilled workers compared with clerical, managerial, and professional workers' families. Yet there are no prices and no income barriers. The explanation given in a 1980 government report is in part the poor nutritional and smoking habits of low earners, in part the demands of their jobs. But it was also contended that the "subjective experience of ill-health is framed by customary expectations and by the degree of inconvenience and cost attached to occupancy of the sick role."[1]

Price in the United States has little to do with most of the delays to seek medical care for acute symptoms. In a 1973–74 survey of persons who reported acute symptoms, 53 percent obtained medical care.[2] Two-thirds of those receiving medical care had delayed four hours or more in consulting by telephone or in person with a physician. Of these, only 4.2 percent stated that "money or transportation problems" were a factor. Thirty-eight percent of those who did not seek medical care thought that their symptoms were not serious enough to warrant medical attention. In a similar vein, 22 percent believed that self-care was sufficient, 26 percent said that they had problems in getting an appointment, and 15 percent mentioned time and weather constraints.[3] Unfortunately, it is impossible to tell from the data whether the severity of the medically treated symptoms were greater than the non-treated. It is also indeterminate whether those persons who delayed four hours or more in seeking medical attention actually had more or less severe symptoms than those who did not delay or never sought care. Once again, the discretionary nature of medical "need" makes it impossible to assume that those whose acute symptoms persisted were the only persons to delay, and then finally seek, medical care.

Patients' and physicians' perceptions of medical need do not always agree, nor do physicians always agree among themselves. A U.S. government publication comments that "in general, the community physicians tended to recommend that a larger proportion of patients contact a physician for a given symptom than did the academic panel. However, agreement was close (within 5 percentage points) across most age categories for several of the more severe symptoms including bleeding, shortness of breath, aching joints, pain or swelling in joints, pains in gut, and sudden weakness. The somewhat milder symptoms of coughing and sneezing showed very large differences consistently across all age groups."[4] Each physician is expected to follow the ethical precept to act solely in the patient's interest. However, when the demands on the physician's time create a need to ration his time, the physician resolves conflicts by making a clinical judgment as to whose need for medical service is the greater and/or cuts the amount of time for each visit. When overwhelmed by demand, physicians refuse to take new patients. To require physicians to allocate medical care in accordance with bureaucratic rules, whether of a private group practice or a government program, may contradict their ethics. Cost containment may be antithetical to best medical practice.

Should prices allocate medical care in the United States just as they allocate other goods and services, for example food, housing, clothing, and transportation? Many people believe that basic medical care is a "right" and should be available to all who "need" it regardless of their ability to pay. However, as we have seen, there is no precise way to objectify and standardize medical need. Many Americans abhor the idea that medical resources should be distributed according to "ability to pay" if income levels differ and individual incomes are the sole source of payment. This accounts for early growth of employer health insurance plans. Because the government programs have eliminated the effect of different incomes on access to care, "price" is acceptable but it is not, under widespread third party payments, an economic price that can "clear the market" or allocate goods and services to maximize total welfare. Prior to Medicaid and Medicare, the price mechanism was not generally acceptable as the primary means of allocation in the United States. But if it is impossible to allocate medical care according to "need," repugnant according only to price, and non-workable with third party payments to use price, how is medical care being allocated or should it be allocated?

Allocation becomes an issue only when a resource is scarce relative to demand. Because third parties other than the consumer are paying an increasing share of the personal health care bills, the demand is surpassing the resources used for medical care. The ensuing price rise does not reduce demand because the consumer does not directly pay the bills. Thus, many scarce resources such as skilled labor and building materials are used for provision of medical services that might be used for a multiplicity of other purposes that consumers might prefer. If existing medical personnel and equipment are fully employed, an individual can attain more medical care only if another receives less care. One person's situation is improved, but at the expense of another.

The allocation of medical care has become a political dilemma in most industrialized countries. Who determines and what criteria are used to decide who receives how much medical care and at what level of quality? Traditional market prices for medical care services do not exist in countries that have government provision or financing of health care. In the United States, federal regulations at the societal level have partly replaced the price mechanism as an allocating device. Regulations are increasingly affecting the availability of new drugs and medical devices. Customary medical practice, and waiting also play an important part in the allocation of medical resources at the individual level. In Great Britain, explicit government decisions to limit its resources for medical care under conditions of no market price have made more important than in the United States the devices used for allocation: government specific regulations, waiting in its various forms, and evolving customary medical practice. Great Britain spends less than 6 percent of its GNP on medical care.

The words "medical care" do not generally include dental care or drugs, prescription and over-the-counter. In these health areas, price is still the dominant allocative device. Private health insurance in the United States covered just 22 percent of dental care expense and only about 8 percent of out-of-hospital, prescribed drugs in 1977.[5] While in some states Medicaid pays for these items, in others it does not. Medicare also does not cover dental care and out-of-hospital prescription drugs. Expenditures for "drugs and drug sundries" and dental services are a declining share of the health care dollar, dropping from 13.6 percent and 7.4 percent, respectively, in 1960 to 8.0 percent and 6.4 percent in 1979.[6] Hospitals, however, increased their share of the health care dollar from 34 percent to 40 percent in 1979 while the share to physicians lost ground slightly, from 21 percent to 19 percent. Because third party payments for dental care are increasing and because there is evidence that consumption of dental care increases as real income rises, an increase in the percent of the health care dollar spent on dentistry can be expected.

To the degree that the Food and Drug Administration (FDA) limits the marketing of new, effective drugs available abroad, government limits accessibility to these drugs to the knowledgeable and those who can afford to purchase abroad. This can be viewed as a form of allocation.

Under a market price system, firms that have enough sales at high enough prices receive revenues that exceed costs and, therefore, remain in business. Those firms whose products do not fulfill these requirements fail. Under cost-reimbursement, as in large parts of the defense and medical industries, firms do not fail when their costs rise substantially because the purchasers will pay the higher prices as contracted. However, over time the number of buyers will decrease as reimbursed costs continually rise. In the medical care sector where the costs are reimbursed by other than consumers, higher costs do not act to discourage continuing purchase. This is unlike the situation in the defense industry.

Demand by consumers can expand in the medical care sector, costs rise rapidly, and the firms whose costs are reimbursed still make profits. An example of this in practice is implied by the competitive bidding of Humana, Inc., in mid-April 1981 for Brookwood Health Services, Inc., against American Medical. All three firms operate hospitals and apparently all three make attractive gains on their equity.[7]

In the medical care sector, cost-reimbursement is the dominant means of payment via the government programs of Medicare and Medicaid, private commercial insurers, and Blue Cross/Blue Shield. It is true that Medicaid and Medicare, and even private health insurance, reimburse at less than 100 percent of the submitted "costs." Under Medicare and private insurance, a patient is responsible for any billed amount that is not reimbursed. Prior to 1966, some bills that are now only partially cost-reimbursed under Medicaid were not paid at all. Hospitals, in most instances, do not bill the actual costs of the goods and services consumed by the patient who requests that the third party pay. It is a common practice for hospitals to use what the economist calls "cross-subsidies." A hospital's billed costs are often not the patient's actual costs. After federal audits, Medicare at times demands return of over-payments made to some hospitals on behalf of their Medicare patients. For example, Stanford University Medical Center returned $1.5 million for over-billing during 1975–77, or about 2.6 percent of total Medicare payments to that hospital for patient care in that period.[8] Hospitals favor different classes of customers. The less seriously ill often pay for part of the costs of the more seriously ill. Hospitals increase their prices to the private consumer to cover the unmet costs of Medicare and Medicaid patients. Thus, some patients cross-subsidize other patients. As long as cost-reimbursement by third parties dominates, consumers have little incentive to protest the high costs of care, and in many instances do not even check their bills.

Because consumers are not fully knowledgeable about the price, quality, and various substitutes for medical care, the market price system alone—even without third party payments—cannot efficiently allocate medical care, although price may allocate as well as it does in some other markets. Perfectly competitive markets postulate complete consumer knowledge of the available selection of goods and services, their prices, and quality. Perfectly competitive markets are not common, and it is illusory to judge any actual market against this theoretical "nirvana" concept.

Quality of services—and medical care is a service—is especially difficult for purchasers to judge because there is no tangible commodity, such as a wool coat, that can be visually examined. However, consumers today are not as ignorant about medical care as consumers 50 years ago. When consumers know little about a service or product which they intend to purchase, they seek advice from persons who do have knowledge of those services or products. Many persons who intend to purchase a home computer or stereo system will first obtain information from their knowledgeable friends. In hiring an architect or a lawyer or a physician, individuals act in similar fashion. In all these instances, many individuals will not have access to knowledgeable persons. Printed informational sources may be substituted. After a primary care physician is selected, he or she may act as an informed adviser to their patients about different types of specialized medical care.

It is often difficult for the mobile person to obtain information about primary care physicians in a new geographical area. It is logical for a person who is contemplating a move to ask his current physician about physicians in the area to which he or she is moving. However, this does not always result in a definite recommendation. County medical societies give, without relevant information, only the names of three physicians. Printed directories of physicians are good sources for an informed choice. Some consumers prefer to select a multi-specialty group practice rather than one physician because they thus avoid future choices that may have to be made in a period of stress about what specialist to see. These consumers rely completely on physician-initiated referrals and that the specialist is a member of a familiar group practice reinforces the referral choice.

It may be easier for consumers to make an informed choice from an array of health insurance plans than from the large number of physicians in an area which is new to them. Choosing a third party payer involves many multi-dimensional aspects of costs and benefits but these are of a nature more readily assessed than the relative quality of many physicians. Employers can supply all the necessary information for a choice among insurers. Employers do not rate physicians. Large companies offering an HMO alternative may have several staff members whose primary responsibility is to select and monitor the various HMOs that they offer employees across the country. However, they do not, probably for legal reasons as well as the time costs involved, attempt to assess the quality of the providers.

Although it is well proven among economists that specialization usually results in higher quality, consumers do not usually think of this aspect when they are having an operation. Yet it is clear from the medical literature that hospital surgical teams that perform a difficult operation several times a month have far better mortality outcomes than do those who perform that operation rarely.

Many consumers do not realize that when they choose a physician they are also choosing a hospital. It is exceedingly idealistic to expect consumers to make informed choices among physicians and hospitals in the face of a considerable lack of information and the uncertainty about the outcomes from medical intervention. Companies can, and do, supply some of the needed information about insurers. If the vertical integration of suppliers and insurers increases, as under IPAs and other HMOs, it might become easier to make more meaningful comparisons among various financial arrangements. With or without such integration, consumer ignorance can be overcome. Health insurance commissioners in various states can make a determined effort to provide the information. During the 1970s, Herbert S. Denenberg,[9] insurance commissioner of Pennsylvania, issued several guides to health insurance plans, dental and surgical care, and even rated the hospitals in that state. Rating physicians would be a more difficult task, but it is possible to provide information about physicians that is useful to consumers but which does not actually entail rating. For example, the *Directory of Specialists*, which is in most large public libraries, lists for each physician: the year(s) and name(s) of the undergraduate and medical colleges from which he/she graduated, and the year(s) and name(s) of the hospitals of his or her internship and residency. It also indicates when physicians passed their specialty boards and gives their employment as of date of publication. This information is readily available, yet most consumers do not know it exists. This is despite newspaper coverage by the *New York Times* and other papers in recent years about the availability of medical directories with an explanation of their medical abbreviations and codes.

The *Washington Post* carried a story on "Cutting Prices: A Guide to Washington Area Surgeons' Fees," published by the Health Research Group. The story pointed to a $1,500 differential for the same surgical procedure.[10] The *Wall Street Journal* wrote a lead story on physician supply indicating the wide range of physician fees. "The prevailing charge for an appendectomy in San Francisco is listed at $541.88, well above Boston's and Washington's $356.50, but far below Manhattan's $784.30."[11] Geographical averages of physicians' "usual, customary, and reasonable" (UCR) fees reimbursed by Medicare are available from the Department of Health and Human Services.

The percentage of the population that has graduated from high school and college is increasing. In 1960, only 25 percent of the population had completed high school while in 1977, 36 percent had. By 1980, the 8 percent of the population that had completed four years of college in 1960 had doubled to 16 percent. Of all persons 25 to 29 years, 85 to 90 percent have completed high school and over one-fourth have completed four years of college. The more educated people are, the easier it is for them to obtain medical information and understand technical writing. There are medical dictionaries to aid in the process. Many educated consumers, when they become seriously ill, are assiduous researchers on the particular illness that they might or do have.[12] Today's consumers are more sophisticated because of the greater availability of medical information in books, newspapers, widely read business periodicals, and popular women's magazines. In many cities there are day-time TV and radio programs on which physicians answer questions that are phoned-in. A sampling of recent periodicals reveals the following health-related columns: "RX for Medical Care: Choosing a Doctor Is No Longer Merely a Question of Where It Hurts," in *Sky*, May 1979, a Delta Airlines' periodical, a copy of which was in every seat-pocket of their airplanes. Almost all "women's periodicals" and most issues of *Newsweek*, *Time*, and *Reader's Digest* (over 20 million circulation) carry regular science or health columns covering information about new medical procedures and drugs, often with citations to the medical literature. *Reader's Digest* also carries one article in each issue on a specific health problem. *Business Week* has intermittent columns on health, and *Fortune* prints in-depth articles on new biological research and its potential for medical advancements. Other business periodicals, such as *Forbes*, have investment-oriented articles on hospitals and new drugs.

In recent years, airlines, on their long flights, have shown free films on health education subjects such as exercise, reduction of stress, and cardiopulmonary resuscitation (CPR). Newspapers, in addition to their usual "Doctor Answers" columns, print feature articles that list self-care alternatives and sources of outpatient care by hospitals and clinics in the newspaper's circulation area. It is not uncommon for these informative lists to include hours that the facilities are open and the prices charged. These popular articles are often surprisingly comprehensive and accurate.

Some of the articles list questions, procedures, and tests from which a patient might evaluate the completeness of a "checkup" examination. One example, from *Business Week* (August 1980), is reproduced below:

What a Competent Doctor Should Be Looking For

Not all physical exams are created equal. They vary according to the doctor giving them. Dr. Charles S. Smithen, a cardiologist and internist at New York Hospital, offers this version of a "typical" physical exam, explaining what he looks for at each step:

Vital signs. Temperature, pulse, and blood pressure, while both lying and standing and in both arms. If the pressure drops sharply in the standing position, it might indicate anemia or internal bleeding. A big difference in pressure between arms might show an obstruction in an artery or a kink in the aorta.

Skin check. Pallor could indicate anemia; jaundice, liver disease; blue lips could indicate poor oxygenation of the body, which might mean emphysema or heart disease; a butterfly rash around the nose and face might signify a rheumatic condition; too many black and blue marks could mean a blood disorder; xanthomas—soft yellow spots around the eyes, palms, or elbows—could come from high cholesterol; and, of course, skin cancers could turn up.

Hair. If it's very coarse and falls out easily, hypothyroidism may be present. If it's too fine and silky, there may be a hyperthyroid condition.

Eyes. The only visible arteries in the body are right behind the eyes, and that is what doctors are checking when they shine the little light in. Both atherosclerosis and severe high blood pressure can be seen. The outer surface of the eye can show jaundice, and, of course, glaucoma. Bulging eyes may mean an overactive thyroid. Drooping eyelids might be a sign of myasthenia gravis, the disease made famous by Aristotle Onassis. They also might mean that a lung tumor is pressing on a specific nerve in the chest. An old stroke or Bell's palsy can also be spotted through the eye exam.

Mouth, nose, and ears. Tonsils and teeth care are checked, as are sinuses. Of course, any visible obstruction is checked out. An extreme archness of the palate can be associated with a mitral prolapse, a heart disorder. Bad breath can imply chronic stomach problems.

Neck. An enlarged thyroid can readily be felt. A check of the jugular vein and the carotid artery can tell a lot about internal pressures in the heart—for example, if the muscles are working properly, or any valves are leaking. Feeling the lymph glands could turn up lymphatic cancer, or even stomach cancer.

Chest. Those chest massages and knocks on the back and chest are generally checks for fluid in the lung. Impulses that come through to a doctor's trained hands can also indicate whether chambers in the heart are enlarged. The check with the stethoscope is for bronchitis and any extra heart sounds, such as murmurs. Emphysema will also show up in the chest examination.

Abdomen. The doctor will feel for the liver, the spleen, and the gallbladder—and if he feels any of them, it probably means they are abnormally enlarged. Kneading the abdomen can also show masses in the bowels. And since the aorta runs down the middle of the abdomen, aneurysms might be detectable.

Extremities. Circulation to the legs and hands is checked. Early arthritis in the hands can be spotted at this point. The nails yield a wealth of information—for example, a skewed angle in the nail bed could imply a heart disorder. Reflex tests—knee jerks, ankle jerks, and the like—show whether the brain's reflexes are working properly.

Rectal exam. The painful proctoscopy is pretty much out of fashion nowadays. Instead, the physician is likely to do a manual rectal, looking for prostate problems or tumors.

Screening tests. Increasingly common stool tests are what have made the proctoscope obsolete. Patients submit stool samples from several different days and the lab checks for blood in the stool. Urine samples can yield information on diabetes, kidney disorders, and blood disorders. Blood tests can indicate almost anything—the calcium level might show parathyroid cancer, alkaline phosphatase readings might indicate Paget's disease, a bone disorder often misdiagnosed as arthritis. Cholesterol problems show up here—in fact, one doctor says that more than 50 diseases can be spotted through blood samples. Resting electrocardiograms can indicate heart disorders, of course. Smithen recommends exercise tolerance tests (EKGS while a patient is on an exercise bicycle or treadmill) and spirometry tests (breathing tests) only for patients over 40 who smoke or who have a history of heart or respiratory diseases in their family.[13]

A handbook, written by a former *Medical World News* correspondent, J. N. Tuck, was published by *New York Magazine* in December 1972. This consumer guide evaluates hospitals in New York City and includes charges and approximate waiting times for appointments with staff physicians. Several local communities have published directories listing office hours and prices of physicians, and whether they accept Medicare and Medicaid patients.

Blue Cross publishes a *Monthly Consumer Report* whose information is directed primarily towards employers who pay their premiums and their enrollees or potential patients. Many university medical centers and county medical associations print handbooks listing physicians by specialty, but the handbooks are distributed internally and sent to referring physicians, not to would-be patients. In January 1979, the Pacific Gas and Electric Company mailed with every bill a leaflet entitled "TelMed: Private Answers to Your Health-Care Questions." That leaflet listed telephone numbers to dial for information recorded on 3- to 7-minute tapes concerning 200 health problems. There are several hundred similar Tel-Med services nationwide, and in some communities the number of Tel-Med tapes number 350. In Pittsburgh, 1,000 calls a day were received during the first twenty-one months of the program. An analysis of the users of the Pittsburgh Tel-Med found that callers tended to be young and well-educated, and that one-fourth had a specific health care followup.[14] With this plethora of information, can physicians continue to maintain that consumers are ignorant, or more ignorant about medical care than other services that they purchase? Or that average consumers who spend money for informational sources about medical care and health do not wish to be, and are not, informed about the state of medical science?

In 1980, the American Medical Association (AMA) amended its code of ethics to state that physicians may "advertise their services and fees" and thus solicit patients. This acknowledges that consumers want more information, and that those with less third party coverage are shopping for price as well as quality. That the AMA's action is also in response to the FTC's actions of 1978 and 1979 against professional associations of health providers that bar, as a matter of "professional ethics," advertising of prices does not detract from the AMA's recognition that the times have changed.

In April 1979, the American Dental Association (ADA) consented to an interim two-year FTC order that bars the ADA from restraining dentists from the use of truthful advertising under its "principles of ethics." According to an agreement with the FTC, the final decision in the ADA and the AMA cases will be identical. Both associations appealed the FTC's rule that a prohibition on advertising violates the antitrust law. The FTC had argued, in 1979, that comparative advertising in a particular industry, not health, should be allowed because it "maximizes one of advertising's greatest consumer benefits, viz. reducing the time it takes to obtain sufficient information to make a rational purchase decision."[15] The FTC interpreted its "eyeglasses rule" in a letter to the Illinois attorney general as pre-empting state laws and permitting advertisements to state "whether an advertised price includes single vision and/or multifocal lenses, refers to hard and/or soft lenses, includes an eye examination, includes all dispensing fees, and includes both frames and lenses." In 1979, the FTC also issued a consent order to require the California Medical Association to stop producing and publishing their commonly used, medical care pricing schedules, Relative Value Schedules, "to withdraw those already published, and to stop giving instructions for their conversion factors."[16] The order does permit them to provide reimbursers lists of procedural terminology and historical prices.

At the state level, repeal of fair trade practice laws is creating a more competitive climate. During the 1980s, advertisement of prices in the various health care markets, including those of group practices, will increase.

GOVERNMENT DECISIONS

Consumer Input

As cost-reimbursement by the government increases, government regulation grows. As a minimum, the costs to be reimbursed need to be defined and approved, checks must be made to show that the service actually occurred, and accounting procedures overseen to avoid fraud and unwarranted manipulation. Regulation has grown beyond this minimum. The federal government has begun to seek consumer input to guide the regulatory process.

In 1980, the federal government proposed regulations about the number of consumers that should be on various private, governing boards in the health sector, including Blue Cross and Blue Shield. For example, the FTC has expressed concern that physicians and hospital administrators monopolize committees of the Blues that in turn decide the fees and costs to be reimbursed. Government seemed to be far less concerned that, by law, physicians dominate Professional Standards Review Organizations (PSROs). The federal government required the establishment of PSROs in 1972 to review quality, appropriateness, and utilization of inpatient hospital, extended nursing home, and ambulatory medical care. The goal was to contain costs by ensuring that the most efficient or least costly level of care is used without sacrificing the quality of care. In practice, the bulk of PSRO activity has been in review of necessity and length-of-hospital stays. Although non-professionals select from computer printouts large deviations from the norms by diagnosis, age, sex, etc., the PSRO review board members are primarily physicians. There was, to the author's knowledge, no consumer input until 1980 when the Fairfield-Westchester Business Group on Health, representing twenty-two large companies, forced acceptance by PSROs in the Connecticut and New York areas to share with industry in utilization review.

Because PSROs monitor quality, government is understandably reluctant to be involved in this less precise area even though PSROs affect physicians' incomes. It is debatable whether, as most physicians claim, only physicians can review utilization rates. Representatives of private industry that pay large premiums are interested in quality and price. The apparent lack of PSRO cost-effectiveness and their probable loss of support under the Reagan Administration, however, may make purchaser or consumer involvement in PSROs moot.

Consumer involvement is intended to offset, to a degree, the greater and thus more effective interest of the providers, i.e., doctors and hospitals. The Federal Trade Commission pays consumers and public interest attorneys for commenting on regulations proposed by agencies such as the FDA. FTC Commissioner Pertschuk explains that public participation funding was "a modest effort to redress the balance of advocacy by reimbursing those few participants who could demonstrate their competence and ability to represent a significant public interest which would otherwise have no voice in the administrative procedure. . . . The real measure of the program is whether it enhances the quality of our rule-making proceedings. . . . Without a doubt, it has."[17]

The question of consumer representation has also been raised in connection with pre-market approval of new drugs to meet safety and efficacy standards. These decisions involve allocation by regulation rather than price. One of the many recommendations of the 1977 *Final Report of the Review Panel on New Drug Regulations* is that a "voting public interest representative be included on each advisory committee so that consumers will have a voice in whether the social benefits of new drugs outweigh their risks."[18] No advice is given on how to select the consumer representative. In this respect, the FTC's experience under the Magnuson-Moss Act in subsidizing individuals or organizations who wish to participate in the Commission's hearings but cannot afford to do so is enlightening. According to one observer, "FTC has been diligently recruiting 'public participation' by selected individuals or organizations—and benevolently writing their testimony for them."[19] By extending this policy to other regulatory agencies, the federal government appears to be reducing the over-supply of lawyers rather than increasing consumer input about regulations. Consumers have traditionally influenced regulations by voting for officials and writing letters to their Congressmen.

The FDA sought more specific consumer participation for proposed regulations on over-the-counter drugs during the 1970s. The FDA appointed one consumer to each of its review panels for the different therapeutic classifications of over-the-counter drugs. During 1974 and 1975, these consumers were non-paid and non-voting members, and as such were considered second-class citizens on these committees that were primarily composed of scientists.[20] This proved an unsatisfactory approach and eventually the consumer members of FDA's advisory committee were paid and allowed to vote. To my knowledge, consumers have never been appointed to FDA's scientific committees on prescription drugs. Although FDA Commissioner Schmidt used consumers on the top National Advisory Drug Committee (NADC), that committee was discontinued by Commissioner Kennedy when he took office in 1978 and has not been restored. Many such committees became "captives" of the agency. The NADC did not, and as a committee assessed that there was a lag in approval of new drugs already being marketed abroad and that some of these drugs were a substantial therapeutic improvement. The NADC began to explore how to improve legislation to speed up approval of new, beneficial drugs. Because the agency had control over the agenda, this activity was hampered.

In October 1979, the FDA announced

> the establishment of a pilot program to pay the expenses of certain consumers, small businesses, and public interest groups who wish to participate in Agency regulatory proceedings but cannot afford it. . . . Other regulatory agencies also have set aside funds to reimburse groups that otherwise could not afford to participate in regulatory proceedings. The programs stem from a 1976 decision by the Comptroller General of the United States who said regulatory agencies could extend financial assistance to people "who require it" and "whose participation is essential to dispose of the matter" before the Agency.[21]

The FDA set aside $250,000 for the first year of this program and set up four criteria for reimbursement: "Be able to contribute substantially to the proceeding, be able to represent a significant point of view that otherwise would not be represented at the proceeding, be able to represent competently the position advocated, and be unable to obtain from other sources enough money to participate effectively."[22] However, the announcement of this policy of using carefully selected (by the agency) consumers and the hearings to which it applies were published only in the *Federal Register*, which the average consumer does not read.

Government regulators who are in the upper civil service grades are probably more risk-adverse by self-selection than the general public. Publicity makes them even more risk-adverse. The input of well-informed consumers who take risks every day could offer some balance in regulation. In 1980, a House subcommittee report to Congress referred to congressional testimony of June 1979 and the General Accounting Office (GAO) report of May 1980 in support of its conclusion in the transmittal letter to the Chairman of the House Committee on Science and Technology (November 25, 1980) as follows: "There is, for certain categories of drugs, a 'drug lag' within the United States as compared with some other technically advantaged countries."[23]

In its conclusions, the report states that the "Hearings' testimony identified more than 30 significant drugs for cardiovascular diseases and a dozen drugs for neurological diseases which had been delayed over the past two decades."[24] Among other recommendations was that the FDA "should draw from processes and mechanisms used by foreign approval agencies in expediting the drug approval process, such as use of committees of experts (such as physicians, academicians, para-professionals, and consumer representatives) in the drug approval process."[25]

In contrast to a few bureaucrats, including 1979 FDA Commissioner Donald Kennedy, who maintained that there is no drug lag but rather a drying up of biological knowledge from which new, significant drugs can evolve, the report denies this premise and further states that the "drug lag" is in regard to "important drugs" that offer therapeutic gains and not duplications of already marketed drugs.[26]

The major avenue for input about government regulation open to all consumers is through their elected representatives. The importance of the consumer as a powerful political force has been illustrated by the successive delays in banning saccharin and the demise of a proposal to classify vitamins as prescription drugs. Consumers are involved in public policy decisions about health. Recognition that the public should be involved in such regulatory decisions was made by FDA Commissioner Alexander Schmidt:

> In the first place, science is no longer as great a mystery as it once was to the general population. But, more importantly, there are growing numbers of decisions we must face in FDA that science cannot serve. These are decisions involving ethical or philosophical or moral judgments.
>
> For example: How much protection does the public want from government? How much should it have? Where is the line between what government should do to protect the people and what the people should do to protect themselves?
>
> Facing the reality that life involves risk and that no amount of government regulation can remove all risk, then how much risk does the public find acceptable—especially in the use of therapeutic chemicals which all have potential for harm as well as benefit?
>
> And whatever its needs and wishes, how much protection is the public willing to pay for, both with dollars and with loss of freedom to do whatever it wishes, right or wrong, wise or unwise, dangerous or safe?

As we in FDA consider issues that move away from science and toward ethics or individual choice, we must look for guidance to the public voice.[27]

Regulation

Government regulations confound the issues and hamper the individual's freedom of choice. Yet, there is need for some government regulation for safety of drugs and foods although no amount of regulation can assure safety. Law suits occur only after harm is done. Regulation can prevent some of the harm from occurring. However, government programs and regulations can also distort the allocation of medical care. The percentage of medical care dollars that goes to the aged has increased more rapidly than the growth in the number of the aged. In 1965, 9 percent of the population was 65 and over, or "aged." By 1979, the number of aged persons had increased to 11 percent of the total population, a 20 percent gain. Meanwhile, expenditures on older persons rose from 24 percent to 30 percent of all personal health care expenditures, an increase of 25 percent. Although some of this increase reflects medical technological advance, it also appears to be at the expense of persons under 19 years of age. With the decline in the birthrate beginning in 1960, individuals under 19 years are a declining part of the population, dropping from 38 percent in 1965 to 31 percent by 1979. This is a decline of only 18 percent, but the younger persons' share of all personal health care expenditures shrank by 25 percent. This may be in accord with the public's wishes. The 1965 distribution was apparently not; otherwise, Medicare and Medicaid would not have passed. However, if or until new legislation is enacted, there is no way of knowing whether the current allocation that regulation affects is or is not in accord with the public's desires.

The Medicare program has resulted in the allocation of more medical resources for complex medical technology to cure the aged, and often to increase their life expectancy without any cure. There have been few counter-balancing programs for early screening of the young with followup care for such problems as poor hearing and eyesight. Wealthier states, such as California, require children to have physical examinations prior to entering a public school and also immunizations against diphtheria, whooping cough, tetanus, polio, mumps, and German measles. Medicaid provides followup care if the child's family cannot afford private care. There are also many state screening clinics, but these are primarily for the aged. In those states with lower per capita incomes, the screening programs for children are few despite Medicaid's Early and Periodic Screening, Diagnosis, and Treatment Program, which began in 1973. Although legislation was passed by the House to broaden and make more effective state screening and followup care for poor children under eighteen years, it was not passed by the Senate. A major argument against spending more money on the politically appealing and in the long run, cost containing measure was that there are thirty other, mostly minor but uncoordinated, public-financed health programs for children. Bringing about an orderly structure to the whole area of preventive health is a challenge that should be tackled by the Reagan Administration.

A recent three-year study measures the high economic costs associated with the major diseases—cancer, coronary heart disease, and stroke—and also with motor vehicle injuries. Using a present-value (1975) equivalent (discounted at 6 percent), the study found that the generated direct medical care costs and the indirect costs of loss of productivity from occurrences in 1975 were $23.1 billion from cancer, $14.4 billion from motor vehicle injuries, $13.7 billion from coronary heart disease, and $6.5 billion from stroke.[28] Obviously, given the current state of medical knowledge, the prevention of automobile accidents deserves a high priority. Although the above costs and the implied benefits from reducing the incidence of disease and accidents do not include pain and psychic harm, they do act as shadow-pricing to help order the priorities of government spending. The emphasis on using the first known year of incidence and the future costs generated is especially appropriate in costing the total benefits from the use of preventive medicine.

Increasingly, visits to physicians are being made for preventive care and this is especially so among women with about 20 percent of their physicians visits in 1977–78 coded as being "diagnostic, screening, and preventive" and not for a symptom, disease, or treatment. The corresponding number for men was 11 percent.[29]

In the United States, the emphasis has been on treatment of the acutely ill with intensive use of technology, while in the United Kingdom, where the percentage of the GNP available for all types of health care is severely limited, the emphasis is on "caring" rather than curing. The emphasis on caring (nearly 8 million home visits were made in 1976), it has been charged, is a deliberate cost-effective political program in the U.K. because it provides more people with health care services for the same expenditure than if "curing" were the primary goal. It is claimed that the more people who benefit from a national health program, the greater the number of votes or political support.[30] Obviously, caring programs affect more people than curing of acute illness, which is also more difficult to do and requires expensive hospital beds and technological equipment.

Government programs in the United States have given the poor access to medical care, but possibly at the expense of the low income worker. The latter pays social security taxes on each dollar earned, income and other taxes in accordance with the law, and does not receive wages usually indexed to cost-of-living. Persons sixty-five years and older who have a double income exemption may receive social security benefits that are indexed and are eligible for Medicare benefits. Although most aged have greater medical needs than the young, most aged also own their own home and other household capital goods. Medicaid provides the poor with more health benefits than do private benefit plans. Low income workers have poorer medical coverage than high income workers. A recent study shows that Medicaid recipients use more medical resources than the poor not receiving Medicaid: "A recipient with average health would visit a physician 50 percent more often and spend nearly twice as many days in the hospital as a similar poor person not on welfare."[31] This is a very significant statement because the level of health in that study was the same for the Medicaid recipient and the poor not on Medicaid. Further, those poor who received government benefits "used medical services about as often, on average, as middle-income people with similar health status, but that the poor not on welfare continued to lag well behind."[32] The non-welfare poor appear to be priced out of the market.

More recent studies of the Portland, Oregon, area have found that, in a prepaid group practice plan, low income enrollees with concurrent Medicaid coverage had consistently higher utilization rates than low income enrollees not under Medicaid. Medicaid coverage was the strongest explanatory variable of this utilization pattern.[33]

In 1977, the poor averaged 5.8 visits per capita as compared to 4.8 visits for those with incomes above $25,000. Because "poor" is defined as persons with less than $5,000 annual income, most of these were not steady workers and most received Medicaid. There is a circular effect in that those who do not work steadily may be ill more often than those who have a regular job. Persons in the $5,000 to $10,000 income bracket averaged 4.9 visits per capita. At 1977 price and wage levels, individuals in this bracket formed the bulk of the low income workers.

In the United Kingdom, where one would anticipate the same results if the poor are on the average less well than those with higher incomes, it seems that the poor receive less resources per ill person than middle and upper income persons. Economist John C. Goodman comments in a 1980 book on health care in Great Britain that "if an individual in the highest social class becomes ill, he can expect that about 40 percent more health dollars will be spent on him rather than on an individual with the same illness in the lower class."[34] *Inequalities in Health*, a 1980 British government report that took three years to complete, documents that rates of consultations with children of the upper social class families are relatively more frequent than with other children and further, "that middle class patients tended to have longer consultations than did working class ones."[35] Moreover, the Report states that because persons in the middle and upper income groups are usually better educated than those in the lower income working class they have, as was early predicted, used the National Health Service to better advantage, and especially so in respect to preventive care. Physicians are likely to be from, and mix socially with, persons in higher income groups. They thus have social class preferences that are very difficult for any government plan to overcome. Further, persons in the working classes live in working-class neighborhoods where the health facilities are of poorer quality.

There are distortions in the allocation of health care resources that the increase in third party payments by private insurance has enlarged. These include, in the United States, the greater use than otherwise would occur of hospitals (as opposed to outpatient and home care), high technology, x-rays, and tests. One area of allocation, however, does not appear to be influenced greatly by government intervention: the urban/rural difference in availability of hospitals, physicians, and other medical resources that exists probably in all countries, in the U.K., and even in the U.S.S.R., where explicit job assignments are made. The U.S.S.R. has not eliminated the differential in numbers or quality of hospitals, physicians, and other health services and goods within that vast country. This is understandable. Within the United States, the Hill-Burton Act increased the number of hospitals in the rural areas, but these are relatively small hospitals that do not attract specialists. The tremendous increase in the number of physicians per capita within the more culturally attractive metropolitan centers of the United States is creating a greater rural dispersion of specialists, all of whom cannot earn a living in the large cities.

However, the relocated specialist without an expensive, well-equipped hospital, will be practicing more primary than specialist care. This outcome is considered desirable by many.

Government requirements for "certificates-of-need" to expand existing hospitals or build new ones have also distorted resource allocation. The certificate-of-need is issued or denied after application by a regional Health Systems Agency (HSA). There are 203 HSAs and about 80 percent are approved by the federal government. In many areas they have been attacked as ineffective in preventing the building of "not-needed" new hospitals while, in other areas, they have been charged with creating a shortage of beds and protecting the established hospitals from new competition. The existence of the certificates-of-need law rests on a belief that hospital growth, whether by the entry of new firms or of the expansion of old ones, must be controlled, and additionally that hospitals compete primarily by purchase of expensive equipment that they may use rarely. Assured government and insurance reimbursements otherwise create an over-supply of beds, which is inefficient and thus more expensive than need be. Thus, one type of government intervention, financing of new hospitals, has created a need for more intervention. Certificates-of-need are also required by law to be obtained by all medical providers, except HMOs, for the purchase of medical equipment costing more than $150,000. By exempting HMOs from the requirement of obtaining certificates-of-need for out-of-hospital equipment, Congress reinforced the belief that successful HMOs will, through competition, restrain costs and therefore charges.

An analysis of 1968–72 data found that this governmental regulation of capital expenditure and "controls did not significantly affect total investment by hospitals . . . resulted in lower growth of bed supplies and higher growth of plant assets per bed than would have been observed in the absence of controls."[36] Some believe that the investment controls have accelerated cost inflation in the 1968–71 period; others believe that the nationwide effect was small because local politics often negated their influence. Often cited is the recent approval, after political intervention, of a new hospital in the over-bedded Boston area.

Under the Health Planning Act of 1974, federal guidelines for the number of hospital beds desirable in an area were published to help the HSAs determine whether or not to approve a hospital's expansion. Some of these guidelines are: a maximum of four general hospital beds per 1,000 persons, existing 80 percent hospital occupancy rates before approval, and delivery of at least 2,000 babies annually in metropolitan areas and 500 babies in a rural area before approving additional maternity wards and delivery rooms. This latter guideline, during a period of declining birthrates, has especially disturbed administrators of some rural hospitals and also the expectant mothers living in those rural areas where delivery rooms and accompanying facilities are at a distance from their homes. How far should a woman, expecting a baby momentarily, be expected to travel over mountainous roads? The rural mountain areas of the West have different needs than the flat, rural areas of the mid-West. Federal "guidelines" cannot be perfect or equitable in a large, geographically diverse country. They are unlikely to do more than persuade those already leaning towards a given position. Because HSAs do not have to decide how to spend a limited number of dollars, their criteria for approval are numerous and sometimes vague. Political considerations become dominant, especially because the federal law requires that the majority membership of the HSA represent the public.

The 1979 extension of the Health Systems Agencies (HSAs) for three years eliminated the earlier requirement that state and local decisions must conform to HHS' national guidelines and carried a significant new provision that the HSAs are to promote competition among providers of health care. However, the legislation also permits HSAs "to allocate the market for institutional and other services not responsive to competitive pressures."[37] The authorizations expire in fiscal year 1982.

The difficult problem is how to contain costs by reducing hospital utilization when the non-used hospital beds are maintained and their indirect costs continue. Loans and grants are available to convert the unused beds for uses other than acute care, but there needs to be a sizeable number of unused beds in one facility to make this feasible.

Deregulation by the Reagan Administration is expected to phase out public monies that support the HSAs. Opponents argue that without HSAs there will be a hospital building boom. The high interest rates for construction money makes this unlikely. However, some business firms that have been involved in HSAs argue for their continuance. Among the compromises suggested is to raise the trigger for a certificate-of-need (CON) to one million dollars. The state CON laws are expected to continue while the federal government plans to phase-out support monies and to develop plans for more competitive health care markets. The latter will take time to put in place and deregulation should therefore be slowed.

PSROs, also mandated by federal law, primarily to review the appropriateness of the length-of-hospital stays, are made up almost entirely of physicians. As such, they maintain standards of custom-ary modes of medical practice and do not use costs and benefits as an over-all frame of reference. Evaluations of the PSRO program by the Department of Health and Human Services annually, the Congressional Budget Office in 1979, and the General Accounting Office in early 1981 and before indicate that considering just the costs of the reviews and the dollars in hospital days saved, the net saving, if any, is very small. To the author's knowledge, no weighing of costs against health outcomes or the health benefits or losses from the briefer length-of-hospital stays is made. The Reagan Administration would reduce this program, about which many physicians complain.

In attempts to contain costs, the HSAs have limited purchases of expensive medical devices such as the computerized axial tomogra-pher (CAT) scanner. HSAs have been backed up by Medicare and insurers by their refusals to reimburse charges for use of unapproved scanners. This remarkable diagnostic tool, whose inventors won the Nobel Prize in Medicine in 1979, has been thus artificially limited in usage. About 1,200 scanners, each costing nearly "one million dollars to purchase, install, and operate" for the first year, had been bought by hospitals and physicians by the end of 1979.[38] The restriction on purchases of this device in the United States forced the rationing of its use. If there are too few such devices in relation to the demand in an area, then machine time must be allocated. Decisions on access are made by a combination of bureaucrats and physicians who decide on the basis of some form, implicit or explicit, of cost-benefit analysis. The government's rationale to limit the CAT's proliferation is based on the high capital and operating costs, potential duplication beyond the "need" for this expensive device, and the cost impact on the government's Medicare and Medicaid programs. Private insurers, and especially the Blues, are denying reimbursement for CAT scanner charges unless their purchase was approved by an HSA and add-itionally met the Blues' review criteria. In 1977, Blue Cross, since receiving its commissioned report from the National Academy of Sciences, has urged limitations on the scanner's use.

A recent example of the CAT scanner's less well known but highly cost-effective use is its ability to discriminate between benign and malignant lung tumors without biopsy or exploratory surgery with attendant hospitalization costs.

The ingenuity of private enterprise is rapidly eliminating the reg-ulatory-imposed scarcity of CAT scanners, and at a savings possibly induced by government regulation. American Medical International,

Inc., ordered $27 million worth of CAT scanner equipment from General Electric, the major manufacturer, with the intention of rotating the CAT scanners among hospitals by moving them in specially-equipped vans. Each participating hospital then needs only $5,000 for a special power outlet and about $250 for the costs of each scan.[39]

CAT scans of the head for diagnosis may be especially cost-effective. Medical technology changes very rapidly. There are several generations of CAT scanners now in use and other innovations that also permit non-invasive diagnostic procedures. To assess reliably the net benefit of any new medical innovation is very costly because, if precisely done, it involves prospective, controlled use of the procedure with a sizeable number of patients over a period of time who are compared with matched patients for whom the already available procedure or drug or other medical intervention is used. It is questionable whether the money and time costs of assessment would be greater than any net losses from the use of a new procedure with questionable efficacy over its foreseeable lifetime prior to obsolescence. In technological assessment as well as drug assessment, more than the dollar costs of treatment and the therapeutic outcomes are involved in a cost-benefit analysis. Ultrasound and CAT scanners have lesser risk and give the patient much less discomfort than invasive arteriograms and also save the patient time as well as money. These latter are non-health benefits of considerable value.

Within the federal government, the Public Health Service (PHS) early discouraged wide use of CAT scanners by applying their four criteria: (1) safety, (2) efficacy, (3) stage of development, and (4) acceptance by the medical community. "Efficacy" is used to mean health outcomes under ideal circumstances while "effectiveness" is generally used to mean health outcomes under usual clinical conditions. Neither term includes non-health benefits to the consumer. The Medical Device Amendments of 1976 charged the FDA to judge the safety and efficacy of medical devices. Data on the latter are often lacking, but the FDA and the Public Health Service's National Center for Health Care Technology advise Medicare on whether it should reimburse for a specific, unusually expensive, medical procedure. Blue Cross and other insurers may use such a decision as a precedent to deny or pay reimbursement. Technology assessment could become a determination of "relative efficacy" when advice on whether reimbursement should or should not be made is tied to the assessment. Determination of the "relative efficacy" of a drug as well as a medical device is exceedingly difficult because each human being is unique. Each individual reacts differently to a given dosage of a drug. The

National Center for Health Care Technology (NCHCT), established in November 1978, is under the PHS unit that decides which new technologies Medicare should not reimburse, as well as which older technologies might be considered obsolete. Additionally, the Office of Technology Assessment (OTA), which released its first study, "Drug Bioequivalence," in July 1974, advises the members of Congress. In 1980, OTA released studies on the methodology and literature reviews about the cost-effectiveness of medical techniques. The American Medical Association (AMA) opposed the establishment of the National Center for Health Care Technology, which has begun to assess specific medical procedures. The American College of Physicians recently issued eight specific efficacy assessments, the first two of which follow.

1. Ultrasonic Arteriography. The use of B-mode ultrasound is not efficacious clinically in peripheral artery occlusive disease but it is indispensable in determining aneurysm size. This recommendation does not refer to the use of a Doppler testing device for peripheral artery occlusive disease.

2. Use of Ultrasonic Arteriography in Distinguishing Diseases of the Carotid Artery System. The use of B-scan and Doppler ultrasound in distinguishing diseases of the carotid artery system are efficacious clinically.[40]

The AMA has also expressed intent to evaluate specific medical techniques. There is agreement that evaluation is needed but disagreement on whether the government or private parties, both physicians and insurers (admittedly at-interest), can best make the assessments. The American College of Physicians (ACP) has testified in favor of the National Center. However, a comparison of the NCHCT assessment list of seventeen high priority technologies, as of December 15, 1980, with that of the ACP's assessments of eight medical interventions published in June 1981 indicates only partial agreement about which procedures most need evaluation. Whereas the ACP has already issued detailed recommendations on the use of ultrasound for cardiac diagnosis, the NCHCT lags and has commissioned an overview paper and scheduled a forum in Winter 1982 on ultrasound for cardiac diagnosis, a technique that the Center terms an established technology with large volume and high cost.

It is obvious that if the Center advises the federal government not to reimburse for specific procedures, this will act to contain costs. Private third party insurers who are aware of these assessments may use govenment assessments in lieu of their own. To refuse reimbursement because a procedure is not medically beneficial for everyone at risk is different than refusing reimbursement because the procedure is not "reasonably cost-effective" for society. Health costs are rising rapidly and it may be that government should pay only for a minimal level of care. If that is the case, let us say so and not hide behind the cloak of scientific judgment that a procedure is not relatively efficacious, or not cost-effective compared with an alternative method of gaining the same end. *Relative* efficacy is more difficult to prove than efficacy.

Is there a need for government assessments? Are government assessments "at-interest" because government pays billions of dollars for Medicare patients? Not until June 23, 1981, was the Center's special report on coronary artery bypass surgery available. This seventeen-page paper reports on an April 21–23, 1981, technology assessment forum on a type of surgery that the Center estimates costs $2 billion annually for over 100,000 operations. The conclusion, as one would expect from a government body, that *per se* must be conservative in face of potential adverse publicity, calls for "further clinical research" and "further investigation and analysis of the economic, ethical, and social aspects of coronary artery bypass surgery"[41] and the report is replete with such vague phrases as "reasonably cost effective" left undefined.[42] However, the Center did make specific recommendations in its preliminary report of a forum on dental radiology held June 29–July 1, 1981. Examples from an "unofficial summary" follow: "Routine dental x-rays should not be taken for detection of caries" and "Radiographs should not be taken for administrative reasons only."[43]

Among the several items that the Center intends to initiate for assessment in the future are total hip replacement. Hip replacement is an established technology. It may not prolong life, but it does improve the quality of life. The Center's concern about costs and long-term outcomes data implies to the aware consumer that cost containment rather than efficacy might be the primary end-point of many of the Center's proposed studies. It is clear that there is over-utilization of some medical procedures and here, as in the U.K., costs can be restrained if the government refuses to reimburse for specific procedures or, alternatively, places an overall cap on total reimbursements. The latter leaves a greater measure of choice.

Government decisions about the desirability of reimbursing for new forms of medical interventions can slow the diffusion of new medical technology and its higher costs and also depress the medical device industry. Conservative government decisions aimed to contain costs may delay "needed" beneficial therapeutic innovations. Rather than the government attempting to assess the cost-effectiveness of medical technologies or to rank medical interventions in accordance with relative efficacy, the government regulations should concentrate on safety. This would leave to the individual patient and physician to make the decision, based on the available data, about whether the patient wishes to have a drug or other medical intervention, often carrying an unknown probability of risk, to gain an unknown probability of benefit. If the costs of the medical intervention are very high, one would suspect that the medical procedure is usually still in the research stage and thus would not fit Medicare's "reasonable and necessary" (for diagnosis, treatment, or improved functioning) criteria for reimbursement.

Cost-benefit analyses of new medical devices are badly needed and are being done and reported on in the medical and economic literatures. Many question whether these assessments can be impartially done by such large third party payers as the federal government and insurers. Physicians not employed by these organizations can make available the needed biological information and economists can indicate the outer bounds of the probable costs and benefits of available options. The implicit, different value judgments about patients' preferences, including their values of a year of life of a specified level of quality, can be made clear. Subsequently, as dissemination of such knowledge improves, consumers/patients will have more information on which to base their decisions.

To measure precisely the net benefit of new drugs or medical procedures for an individual and then to extrapolate that to the subgroup of the population likely to benefit is difficult. However, I maintain that in doing even an imperfect cost-benefit analysis, data are ordered, value judgments detected, and a wider set of data become available because non-health benefits and non-health costs of the individual are included. Probably even more important, cost-benefit analysis at the societal level of the potential impact of a change includes, in the estimation of the societal net benefit, the loss of benefits to those at risk to the disease in question.[44] A few government publications are beginning to recognize this, and the Reagan Administration is requesting greater use of cost-benefit analyses in its attempt to deregulate all industry, including the health industry. An influential publication by a special advisory body to Congress, the Office of Technology Assessment, states:

Performing an analysis of costs and benefits can be very helpful to decisionmakers because the process of analysis gives structure to the problem, allows an open consideration of all relevant effects of a decision, and forces the explicit treatment of key assumptions.[45]

Health Systems Agencies, the Environmental Protection Agency, the Occupational Safety and Health Agency, and all other federal groups that make policy decisions about health implicitly or explicitly make cost-benefit analyses, even to the extent of evaluating life. This is especially true of agencies dealing with automobile and airplane safety. Prevention of accidents that create heavy demands for medical care restrain health care costs better than do savings in treatment costs.

Extensive cost-reimbursement and consumer/physician ignorance of costs and benefits weaken the market price system as an effective method of allocation and set the stage for regulatory guidelines on capital expenditures. Knowledge about the costs and benefits of new medical procedures can certainly be improved. Weakening the reimbursement effect, however, is more difficult. As long as a large part of suppliers' costs are automatically reimbursed, regulation over capital expenditures, or alternatively, requiring uniform accounting, makes sense. The problem is complex because cost-reimbursed bills are not always a sizeable part of every provider's revenues. For those providers, primarily extended care facilities and physicians, whose cost-reimbursement is a smaller factor than in the case of hospitals, regulations limiting their capital investment impede their ability to compete. It makes better economic sense to place all providers at risk for their costs than to regulate their activities. If hospitals were forced to follow the same accounting rules that industry does under cost-reimbursement, then costs could be contained through greater accuracy and a gradual reduction of the numbers of regulations would become viable. To continue with extensive, inflationary cost-reimbursement and ineffective regulation means spiralling health care costs. Existing exemptions for HMOs permit some to "over-invest" in expensive equipment. If there are exemptions from the regulations, they should be proportionate to the percentage of revenues cost-reimbursed, not to whether or not services are paid for on a prepaid per capita or fee-for-service basis.

The high percentage of catastrophic medical expense coverage has resulted in a greater use of medical tests, x-rays, and other forms of medical care during the last weeks of life than would probably be chosen if consumers had complete information and paid for a larger part of their medical care. Using sizeable copayments as a cost control has to be balanced against the ethics of permitting a rare individual's inability to pay a copayment resulting in a denial of needed medical care. This situation is eliminated under Medicaid. Copayment requirements could be increased with income.

Older persons use an ever-increasing amount of intensive care resources. Yet, at the same time, expenditures on preventive health care per capita appear to be declining. National health policy has evolved in response to the exigencies of acute symptoms. The result is increasingly to extend life expectancy at age 65 rather than to reduce the number of early deaths, those before age 65. But, the quality-adjusted life years gained from preventing deaths at an early age are far greater than those from extending life expectancy at age 65. One estimate is that "although only 36 percent of all deaths in the United States in 1974 were early deaths, i.e., deaths of people under age 65, those early deaths accounted for 83 percent of the 'quality-adjusted life-years' lost."[46]

The concerns of the average person about the quality of life in later years as average life expectancy increases are great. Some physicians and scientists believe that "the amount of disability can decrease as morbidity is compressed into the shorter span between the increasing age at onset of disability and the fixed occurrence of death. The end of the period of adult vigor will come later than it used to."[47] These thoughts have not yet permeated the popular press. There has been a dramatic rise in the number of living wills, legal battles over the rights of near-terminal patients to refuse medical care, and the passage of state laws such as California's "right-to-die" law. This concern is not limited to older persons. A May 1980 survey of the young female readers of *Glamour* found that "87 percent believe that every patient has the right to decide to die when further medical help holds no hope for cure" and "75 percent would prefer to spare themselves the discomfort and . . . the high cost of life-prolonging treatment."[48]

The concept of a person's right to informed consent before any medical intervention is relatively new, emerging only in the 1940s. Patients believe that most physicians abide by the well-known medical precepts "to do no harm" and to save life. By the 1980s, the great advances in medical technology made unacceptable to many the traditional definition of death. The economic implications of the high cost of support medicine without promise of cure or maintenance of an unacceptable, to some, level of quality of life had increased many patients' desires to participate in decisions about their health. In a speech given in September 1980 at the World Congress on Health Economics, Leyden University, the Netherlands, I said that "in cases of terminal disease where death is judged to be imminent, a low probability of an anticipated benefit to health may be assessed as worth the risk of a high probability of incurring a severe adverse effect. This is because the record of alternative, existing treatments make some patients believe that they have 'little to lose.' "[49]

Some individuals do not wish to make the anxiety-provoking decisions about the course of their medical treatment. They prefer that the physician alone make the decision. However, practicing physicians are beginning to realize that their ethical and other values may differ from those of their patients.

Cooperation with a medical regimen is greater among informed than uninformed patients. There are also legal requirements to give full information to patients and non-conformance to these may result in a malpractice suit. I commented in the same Leyden speech: "To inform patients fully about the probabilities of adverse effects and outcomes is time-consuming. Many physicians argue that most patients do not want the information and, moreover, will not understand it. The hypothesis that a sufficient number of persons, those 'at the margin,' will not understand the risks and benefits written in clear (nonmedical) language needs testing."[50]

Physicians cannot be expected to abandon their training and traditions because of technology's rapid advances in medicine, but they are, in greater numbers, sharing clinical decision-making with those most affected: their patients.

There are agonizing concerns involved in deciding whether life-support equipment should be used to sustain an unconscious patient who has no hope of returning to consciousness or a normal life. When a government bureaucracy implicitly or explicitly allocates additional resources to life-sustaining technologies, there may be thousands of individuals who go without needed medical care and nutritious food or incur unspoken, unknown losses. Allocating resources by bureaucratic decisions does not avoid placing a value on life and does redistribute the gross national product. The ethical and religious beliefs that the value of any life is "beyond price" and what value is placed on life in such decisions are hidden. As medical technology advances, values placed on life increase. Older individuals receive more care than they would have five or ten years ago because the new technology increases the chances of success.

The age at which kidney dialysis is now performed in the United States has, in some cities, reached 80 years. Successful heart transplants are defined as living five additional years of life. Persons with one successful heart transplant are expected to require a second heart transplant because the disease process that destroyed the first heart will affect their new heart. The number of organ transplants will dramatically increase in the future because of a new drug, Cyclosporin A, that reduces the body's tendency to reject a transplanted organ and, unlike other drugs that do this, also does *not* lower the body's resistance to infection. Thus, depending on the financing, this area of medical costs is explosive. Ethical questions can be raised about a few individuals having successive transplants of not only one organ but of two or more. A poorly working heart affects lungs and kidneys. Eventually all body systems will fail, but by successive, expensive transplantations some persons can live longer than others. But at whose cost and with what ethical implications?

No one speaks for those persons who, as a result of the high costs of the dramatic organ transplants, may not receive high quality, more routine medical care and also have less to spend for good food and housing. Because of higher taxes to support rising Medicare and Medicaid costs and higher medical care private charges to make up for the losses at hospitals where costs are not fully reimbursed, other resources for health will be diminished. Few speak to this use of scarce resources because the tradeoffs are not self-evident. One who has written is Ernest Gruenberg, of Johns Hopkins University, School of Hygiene and Public Health:

> Our technological successes defy death's claim on the sick and the weak. We are proud of these successes, and perhaps it is partly our pride which prevents us from seeing that the successes result in the prolongation of sick lives. . . .
>
> Our life-saving technology of the past four decades has outstripped our health-preserving technology.[51]

The arguments about who shall receive and who shall pay center around legal liabilities and complex ethical questions. Economists are attacked as unfeeling because they seem, to the uninformed, obsessed with determining the worth of a life in the course of answering those questions. In truth, economists are merely making explicit what has long been insufficiently exposed: the value of life is always a factor in such decisions and this factor, like any other, must be expressed to avoid insensitive decisions. Kidney transplants cost about $25,000, but in addition the recipients need medical care to guard against rejection for the rest of their lives. A *London Times* story reported:

> —. . . Even after the new provision of 400 extra machines announced in the April budget . . . that between 750 and 1,000 people aged under 60, of a total of about 2,000 developing renal failure, would not be able to obtain treatment and so would die every year.

> —Necessarily rough estimates of values of life inferred from policy decisions not to provide treatment for chronic renal failure in a patient aged 50 implied a value of £30,000. However, changes in building regulations made after the collapse of the Ronan Point block of high rise flats which resulted in the deaths of some residents implied a valuation of £20 m.[52]

The cost of kidney transplants and hemodialysis in the United States is usually covered by HMOs, many private insurers, as well as by Medicare. Different lives may have different values, and even their rank order may be changed when evaluated by different means. Some, however, believe that each life has equal value. A cost-benefit analysis based on discounted future earnings will favor high income persons over low income persons and young over old. Even when other parameters are included such as the value of a mother to the welfare of her small children, higher income persons usually are still estimated to have a higher "value of life."

Early decisions on who would or would not receive kidney dialysis and an organ transplant were made on an informal, intuitive kind of cost-benefit analysis.[53] Medical factors such as a psychologically stable patient and sociological factors, for example that there be some adult other than the patient in the household, were and are important. To the degree that economic rewards are related to individuals' contributions to society, cost-benefit analysis favors those who contribute more to the general welfare.

By 1980, many individuals recognized a need to halt the potential over-use of medical care on their own behalf. The number of physician visits per capita has been declining. Self-care is increasing. This concern has been extended to over-all resource planning. Is 10 percent or more of our GNP being spent on health too high? Is it too low? Elected officials, appointed judges, non-elected bureaucrats of administrative agencies, and members of HSAs and PSROs are making an extraordinary high number of decisions about how to allocate scarce resources for medical care. Would it be better to return these decisions to physicians and to patients who are better-informed than their counterparts prior to World War II, by capping the growth in the expenditures of large government programs? Because of the rapid increases in medical technology, the needed decisions about what government will or will not reimburse are multiplying. Because of the inherent conservatism of government, a new technology may become obsolete before a decision is made. Government can continue not to reimburse for the clearly research procedures. A decision not to reimburse does not deprive those who can afford it to purchase a research procedure.

Far more costly in terms of total expenditures are some of the established procedures, such as coronary artery bypass surgery and other high cost and high utilization procedures that the National Center for Health Care Technology are evaluating for Medicare reimbursement. Coronary artery bypass surgery does not in many cases extend life but does improve the quality of life. It is this type of procedure where the individual patient's assessment of the value to him or her is very important. Methods to measure the quality of life are just now being developed. Without an objective method of measurement, who can or should decide who may benefit? A hopeful beneficiary may over-estimate the value of the benefit, while those who pay for it may under-estimate the benefit.

Alternatively, Medicare can deny reimbursement, reimburse a percentage of the fee, or (unlikely) pay the entire bill—but the Center's decision is made for all patients as a group, not on an individual clinical basis. Income levels and medical needs differ among this group (and any other group defined by diagnosis) and some, if reimbursement is denied, will be able to purchase through their own resources, insurance, loans, and other means the procedure, while others will not. Some who will be able to afford the procedure will decide against it. Some fee-for-service surgeons, who are increasingly in over-supply, might encourage more, otherwise clinically unwarranted, operations if government reimbursement is assured. These are only some of the factors involved in this type of bureaucratic decision. The Congressional Budget Office's proposal to contain Medicaid costs by placing a financial lid on that program's future total costs avoids the necessity of hundreds of government decisions in order to place limits on the use of resources for medical care. Those who argue for a voucher system point out that this also would obviate the necessity for government to make these kinds of decisions.

The public, through elected officials, can agree or disagree with the method of limitation and the percentage of tax revenues used for medical care. As already stated, a large part of physicians' bills paid by Medicare and all of Medicaid payments are met from general revenues, federal and state.

An example of a clinical type of decision made by the government is the Food and Drug Administration's issuance of "compassionate INDs" (Investigational New Drugs), a method by which an unapproved drug is released to a special physician-investigator for use in the treatment of individual patients.

An acting director of a division of the FDA's Bureau of Drugs writes that

'compassionate INDs' . . . have been generally accepted (though unwritten) policy for some time. As any NDA (New Drug Application) nears approval and the public becomes aware of the promising new drug, there are usually many requests to obtain the drug prior to marketing. In certain cases, such as patients unresponsive to other drugs, it is difficult if not impossible to refuse. Other examples are in cases of a patient having taken a drug in a foreign country and now residing in the United States, or patients with diseases for which there is no known treatment, although the drug may not have been shown to be safe and effective. An individual benefit-risk decision is made on a case by case basis.[54]

U.S. government regulators decide on the merit of clinical use of a therapeutic drug for an individual without ever seeing that individual. Allocation is impersonal, and the drug remains potentially available only to the very knowledgeable. Patients and physicians who do not know of the drug have no opportunity to use it, even under the most propitious circumstances. This is a high price to pay for lack of knowledge.

"Tragic Choices"

Decisions by the federal government whether or not to pay for a lifesaving medical intervention or procedure that improves the quality of life but not the length of life differ in an ethical sense. The latter are closely allied to those empathetically labelled "tragic choices." Scarce resources make many choices painful; however, tragic choices involve a conflict among "the values accepted by a society as fundamental."[55] Regulatory actions can create situations of tragic choices. The late approval, in 1978 (initially in France, 1967), of a drug effective in controlling multiple epileptic seizures in children created a situation of tragic choice for some informed parents. Prior to the drug's approval, the parents had to choose between complying with the law or breaking the law to benefit their children. It was difficult, but not "tragic" for the government to decide whether the risk to the children suffering multiple seizures was worth the therapeutic benefit.

It is tragic to be forced to choose between obeying the law and watching one's child have multiple seizures or to break the law to use a drug that has a favorable track record in other countries and promises relief to the child. In some cases, the knowledgeable parents of these children, if financially able, paid to bring the unapproved drug into the country or, if well-connected, induced their friends to bring it in for their child's use. Alternatively, some parents obeyed the law and endured watching their child have multiple seizures each day until the drug was approved. A report by a congressional subcommittee states that the drug in question, sodium valproate, "is regarded as the greatest advance in the treatment of epilepsy in 40 years."[56] The report also notes that it helps persons with several other forms of epilepsy that the FDA has not approved for treatment with this drug.

The denial of options to the knowledgeable consumer is a consequence of bureaucratic rigidity and fear of publicity if a severe, adverse effect appears in an identifiable person. People who do not receive the drug are usually not identified.[57] A "compassionate IND" is not made available unless one's physician knows about it and is willing to apply. The non-knowledgeable consumer is deprived of a choice.

During late 1979 and early 1980, federal government officials vacillated on whether or not Medicare should pay for heart transplants for only those patients operated on by Stanford University's medical team that had achieved a 50 percent, five-year survival rate, a rate higher than for other cardiac transplant centers. Some believe that a 50 percent survival rate for five years removes a medical procedure from research status to clinical medicine. When a heart patient was turned down by the Stanford Medical Center, which has its own criteria for acceptance, the patient went to the University of Arizona Medical School for heart transplantation. A ruling by an administrative judge of the Social Security Administration extended Medicare reimbursement to heart transplants performed by the University of Arizona. The ruling was appealed by the Department of Health and

Human Services (HHS) to the Supreme Court. The ruling had opened up issues of equity and new fears of rapidly rising costs of Medicare. In 1980, HHS denied reimbursement by Medicare for any heart transplantations during a two-year moratorium.

There are about twenty medical centers where such surgery can be done. If reimbursement is assured, the number of new centers will tend to multiply so that the long-run costs will grow to billions of dollars. There is a physical limit to the number of available donor hearts. The University of Utah is planning to implant, in 1982, an artificial heart that its scientists have developed and tested in animals over many years. It is awaiting only FDA's approval for use in human subjects. This medical device will be used essentially to tide over heart transplant candidates until donor hearts become available. This experimental procedure is estimated to cost from $25,000 to $75,000. Additionally, heart-lung transplants were being performed in 1981 at Stanford University Medical Center, and improved medical techniques and a new drug are expected to make all organ transplants more common.

When the government pays the bill, the number of persons for whom organ transplantation is "reasonable and necessary" will increase dramatically. One indication is the nine-fold increase in patients for kidney transplant and dialysis since Medicare reimbursement began.

As of this writing, Medicare reimbursement for any heart transplantation is not assured. Most insurance companies, as well as Blue Cross and Blue Shield in most states, do not pay for heart transplants. Sometimes a community or private club will raise money to pay the costs. Many in our society still consider heart transplants experimental. Government research grants have paid for some of these costs in the past. Alternative uses of the resources consumed in this expensive procedure (ranging from about $60,000, without surgical fee, to $100,000)[58] could yield substantial benefits to more than a single person.

Several approaches to a cost containment, reimbursement policy for heart transplantations were considered by HHS during 1980: (1) perform a cost-benefit analysis for each individual operation proposed, (2) define criteria for acceptability of (a) the individual patient and (b) the operating team, (3) require the medical center to estimate the implied value of life that it uses in its decisions and also require that value to be within a range set by government regulations, (4) continue to refuse reimbursement until survival rates reach a higher level of "success," and (5) establish a total "dollar cap" and let physicians determine for whom the limited dollars are spent, as during the experimental period of kidney transplants.[59] Under the latter policy, those who apply late in the year may not find funds available even though their "case" for reimbursement may be better than those already operated on. The tradeoffs in any such decisions are complex and poorly understood. Decisions about who gets life-saving resources mean that values of life are being assigned to individuals. This is in conflict with ethical and religious teachings. However, even if the value is not made explicit, any choice in the face of scarce resources implies a value was set.

It is clear that the combination of increasing regulation and advances in medical technology is increasing the number of "tragic choices" for society. Recently the federal government has contracted for a study to answer "whether the costs that these (heart) patients will bear in the absence of public funding—bankruptcy, sickness, and death—are justified by the benefits that the rest of us derive from not paying for expensive programs."[60] This implies the use of cost-benefit analysis for allocation of resources across all uses of society.

WAITING (AND LOTTERY)

Those who argue for egalitarianism in the distribution of medical care believe queuing or waiting for one's turn to be the fairest method of allocation, while others favor a lottery.

The lottery is an alternative method of allocating scarce medical resources that many consider at least as egalitarian as waiting. Persons waiting for a kidney transplant are not biologically alike, however, and do not necessarily have equal chances of surviving a kidney transplant. Their biological differences are noted to determine the limits of a lottery pool from which physicians may choose kidney recipients. Physicians generally prefer to operate on those patients who have the best chances for success. In most instances, this favors a pool of younger persons. In recent years, however, the age limit for successful kidney transplants has risen and the number of persons per one million population treated in the United States is higher than in other countries.

Many favor the apparent egalitarianism of waiting and its implied lottery of "first come, first served" because then a higher income person cannot buy medical care at the expense of the poor. Waiting, as previously discussed, is not necessarily as egalitarian as its proponents state. Those who die while waiting for an operation obviously had a higher value of a unit of time than those who wait longer and do not die. Some opponents to egalitarianism as the sole criterion for distribution argue that equal access to the "best" care is impossible because the ability of physicians and availability of resources differ. The larger the amount of real resources per capita that is available and willingly paid for, the less important are the criteria used. Countries with very low incomes per capita cannot afford organ transplantation.

In the United States, the marginal benefit and the marginal cost of an additional unit of medical care is usually expressed in money terms, occasionally with time costs included, but in the United Kingdom (U.K.) it is expressed solely in terms of time:

> . . . time spent travelling to the medical facilities, time spent queueing once arrived (including waiting in a hospital bed for treatment) and time spent on treatment and convalescence. The marginal disutility of health care consumption will therefore be the product of the time spent on consumption of a unit of health care and the marginal disutility of such time. Now it seems likely that both of these will be generally smaller for high socioeconomic groups. The time spent travelling and queueing will be less because (a) they have more cars and are less reliant upon public transport; (b) they have more telephones and hence can make appointments which diminish time spent queueing once arrived; and (c) the areas in which they live are better endowed with medical facilities than the areas where the lower groups live, so that they have less distance to travel. . . . The marginal disutility per unit of time spent in health care consumption is also likely to be less for the higher groups, since professional and managerial workers, being paid in general on a monthly or yearly basis, are less likely to lose income for time lost in working hours than workers in manual occupations who are paid by the hour or day. Overall, therefore, the marginal disutility of time spent consuming health care is likely to be less for higher groups than for lower ones.[61]

Regardless of income, available time for waiting for hospital admittance varies for patients. Under the British system of first-come, first-served, some who come later to the waiting list for surgery and hospital admission may be better biological risks than those who come earlier. Even the size of the waiting list for hospital beds (over 600,000 in 1976) is not a good indicator of unmet medical need. Are many people placed on a waiting list as a precautionary measure?

How rapidly do people who decide against surgery under National Health Service (NHS) auspices inform those who placed their name on the list about their decision? On the other hand, the general practitioner (GP) who acts as a gatekeeper to all specialized services, including that of the gynecologist, "is less apt to refer a patient to the hospital if he knows that the waiting list for the specialty service required is long. . . . New or improved hospital facilities often trigger an initial spurt in the waiting lists as GPs step up referral rates in line with their perception of resource availability."[62] At the end of 1976, the total waiting list for surgical beds was 580,000, almost double the average number of occupied beds. Although there is a great disparity from a couple of days to two years or more of waiting, of the 1,447 "urgent" cases on September 30, 1976, 966 had waited over one month.[63]

Age and disease category classifications, setting up different lists or pools, appear to exist in many countries. Waiting and lottery are thus used to allocate among persons of a specified group. Within the U.K., where the more urgent operations are handled first, "those patients needing operations for hernia, varicose veins, thyroid problems, hip joint replacement and the like simply wait their turn or go to a private hospital."[64]

Although most observers of the British NHS place medical urgency at the top of the criteria to allocate a hospital bed, some would permit other factors sometimes to over-ride. These other criteria include the length of time a person has already waited, "family, social and economic circumstances of patients,"[65] and comparison of their medical condition with those who are already inpatients. Because the length of hospital stays in the U.K. are much longer than in the U.S. and other countries, the latter could be very important. Without criteria for weighting and thus combining all factors into one over-all measure, policy-makers can rationalize any choice that they prefer.

Medical criteria are not precise, but vary according to the individual standards of each specialist or consultant. If the pricing system is rejected, a "social and humanitarian cost-benefit exercise . . . and the setting of norms that represent nationally promulgated needs formula" are, in the opinion of some British economists, needed.[66] As in most government decisions involving health, the increase in costs is better documented than increments in benefits. The dilemmas that centralizing decisions in a political body about who gets what amount of medical care creates are posed in the following quotation:

> Charges against the NHS, or claims for it, that it is either an inhumane, uncaring bureaucracy or the triumph of social

responsibility over selfishness, are ultimately tested. This is the
ultimately irreducible element where the uncompromising moral
choices have to be made by someone. Their task will, however,
have been eased to the extent that what can be quantified has
been quantified and what lower-level value judgements may
properly be made have been made. By clarification of the issues,
by a narrowing down of the grey areas, by eliminating as far as is
humanly possible all that is not inherently imponderable, the act
of faith we are making says that we shall begin to approach the
fulfillment of the objectives of the NHS. And it *is* an act of
faith—one cannot *prove* that less ignorance of the facts of ill
health and medical efficacy and more explicit analysis of the
issues of choice lead to better policy. But in view of the
alternatives, one *has* to believe that they do.[67]

This is also both a defense and a critique of the use of cost-benefit
analysis to make public policy decisions.

The U.K.'s system of explicit rationing has resulted in a very different distribution of the medical care dollar than in the United States.
For example, the aged explicitly receive less medical care than persons
in younger age groups. The wait for a hip replacement operation
may become longer the older one is, and there is an unspoken rule
"that no one over 65 . . . is admitted to medical wards where an
immediate medical evaluation could be made. Even if the patient is
unconscious, that patient waits for the geriatric bed for which there
are queues." The physician-author of the above quotation continues:
"The hospital apparently had 20 unconscious patients waiting to be
admitted. They sent a trained health visitor round (sic) to assess the
priority of these cases, presumably to see who was most unconscious."[68] Denial of medical care to older people in favor of younger
people can be rationalized by comparison of their discounted streams
of future earnings. To extend life at only older ages is increasing the
need to tax workers to support the aged.

A study done in Denmark in 1975 asked the question, "In view of
the scarce resources in the health sector, how ought the impact of
allocating these resources to various diseases be evaluated?"[69] Three
methods of evaluation were considered: the percentage decrease of
all deaths, the gain in life expectancy that would occur if those deaths
due to the disease were eradicated, and the change in the ratio between
productive and non-productive groups that would result from eliminating the disease as a cause of death. Although the effect of eliminating most diseases as measured by mortality or life expectancy was
positive, these measurements overlook the quality of life. Increased

life expectancy, if it means an increased number of days lying in bed, should be a discounted measure. The effect of eliminating most diseases as measured by a gain in goods and sources services produced was computed to be negative. The proportion of persons of productive age who would enjoy longer lives would be less than among older persons. However, if accidents as a cause of death were eliminated, the distribution of the population between the productive and non-productive age groups would remain stable.

Cost-effective use of the limited number of beds, despite a deliberate policy of withholding monies for new hospitals, has not been practiced in the U.K., where the average length-of-stay was, in 1974, twelve to thirteen days in acute hospitals compared to eight days in the U.S.

The wait for hospital beds under Great Britain's NHS varies by region and availability of beds, specialists and consultants. An American economist writes that "in the Liverpool-Wellington area, children in need of hole-in-the-heart surgery face a two- to three-year wait which doctors believe may jeopardize their chance for survival."[70]

Even though Sir William Beveridge stressed that preventive care would be gradually provided when he pushed NHS through Parliament in 1946, preventive medicine is rare under NHS even today. The average physician visit is five minutes, too short for informal health education. Physical checkups without significant symptoms are rare. In 1976, only 8 percent of women 15–64 years of age had a pap smear, or cervical cytology. Although this procedure may be over-used in the U.S., it appears to be under-used in the U.K., where "it is widely accepted that a seemingly healthy adult requires little if any recourse to the medical system."[71] Partial acceptance of this view might be for the better in the U.S. where the reverse concept, that "everyone is a patient," has become the norm. Examples of this American attitude are recent advertisements urging consumers to attend health preventive days, run not only by local community colleges and universities but also by well-known medical groups. One of these follows:

LOW ENERGY? OVERWEIGHT? STRESSED?

At The Healthing Center (TM), part of Straub Clinic & Hospital, we spend all our time helping people succeed—at making healthy lifestyle changes.

Now we're introducing a special, one-day Healthing workshop designed to help you start eating better, exercising and handling stress creatively—so you too can look and feel great!

SPEND A DAY WITH US—
AND TURN YOUR LIFE AROUND!

This month's one-day workshop, scheduled for SATURDAY, AUGUST 23, includes a Healthing luncheon. Workshop price $60.00. Call us at 523-2311 (weekdays) for details and reservations.

THE HEALTHING CENTER (TM)

Straub Clinic and Hospital, Inc. [72]

EVOLUTIONARY APPROACH

This approach to allocation has been described as an "attitude . . . of the avoidance of self-conscious choice: The method of choosing is not explicitly chosen and may not even be known by the mass of the people. The actual allocations evolve in the society without any explicit selection . . . thus avoided are the costs of fundamental values in conflict."[73] Here, there is no concept of an optimum allocation; the results are random and the alternative costs are concealed.

Traditionally, medical care has been provided according to religious and moral codes which eschew the idea that a value of life is implicitly established when saving a life. Although many physicians also do not acknowledge this fact, most policy-planners and physicians involved in organ transplants do. The great variation among nations in the number of patients with chronic kidney failure per one million population who are being treated by dialysis or have a functioning transplant reveals the difficulties involved when no single criterion or allocative rule is used. Because the biological measurements often are in terms of a continuum, it is difficult to defend a cut-off point that marks some patients as sick enough to need a particular treatment while others are not. The per capita income of a country, the percent of GNP spent on health, different cultural values, different levels of technology, and the different values placed on life all play a role in the evolution of customary medical practice and its financing.

In 1974, the number of individuals who benefited from treatment of chronic renal failure in the United States was under 20,000. In 1980, it was over 60,000 persons. Because of the availability of more powerful antibiotics and immunosuppressive drugs, persons over 60 years are a good medical risk not only for dialysis but also for transplantation. Therefore, many more persons can benefit from treatment if the money to pay for their care is available. The costs of the treatment of renal failure have risen rapidly to nearly 10 percent of Medicare's Part B expenditures, thus leaving only 90 percent of that money to pay for medical treatment of 20 million or more aged as opposed to almost 10 percent being spent for about 60,000 end-stage renal dialysis patients.

In the United States, the number of persons receiving dialysis or transplantation greatly increased after 1972 when Medicare began to pay for such care. In 1981, the in-hospital costs of hemodialysis per treatment ranged from the lowest guaranteed rate reimbursed by Medicare of $138 to about $400. The high end of reimbursed costs is because of the numerous exceptions to the fee screens used under the 1978 legislation with its subsequent "reasonable cost" reimbursement. The per-treatment costs of the free-standing, primarily for-profit facilities to which one-third or somewhat more such patients go are lower than most hospitals' costs. This is primarily because the free-standing facilities specialize in kidney dialysis and provide no other medical services. Hospital administrators argue that they have a substantially sicker group of people receiving hemodialysis treatment than do the specialized centers.

Economists doubt that the case-mix differs enough to substantiate an ever-widening differential, now over $250 per treatment, in favor of some hospitals. Economists are also concerned about the tremendous decline in the less expensive dialysis at home, from 40 to 10 percent of all patients using kidney dialysis. The geographic differentials in use of home dialysis are great: from 1 or 2 percent in Los Angeles to about 60 to 75 percent in Seattle and a few other large metropolitan areas. The low Los Angeles percentage persists despite the apparent rule among Kaiser's urologists that at-home or special-facility dialysis centers are to be prescribed.

Economists believe in specialization. I am skeptical that either the patient case-mix of hospitals is so different from that of the free-standing facilities or that Kaiser's enrollees who have terminal kidney disease are so different from those with that disease in the general population that the sizeable reimbursement differential is warranted. Hospitals have higher labor costs than the free-standing facilities. However, it would save Medicare a substantial amount of monies if it cut drastically hospital reimbursement for this procedure to an amount equal to, or only slightly above, that of the free-standing clinics. This would create incentives to induce more people to use the less expensive alternatives. Not only would this save dollars per treatment but also the administrative costs of checking on the high levels of costs claimed by many hospitals. A long-run goal should be to induce most hospitals not to provide a type of care that can be provided at lesser costs by other organizations and at home. Quality of care seems to have been of little concern in formulating policy on this matter because most patients having hemodialysis are knowledgeable about the technique, and survival data show that at-home dialysis has as good or better a record than institutional dialysis. What is of concern is the inappropriate use of too costly facilities and the use of accounting to mask the actual costs. The numbers receiving hemodialysis can be expected to increase greatly. Government policy is discouraging home dialysis. A 1981 study done by economists under contract to HHS asks: "Why should decision-makers have such difficulty expressing a clear policy preference for the dialysis treatment that has the least cost when survival data show it to be as good, if not better, than institutionalized dialysis?"[74]

As of December 31, 1976, Spain had 39.3 chronic kidney failure patients per 1 million population being treated; Austria, 65.8; United Kingdom, 71.2; Canada (as of 1975), 73.4; and Sweden, 99.3. At the other end of the scale were Switzerland, 150.0; the United States, 120.0, and in 1980, about 300; and the Netherlands, 108.5.[75] These variations cannot be adequately explained by variations in medical need. Premeditated rationing by government drastically limiting resources (U.K.) may result in one extreme and the open-ended cost-reimbursement with no explicit limits (U.S.) in another.

COST-BENEFIT

The importance of cost-benefit analysis in making decisions to allocate scarce resources for medical care lies in its potential ability to act as a substitute for competitive price allocation, which does not exist in the medical care market. In some countries, the government provides all medical care. Because of the extent of third party reimbursement in the United States, there is little normal feedback of changes in demand by consumers to those health providers who receive most of their revenue in the form of cost-reimbursement. Feedback is necessary for a market price system to operate. Feedback is not necessary from all consumers, but only from a proportion sufficient to affect some providers. To establish "perfect competition" is an impossible task both theoretically and politically. However, it seems possible to increase the competitiveness of the health care markets sufficiently to decrease the existing amount of government regulation.

Because some government regulations probably will be retained for a long period of time, it is wise to explore the potential of using some form of cost-benefit analysis to guide policy-makers. However, because it is difficult to ascertain medical outcomes derived from medical intervention, the data on which to base cost-benefit analyses are limited. Even if evaluations of technology as used in medical practice were readily available, there is no guarantee that physicians in clinical practice will readily adapt to the findings or that consumers will overcome ignorance. However, deliberate efforts can improve the flow of information to providers and consumers, but at this time the search costs (time and money) are still quite high. Many reliable medical information services are available to physicians but are not generally known to consumers. Obtaining information is a business expense for physicians, but the high cost of obtaining up-to-date medical information cannot be expensed against income by consumers. Moreover, consumers' needs for information are selective and sporadic.

One can question whether an imperfectly competitive market (but with more information) might allocate resources as well as regulations based on very limited data bases.

To obtain a net benefit of a medical intervention, it is necessary to sum all the costs and all the benefits in terms of dollars. The net benefit is the excess of benefits over costs. To allocate resources in an optimal fashion, money is then spent where the net benefit is greatest. Cost-benefit analysis thus could, where the data are available, substitute at the national level for the business firm's use of the return-on-investment (ROI) criterion to make its capital expenditure decisions. However, to perform a cost-benefit analysis even of one type of medical intervention, for example the impact of a new medical device, involves many variables, some of which are unknown and others which cannot be easily priced. The value of relief from anxiety that a CAT scan can give when a brain tumor has been suspected is high but difficult to quantify. Other limitations include differing valuations of extended days of a given quality of life of people at different ages. Many believe, however, that, despite these limitations and the ethical issues involved in valuation of life, the mere act of structuring a policy-maker's thinking along the lines of benefits and costs (with or without valuations) is helpful in making any specific decision: whether to approve a new drug, reimburse for a given medical procedure, or finance a specific research project.

To use cost-benefit analysis for over-all resource allocation is much more difficult. Benefits in some decisions in the health sector are more subject to difficult-to-measure quality differentials than in other industries. Moreover, arguments about the techniques of valuation of the days of life that a medical intervention might save have not been settled.

Cost-benefit analysts often evaluate a life using a discounted stream of potential earnings approach plus an estimate of the value of imputed income, for example, from doing household chores, but rarely add in shadow prices for the intangibles of love, parentage, and similar variables. Other analysts prefer to value additional days-of-life on the basis of how many dollars an individual would be willing to pay to increase his or her probability of a longer life expectancy. This method is theoretically superior because there is no fall-off to near zero values upon retirement. Empirical data to support this approach are not consistent. Joanne Linnerooth writes in *Economic Inquiry*: "As a person's survival chances decrease, his willingness to pay increases at an increasing rate."[76] In other words, as one approaches death the value of money falls, especially if one has no descendants who will be heirs.

Other approaches used to evaluate life include a discounted value of future consumption by non-workers and comparison of premium wages paid for very risky jobs above less risky jobs requiring equal skill. Combination approaches that employ different parameters over a range of values are also used. Whatever the method, it is generally accepted that the value of life is greater than the value of a person's future stream of discounted earnings.

Assumptions are made and value judgments are used in all methods. Further, there "is no testable relationship between the willingness to pay and the human capital approaches to placing a value on the loss of a human life."[77] In 1980, $300,000 to $500,000 was the dollar range used by some economists for the value of one life. These amounts are greater than the average person's discounted life-time earnings. As already discussed, government regulators generally place much higher values on lives saved. John P. O'Neill, of OSHA, explained in 1979 that "we do not use a cost-benefit analysis. . . . We're not making a balance, we're making a judgment."[78]

An advantage of the cost-benefit technique for allocation of resources within a society is that it permits comparison between the net benefit of a new medical intervention, drug, or medical device with those of existing modalities.

Cost-benefit analyses can help choose not only the most cost-effective method of obtaining a single goal but within limits can help rank, or at least compare, substitute and complementary goals of national health policy. Cost-benefit analysis suffers from uncertainties, but in no greater degree than the decision-making that characterizes the existing mixed system. The decisions about allocation by Health Systems Agencies and provider-dominated utilization review panels are often political.

Although federal agencies have attempted cost-benefit analyses of proposed regulations as was required by the inflationary impact statements under Executive Order No. 12044 in 1978, they generally have not used this method. However, in Fall 1978, the U.S. Circuit Court of Appeals set aside OSHA's benzene exposure rules because OSHA did not show "a reasonable relationship" between anticipated benefits and costs. The Reagan Administration is placing greater emphasis on the use of cost-benefit analysis to assess the worth of regulations. However, this is far different from using the technique to allocate scarce resources for the maximum welfare. Although in the private sector there are studies to develop common, unitary measures of benefits from different medical interventions, these are still in the experimental stage. The use of a monetary valuation and its limitations has already been discussed.

Currently, I am developing a method that uses, as a common measure, "hours" spent on work, unpaid household chores, and leisure. Because time costs have replaced, in many countries, money costs as an allocator of medical care and because individuals have a limited number of hours as well as money, this measure seems appropriate and avoids the ethical dilemmas of monetary valuation. Moreover, "hours lost from paid work" is a common tool of the economist. If this approach proves feasible, it would still be possible to use a cost-benefit approach by translating the hours into dollars for optimal allocation of health care dollars.

What is the current practice of using cost-benefit analysis? Congress obviously believes that such analyses should be done and at least be used as guides for specific decisions. The Office of Technology Assessment in its November 1980 report to Congress states that, although some form of cost-benefit analysis "is useful for assisting in many decisions, it should not be the sole or prime determinant of a decision."[79] There are some academics and others who believe that over-all resource allocation decisions can be based on cost-benefit analysis. I believe that the increasing number of non-government, decision-analysis or cost-effective studies will eventually yield better guides to resource planning for a given purpose or end-point but not for comparing allocative decisions involving different goods or end-points. For example, cost-benefit analyses on whether a hospital should or should not buy within its limited budget a CAT scanner rather than other equipment are relatively simple. Somewhat more difficult is whether HHS should or should not within its limited budget support screening of a targeted, at-risk population for hypertension. However, it becomes far more complex when the question to be answered is whether incremental amounts of money be spent on heart transplantation, school lunch programs for the poor, or basic health research. The number of variables become very large, time spans until pay-offs differ, and the beneficiaries under each program also differ so that comparative assessment under different value judgments becomes necessary.

Most public policy-makers here and abroad do not use cost-benefit analysis even to assess whether medical intervention, a new medical device, or a new drug has greater net benefits than costs. Yet "in one disease alone, phenylketonuria, hospitalized patients would incur a net cost over current treatment of $50,000,000 annually were it not for programs of neonatal detection and dietary therapy"[80] instituted upon detection. Government policy-makers prefer not to expose how their decisions are made, and they are especially loathe to clarify, whenever a decision involves life and death, how much they have assumed a life to be worth. One economist has estimated that for government "supported, operated, or mandated" health programs, the implicit cost per life saved ranges from $72,000 for a kidney transplant to well over $1 million in occupational and environmental regulations to protect health. For example, it is estimated that the implied value of each life saved under OSHA's coke oven emission standard is anywhere from $4.5 million to $158 million, and, under OSHA's proposed standard for occupational exposure to acrylonitrile, the value of each life is upwards of $625 million.[81]

It is obvious from the above that public decision-makers would offend many people if the assumptions behind their regulations were known. Systematic decision-making methods about allocation of scarce resources of health are not likely under government regulation.

There are few published cost-benefit analyses of specific medical procedures. A 1980 British cost-benefit calculation found that "heart transplants are a good buy . . . for a man, aged, 25, married with two children and earning £5000 ($11,500) a year before falling ill."

The British estimate of the direct medical costs was, in 1980, $60,000. The positive net benefit is mainly because of the government's "cost of maintaining him and his family in benefits over four years of his immediate death . . . of $69,000 and the government cost of his survival as an invalid $71,300."[82] The study used the Stanford University Medical Center's survival rates and gave the individual an 80 percent chance of returning to work after one year. This analysis may be criticized for incompleteness and because its assumptions "loaded the dice," but it is noteworthy that it was done at all and published in *The Sunday Times*.

Other examples of cost-benefit analysis that could be used to allocate medical intervention under the British National Health Service (NHS) concern hip replacement operations for older persons with arthritis. In 1976, it was estimated that a total hip replacement for persons under age 60 yields a monetary benefit-to-cost ratio of at least ten to one while for those aged 60 to 70 years, the ratio is only two to one. In 1974, one-half of 1 percent of the total cost of NHS was for these operations. In that same year, 5,000 hip replacement operations were performed privately, indicating that the supply was substantially less than the demand.[83]

Cost-benefit analysis as well as politics has probably played a role in increasing the quality of day-to-day care in the U.K. received by aged persons. It is clearly more economical to provide routine medical care services in the homes of aged persons by well-trained nurses than to use long-term nursing-home care. Mary-Ann Rozbicki, in a paper prepared for the U.S. State Department's Executive Seminar, writes that "house calls by home nurses and health visitors totalled nearly eight million in 1976, the equivalent of 14 percent of the population. . . . [The] purposes ranged from care for post-operative and chronically ill patients to prenatal and infant care as well as family planning and nutrition."[84] Rozbicki comments somewhat later in the same paper:

> British health authorities thus find it much easier to adopt "cost effective" allocation procedures than would their counterparts in this country. In weighing the choice between a more comfortable life for the millions of aged or early detection and treatment of the far fewer victims of dread diseases, they have favored the former. In choosing between a fully equipped hospital therapy and rehabilitation center or nuclear medicine technology, they have favored the former. The sheer numbers involved on each side of the equation would tend to dictate these choices by government

officials in a democratic society. But, another element appears to affect the decision as well; those involved in the allocation process appear to affix a relatively low value to the benefits that medical technology can produce.[85]

Many of the examples of cost-benefit analysis actually being used by governments in formulation of policy come from the British experience. This is because the British have limited the percent of GNP that they will spend on health and this makes allocation or rationing obvious. Most other countries have not deliberately capped total expenditures for health. The British believed that

> In the 1940s, it was possible . . . that the demand for health care was finite, and not beyond the resources of the economy to satisfy.

> . . . to provide a service 'to meet all reasonable requirements' dooms them to failure. It is time the British people were told this; it is time the N.H.S. told the community what level of service it can expect with the resources emerging from a declining economy. But before this can be done the statute book must surely be relieved of what has become an embarrassing piece of fantasy.[86]

The British-planned priorities continue not to be met. The 1980 British government's report on *Inequalities in Health* documents that "there is generally little sign of health inequalities in Britain actually diminishing and, in some cases, they may be increasing . . . the causes of health inequalities are so deep-rooted that only a major and wide-ranging programme of public expenditure is capable of altering the pattern."[87] Further, the amount of expenditures needed is unrealistic given Britain's economic situation and there is no firm belief that, if more is spent, it will correct the identified problems of inequality. Although inequalities referred to include differences by socioeconomic classes and geographical areas in mortality and disability rates, the 417-page report also stresses the need for more consumer health education with a particular focus on the schools, vaccination and immunization programs, cost-effective targeted screening, and anti-smoking programs. The report's first recommendation is "to give children a better start in life."[88] In actuality, expenditures benefiting children and the mentally handicapped, who are unable to vote, have been experiencing cuts rather than gains.

Despite the British Secretary's intent in the 1970s to shift spending priorities "in favour of services for the elderly, for the mentally ill

Table 13. Great Britain, Southwestern Region:
Growth in Revenue Expenditure on Health,
1975–76 to 1977
(Excluding Personal Social Services)

Service	Actual Percent	Planned[a] Percent
Acute	+ 1.6	+ 1.2
Primary care	+ 1.0	+ 3.8
Elderly and physically handicapped	+ 1.0	+ 3.5
Mentally ill	+ 0.4	+ 1.5[b]
Mentally handicapped	− 1.5	+ 1.6
Children	− 1.7	+ 2.2
Maternity	− 2.7	− 1.8
OVERALL:	+ 0.9	+ 2.9

[a]*The Lancet* (March 25, 1978), p. 659. Illustrative national average growth-rate of expenditures per annum from U.K. Department of Health and Social Services, *Priorities for Health and Personal Social Services in England* (Royal Stationers: Government Document, 1978).

[b]Calculated.

and handicapped, and for children . . . while slowing down the expansion of acute s rvices,"[89] this was not accomplished. It has been charged that health expenditures in the U.K. have been shifted more to the elderly and chronically ill and also to those areas with greater population and thus to those with voting power.

The British, with almost a completely tax-financed system, have similar problems of inefficient allocation of medical care as the United States. British economists at the University of York, Alan Maynard and Anne Ludbrook, explain the British problems in containing health care costs in the same fashion as do economists describing the American problems in containing health care costs.

The basic problem is that the primary decision makers in the resource allocation process, the general practitioner in primary care and the consultant in the hospital, have little incentive to pursue rigorously cost-effective medicine. . . . The doctor is the decision maker but not the budget holder: he assesses the benefits of therapy but rarely has to compare these with the costs of treatment and the opportunities foregone in treating the patient under his care as opposed to the patient in the queue or undiagnosed outside the community.[90]

The authors of the above criticism write further:

We consider now the impact of a more fundamental reform of health care arrangements, i.e., the introduction of a 'free market,' with prices charged for health care services, accompanied by voluntary public and/or private insurance. The advocate of the market forecasts that the efficiency of this form of allocative mechanism will be superior to that of a State institution such as the NHS. Clearly, if this forecast is correct it is a powerful argument in favour of the market as it might enable us to reduce the resource wastage that exists in the NHS. However, there are two major obstacles to the achievement of an efficient outcome in the health care market, namely uncertainty and the monopoly position of the suppliers (doctors).[91]

Apparently, arguments for more competition in the health care markets are being listened to in the U.K. as well as in the U.S. However, in both countries, the inherent factor of uncertainty and the imposed factor of licensure raise doubts as to the potential efficacy of the competitive approach. More information would reduce some of the uncertainty, and the necessity for more information is one of the major themes of this book. I have already discussed the inconsistency of having licensure in a competitive market. Politically, it does not appear viable to replace physician licensure with accreditation, as has been proposed for other health care providers. However, weakening or eliminating licensure of physicians is being discussed in the executive offices of California in Sacramento, and hearings on licensure of physicians are planned for Fall 1981. Even with retention of physician licensure, other factors can work to create as competitive a market in health care as exists in some other markets. The licensure of physicians and their political power to retain it need not be a roadblock to the other reforms being put in place. Once some measure of competition is achieved, physician licensure can again be evaluated.

The number of physicians is rising, which alone can act to reinforce competition. As lesser trained physician extenders become increasingly directly reimbursed and the diversity of insurance and medical organizations of suppliers increases, the viability of an imperfect market acting to allocate medical resources in a fairly efficient manner seems promising. The viability would be greater if all licensure were replaced by certification. If some licensing boards are retained, the majority of their members should not have a vested interest.

Cost-benefit and other forms of decision analysis as used by the economist is being recognized as useful in making clinical decisions. Although physicians and patients usually dislike using monetary units or any numerical measure to describe costs of pain or benefits of relief from pain or, especially, value of life, increasingly the ranking of options is occurring. There are even available examples of the numerical ordering of health benefits for the individual in monetary terms:

> If restoration of normal health were given a utility value of 100 units and if death following a prolonged painful illness were given a utility value of 0 units, a dollar expenditure of $5000 might be assigned 20 or 30 units, an anaphylactic reaction to a drug might be assigned 10 units, and improvement of health to the point where the individual could return to work on a part-time basis might be assigned 60 or 65 units.[92]

There are needed cost-benefit analyses of specific medical devices, surgery, drugs, alternative combinations of treatment, and places of treatment. The method, however, needs to be greatly refined to reflect the probability of added days of life of a given quality from the medical intervention. Such analyses can help to reveal value judgments made in choosing between alternatives. The distributional effects should always be made explicit. Although the estimates of costs and benefits in a cost-benefit analysis may be incomplete, cost-benefit analysis permits ordered thinking and an indication of the range of a potential benefit.

SUMMARY

The world-wide nature of the problem of optimum resource allocation for health is evident in many different forms. Recently, American newspapers have carried stories of misallocation of health resources in the U.S.S.R. stemming from the over-use of free emergency services to the detriment of seriously ill persons waiting for a physician who is often tied down by non-essential calls. As early as 1972, the *Los Angeles Times* printed a story concerned with the allocation of medical care within the U.S.S.R.

> Long considered one of the successes of the Soviet system of delivering free public health care, the emergency home service is undergoing major reforms to eliminate abuses which hamper its efficiency.
>
> In the past, when it was necessary to pay for a visit, doctors were not called for trifling reasons, Dr. Mikhail Bogomolsky, an emergency aid physician, said recently. . . .

But now, with free medical service, everybody wants a profoundly scientific cure. Well, that is all right in a way, but in some cases "we have to use a cannon against sparrows," as a Russian saying has it, Dr. Bogomolsky said.[93]

Regardless of the type of "misallocation," the problem arises because there is a "shortage" when no market price covering the resource costs exists to clear the market. In most countries, the rural sector suffers from the maldistribution. In many countries, some solution is being sought as costs, even when there are no markets prices, soar in response to the demand. Solutions that remove the "financial barrier" and do nothing about the problems of allocation beg the question.

The allocation of medical care becomes synonymous with rationing medical care. Rationing of scarce resources can be implicit (not specific to any group or person) or explicit. In the United States, there has been no effective limit on health expenditures because its resources per capita are relatively large. Rationing can be veiled behind government legislation and regulations that exist primarily for purposes of remedying the more obvious inequities. Medicaid was passed to remove financial barriers to medical care for the poor. Similarly, Medicare was passed to aid the aged who, by the necessity of being closer to failing health and death, have greater "need" for medical care. Rationing by the physician "gate-keeper" is more obvious than rationing by regulation.

From a cost-benefit point of view, more dollars spent on research and prevention should yield higher net benefits than additional dollars spent to extend the lives of elderly people, for whom there may be no cure and whose quality of life may be diminished. Funding of biomedical research is partly by government, partly by private industry, and only minimally by universities. The federal government has been decreasing its investment in research trainees and at the same time has created new roadblocks for private companies planning to market new, beneficial drugs and medical devices. The Reagan Administration is anticipated to reduce the regulatory hurdles. A new development has been alliances between industry and universities to develop further basic and applied research.

In either a relatively private market system or a government-run, national system of health care, decision-making by the physician is divorced from efficient allocative decision-making. The closer the health care markets come to competitive markets with their attributes of full information and free entry, the closer will be the efficient allocation of scarce resources.

As the percentage of the GNP spent on health care increases, it dramatizes the conflict between health care and other needs of society. When 10 percent of the GNP is being spent on health, there is obviously less funding available for needs other than medical care. It has been estimated that, by 1990, 12 percent of the GNP in the United States will be spent on health, double the 6 percent of GNP spent on health in 1965. The next twenty-five years will not see a further doubling of that percentage but, rather, a slowdown in the rate of increase. If costs are not contained, what would increases beyond even 10 percent of GNP mean for other worthwhile expenditures of government?

X. POLICY RECOMMENDATIONS

The United States has been fortunate in that until recently the 9 to 10 percent of its GNP being used for health has been large enough to yield sufficiently ample per capita resources, so that difficult allocation decisions have been minimal. This has not been true for those countries with small, per capita national incomes. However, new advances in medical technology have changed the situation in the wealthier nations. The controversy over the financing of heart transplants and other costly medical procedures continues. Artificial organs, especially the artificial heart, may remove, in the foreseeable future, the existing, natural and legal limitations of a shortage of suitable organs. The cost of medical care over one person's lifetime is rapidly increasing as one expensive procedure saves a person only for that same person to live to incur another expensive procedure. Until research finds cures, the best approach to contain costs is a combination of more consumer health education and steps to make the health care markets more competitive. The two are linked: better informed consumers are needed for competitive markets to work.

In the private sector, in 1980, the Massachusetts General Hospital discontinued, when at the same time the Mayo Clinic established, a heart transplantation program. The federal government has estimated annual costs for the first few years of a federally financed heart transplantation program at only $3 billion. Continuing developments in drugs and medical procedures for organ transplants could make this a very expensive program. Although legislative debate in the past has centered on national health insurance, the state of the economy with only level or low real growth as well as politics are dictating budget cuts in the 1980s. The only probable form of expansion of government health insurance is catastrophic expense insurance, which is far less costly than comprehensive, first dollar coverage insurance. Given the income distribution and levels of taxation in the United States, any sizeable expansion of the existing Medicare and Medicaid type programs would result in sizeable redistribution of incomes away from some to others who are in the middle and higher income tax brackets.

Medical technology is advancing so rapidly that additional potential medical care costs are very high because of the probable inappropriate use of some of the new techniques and the rapid obsolesence of the technology. An example of the potential duplicative uses of medical technology are the CAT scanner, ultrasound, nuclear magnetic resonance and x-rays, which obtain body images and may sometimes, but not always, be used to repeat known knowledge when there is no medical need for more data. This is not to argue against innovation but to point out the cost implications if the consumer is ignorant and also price does not allocate. Because of the high costs to the consumer of obtaining current and accurate medical information, the consumer uses the physician to advise about purchases in a fashion similar to that of other professionals. However, in the medical care sector the third party umbrella is increasingly pervasive. The physician, as do many other professionals, benefits from the higher costs of the services. Under these circumstances, how should society decide who should get what treatment and who should pay for it? In the cases of catastrophic medical expense, how should the value of life itself be determined?

CATASTROPHIC EXPENSE

A national policy option debated in Congress for many years is government-financed or government-mandated catastrophic or major medical expense insurance coverage for all persons. The main argument for this type of insurance is that everyone, including those who are working or have any source of income, dread the often unexpected, expensive treatment costs of a chronic disease such as cancer, kidney failure, or injuries from a severe accident. The permissible deduction from federal income taxes of those medical expenses that are above 3 percent of adjustable gross income does not help persons who pay no income tax although it does help those with higher incomes. In 1981, the special medical deduction plus the exclusion from taxes of health insurance premiums paid by employers and the $150 individual itemized deduction for health insurance premiums equaled a total indirect subsidy of nearly $18 billion.[1] Employees receive a tax subsidy because the health insurance premiums paid on their behalf are compensation that is not subject to income tax.

Economist Alain Enthoven has evolved a unique, catastrophic coverage plan that would eventually eliminate this tax subsidy and replace it with a tax credit issued upon purchase of health insurance. The tax credit would be a percentage of the actuarial cost of providing health care to families with similar income and demographic characteristics.[2] Enthoven suggests a tax credit per family equal to 60 percent of the actuarial, community-rated costs for nonpoor families. Enthoven would thus eliminate the link between employment and health insurance coverage so that providers would have to satisfy consumers, not employers, and he implies that non-coverage among adults would lessen. Payments to plans or insurers made by consumers above the suggested 60 percent tax credit would come from their pockets. In effect there would be a 40 percent cost corridor at time of purchase of insurance rather than only a cost corridor at the time of consumption of medical care.

Under Enthoven's plan, employers may pay premiums for their employees but the employees must then pay income and social security taxes on the resulting income-in-kind. However, exceptions are made if the premiums are community-rated for a "qualified" government plan with specified benefits and the premiums are below a fixed amount. If the plan is "qualified," the employer may continue to expense as labor costs the premiums or HMO per capita charges below a fixed amount. Whether an employee would gain or lose under these complicated financial arrangements would be dependent on variables, such as the previous level of employer benefit payments and the new standardized levels of premiums for selected demographic groups and areas. Employers would not be able to expense premium costs that are higher than the appropriate levels. Those families selecting more expensive plans would probably themselves have to pay the premium amounts above the standard in order to get the additional benefits.

Although Enthoven's plan breaks the link between the job held by the head of the family and the amount and adequacy of health insurance coverage, it does so at some sacrifice of consumer choice by individuals in families where both husband and wife work because each family could choose only one health plan. Enthoven argues that this would eliminate most duplicate coverage and the potential for duplicate payments. A two-worker family living apart, possibly temporarily for career reasons, thus would not be able to choose separate plans. More importantly, two-worker families living together might have to compromise heretofore respected reasons for each worker's making a different choice. Also, unless the employer gives cash or other benefit equal to the loss of the earned health insurance premiums, workers who are denied the benefits from their employers' plans suffer a loss in wages. Presumably they would receive a rebate, but Enthoven does not mention this.

Enthoven's plan also envisages only community-rated plans and thus reduces employers' incentives to promote better health among their employees. Enthoven's "Consumer Choice Health Plan" (CCHP) would at least in the initial stages require a great deal of government regulation in setting up the qualified benefit packages. It does more than encompass catastrophic health expense coverage with its $1,500 out-of-pocket expense for deductibles and copayments. CCHP has been criticized because, by insistence on community rates, comprehensive health benefits, and taxation provisions, it appears to favor large, established HMOs. It is not easy to summarize all the complex provisions of CCHP in a few paragraphs and it is suggested that the interested person read Enthoven's own description and then make his or her own judgment.

Another well-known policy approach that centers only on catastrophic expense is Martin Feldstein's major risk insurance plan which has a deductible that increases as personal income increases.[3] In addition, government guaranteed loans would be made available for families to post-pay medical bills. If simplicity has virtue, Martin Feldstein's plan, first proposed in 1971, should not be ignored. Both Enthoven's and Feldstein's plans would, after an expense limit paid out-of-pocket is exceeded, provide virtually comprehensive coverage. Enthoven's plan, however, claims more cost containment than Feldstein's, but the latter has the virtue of administrative simplicity and interferes less with the organization of medical care. Feldstein's plan has been criticized like all pure catastrophic expense coverage plans have, because it does not have a mechanism to prevent over-utilization once the out-of-pocket deductible is met. This argument is discussed further within the general analysis of catastrophic health insurance that follows.

For persons who suffer from one catastrophic disease, kidney failure, the federal government now pays for treatment of that disease. Expansion of coverage for catastrophic expense, disease-by-disease seems less rational than expansion related to the expense of the treatment and income of the afflicted individual. In the famous Karen Quinlan case, the issue of costs and who pays for them, and also the real resource costs to society, were ignored by the judiciary. Ethical principles, not tradeoffs, were the deciding factors.[4]

A line of demarcation between high medical expenses and catastrophic medical expenses is difficult to draw. Medical expenses are usually defined to cover only traditional medical care. The expenses may be defined in terms of total dollars spent out-of-pocket (costs above payments by third parties) or as a percentage of income spent out-of-pocket. The insurance concept of catastrophic expense as it is debated in Congress implies that persons have the means to pay routine medical care expenses through other insurance, from a high income, or liquidation of large assets. The poor would continue to be covered under Medicaid, which has first dollar coverage.

Some young, healthy persons may purposely avoid first dollar insurance coverage as a self-perceived waste of their money and may utilize preventive measures other than medical care as a partial substitute. These persons, although less likely to experience high medical expenses, do not have the presumed floor on which catastrophic insurance can build but would be covered by Medicaid if their financial resources are exhausted by unforeseen medical bills. Persons covered by Medicaid have virtually complete catastrophic coverage in most states. Under Medicare, persons have a limited form of catastrophic insurance. Private health insurance coverage under major medical or catastrophic expense insurance has greatly increased. It is estimated that about two-thirds of the population have such coverage under private insurance. Most of the premiums for private catastrophic coverage are paid for by employers. Unless the tax laws change, private major medical insurance will grow.

Private major medical plans usually have dollar deductibles of $300 to $2,000, a continuous cost corridor, and an over-all life-time limit, some as high as one million dollars. Even with these restraints, costs higher than the insurer anticipates may occur. Insurers impose their own standards of "reasonable and customary" charges in a given area. Thus, in periods of rapidly rising prices, protection of the privately insured is decreasing as is that of those under Medicare.

Many of the private plans, including those of HMOs, exclude some types of health care such as unlimited ambulatory mental health services and nursing-home care that separately can amount to extraordinary expenses. However, most proposed national legislation also does not cover these items. Fortunately, about 75 percent of all hospital stays are less than 10 days. More than 90 percent of hospital stays end before 30 days, and less than 1 percent exceed 100 days.[5]

Catastrophic expense insurance applies only to those amounts which the individual pays out-of-pocket. If a $5,000 deductible is used, about 2.5 million non-institutionalized persons would have exceeded that amount in 1977; if $2,500, about 7 million. With lower deductibles, the persons affected rise rapidly. There were 20 million, or about 10 percent of the population, with total annual medical expenses over $1,000 in 1977.[6] In fiscal year 1978, 7 million families had *out-of-pocket* medical expenses greater than 15 percent of their gross income. About 20 million families had *total* health expenditures greater than the 15 percent cut-off.

Government catastrophic medical expense benefits based on the out-of-pocket expenses exceeding a percentage of income rather than given dollar amount spent will, if tax financing remains the same, redistribute income to the poor. A requirement of prior spending of 15 percent of income was more liberal in 1977 than a $5,000 requirement. On the basis of the 1977 Congressional Budget Office (CBO) estimates used here, the 15 percent cut-off was comparable to an absolute dollar amount of $2,500.[7]

A major argument against mandating any type of national catastrophic health insurance or provision for it by employers is that it rewards over-utilization of expensive technology once the deductible is spent and that, therefore, the most expensive procedures will be commonly used to keep persons alive, some in a state of "living death" at higher dollar and emotional costs to them and their families, and also at health care costs higher than otherwise to the taxpayer. Proposals are being made to restructure physician reimbursement to provide incentives for physicians to be more selective in ordering multiples of the less expensive technologies and more discerning in involving the patient and family in use of the very expensive medical technologies. The potential over-all impact of these proposals is not known.

To cost out the various legislative proposals for catastrophic health insurance is difficult. Under-estimates of future costs of any type of health care program are common. Cost-sharing through deductibles, copayments, and cost-corridors will restrain increases in demand. However, the degree of restraint is dependent on the size of those factors and consumer response. Also, legislative changes are expected to place limits on the amounts that employers can expense as health insurance premiums. That copayments of whatever variety restrain demand over a period of time has long been debated. Countries that spend the larger shares of their gross national product on health use several sources to pay the bills. However, that they spend a greater percent of their GNP may be because, when the entire bill is paid by one source, a government, it usually is a predetermined, budgeted amount. Under the mixed system of the United States and some other countries, the total is open-ended. Many HMOs have copayments along with a predetermined, negotiated annual charge. Legislative proposals for catastrophic health expense coverage have open-ended reimbursement, some with the mandated benefits to be paid for by employers. By definition, catastrophic health insurance contracts have sizeable deductibles. Most private contracts additionally have requirements of copayments of expenses incurred beyond the deductible.

Recent studies done at the Rand Institute have used both insurance claims and premiums and also actual expenditures over a two-year period of a sample of about 400 families in Dayton, Ohio. Both types of studies found that the amount of out-of-pocket expenditures required does affect total expenditures on medical care. This is what traditional economists would anticipate. Using data based on insurance claims and premiums, Joseph P. Newhouse's preliminary results suggest that "demand for care is on the order of 50 percent higher when care is free than when it is subject to an income-related catastrophic insurance plan."[8]

The preliminary results of another Rand study using the actual two-year data of nearly 400 families in Dayton, Ohio, from 1974–76 are that "expenditures on medical care do vary with insurance, income and covariates. The co-insurance elasticity of demand is on the order −0.2 and most of the response to changes in prices from changing the co-insurance rate occurs between zero and 25 percent."[9] These new data indicate that catastrophic health expense coverage may, if properly designed, effectively contain demand and thus costs.

However, the only major U.S. government experience with coverage of catastrophic expense has been Medicare's coverage of treatment for terminal kidney disease. In April 1974, HEW estimated the first-year costs of kidney dialysis and transplantation at $240 million. The total cost of the program in 1981 was nearing $3 billion annually. Until the legislation was amended in the late 1970s, costs were expected to reach $6 billion for 75,000 patients by 1992. The increase in costs is because of the increase in the numbers who are receiving treatment, switches to more expensive treatment, and inflation. This experience points to the problem of containing costs when catastrophic expenses are paid even after a deductible and with a cost corridor. Although copayments may not appear during an inflation to restrain costs, they do cut potential expenses that would have occurred without copayments. To require employers to provide catastrophic health expense coverage is, for those employers who do not already provide this benefit, equivalent to a new payroll tax levy. Thus, this would, as would similar increases in social security taxes, depress the economy. In most instances, employers will in the long run adjust to higher payroll taxes either by reducing their number of employees or reducing the rate of increase in wages.

Whether one supports catastrophic medical expense coverage for all persons depends on how it is financed and one's value judgments. What are its potential benefits in an equity sense of the well paying for the medical care of the very ill? Can employers substitute premiums for catastrophic health insurance for some part of the health insurance premiums which they already pay by increasing the co-payment for which the consumer is responsible? Employees of a few companies (TRW, Inc., American Can, Morgan Stanley, and others) are being offered a basic benefit package to which they can, at the employer's expense, add those optional items that they prefer.[10] If the optional items were paid for by the employees, this would be close to Enthoven's CCHP. Education of consumers and flexible benefit packages could be used to reduce first dollar coverage and favor catastrophic, medical expense coverage.

Cost containment through consumer education, living wills, and other measures might offset the technological imperative to keep terminal patients alive by artificial means even when, given the current state of technology, they have no hope of recovery. Patients have always had the right to refuse treatment, but in an increasing number of cases patients may become comatose before they have made a decision. Many states have passed "living will" laws to give individuals greater control over whether or not they want extraordinary life-support measures used to prolong their lives. The legislatures of many additional states have similar bills on their agendas.

In this debate, my value judgment is that the well should pay at least in part for the catastrophic health expenses of the very ill. This judgment does not, however, rule out concomitant use of the tax system to discourage unhealthy habits of living, cost-effective measures to encourage prevention of disease and accidents, and efforts to improve audit of government spending. The growth of courses on medical ethics in medical schools is encouraging, as is the increasing number of courses at all levels of university education on the economics of health.

Federal direct financing of all expenses to treat catastrophic illness, although ethically appealing, appears unwise. Experience under Medicare's 1972 amendments to pay for kidney dialysis for all who "need" such treatment indicates how the numbers per 100,000 treated can greatly increase when, as with many diseases, there is a continuous progression from somewhat ill to very ill. There is no agreed upon cut-off between somewhat ill and very ill in the cases of terminal kidney disease, diabetes, and hypertension. In 1978, 19 percent of end-stage kidney disease patients under Medicare were over sixty-five years of age. As life expectancy increases, the incidence of chronic disease increases. As medical advances continue, individuals at older and older ages can be successfully treated.

Federal payment for treatment of terminal kidney disease also indicates the progressive increase in the number of regulations needed even to approach control over the costs. Without detailed regulations defining when a disease is terminal, the appropriate levels of care required at different disease stages, the acceptable quality of care, and the accounting procedures used, etc., the government has an explosive, open-ended commitment under cost-reimbursement of procedures.

British economist Michael H. Cooper comments that "need is not an absolute state but a matter of judgment and opinion. It is one of many possible points along one of many possible continuums. Each doctor is liable to have his own dividing line between states that are categorized as being in need and those free of need."[11] The dividing line appears to shift if someone other than the patient pays for the care.

For all these reasons, some persons question whether government should finance an additional share of catastrophic health expenses. Gradual expansion of such coverage, disease by disease, seems to be an unwise course. It may be wiser to wait until the consensus is that the economy can afford such coverage for all persons incurring extraordinary medical expenses irrespective of the disease in question. Medicare provides catastrophic expense coverage for the aged. The public needs to decide how to spend additional resources: whether society wants to shift existing resources away from other uses or whether it may wish to use additional new, real income for catastrophic health insurance, or more benefits for the retired, or preventive health care for children, etc. These are political decisions. After the hard choices are made and the interrelationships, especially with government and private pension policies, recognized, the direction of national health policy can be more wisely set.

For society to make informed decisions, data are needed about anticipated changes in health outcomes: changes in mortality rates and the incidence and duration of illness resulting from spending more dollars on medical care, including that for preventive care. Although cost-benefit analysis that attempts to assess the value of a medical intervention can be attacked because some value judgments are used, the latter can always be revealed. Moreover, if the value judgments used in deriving the value of an added year of life of a given quality are the same for alternative expenditures, the cost-effectiveness of those alternative expenditures can be compared. Of possibly greater concern is the lack of hard data on the biological effects of medical intervention on which cost-benefit analyses depend.

There are those who believe that "any medical program that is ambiguous enough to require cost-benefit analysis is too ambiguous to be resolved by cost-benefit analysis."[12] However, even the author

314 Policy Recommendations

of this quotation admits that the act of cost-benefit analysis will make the policy-maker better informed. Final decisions on the allocation of medical care are political decisions, and the voters have not yet had the opportunity to make an informed choice.

In 1971, I wrote that "it is recognized today that the individual's state of health or illness is a continuum, ranging from optimum adaptation to environment and no disease to maladaptation with various levels of disease. This concept puts stress on prevention and early detection of disease—as well as on the care of symptoms and, if possible, rehabilitation."[13]

Because of shortages of natural resources, medical care has primarily treated symptoms with the exception of a few proven methods of preventive care. These include vaccines and immunization against such diseases as polio, diphtheria, and the prophylactic use of some drugs. As the nation's GNP per capita grows, however:

> prevention of disease is being proposed with increasing frequency as a strategy to moderate the increase in medical-care expenditures. Acceptance of prevention, however, does not extend to all technologies or to all age groups. Primary prevention, the prevention of the occurrence of disease, has received greater professional, consumer, and public support than secondary prevention, the screening and subsequent treatment of disease in its early stages. Among methods of primary prevention, immunizations for children have been accepted to a greater extent than those for adults. Medicaid, for example, supports childhood immunization, but Medicare excludes preventive vaccinations from coverage.[14]

Recently, screening for early presymptomatic disease followed by health education has been proposed as a method of delaying symptomatic disease, increasing the quality of life, and even prolonging life. Screening for a specific disease where it is cost-effective is being encouraged.

In 1980, because not all diseases can be effectively treated, followup medical care after screening cannot always be used. Screening for diseases for which treatment is not available is not acceptable. Screening may result in the reporting of a large number of "false positives." These indicate that persons have a disease that they do not actually have and thereby creates anxiety and the need for retesting. Screening may also result in some false negatives.

Screening is a viable technique to allocate medical resources. Consumers, at entry to the medical care system, can be given a battery of tests by a paramedical staff under physician direction. This method is used primarily by Kaiser-Permanente and some other prepaid groups to direct only the sick to physicians and to direct other persons, such as the worried-well, to health education personnel. This technique is not accepted by all physicians. Its importance to the economist is that, because of the size of third party payments, price does not allocate medical care. Because resources are scarce in relation to wants, some method of allocation is needed.

Whether multiphasic screening can allocate scarce resources optimally in relation to medical need is still being debated. The larger the number of tests given at one time, "multiphasic screening," the less the cost of each test. There is, however, no agreement for each of the tests commonly given or about the precise criteria that indicate treatment for abnormalities.

Some believe that there should be mass screening to detect specific asymptomatic disease in its early stages, such as hypertension. However, in 1978, medical opinion was that "there is no hard evidence that any therapy will change the natural history of the disease."[15] There is some evidence that asymptomatic persons labeled as hypertensive have a diminished feeling of well-being and may even increase significantly their number of days absent from work.[16] Recent studies indicate that treatment of persons with moderate hypertension with new drugs does significantly reduce stroke and heart attacks. For the treatment to be effective, the patient must comply with the drug regimen. Adherence to the prescribed therapy is low. Government policy to encourage mass screening for this disease seems unwise given the information available at the beginning of the 1980s. Screening targeted to those sectors of the population whose demographic factors (age, sex, and race) make them most at-risk may be cost effective.

Some argue that health education of the consumer can be used to change life-styles so that mortality and morbidity outcomes will improve. There is increasing evidence to support this. Mortality from heart disease, the leading cause of death in the United States, has declined over 20 percent since the mid-1960s while, in Sweden and in some countries behind the Iron Curtain, there has been an upturn in heart disease deaths for males. Chapter VIII has a lengthy discussion about the lack of data to access what part of the decline in cardiovascular disease derives from life-style changes and what part from better medical care. The London *Financial Times* of September 9, 1981, reported that 10 to 27 percent lower insurance premiums for nonsmokers were being charged by the Scottish Mutual Assurance Society.

A U.S. government publication points out some of the difficulties in screening for diseases before the clinical symptoms are present and then encouraging individuals to change their way of life in order to postpone the day when the clinical symptoms can no longer be ignored.

> A feature of cardiovascular disease and many other multifactorial diseases that complicates the design of prevention programs is that they usually develop over a long period of time. For this reason, achieving and sustaining motivation to reduce risk from factors such as smoking, dietary habits, or reactions to stressful situations is difficult. In contrast, the "benefits" of unhealthful habits are often immediate gratification, fulfillment of the desire for certain unhealthful foods, or cigarettes. Powerful stimuli in the social environment, including advertising, promote unhealthful choices.[17]

As early as 1952, according to testimony in the Senate, "there is evidence which suggests that, dollar for dollar, spending on visits to doctors and on drugs may not be as effective in increasing the health of low-income groups as spending on housing and food."[18] Almost thirty years have passed and evidence to support the above has accumulated despite the slow growth of nutrition as an accepted science. Patient education is being performed in physicians' offices, hospitals, clinics, and schools. But the media, and especially television, have had a greater impact through spots, regularly scheduled question-and-answer programs with a physician-expert, and story lines with medical content. Economist Charles E. Phelps writes that "personal behavioral decisions such as smoking and dietary patterns appear to have dramatic effects on health and mortality. Public policy appears to be better directed toward inducement of such health-producing behavior than inducement of further medical preventive procedures."[19]

Many large companies that self-insure health benefits and have in-house education programs to change health-related ways of living—smoking, nutrition, and exercising—also believe that long-run cost containment will result from such programs. These companies often provide in-house physical fitness facilities, which help their employees to be healthier during their work years and also appear to increase their life expectancy. Many large companies pay for insurance benefits for their retirees, and the substantial increases in these costs have added to the over-all premium costs of the companies' health insurance plans. Companies and individuals must keep up to date on future changes in entitlement ages for social security benefits and review their retirement plans in relationship to future health insurance costs.

Over the long run, many preventive services may be cost-effective because they may improve an individual's health and ability to work. This is despite the immediate or short-run costs of immunization, screening, and followup treatment. Immunization may save direct medical care costs for a specific disease. Screening and treatment for glaucoma may save later, more expensive surgical costs as well as yielding a much higher quality of life than if the disease were not discovered until irreversible loss of vision occurred. It is questionable, however, whether the benefits where screening and treatment postpone death would also offset the future costs of treatment of other diseases that eventually most persons incur as they grow older.

Although cost-effectiveness may be an attribute of some preventive health expenditures, it is not true of all. It is also true that in many instances those who pay for preventive care are not usually the same persons who benefit from it. If Medicare paid for such care, a large part of the costs would come from general revenues and it is likely to add to the inter-generational transfers from the young to the old that exists under the social security program.

Important areas where benefits have outweighed costs are the use of vaccines against polio and also vaccines against rubella measles by female youngsters who will, if they incur the disease at some future date when they are pregnant, have a relatively high risk of bearing defective children.

Some observers view expenditures on cost-effective preventive care to be limited in the near future. But many companies, some insurers, and the federal government believe that, although there is no immediate pay-off from consumer health education and preventive medicine, a cost containment effect will occur in the not too distant future. For example, Blue Cross has been exploring the possibility of marketing cancer-screening insurance policies. Such policies would cover costs of prevention through health education, screening for early presymptomatic, treatable cancer, and finance followup medical care. The goal is to detect treatable cancer while it is still localized. Although there is currently no cure for most types of cancer, long remissions of leukemia and Hodgkin's disease do occur and are sometimes assessed as cures. The purpose of the screening is to control the spread of cancer and to induce such remissions. Whether such screening insurance is cost-effective depends partly on whether the patient delays in seeking definitive diagnosis and treatment, partly on the availability of effective treatment, and whether the treatment itself induces a new type of cancer. Such insurance policies are likely to be marketed primarily to middle and high income persons who appear to be at lesser risk to cancer than low income, low-occupational status persons. It is illegal in Massachusetts to sell insurance that provides health expense coverage only in cases of cancer.

Detection of cancer-inducing environmental factors and food additives is also part of prevention. There is need, however, to quantify the probability of risk and benefits from all sources and then to select rationally how government monies should be allocated for the greatest benefit per dollar spent. Cost-effective preventive health measures will be sought and implemented by the government and private parties in many areas during the 1980s. There is a danger in seeking to reduce risks to a very low, possibly unreasonably low, level that the regulation-induced methods will also decrease the gross national product. The Reagan Administration believes that there is already over-regulation of the environment, manufacturing processes, foods, and drugs in this sense. The Reagan Administration also recognizes that one cannot live without risk.

COMPETITION AND REGULATION

I foresee two probable developments during the 1980s: a strong federal government drive for more competitive markets with decreased government regulation or, alternatively, only a flirtation with that approach and the continuance of present financial arrangements, continued slow growth of HMOs, and increased government regulation. Those who support costly government regulation, especially of new capital health expenditures, argue that use of medical technology will otherwise snowball needlessly under third party payments. The extensive charges that have been made concerning the over-use of technology have not been answered by existing or proposed regulations. The number of x-rays and tests ordered may be excessive because some reimbursement practices encourage their use and some physicians practice defensive medicine in order to protect themselves against malpractice suits. There probably is some excessive surgery. This may stem from an over-supply of surgeons who are protected by licensure as well as surgeons being encouraged to operate because otherwise they do not earn a "fee-for-service" payment. Also, not all hospitals restrict even specialty surgery to board-certified surgeons.

Licensure is regulation. There are many economists who would replace all licensure with certification. However, this would not reduce surgery. A better informed public would act to restrain excessive surgery.

The American Medical Association (AMA) states its case against removal of licensure: "To the extent that increased competition is associated with the idea of removing licensure restrictions, as some competition advocates suggest, then surely AMA's concerns for the quality of care require careful, selective support for only those pro-competition measures that do not diminish the quality and excellence of the health care delivery system in this country."[20] I do not foresee elimination of physician licensure in the United States in the near future.

The claimed inappropriate use of artificial measures that prolong the lives of dying patients is a result of all the factors already discussed including the continual innovation of medical technology. Although information to the consumer acts to restrain the inappropriate use of scarce resources, a reduction in the level of percentage of the bills reimbursed, as many proponents of more competition suggest, would also restrain demand. If demand were contained, a more rational restraint on the costs derived from new technology might occur than if regulations are imposed over who can use what technology. More information and also an over-all reduction in third party coverage modified by the size of expense as well as income levels would not hamper innovation and the appropriate use of technology. This approach is preferable to detailed regulations tailored to curb the excesses because they interfere with the practice of medical care. It may be wiser to reduce the existing regulations, including much of the body of licensure law, that controls who is allowed to perform a given medical procedure and concomitantly provide the public with extensive information about options among certified providers along with their qualifications and pricing.

Although the congressional extension in 1979 to mid-1981 of the Health Systems Agencies required that the states collect annually the prices of the twenty-five most used health services and make this information available to the public, little evidence of conformance exists. As of this writing, mid-1981, I have not seen any official price lists published in the state where I live (California), nor have my geographically scattered friends reported any such lists. For such prices to be useful in promoting competition, they need to be available to members of the public *before* they are ill, not after they go into a hospital or see a physician. Posting of prices at health facilities is not common and the posting does not meet the need for early information that advertising satisfies.

Effective regulation of the use of new technology also needs a data base, including costs, probabilities of the risks, and the benefits of that technology. In most instances, that data base does not exist and government regulations that pretend to have the hard data sometimes are reversed when the data do become available.

It is often argued that the federal government should support research to assess new and old medical technology in order to ensure that Medicare and Medicaid funds are being wisely spent. If government itself does these evaluations, it would fall into the same trap that FDA's assessment of new drugs and medical devices does: overemphasis on risk and under-assessment, especially of the non-quantifiable costs and benefits. The technical complexities of cost-benefit analyses have already been discussed as well as the underlying questions about value judgments.

As I wrote in a chapter of the Hoover Institution's book *The United States in the 1980s*:

> The National Center for Health Care Technology was established in November 1978 to recommend for which new technologies Medicare should not reimburse payment as well as which older technologies they consider obsolete. Governmental decisions of this nature will slow diffusion of new medical technology and its costs, but will also depress the medical device industry and delay more beneficial, new therapeutic innovation in this area. If competent physicians set standards of medical need for different technologies and agree on guidelines, they would guard against inappropriate use of the newer technology and high concomitant costs from duplication. Cost-benefit and cost-effective studies of new medical devices are badly needed, but a government agency cannot be an impartial expert. If physicians make available the needed biological information, economists can spell out costs and benefits under different sets of value judgments and consumer-patients will have more information on which to base decisions.[21]

Since the above has been written, private foundations have been supporting efforts to assess medical technology. In April 1980, private funds were used to present a symposium in Boston on "Critical Issues in Medical Technology: Innovation, Diffusion, Utilization, and Cost." The American College of Physicians has reported evaluations of some of the new medical and surgical techniques. Third parties, and especially the Blues, have denied reimbursement for some procedures. Insurance companies, through denial of reimbursement, are already affecting the obvious over-use of tests and x-rays. Although each of the private parties may have a self-interest in the evaluations, government also, as a third party reimburser, has an interest. It is better to have several diverse private groups make assessments rather than a single assessment by the federal government.

There is need for impartial assessment and for that assessment to be made known to the general public. However, the decision whether or not to perform a medical procedure in a specific case should be made by the patient and physician. If the procedure has a poor track record and the patient is dissatisfied, the route to a malpractice suit is open. Bad publicity alone is a deterrent.

Rather than more regulations, national health policy in the future is likely to involve an increase in all facets of competitive marketing: on the demand side, more information to the consumer; and, on the supply side, continuing use of antitrust law. Big business, a major payer, and possibly trade unions will take the leads as counterweights to restrain increases in the costs of medical care and health insurance premiums. Business can expand its newly adopted role of informed customer in its purchases of health insurance. Large companies can attempt to control health care costs by their use of self-insurance and direct provision of medical care as a buying power leverage in negotiating health insurance premiums for specific benefit packages.

Similarly, business can affect the prices charged by some providers of care, such as HMOs and hospitals. Businesses, by forming coalitions, have given notice that they intend to monitor utilization and charges as well as take an active role in containing costs. Among the groups that have been formed are the Washington, DC Business Group of over 170 companies, the Chicago Mid-West Business Group on Health, Employers Health Cost Committee of San Diego, Maryland Health Care Coalition, and the Penjerdel Council of about forty-five companies in the Philadelphia area. The major goal of these groups is to encourage hospitals to be more efficient: have joint purchasing plans with other hospitals, plan cash flow, intensify their utilization review of the number of hospital days, and use the best available financial arrangements to provide the capital for needed expansion and equipment. Additionally, many companies are acting to increase their employees' use of home health care as a substitute for nursing home and hospital care and also offering employees the choice of enrolling in HMOs.

Almost all large companies make available accurate information about health care through employee newsletters or special summaries. Mobil publishes informative letters. For example, "Smoking and Exercise: How the Two Habits Influence One Another" (November 1979) compresses available data into a surprisingly brief statement that forcefully concludes: "Runners may be a self-selected group of health-conscious individuals, but it is also true that many people stop smoking as a direct result of becoming involved in a vigorous exercise program. The often-cited problem of weight gain after an individual stops smoking can also be minimized with participation in a vigorous exercise program."

Many companies have special physical fitness programs, give training, or pay for courses in accounting and finance that will help their employees who are on boards of hospitals or other health care organizations. IBM, for example, gives or pays set amounts for employees and their spouses to take courses in exercise, smoking cessation, stress management, weight management, and other areas. This policy is obviously aimed at improving worker productivity and reducing the demand for medical care.

Insurance premiums reflect health costs. Corporations and trade unions have large monetary incentives to hold down the costs. The Ford Motor Company and many other large industrial firms pay $2,300 in annual health insurance per employee. If these premiums were lower, wages might be higher. The automobile industry's medical benefits cover both their current employees and their retirees. As their employees live longer, the company's pension costs and health insurance premiums rise. Companies with such plans tend to support more extensive federal health insurance benefits because these would lessen the companies' health insurance premiums. It is of interest that "Blue Cross-Blue Shield of Michigan . . . agreed to take a $17.5 million loss in an effort to help Chrysler Corporation obtain loan guarantees."[22] Business *can* and does exert leverage on insurance companies.

The Fairfield (Connecticut)/Westchester (New York) Business Group on Health, made up of representatives of twenty-two large companies with nationwide health insurance coverage of 4.5 million persons, for whom it pays $2.2 billion in premiums, made public its first annual report (June 30, 1980). This is an action-oriented group involved in insurance plan design to help reduce inpatient hospital care, and, in PSROs, to minimize the unnecessary use and foster the appropriate use of a variety of health services. The business group also provides educational programs for persons serving on health boards. Its greater involvement than other similar groups is evident: "The PSRO committee is attempting to develop a common approach to utilization review for the member companies. Initial and ongoing discussion for this purpose has been established with the PSROs covering the two counties and with the area hospitals."[23]

The Director of Benefits and Personnel Services of IBM testified before the Price Advisory Committee to the Council on Wage and Price Stability that IBM is conducting analyses to look "at things like reasonable and customary costs. We are also looking at length of stay, utilization, by group, by hospital. We are looking at things like Friday admission for Monday morning elective surgery."[24] Business is becoming involved in peer review! Large business is leading the way for informed consumer choice.

A major cause of high medical costs is high utilization. This is because "the complex of perverse incentives inherent in our dominant financing system for health care . . . rewards providers of care with more revenue for giving more and more costly care, whether or not more is necessary or beneficial to the patient."[25] If employers pay the lowest available alternative amount among health insurance premiums and HMOs per capita charges for a given set of benefits, the employee who selects the more costly financial arrangements would pay the excess. Employers have a responsibility to give full information about all the plans which they offer. This should include, for HMOs, their arrangements for review of quality and for insurers, their claims review rules that reduce the percentage reimbursed to providers when they are believed to have overcharged. The federal government has compelled all firms of twenty-five employees or more to offer available HMOs as alternatives to existing arrangements. Thus in 1980, The Gillette Company offered its Boston employees the opportunity to join the Harvard Community Health Plan or the Matthew-Thornton Plan. Thirty-one employees voted to join the former; four, the latter; and 2,981 remained with the Gillette provider plan coupled with Blue Cross, most of them choosing the family coverage option.

Making available choices does not ensure that they will automatically result in a fully competitive market. The only area of the country that gives some evidence of active competition with possible cost containment is the Minneapolis-St. Paul area, where the employers did the selling job. Even here, however, the impact has been questioned because, when HMO enrollment doubled, hospital utilization remained the same or increased slightly in those cities. As Harold Luft states, this is "consistent with both the notions of no major competitive response and the selective enrollment of low utilizers in HMOs."[26] It is true, however, that medical care prices in the Twin Cities have risen less than in the rest of the United States and less than the cost-of-living in those cities. This is not true for other large cities where HMOs are serving 12 percent or more of the population with the possible exception of Honolulu. Modern medical care delivery in Hawaii evolved atypically by competition with the direct provision of medical care by plantation owners. Hawaii has far fewer hospital beds per 1,000 population, a relatively younger population than is usual, and also a very temperate climate. For these and other reasons, most economists do not generalize from the Hawaiian experience.

New forms of delivery of care are developing, as are new, more competitive forms of insurance coverage and other financial arrangements. Insurers will be forced to bargain harder with providers about the terms of payment. One group that considers itself especially threatened by the competitive strategy is the teaching hospitals. Eli Ginzberg recently put it this way: "I see nothing except trouble ahead if the nation's teaching hospitals are forced to compete with community hospitals in providing routine services, since the former's per diem costs are 1-1/2 to two times as high as the latter's, as a result of their diverse output, which goes far beyond performing an appendectomy or hysterectomy and involves such critically important societal goals as training the new generation of physicians and adding to the pool of knowledge and technique."[27] The economist wonders why teaching hospitals still perform routine operations. Why cannot the training for these be provided in community hospitals, even if at some small sacrifice in quality of medical education? Substantial cost-savings and greater diffusion of medical knowledge to more rural areas would occur. Teaching hospitals should be reserved for the more complex, specialized areas of medicine. Interns can be rotated among hospitals as they have been in some of the rural mountain states that have no medical schools.

Consumers are becoming more involved in decisions about their own health care. They are beginning to shop for quality and price in response to increasing advertisements. The AMA's initial lifting of the ban on physician advertising resulted in a Hawaiian newspaper announcing that a "Consumer Directory of Physicians, Dentists and Health Care providers with educational/work background, fee schedules and other practice-related information is available for review at all state libraries including the Maui Bookmobile and MCC (Maui County Community) library."[28] However, in 1981 the AMA appealed the striking down of its ban and further evidence of price advertising has not been seen. Prices of prescription drugs and medical procedures are not being advertised. Without pricing information, a competitive market will not replace regulation. Only if the trends leading towards more competition are successful can there be a gradual deregulation of the presently over-regulated health industry without medical care prices rising faster than the general inflation. The path of less regulation and more competition is not acceptable to all providers, but it holds out greater promise for long-run cost containment and greater freedom for providers than the continuance and elaboration of detailed regulations coupled with cost-reimbursement.

As government regulation and government control over financing of health care have increased, the problem of protecting the patient's privacy has also increased. When federal and state governments pay for the delivery of medical care, they bear a responsibility to assure that they are getting their money's worth. Computer records of utilization and costs by provider and patient are kept by hospitals, clinics, and group practices in order to provide the government and other third party payers the information requested before making payment. Many patients' health records are thus likely to be in a computer data bank; relatively few will remain in the files of a physician in solo practice, who may not use a computer. However, patients in many states do not have a "general right to see their own records, either before the data is released to third parties or as a matter of patient interest during regular care."[29]

The author concurs with the *Report of the Project on Medical Records and Citizen Rights*, which states:

As a general matter, patients should have a right to full information about their health conditions. Where health data is to be used to make judgments about service payment and claims, or in any non-medical social and governmental programs, the individual should have an absolute right to inspect what is to be released from his/her record. In chronic and acute care, patients should also have a right to see any part of the medical record, including the medical professional's working notes, if they insist upon this after the medical professional has had a chance to explain directly to the patient why he or she feels that such disclosure would not be in the patient's best medical interest. A special procedure is suggested for patient-access problems in psychiatric care.[30]

A COMPETITIVE STRATEGY

I support a competitive approach to containment of health costs through provision of a voucher for everyone. The voucher may be spent not only as a premium for health insurance or a per capita payment under a prepaid plan but also, after catastrophic coverage has been obtained for oneself and all dependents, for direct purchase from accredited health care providers. The emphasis then shifts to substantial doses of deregulation, while Alain Enthoven's version of a consumer-choice health plan implies concomitant use of many regulatory requirements. I also object to Medicare and Medicaid reimbursement of a consumer's choice being limited to only a qualified health care plan with community-rating set by actuarial category. The acceptance by many policy-makers of HMOs as the sole means of ensuring a semblance of competition in the health care markets appears to have cut off development of other ways to increase the competitiveness of these markets. The choice open to consumers should encompass all types of plans: those of commercial insurers and the Blues that have experience-rating and also those of solo practitioners who are willing to risk a prepaid, per capita arrangement.

The latter arrangement might be especially suitable for pediatricians who are being squeezed out of the market where HMOs are strong.[31] The solo pediatrician could, under prepayment arrangements, cover ambulatory care of children including well-baby care, immunization shots, and checkups. Although HMOs do cover these items, most private health insurance plans do not. Pediatricians could compete with HMOs by offering their own per capita arrangements and also by holding office hours during some evenings and Saturday mornings. A major group of children who receive lesser amounts of medical care are those whose mothers work. The pediatrician could self-insure against the rare expenses of hospitalization among children. Further, the solo general practitioner could explore the same route and possibly work out with a hospital and an insurer a similar plan for adult patients.

My proposal for more competition via vouchers to consumers is perforce a two-phase one because it recognizes that some employees are receiving well over $2,000 annually in tax-free health premiums and other employees far less than $1,000. This fact is also recognized by the transition provision in the Gephardt-Stockman Bill, introduced June 9, 1980. Its solution is to freeze employer contributions for premiums above a given amount until inflation pushes the lesser employer-paid health insurance premiums into the same bracket. This, unless inflation continues at a high level, will take several years.

Under my proposal, the employer would be required to pay for a voucher equal to the lower of: 110 percent of the lowest charge *or* of the second lowest charge in the area by HMOs or insurers for an employee. The second lowest charge, if not more than 10 percent above the lowest, seems to be a more desirable level of health insurance premium than the lowest, at least during a transition period. The 110 percent would encourage competition by new plans and not over-protect established plans that have earned surpluses to draw on. During the second phase, the government would issue a voucher to Medicare patients equal to higher amounts in accordance with the actuarial experience of age groups: 65–74 years and those 75 years and older. I would delay using vouchers for Medicare patients until information about existing plans and medical care providers has been more widely disseminated. Younger persons who are working can get information from employer clearinghouses and also from the government. It takes time to set up channels of communication. Persons 75 years and over, moreover, are likely to be in greater need of medical care than those 65–74 years and both age groups need more medical services on the average than younger persons. It is hard to get older persons who are ill and have an established physician relationship to switch providers as was noted earlier in Chapter VII.

The voucher amount is determined by the HMO charge or insurance premium that would pay for all medical care of the employee, but with specified copayments and customary exclusions. The employee could elect to cover dependents and pay for this, or, alternatively, use the voucher for only catastrophic expense coverage for himself and dependents thus gaining some discretionary health expenditures. By mandating a voucher equal to the coverage cost of comprehensive care for a single employee, there is no need to strike the benefits of a second worker in a family. This voucher plan is close to the existing Stanford University plan that pays, in addition to catastrophic expense coverage for employees, up to a set amount for each employee and that amount also covers part of the premium cost for one dependent. My voucher plan differs in that the employee can spend a voucher for health services from any provider with accreditation or certification or licensure that he or she wishes. The em-

ployee does not have to use employer-approved arrangements. A
sensible option for any employee would be to purchase catastrophic
health expense for all dependents, when they are not covered by the
employer. Catastrophic insurance plans are all low-cost policies.
The voucher system would permit wider competition and world-
wide availability. In a two-worker family, fewer duplicate benefits
would be available. A plan to eliminate duplicate payments could
be worked out. Under current arrangements, some two-worker families are "over-insured." Elimination of one spouse's benefits would
be equivalent to a wage decrease because health benefits are in lieu
of wages. The insurance company or an HMO, not the employer or
the employee, is the beneficiary of this solution. Vouchers on an
individual not a family basis would avoid this problem.

A voucher system could permit direct payment of physical therapists, acupuncturists, and others. The consumer who has an excess
voucher would determine whether to use it for traditional medical
care, substitutes for medical care, or, it might be possible, as has been
proposed by the Louisiana State Medical Society's plan and as is being
practiced in a few firms and local governments (teachers in Mendocino
County, California), to invest under a special arrangement the money
for some future medical bills that are not met by a catastrophic expense
insurance plan. The Louisiana Plan, Consumers Health Investment
Plan (CHIP), proposes complete catastrophic expense coverage with
a high deductible and also proposes that the consumer (or employer)
invest the dollars saved that would otherwise have paid the premiums
for the more expensive first dollar coverage. Retirement plans restrict
the use of money until retirement. A health fund plan could restrict
the use of money for only purchases of health services and goods.

This too-briefly outlined proposal combines a competitive approach
with catastrophic expense coverage. This is a working proposal; the
details are not set in concrete. Fifty-five percent of the uninsured are
dependents of persons in the labor force. This plan should give them
catastrophic expense coverage because it always permits the employee to use the voucher to purchase first only catastrophic expense
coverage for himself and all dependents and then to use the excess
in other areas of need. Thus, persons with different family obliga-
tions and different expectations from health providers could make
different choices. The federal government may reserve the option
of not honoring with cash, vouchers used for services of non-ac-
credited health care institutions and providers.

The most difficult area of this plan is implementation of a cap on
the amount that employers can expense. That precise amount may

best be set only after analysis of the now available Medicare cost data, followed by political negotiations. For those companies paying higher premiums than the voucher amount, a dollar refund of the excess could be returned to the employee in the form of higher wages and the company cannot expense premiums above the voucher amount. Some employee objections to this can be expected. For companies whose premium expenses are below the cost of the voucher, a period of time could be permitted for a gradual increase in allowable, expensed premium payments until they are equal to the amount of the voucher. This increase would admittedly replace part of otherwise anticipated wage rate increases, but, because most employees prefer tax-free premium dollars to wages subject to taxes, the employees' objections should be few. The employer could act as a clearinghouse for the detailed information about the costs and the benefits of the insurance and HMO plans available in the area. Insurers and the HMOs would supply the material; the employer would not be responsible for the correctness of the information. The employee could choose among substantially similar, fairly competitive benefit coverages and would clearly not be limited to prepaid group plans or HMOs, or even the standard insurance packages. The employee could select, "cafeteria style," an individual package tailored to his or her needs.

The federal government would not loan to, or otherwise financially support, HMOs and they could be either community-rated or experience-rated plans. Thus, the financial incentives for industry to maintain healthy work environments and provide health and safety education would continue because experience-rating reflects in lower premiums the lower costs of employee groups that have better health records. Financial incentives could also be developed for individuals to continue, or even initiate, healthier personal habits.

Once the framework for the employed is in place, a plan for the unemployed should be developed. Employees might elect in excess of the basic catastrophic coverage for themselves and their dependents, that catastrophic coverage continue for six months or for longer periods of unemployment. It is assumed because of recent employment that they could pay for the more routine medical expenses for several months. If the person is unemployed over a period of time, then a voucher equal to Medicaid's per capita expenditure in the past year for the average of community-rated groups in the area could be provided by the federal government. This is only one plan for the unemployed; others might be better. Those who are unemployed and whose medical bills exceed the voucher amount would be eligible, without payment, for treatment in county hospitals and teaching hospitals. Their medical costs incurred in the teaching hospitals could be met from federal revenues earmarked to support training costs of new physicians. Clearly, hidden cross-subsidies among the ill now support the training costs of physicians. The state and local monies needed for the poor could be handled by pooled, state insurance funds paid under Medicaid.

The government, instead of regulating and subsidizing the organizations that provide medical care, would compile detailed information about all available financial arrangements and benefits from data required and supplied by insurance companies, HMOs, and other providers. The data summaries would be available to consumers. The purpose is to educate consumers to be prudent purchasers, to know what to look for in advertisements, and to have comparative knowledge. After a three-year period, the government information bureau would be reduced in size because, with rare exceptions, it would primarily be updating existing information. Advertisements by that time should have become common. HMOs and health insurance plans are already advertising in California newspapers and on television. The advertisements are noteworthy in that no prices are given and also omitted are details about payment of referrals to specialists and pre-certification requirements for hospital admissions. If advertisements provide more information, the government information bureau could be phased out.

Financial incentives under fee-for-service practice induce more than optimum consumption of medical care, but financial incentives under prepaid group practice induce less than optimum consumption. At the same time, actual optima are unknown. It is essential, therefore, to keep available a wide variety of options. A voucher system, with most of the details as yet to be worked out, may offer the most promise of the widest selection. After experience with this system, Medicare patients might be included in the program. Additionally, the government could experiment with promising those individuals on Medicaid a percentage of the cash equivalent for all monthly vouchers that at the end of the calendar year remain unused.

TEN SPECIFIC RECOMMENDATIONS[32]

1. The most important of the author's recommendations involves the education of consumers about what medical care can and cannot

do, and about what they can do to improve their own health. More dissemination of information through advertising, directories of physicians by specialties, and of hospitals with representative charges, staffs, and tertiary care specialists is needed. Most public libraries purchase the national directories of physicians by specialties and the *Physician's Desk Reference* (PDR), which contains manufacturers' descriptions (FDA approved) of prescription drugs. But most persons apparently are not aware that these informational sources exist. There is also a need for new compilations about HMOs, hospitals, nursing homes, health insurance benefits, and alternative medical technologies written in language consumers can understand. Unless consumers are knowledgeable about what they buy, the market cannot approach a competitive market.

2. Certification should replace licensing of all allied health manpower jobs. The majority of any licensing board should not consist of either those persons who already hold that license or those practicing an occupation competitive with the one being licensed. Substitution for physicians and dentists by less expensively trained personnel should be encouraged through direct reimbursement of them by third party payers. Then those who wish to can work independently of an employer, and consumers who wish to purchase less expensive and lesser quality care may do so. Reimbursement to these certified persons would be at a lesser rate than if the physician or dentist had performed the task. When group practices and hospitals submit charges for work done by lesser-trained persons, their accounts should indicate it and reimbursement should be made at the lower prices.

3. Federal and state governments should encourage growth of new HMOs, both for-profit and non-profit. If HMOs are truly competitive, they should be able to obtain commercial loans for start-up capital costs. Quality controls within HMOs remain a problem. HMOs should be routinely audited. Business, through its various area groups on health, can combat the runaway costs of company health benefits plans by contributing specialized knowledge in the areas of effective quality controls and cost containment. Travelers Insurance Company estimated in September 1980 that health insurance "premium costs are rising by 14 percent to 20 percent"[33] and that business will spend $63 billion in 1981, up from $43 billion in 1978. It is primarily hospital costs that are rising so fast, possibly in anticipation of a cap on hospital costs.

4. Elimination of 90 percent of the fraud and about 70 percent of the abuse in existing government programs is necessary. It is easier to detect fraud. There are not always agreed-upon definitions of what is abuse. To achieve 100 percent purity almost always costs more than it is worth.

5. Medicaid and Medicare should be retained, but with some modifications. Data indicate that introduction of small copayments among Medicaid patients may reduce ambulatory care but increase inpatient hospital care. Further research is needed. Insurance coverage for out-of-hospital surgicenters as well as health care received at home should be more widely available.

6. The federal government should require all employers who have more than a minimum number of employees to offer some form of catastrophic health expense coverage for their employees and dependents. This should not be enacted until fraud in existing government programs has been virtually eliminated. Bidding for such insurance contracts should be competitive. The premium for a high deductible is relatively low because low-incidence but high-expense items are usually covered. Cost-sharing is not required after the high deductible is met. Reimbursement for technologies that are limited should be spelled out: for example, (1) plan does not cover organ transplants and (2) plan does not cover more than twenty outpatient psychiatric care visits annually. The premium costs for an employed population are lower than for the total population. Government and private catastrophic health insurance by disease category, kidney disease and cancer, should be replaced by general catastrophic health insurance, but initially with safeguards.[34]

7. For those who are self-employed and therefore pay higher individual premiums as compared to group coverage, as well as others who are uncovered by private and government plans, a minimum level of catastrophic expense benefits (government determined) should be made available by insurers who bid competitively on the benefit package.

8. The federal government should limit the level of health insurance premiums that employers can continue to expense and which employees also do not count as income for tax purposes. This is an open-ended subsidy, which distorts consumer spending and allocation of resources.

9. Congress should, after debate, spell out the meaning of the requirement "substantial evidence" of efficacy to market a new drug or remove efficacy as a criterion. Knowledgeable and wealthy Americans can obtain proven beneficial drugs from abroad while the poor cannot.

10. Deregulation of the health care industry is desirable. The experience of the health sector with price control and its aftermath should discourage any new attempts in this direction. It is worth noting that, although the American Medical Association (in the Summer of 1980) withdrew its objection to physicians' advertising prices, the AMA appealed (in early 1981) the ruling that prohibits it from declaring advertising by physicians to be unethical. There is needed advertisements of unit pricing of prescription drugs and other medical goods and services. The FTC antitrust actions in the health sector should continue, but with political discretion in view of changing court interpretations of permissible antitrust action in non-profit industry and the insurance sector. Without price advertisements that by implication will also include quality indicators, a competitive market will not replace regulation in the health sector.

As an economist, I have written this book from the point of view that medical care is a service like other services, such as education. Those physicians who believe that medical care is a unique "personal service employing individual knowledge, human concern, judgment, experience, and that it is based ultimately in trust"[35] should consider that these attributes apply to all professions. Far from destroying those qualities, the competitive market will enhance them. Competition encourages high quality and low prices; government regulation does not.

NOTES

CHAPTER I.

1. Maurice Fox, "Why People Are Mad at Doctors," *Newsweek* (January 10, 1977), p. 4.
2. Medicaid is a grant-in-aid program to provide medical services to persons who have low incomes and cannot pay for such services. The federal government pays from 50 to 81 percent of the bills; the higher percentages occur in those states with lower per capita income.
3. President Jimmy Carter, "Remarks before the American Society of Newspaper Editors, Washington, DC, April 11, 1978," in *Weekly Compilation of Presidential Documents*, Vol. 14, No. 15 (Washington, DC: Government Printing Office, April 17, 1978), p. 725.
4. Committee of Enquiry into the Cost of National Health Service, Cmnd 9663, "Guillebaud Report" (London, England: Her Majesty's Stationers Office, 1965), p. 50.
5. Zachary Y. Dyckman, "Physicians: A Study of Physicians' Fees," U.S. Council on Wage and Price Stability (Washington, DC: Government Printing Office, March 1978), pp. 119-120.

CHAPTER II.

1. Gerald Sparer and Arne Anderson, "Utilization and Cost Experience in Low Income Families in Four Prepaid Group Practice Plans," *New England Journal of Medicine*, Vol. 289 (July 12, 1973), p. 68.
2. Department of Health, Education, and Welfare, "Diabetes Data . . . 1977," Pub. No. (NIH) 78-1468, p. 20.
3. "Diabetes mellitus is a metabolic disorder in which the ability to oxidize carbohydrates is more or less completely lost, usually due to faulty pancreatic activity . . . and consequent disturbance of normal insulin mechanism." *Dorland's Illustrated Medical Dictionary*, 25th ed. (Philadelphia: W. B. Saunders, 1974).
4. "Office Visits to Internists," *Vital Health Statistics*, U.S. Public Health Service, Series 13, No. 36 (December 1978), p. 9.
5. Spina bifida is "a developmental anomaly characterized by defective closure of the bony encasement of the spinal cord, through which the cord and meninges may . . . or may not protrude." *Dorland's Illustrated Medical Dictionary.*
6. W. M. McCrea, "Paediatrics and Preventive Medicine," in *Clinical Practice and Economics*, ed. by C. I. Phillips and J. N. Wolfe (Kent, England: Pittman Medical, 1977), pp. 33-34.
7. Selma Mushkin, L. C. Paringer, and M. M. Chen, *Returns to Biomedical Research: 1900–1975* (Washington, DC: Georgetown University Public Services Laboratory, October 20, 1976), p. 11.

8. Victor R. Fuchs, "The Growing Demand for Medical Care," in *Essays in the Economics of Medical Care*, ed. by V. R. Fuchs (New York: National Bureau of Economic Research, 1972), p. 65.

9. U.S. Congress, House, Committee on Ways and Means, "Background Information on Kidney Disease Benefits Under Medicare" (Washington, DC: Government Printing Office, June 24, 1975), p. 6; Richard A. Rettig and Ellen L. Marks, *Implementing the End-Stage Renal Disease Program of Medicare* (Washington, DC: Health Care Financing Administration, March 1981), p. 3.

10. U.S. Congress, House, Committee on Ways & Means, "Administration by the Social Security Administration of the End Stage Renal Disease Program" (Washington, DC: Government Printing Office, October 22, 1975), p. 2.

11. A range of co-insurance rates was used. Joseph P. Newhouse and Charles E. Phelps, "New Estimates of Price and Income Elasticities of Medical Care Services," in *The Role of Health Insurance in the Health Services Sector*, ed. by R. Rosett (New York: National Bureau of Economics Research, 1976), pp. 283-284, 314.

12. Robert M. Gibson and Marjorie Smith Mueller, "National Health Expenditures, Fiscal Year 1976," *Social Security Bulletin*, Vol. 40, No. 4 (April 1977), p. 14.

13. Robert M. Gibson, "National Health Expenditures, 1979," *Health Care Financing Review*, Vol. 2, No. 1 (Summer 1980), p. 3.

14. American Hospital Association, *Hospital Guide: 1979* (Chicago: American Hospital Association, 1979), p. 321.

15. Patricia Munch, "Economic Incentives to Order Lab Tests: Theory and Evidence," in *Socioeconomic Issues of Health, 1980*, ed. by Douglas Hough and Glen I. Misek (Monroe, Wis.: American Medical Association, 1980), p. 78.

16. Marcia Daniels and Steven Schroeder, "Variation among Physicians in Use of Laboratory Tests. II. Relation to Clinical Productivity and Outcomes of Care," *Medical Care*, Vol. 25 (June 1977), p. 482. See also Steven A. Schroeder and Jonathan Showstack, "The Dynamics of Medical Technology Use: Analysis and Options," in *Medical Technology*, ed. by Stuart Altman and Robert Blendon, U.S. Public Health Service No. 39-3216 (Washington, DC: Government Printing Office, 1977).

17. Daniels and Schroeder, "Variation among Physicians," p. 483.

18. Karen Davis and Cathy Shoen, *Health and the War on Poverty: A Ten-Year Appraisal* (Washington, DC: Brookings Institution, 1978), pp. 53-54.

19. *Ibid.*, p. 213.

20. LuAnn Aday and Ronald Andersen, *A New Survey on Access to Medical Care*, Special Report No. 1 (Princeton, New Jersey: The Robert Wood Johnson Foundation, 1976), pp. 10 ff.

21. Michael Grossman, *The Demand for Health: A Theoretical and Empirical Investigation* (New York: National Bureau of Economic Research, 1972), p. 16.

22. Myron J. Lefcowitz, "Poverty and Health: A Re-Examination," *Inquiry*, Vol. 10 (March 1973), p. 12.

23. Aday and Andersen, *A New Survey*.

24. Martin Anderson, *Welfare* (Stanford, Calif.: Hoover Institution Press, 1978), p. 19. Data from Edgar Browning, "Redistribution and the Welfare System" (Washington, DC: American Enterprise Institute, 1975), pp. 14-30.

25. Ronald Wilson and E. L. White, "Changes in Morbidity, Disability, and Utilization Differentials between the Poor and the Non-poor," *Medical Care*, Vol. 15 (August 1977), p. 640. See also *Health: United States, 1980* (Washington, DC: 1980), p. 242.

26. U.S. Department of Health and Human Services, *Health: United States, 1980* (Washington, DC: Government Printing Office, 1980), p. 243.

27. Diana Dutton, "Explaining the Low Use of Health Services by the Poor: Costs, Attitudes, or Delivery Systems?", *American Sociological Review*, Vol. 43 (June 1978), pp. 348-368.
28. Aday and Andersen, *A New Survey*, p. 26.
29. U.S. Department of Health, Education, and Welfare, *Health: United States: 1976–1977*, Pub. No. HRA 77-1232 (Washington, DC: Government Printing Office, 1977), p. 209.
30. Whether "moral" or "natural" rights is used is partly a semantic issue.
31. Sidney Hook, *Pragmatism and the Tragic Sense of Life* (New York: Basic Books, Inc., 1974), p. 19.
32. *Ibid.*, p. 13.
33. Arthur Okun, *Equality and Efficiency* (Washington, DC: Brookings Institution, 1975).
34. Charles Fried, *Right and Wrong* (Cambridge, Mass.: Harvard University Press, 1978), p. 131.
35. Robert Nozick, *Anarchy, State, and Utopia* (New York: Basic Books, 1974).
36. *San Francisco Chronicle* (June 2, 1975), pp. 1, 18.
37. *Los Angeles Times* (June 20, 1975), Part I, p. 32.
38. California Legislature, Joint Legislative Audit Commission, Department of Health, "Prepaid Plans" (July 1974), p. 19. (Mimeo)
39. Darling vs. Charlestown Memorial Hospital, 33 Ill. 2d 326, 211 N.E.2d 253 (1965).
40. Manlove vs. Wilmington General Hospital, 53 Del. 338, 169 A. 2d 18; 54 Del. 15, 174 A.2d 135 (1961).
41. Manlove, 54 Del. at 22–23, 174 A. 2d 139 (October 2, 1961), 135.

CHAPTER III.

1. *Special Analyses, Budget of the United States Government, Fiscal Year 1979* (Washington, DC: Government Printing Office, 1979), p. 253.
2. U.S. Public Health Service, *Supply of Manpower in Selected Health Occupations* (Washington, DC: Government Printing Office, 1980), p. 59.
3. U.S. Public Health Service, *Health Resources Statistics* (Washington, DC: Government Printing Office, 1975), p. 159.
4. U.S. Department of Health and Human Services, *Health: United States, 1980* (Washington, DC: Government Printing Office, October 1980), p. 270.
5. See "Physicians for a Growing America," in *Report of the Surgeon General's Consultant Group on Medical Education* (Frank Bane, Chairman) (Washington, DC: Government Printing Office, 1959).
6. W. Lee Hansen, "An Appraisal of Physician Manpower Projections," *Inquiry*, Vol. 7 (March 1970), p. 110.
7. *Special Analyses, Budget of the United States Government, Fiscal Year 1977* (Washington, DC: Government Printing Office, 1977), p. 195.
8. *Ibid.*, p. 201.
9. *Special Analyses . . . , Fiscal 1979*, p. 252.
10. *Supply of Manpower*, p. 1.
11. American Medical Association, "Undergraduate Medical Education," *Journal of American Medical Association*, Vol. 240, No. 26 (December 22-29, 1978), p. 2831.
12. U.S. Public Health Service, *Health Resources Statistics* (Washington, DC: Government Printing office, 1978), p. 21.

13. *Supply of Manpower in Selected Health Occupations: 1950-1990*, HRA No. 80-35 (Washington, DC: Government Printing Office, 1980), p. 4.

14. Merlin Duval, "Health Manpower: The Factors and Issues," in *Manpower for Health Care* (Washington, DC: National Academy of Sciences, Institute of Medicine, 1974), p. 12.

15. U.S. Department of Health, Education, and Welfare, *Health: United States, 1977*, Pub. No. HRA 77-1232 (Washington, DC: Government Printing Office, 1977), p. 314.

16. Uwe Reinhardt, "Health Manpower Forecasting," in *Manpower for Health Care* (Washington, DC: National Academy of Sciences, Institute of Medicine, May 1974), p. 50.

17. *U.S. Department of Health, Education, and Welfare Report* (Washington, DC: Government Printing Office, 1978), p. 64.

18. See, for example, Walter Oi, "Scientific Manpower Forecasts From the Viewpoint of a Dismal Scientist," in National Science Foundation, *Scientific and Technical Manpower Projections . . . Proceedings*, April 16–18, 1974 (Washington, DC: Government Printing Office, 1974), pp. 177–230.

19. *National Commission on the Cost of Medical Care, 1976-1977*, Commission Recommendations, Vol. 1 (Monroe, Wisc: American Medical Association, 1978), p. 13.

20. "Primary Specialties," American College of Surgeons Press Release, June 20, 1977, *Medical Care Review*, Vol. 34, No. 7 (July 1977), pp. 799-800.

21. H. R. Mason, "Revitalizing Primary Medical Care: Role of the Profession and Federal/State Governments," in *Socioeconomic Issues in Health* (Chicago: American Medical Association, 1977), p. 47.

22. *Ibid.*, p. 52.

23. *Health: United States*, 1980, p. 119.

24. Barbara Kehrer and James Knowles, "Determinants of Patient Waiting Time in Medical Practice," Presented at the National Bureau of Economic Research Conference (Rochester, N.Y.: May 31–June 1, 1974).

25. *Ibid.*, p. 10.

26. *Ibid.*, p. 11

27. American Medical Association, *Profile: Medical Practice, '74* (Chicago: American Medical Association, 1974), p. 22.

28. A patient's total time spent obtaining medical care includes, additionally, time in traveling to the physician's office and time spent having x-rays, tests, etc.

29. A true market price is absent because of third party reimbursement. When a third party such as the government pays part or all of the bill, the patient, at time of consumption, pays substantially less than the true costs of all the resources used in providing the care.

30. Eli Ginzberg and Miriam Ostow, *Men, Money and Medicine* (New York: Columbia University Press, 1969), p. 110.

31. "The Silent Treatment, Part 1 of the 'Disease Nobody Knows,'" Live on 4 Special Report, Aired on May 19, 1981 (San Francisco: Chronicle Broadcasting Company, 1981), unpaged. (Mimeo)

32. This section is an update of a paper by Dr. Rita Ricardo-Campbell, "The Effect of Emerging Health Roles on Financing and Health Payment Plans," Presented at the American Association for the Advancement of Science (AAAS) Meeting (New York: January 31, 1975). (Available on microfilm. Ann Arbor, Mich.: University of Michigan Hospital Management Studies, School of Public Health, 1975.)

33. Michael Litke, *Employing the Physician's Assistant or Nurse Practitioner* (Boulder, Colo.: Western Interstate Commission for Higher Education, 1974), 42 pp. (Mimeo)

34. The American Nurses' Association, in a non-official paper (mimeo dated July 9, 1973), has defined "nurse practitioner" as a registered nurse with an expanded role to cover twelve functions, such as taking a health history, assessing health-illness status, entering a person into the health care system, managing a care regimen, teaching, counseling, etc., but does not list either diagnosis or establishing a care regimen except for "normal pregnant women." At least one study, "Comparative Diagnostic Abilities of Child Health Associate Interns and Practicing Pediatricians," states that some physician substitutes do make diagnoses and, further, that "CHA interns can diagnose the problems of ambulatory pediatric patients with an accuracy comparable to that of pediatricians." L. Fine and H. Silver, *Journal of Pediatrics 83*, (1973), pp. 332-335. Some other pediatricians dispute this.

35. See R. Zeckhauser and Michael Eliastam, "The Productivity Potential of the Physician Assistant," *Journal of Human Resources*, Vol. 9:1 (Winter 1974), for a production function methodology which, with assumptions as to who may do what and using empirical data of an urban delivery system, concludes that a well-trained physician assistant, if used maximally with an optimum mix of production factors, can, under supervision, "replace half of a full-time physician."

36. U.S. Department of Health, Education, and Welfare, *Interim Report of the Graduate Medical Education National Advisory Committees*, HRA No. 79-633 (Washington, DC: Government Printing Office, April 1979), pp. 228-229. (Mimeo)

37. U.S. Department of Health, Education, and Welfare, *Health: United States, 1979*, PHS No. 80-1232 (Washington, DC: Government Printing Office, 1979), p. 78. (Prepublication copy)

38. *Ibid.*, p. 80.

39. W. O. Spitzer, David L. Sackett, John C. Sibley, *et al.*, "The Burlington Randomized Trial of the Nurse Practitioner," *New England Journal of Medicine*, Vol. 290 (January 31, 1974), pp. 251-256; D. Sackett, M. Gent, I. W. Hay, *et al.*, *Annals of Internal Medicine* (February 1974), pp. 137-142.

40. "For 'New Nurse': Bigger Role in Health Care," *U.S. News and World Report* (January 14, 1980), p. 60.

41. Barbara H. Kehrer and James C. Knowles, "An Economic Analysis of Prices Charged for Medical Services" (September 1974), p. 161. (Mimeo)

42. *Cost Effectiveness of Physician's Assistants*, HEW Contract No, 1-MB-44173(P), Final Report (Portland, Oreg.: U.S. Bureau of Health Resources Development and Kaiser Foundation Health Services Research Center, 1974–76). (Mimeo)

43. *Ibid.*, p. 51.

44. *Ibid.*, p. 84.

45. See "Nurses Seeking More 'Equality,' " *New York Times* (November 3, 1974), p. 68, as well as various newspaper articles about the 1974 nurses' strike in the San Francisco Bay area.

46. R. D. Fraser, *Selected Economic Aspects of Health Care Sector in Ontario: A Study for the Committee on the Healing Arts* (Toronto, Canada: 1970), p. 226.

47. Philip Enterline, "Effects of 'Free' Medical Care on Medical Practice: The Quebec Experience," *New England Journal of Medicine* 288 (May 31, 1973), pp. 1152-1155.

48. *Interim Report of the Graduate Medical Education National Advisory Committees*, p. 244.

49. Herbert Lerner, *Manpower Issues and Voluntary Regulation in the Medical Specialty System* (New York: Prodist, 1974), p. 94.

50. Charles R. Link and Russell F. Settle, "Wage Incentives and Married Professional Nurses: A Case of Backward-Bending Supply," *Economic Inquiry*, Vol. XIX (January 1981), p. 144.

51. *Health: United States, 1978* (Washington, DC: Government Printing Office), p. 347.

52. George Stigler, "The Theory of Regulation," *Bell Journal of Economics and Management Science*, Vol. 2, No. 1 (Spring 1971), pp. 3-21.

53. *Honolulu Advertiser* (June 4, 1979), p. A5.

54. *New York Times* (December 3, 1978), p. 36.

55. Keith Leffler, "Physician Licensure: Competition and Monopoly in American Medicine," *The Journal of Law and Economics*, Vol. 21, No. 1 (April 1978), p. 166.

56. See discussion between Frank A. Sloan, "Real Returns to Medical Education: A Comment," *Journal of Human Resources*, Vol. 2, No. 1 (Winter 1976), pp. 118-126, and Cotton M. Lindsay, "More Real Returns to Medical Education," pp. 127-129.

57. Frank A. Sloan and Roger Feldman, "Competition Among Physicians," in Federal Trade Commission, *Competition in the Health Care Sector Proceedings* (Washington, DC: Government Printing Office, March 1978), p. 123.

58. *Medical Education in the United States*, Compiled by Sylvia I. Etzel, *JAMA*, Vol. 243, No. 9 (March 7, 1980), p. 852.

59. Leffler, "Physician Licensure," p. 185.

60. Paul Wing, *Planning and Decision Making for Medical Education: An Analysis of Costs and Benefits* (Berkeley: University of California, Ford Foundation Program for Research, 1972), pp. 103-104. (Mimeo). The total direct costs, defined to include "capital," of education for a new physician are estimated to be $77,200 in 1969–70. Students are estimated to have paid only 15 percent of the operating costs, under $3,000, or about 4 percent of total costs.

61. *Ibid.*, p. 101, and author's estimate.

62. Thomas D. Hall and Cotton M. Lindsay, "Medical Schools: Producers of What? Sellers to Whom?", *Journal of Law and Economics*, Vol. 23, No. 1 (April 1980), p. 57.

63. Thomas Gale Moore, "The Purpose of Licensing," *Journal of Law and Economics*, Vol. 4 (October 1961), p. 103.

64. *F.T.C. News Summary*, No. 6 (March 9, 1979), p. 2.

65. William D. White, *Public Health and Private Gain: The Economics of Licensing Clinical Laboratory Personnel* (Chicago: Maaroufa Press, 1979), Quoted in *New England Journal of Medicine*, Vol. 301 (November 8, 1979), p. 1070.

66. Leffler, "Physician Licensure," p. 186.

67. Lee Benham, "Guilds and the Form of Competition in the Health Care Sector," Center for the Study of American Businesses, Working Paper No. 20 (St. Louis: Washington University, August 1977), p. 7.

68. Zachary Y. Dyckman, *Physicians: A Study of Physicians' Fees*, U.S. Council on Wage and Price Stability, Staff Report (Washington, DC: Government Printing Office, March 1978), p. 43.

69. "Briefing—Califano to Med Schools: Cut Back Class Size," *Science* (November 17, 1978), p. 726.

70. The importance of uncertainty in physician decision-making was pointed out by Kenneth Arrow, "Uncertainty and the Welfare Economics of Medical Care," *American Economic Review*, Vol. 53 (December 1963), pp. 941-973. My thinking about uncertainty's importance in withholding knowledge from the consumer reflects discussions with several physicians about patient comprehension of drug labels, labelling of drugs, and the ethics of the use of placebos in controlled clinical trials.

71. Lowell S. Levin, Alfred Katz, and Erik Holst, *Self-Care: Lay Initiatives in Health* (New York: Prodist, 1976), pp. 22, 29.
72. *Ibid.*, p. 108.
73. *Ibid.*, pp. 22-23.
74. Gretchen H. Shapiro, "A Time of Transition," *Forum on Medicine* (July 1980), p. 480.
75. M. Belsky and L. Gross, *How to Choose and Use Your Doctor: Beyond the Medical Mystique* (New York: Arbor House, 1975).
76. Arthur Freese, *Managing Your Doctor* (New York: Stein & Day, 1975).
77. Arthur Levin, *Talk Back to Your Doctor* (New York: Doubleday & Co., Inc., 1975).
78. *Ibid.*, p. 109.
79. Bruce Stokes, "Self-Care: A Nation's Best Health Insurance," *Science*, Vol. 205, No. 4406 (August 10, 1979), p. 547.
80. Lou Crown and Jeanne Floy, "Midpeninsula Health Service: Consumer Control of Health Care," *Self-Determination*, Vol. 1, No. 2 (June 1977), p. 24.
81. Federal Trade Commission, *Advertising for Over-the-Counter Drugs*, Staff Report, May 22, 1979, Public Record No. 215-51, 16 CFR Part 450 (Washington, DC: Government Printing Office, 1979), p. 10.
82. Mitchell Balter, Comments in *The Efficacy of Self-Medication*, ed. by Joseph D. Cooper, Interdisciplinary Communication Associations, Inc. (Washington, DC: Smithsonian Institute, 1973), p. 90.
83. Michael J. Halberstam, as quoted in FTC, "Advertising for Over-the-Counter Drugs," p. 9.
84. Milton Golin, "How Baltimore 'Rescued' Its City Hospitals," *American Medical News Impact* (October 26, 1979), as quoted in *Medical Care Review*, Vol. 36, No. 11 (December 1979), p. 1195.
85. "The Chain: A Survival Formula for Hospitals," *Business Week* (January 26, 1978), p. 113.
86. *Ibid.*, p. 162.
87. Vince DiPaolo, "AHS Studies Service Effectiveness," *Modern Health Care*, Vol. 9 (May 1979), p. 52.
88. See H. S. Ruchlin, D. D. Pointer, and L. L. Cannedy, "A Comparison of For-Profit Investor-Owned Chain and Nonprofit Hospitals," *Inquiry*, Vol. 10 (December 1973), pp. 13-23; J. Rafferty and S. O. Schweitzer, "Comparison of For-Profit and Nonprofit Hospitals: A Re-evaluation," *Inquiry*, No. 11 (December 1974), pp. 304-309; and, Carson W. Bays, "Case-Mix Differences Between Nonprofit and For-Profit Hospitals," *Inquiry*, Vol. 14 (March 1977), pp. 17-21.
89. "The Money in Curing Hospitals," *Business Week* (June 25, 1979), p. 58.
90. Lenore Schiff, "Great Expectations at the Proprietary Hospitals," *Fortune* (December 1977), p. 57.
91. Ann Hughey, "Health Care," *Forbes* (January 5, 1981), p. 132.
92. Harold Luft, John P. Bunker, and Alain C, Enthoven, "Should Operations Be Regionalized? The Empirical Relation Between Surgical Volume and Mortality," *New England Journal of Medicine*, Vol. 301 (December 20, 1979), pp. 1364-1369.
93. C. Brierly, "For-Profit Hospitals: Can They Really Work Together With the Money Boys?", *Prism* (April 1975), p. 16.
94. Ellen Paris, "A Painful Recovery," *Forbes* (September 17, 1979), p. 102.
95. *The Lancet* (April 14, 1979), p. 837.
96. U.S. Congress, Senate, Committee on Finance, Staff Report, *Cost and Utilization Control Mechanisms in Several European Health Care Systems* (Washington, DC: Government Printing Office, February 1976), p. 3.

97. George Chulis, *Medicare: Use of Skilled Nursing Facility Services, 1969–73*, U.S. Department of Health, Education, and Welfare, Health Insurance Statistics (Washington, DC: Government Printing Office, February 2, 1977), H1-75.

98. U.S. Department of Health, Education, and Welfare, *Health Care Financing Review, Summer 1979* (Washington, DC: Government Printing Office, 1979), p. 10.

99. Gibson and Mueller, "National Health Expenditures," p. 5.

100. U.S. Department of Health, Education, and Welfare, *Health: United States, 1979* (Washington, DC: Government Printing Office, 1979), p. 239.

101. Thomas R. Burke, "A Survey and Critical Evaluation of Long-Term Care Reimbursement Policies Under Medicaid," *U.S. Journal of Long-Term Care Administration* (Spring 1975), p. 12.

102. Barry Chiswick, "The Demand for Nursing Home Care: An Analysis of the Substitution Between Institutional and Noninstitutional Care," *Journal of Human Resources*, Vol. 2, No. 3 (Summer 1976), pp. 295-316. Chiswick's analysis supports this statement by use of cross-sectional and time analyses and concludes, "This increased demand will not be the consequence of public policy, but will clearly impact on public policy."

103. U.S. Public Health Service, *Health Resources Statistics, 1976–77* (Washington, DC: Government Printing Office, 1977), p. 329.

104. U.S. Department of Health, Education, and Welfare, *Health: United States, 1978* (Washington, DC: Government Printing Office, 1978), p. 325.

105. U.S. Department of Health and Human Services, *Medicare—Use of Home Health Services, 1977*, Prepared by Wayne Callahan (Washington, DC: Government Printing Office, January 1981), p. 7.

CHAPTER IV.

1. Harold Demsetz, "Information and Efficiency: Another Viewpoint," *Journal of Law and Economics*, Vol. 12 (April 1969), p. 1.

2. Guido Calabresi and Philip Bobbitt, *Tragic Choices* (New York: W. W. Norton, 1978), p. 115.

3. U.S. Department of Health, Education, and Welfare, *Social Security Handbook*, Pub. No. SSA 73-10135 (Washington, DC: Government Printing Office, February 1974), Section 2234, p. 376, Section 2209, p. 361.

4. Harold N. Titmuss, "Ethics and Economics of Medical Care," *Medical Care*, Vol. 1 (January–March 1963), p. 22.

5. *Health: United States, 1979*, p. 180.

6. Steven Schroeder, "The Increasing Use of Emergency Services: Why Has It Occurred? Is It a Problem?", *Western Journal of Medicine*, Vol. 130 (January 1979), p. 67.

7. Martin S. Feldstein, "The Welfare Loss of Excess Insurance," *Journal of Political Economy*, Vol. 81 (March–April 1973), p. 252.

8. Isaac Ehrlich and Gary Becker, "Market Insurance, Self-Insurance, and Self-Protection," *Journal of Political Economy*, Vol. 80 (July–August 1972), p. 641.

9. *Ibid.*

10. Gordon Trapnell, *The Cost of a National Prescription Program* (Nutley, New Jersey: LaRoche Laboratories, September 1979), p. 46.

11. *Health: United States, 1979*, p. 182.

12. Ronald Deacon, James Lubitz, Marian Gornick, *et al.*, "Analysis of Variations in Hospital Use by Medicare Patients in PSRO Areas, 1974–77," *Health Care Financing Review* (Summer 1979), pp. 87, 100.

13. *Ibid.*, p. 88.
14. Nancy Martin, "Already There's Something Better Than Peer Review," *Medical Economics* (November 23, 1970), p. 35.
15. Gene A. Market, *Per-Case Reimbursement for Medical Services*, Department of Health, Education, and Welfare, National Center for Health Services Research, PHS 79-3230 (Washington, DC: Government Printing office, October 1978).
16. Brian Biles, Carl J. Schramm, and J. Graham Akinson, "Hospital Cost Inflation under State Rate-Setting Programs," *New England Journal of Medicine*, Vol. 3, No. 12 (September 18, 1980), pp. 664-668.
17. *Congressional Quarterly* (March 17, 1979), p. 426.
18. Craig Coelen and Daniel Sullivan, "An Analysis of the Effects of Prospective Reimbursement Programs on Hospital Expenditures," *Health Care Financing Review*, Vol. 2, No. 3 (Winter 1981), p. 1.
19. Ake Blomqvist, *The Health Care Business*, p. 122.

CHAPTER V.

1. American College of Physicians, *Observer*, Vol. 1, No. 5 (May 1981), p. 3.
2. Cornelius Ryan and Kathryn Morgan Ryan, *A Private Battle* (New York: Fawcett Popular Library, 1979).
3. Edward J. Carels, Duncan Neuhauser, and William B. Stason, *The Physician and Cost Control* (Cambridge, Mass.: Oelgeschlager, Gunn & Hair, 1980).
4. R. Anderson, J. Lion, and Odin Anderson, *Two Decades of Health Services: Social Survey Trends in Use and Expenditure* (Cambridge, Mass: Ballinger Publishing Company, 1976), p. 193.
5. U.S. Department of Health, Education, and Welfare, *Office Visits to Internists: United States, 1975*, PHS 79-1787, Ser. 13, H. 36, Vital and Health Statistics (Washington, DC: Government Printing Office, 1978), p. 28.
6. Sandra Greene, Dennis Gillings, and Eva Salber, "Who Shops for Medical Care in a Southern Rural Community—How Much and Why," *Inquiry*, Vol. 16 (Spring), p. 68.
7. The more precise rate of motor vehicle accidents for the purpose of measurement of success in prevention of accidents would include the mileage as part of the rate, not only the population. U.S. Department of Health, Education, and Welfare, *Vital Statistics Report*, "Annual Summary to the U.S., 1977," Provisional Mortality Statistics, Vol. 26, No. 13 (December 7, 1978), p. 8; U.S. Department of Health, Education, and Welfare, *Final Mortality Statistics*, Vol. 28, Supplement, No. 1 (May 11, 1979); U.S. Department of Commerce, Bureau of the Census, "United States Statistical Abstract, 1978" (Washington, DC: Government Printing Office, 1979), p. 25, for data prior to 1968.
8. William Haddon, Jr., "The Second Annual William S. Stone Lecture of the American Trauma Society," *Trauma*, Vol. 18, No. 9 (September 1978), p. 652.
9. Sam Peltzman, "The Effects of Automobile Safety Regulation," *Journal of Political Economy*, Vol. 83, No. 4 (August 1975), p. 717.
10. U.S. General Accounting Office, "Effectiveness, Benefits and Costs of Federal Safety Standards for Protection of Passenger Car Occupants," CED-76-121 (Washington, DC: Government Printing Office, July 7, 1976).
11. "Accidents, Speed, and the Road Environment," *British Medical Journal*, Vol. 2 (December 9, 1978), p. 1619.
12. "Human Factors in Road Accidents," *WHO Chronicle* (May 1969), p. 207.
13. *Health: United States, 1980*, pp. 243, 239.

14. U.S. Department of Commerce, Bureau of the Census, "Money Income and Poverty Status of Families and Persons in the United States: 1978," *Current Population Reports,* Series P-60, No. 120 (Washington, DC: Government Printing Office, 1978), p. 24.
15. If the telephone visits were rounded to one place, they would be at 0.6 for both low and high income groups. *Health: United States, 1979,* p. 186.
16. Charles E. Phelps, "Effects of Insurance on Demand for Medical Care," in *Equity in Health Services,* ed. by Ronald Andersen, Joanna Kravits, and Odin Anderson (Cambridge, Mass.: Ballinger Publishing Co., 1975), p 127.
17. Unless otherwise indicated, data in this section came from Dorothy P. Rice and Thomas A. Hodgson, "Tables and Charts for Scope and Impact of Chronic Diseases in the United States," National Center for Health Statistics, U.S. Department of Health, Education, and Welfare (Washington, DC: Government Printing Office, 1979).
18. John R. Moore, Jr., "On the Accuracy of a Self-Reported Measure of Chronic Illness Prevalence," Technical Report No. 37 (Stanford, Calif.: Stanford University Graduate School of Business, February 1974), p. 11.
19. Carl B. Lyle, Jr., William B. Applegate, David S. Citron, *et al.,* "Practice Habits in a Group of Eight Internists," *Annals of Internal Medicine,* Vol. 84, No. 5 (May 1976), p. 598.
20. *Ibid.,* p. 596.
21. Ivan Illyich, *Medical Nemesis* (London: Calder and Boyars, 1975).
22. "There is no support in these data for the notion that deductibles deter preventive care . . . , the data are not well suited to test this hypothesis." Joseph P. Newhouse, John E. Rolph, Bryant Mori, *et al.,* "An Estimate of the Impact of Deductibles on the Demand for Medical Care Services" (Santa Monica, Calif.: Rand Corporation, October 1978), p. 34.
23. "Three Years Later: The Swine Flu Debacle Still Haunts the Government," *National Journal,* Vol. 12 (September 1, 1979), p. 1445.
24. *Ibid.*
25. Most data from the *National Health Interview Survey* have a relatively high probability of statistical error because only a small sample was interviewed. Poor recall and resistance to answering questions about income are two areas that contribute to the error.
26. *Health: United States, 1980,* pp. 405-406.
27. U.S. Department of Health, Education, and Welfare, U.S. Public Health Service, "Physician Visits: Volume and Interval Since Last Visit, United States 1975," Series 10, No. 128 (Washington, DC: Government Printing Office, 1979), p. 11.
28. U.S. Department of Health, Education, and Welfare, "1977 Summary: National Ambulatory Medical Care Survey," Advance Data Series, No. 48 (April 13, 1979) (Washington, DC: Government Printing Office, 1979), p. 6.
29. R. R. Campbell, "Economics of Health and Public Policy" (Washington, DC: American Enterprise Institute, June 1971), p. 26.
30. Anne-Marie Foltz and Jennifer L. Kelsey, "The Annual Pap Test: A Dubious Policy Success," *Milbank Memorial Fund Quarterly,* Vol. 56 (1978), pp. 432-435.
31. Jonathan E. Fielding, "Success of Prevention," *Milbank Memorial Fund Quarterly: Health and Safety,* Vol. 56 (1978), p. 284.
32. S. Ramcharan, J. L. Cutler, Robert Feldman, *et al.,* "Multiphasic Checkup Evaluation Study," *Preventive Medicine,* Vol. 1 (1973), p. 216.
33. Gina Bari Kolata, "Lawsuit Points up Debate over Exercise Electrocardiograms," *Science,* Vol. 202 (December 15, 1978), p. 1175.

34. R. B. Haynes, David L. Sackett, D. Wayne Taylor, *et al.*, "Increased Absenteeism from Work after Detection and Labeling of Hypertension Patients," *New England Journal of Medicine*, Vol. 291 (1978), pp. 741-744.
35. Lewis Thomas, "On the Science and Technology of Medicine," *Daedalus*, Vol. 106 (Winter 1977), p. 45.
36. Helen H. Avnet, "Physician Service Patterns and Illness Rates" (New York: Group Health Insurance, Inc., 1967), pp. 28-29.
37. Gilbert R. Ghez and Michael Grossman, "Preventive Care, Care for Children, and National Health Insurance," in *National Health Insurance: What Now, What Later, What Never?*, ed. by Mark V. Pauly (Washington, DC: American Enterprise Institute, 1980), p. 152.
38. U.S. Department of Health, Education, and Welfare, National Institute of Health, *Proceedings of the Conference on the Decline in Coronary Heart Disease Mortality*, by Richard Havlik and Manning Feinleib, NIH Pub. No. 79-1610 (Washington, DC: Government Printing Office, May 1979), p. xxiii.
39. The data are age-adjusted and the adverse effects of smoking, obesity, and hypertension are accounted for separately. There are no corrections for "diet and psychosocial factors." R. S. Paffenberger, A. L. Wing, and R. T. Hyde, "Physical Activity as an Index of Heart Attack Risk in College Alumni," *American Journal of Epidemiology*, Vol. 108 (September 1978), pp. 161-175.
40. *Ibid.*, p. 173.
41. Michael Grossman, *The Demand for Health*, National Bureau of Economic Research (New York: Columbia University Press, 1972), p. 17.
42. Sidney Abraham and Margaret Carroll, "Food Consumption Patterns in the United States and Their Potential Impact on the Decline in Coronary Heart Disease Mortality," in *Proceedings of the Conference*, p. 257.
43. Gilbert R. Chen and Michael Grossman, "Preventive Care: Care for Children and National Health Insurance," Working Paper No. 417 (Cambridge, Mass: National Bureau of Economic Research, Inc., 1979), p. 41.
44. Robert Wood Johnson Foundation, "New Approaches to Child Care Services Focus Attention on the Nation's Schools," Special Report, No. 1 (Princeton, N.J.: 1971), p. 5.
45. *Ibid.*, p. 8.
46. *Ibid.*, p. 15.
47. U.S. Department of Health and Human Services, *Health: United States*, PHS, Pre-print Copy, Pub. 81-1232 (Washington, DC: Government Printing Office, 1980), p. 410.
48. R. R. Campbell, "Economics of Health," p. 100.
49. "Save Health Care Dollars for Company," EBPR Research Report (Chicago: Charles D. Spencer and Associates, June 1979) (Mimeo); William Greer, Warren Kanbrowitz, and Philip White, "Comprehensive Care Through Physicians Serving in Both Corporate and Private Practice," in *Background Papers on Industry's Changing Role in Health Care Delivery*, ed. by Richard Egdahl (New York: Springer-Verlag, 1977), Chapter 5.
50. William Greer, *et al.*, "Comprehensive Care," p. 56.
51. *Ibid.*
52. *Consumer Exchange* (Chicago: Blue Cross and Blue Shield Association, February 1980).
53. *Environmental Quality*, Tenth Annual Report on the Council on Environmental Quality (Washington, DC: Government Printing Office, December 1979), p. 655.

54. *Ibid.*, p. 17.
55. *Ibid.*, p. 78.
56. *Special Analyses* . . . , *Fiscal 1977*, p. 200.
57. Monsanto Chemical Company has committed substantial monies to Harvard University for a ten- to twenty-year period for basic research in biochemistry and the biology of organogenesis.
58. "Carter Plan to Spur Industrial Innovation," *Science*, Vol. 206 (November 1979), p. 800.
59. "Recombinant DNA: Warming Up for Big Payoff," *Science*, Vol. 206 (November 9, 1979), pp. 663-665.
60. "HEW Prices the Spending Priorities in Slicing NIH's Basic Research Pie," *National Journal*, Vol. 12 (February 26, 1980), p. 278.
61. Dorothy P. Rice and Thomas A. Hodgson, "Social and Economic Implications of Cancer in the United States," Paper presented to the Expert Committee on Cancer Statistics of the World Health Organization and International Agency for Research on Cancer at Madrid, Spring, June 20–26, 1978.
62. Patricia Harris, Secretary, Department of HHS, *National Journal*, Vol. 12, No. 7 (February 16, 1980), p. 277.

CHAPTER VI.

1. Such a central authority would probably need to be governmental because autonomous, effective cooperation by the suppliers of medical care is unlikely and, in any case, would probably be in violation of antitrust laws.
2. *Health, United States, 1979*, pp. 205, 212; U.S. Department Health and Human Services, *Supply of Manpower, 1980*, p. 3.
3. "The Rush to Corporate Practice," *Medical Economics*, Vol. 49, No. 21 (October 9, 1972), p. 253.
4. *Profile of Medical Practice, 1980* (Monroe, Wisc.: American Medical Association, 1980), p. 231.
5. "Rush to Corporate Practice," p. 304.
6. *Profile of Medical Practice, 1980*, p. 232.
7. Frank P. Grad, "The Antitrust Laws and Professional Discipline in Medicine" (December 1977), p. 43. (Mimeo)
8. *Ibid.*
9. U.S. Congress, Senate, Committee on Finance, Hearings, July 1–2, 1969, "Medicare and Medicaid: Problems, Issues, Alternatives," Staff Report (Washington, DC: Government Printing Office, February 1970), p. 71.
10. James R. Cantwell, ed., *Profile of Medical Practice, 1975–76* (Chicago: American Medical Association, 1976), p. 9.
11. *Ibid.*, pp. 10, 13.
12. *Ibid.*
13. *Ibid.*
14. Gerald Meier and John Tillotson, "Physician Reimbursement and Hospital Use in HMOs," U.S. Department of Health, Education, and Welfare, Health Care Financing, Research, and Demonstration Series, Report No. 8 (Washington, DC: Government Printing Office, September 1978), p. 22.
15. *Profile of Medical Practice, 1978*, rev. ed. by John C. Gaffney *et al.* (Monroe, Wisc.: American Medical Association, 1979), Table 33, p. 212.

16. Figure quoted was in 1975 testimony by Roger O. Egeberg, then Assistant Secretary for Health, Department of Health, Education, and Welfare. Zachary Dyckman, "A Study of Physicians' Fees," Council on Wage and Price Stability (Washington, DC: Government Printing Office, March 1978), p. 92.

17. Sharon Henderson, "The Malpractice Problem and Its Effects on Medical Practice," *Profile of Medical Practice, 1978*, rev. ed., ed. by John C. Gaffney (Monroe, Wisc.: American Medical Association, 1979), p. 5.

18. Richard M. Bailey, "A Comparison of Internists in Solo and Fee-For-Service Group Practice in the San Francisco Bay Area," *Bulletin* (New York: Academy of Medicine, November 1968), pp. 1299, 1301.

19. For this point, I am indebted to Patricia Munch Danzon, Senior Research Fellow, The Hoover Institution, Stanford, California.

20. Robert S. Lawrence, "The Role of Physician Education in Cost Control," in *The Physician and Cost Control*, ed. by Edward Carels, Duncan Neuhauser, and William B. Stason (Cambridge, Mass.: Oelgeschlager, Gunn, and Hain, 1980), p. 158.

21. Dyckman, *Physicians*, p. 119.

22. *Ibid.*

23. Gaffney, *Profile*, p. 204.

24. *Ibid.*, p. 194.

25. Marshall J. Orloff and Leon B. Eilwen, *Surgery in the United States: A Summary Report of the Study on Surgical Services for the United States* (Chicago: American College of Surgeons and the American Surgical Association, 1975), p. 183. See also "Surgical Research," in Blair Burns Potter, *Surgery in the United States* (Chicago: R. R. Donnelly & Sons Co., 1975). See also R. Ricardo-Campbell *et al.* "Preliminary Methodology for Controlled Cost-Benefit Study of Drug Impact: The Effect of Cimetidine on Days of Work Lost in a Short-Term Trial in Duodenal Ulcer," *Journal of Clinical Gastroenterology*, Vol. 2 (1980), pp. 37-41.

26. *Health: United States, 1979*, p. 118.

27. William B. Schwartz and Neil K. Komesar, "Doctors, Damages and Deterrence: An Economic View of Medical Malpractice," R-2340-NIH/RC (Santa Monica, Calif.: Rand Corporation, June 1978), p. 12.

28. Kathryn M. Langwell and Jack L. Werner, "A Probability Model of Medical Malpractice Claims," Center for Health Services, Research and Development, Western Economic Association Meeting (Las Vegas, Nev.: American Medical Association, June 19–21, 1979), p. 13. (Mimeo)

29. Schwartz and Komesar, "Doctors, Damages, and Deterrence," p. 16.

30. James Reynolds, "Catching On: Complete Physicals Without M.D.'s," *Medical Economics* (December 21, 1970), p. 81.

31. *1974 Revision of the 1969 California Relative Value Studies*, 5th ed. rev. (San Francisco: California Medical Association, 1975), p. 22.

32. *Ibid.*, p. 19.

33. *Ibid.*, p. 26.

34. Mark S. Blumberg, "Health, Health Care Use, and Type of Private Coverage," *Milbank Memorial Fund Quarterly: Health and Society*, Vol. 58, No. 4 (Fall 1980), pp. 653-654.

35. United States, *Public Health Reports*, Vol. 85, No. 1 (January 1970), p. 87.

36. Boston, New York, Newark, Buffalo, Philadelphia, Pittsburgh, Washington DC, Baltimore, Atlanta, Miami, Tampa-St. Petersburg, Chicago, Detroit, Milwaukee, Houston, Dallas, St. Louis, Denver-Boulder, Cleveland, and Nassau-Suffolk, N.Y., see p. 21.

37. The White House, Congressional Budget Office, "America's New Beginning: A Program for Economic Recovery" (February 1981), Section 6, p. 18. (Mimeo)

38. National Institutes of Health, Committee of the Institute of Medicine, "Health Maintenance Organizations: Toward a Fair Market Test," Policy Statement, PB-239 505 (Washington, DC: National Academy of Sciences, 1976), p. 13.

39. Dyckman, *Physicians*, p. 101 and Appendix IV.

40. Joel H. Broida, "Impact of Membership in an Enrolled, Prepaid Population on Utilization of Health Services in a Group Practice," *New England Journal of Medicine*, Vol. 292, No. 15 (April 10, 1975), pp. 478-483.

41. Harold S. Luft, "Health Maintenance Organizations: Competition, Cost Containment, and National Health Insurance," in *National Health Insurance: What Now, What Later, What Never?*, ed. by Mark V. Pauly (Washington, DC: American Enterprise Institute, 1980), p. 291.

42. Paul Eggers, "Risk Differential between Medicare Beneficiaries Enrolled and Not Enrolled in an HMO," *Health Care Financing Review* (Winter 1980), p. 98.

43. Ibid., p. 93.

44. Mark S. Blumberg, "Health Status and Health Care Use by Type of Private Health Coverage," *Milbank Memorial Fund Quarterly*, Vol. 58, No. 4 (Fall 1980), pp. 633-655.

45. "Proposal Advances in House to Get Elderly Americans Into Prepaid Medical Plans," *Congressional Quarterly* (October 27, 1979), p. 2393, and other sources. The *Congressional Quarterly* reports only "one plan" and 1.5 percent. There has been some increase since 1979.

46. *Lifeguard, A Federally Qualified Health Maintenance Organization: A Summary of Contract Provisions* (Campbell, Calif., 1979). (Brochure)

47. TakeCare, "With Most Health Care Plans It Doesn't Pay to Stay Healthy," *The Peninsula Times Tribune* (April 24, 1980).

48. U.S. Bureau of Labor Statistics, Chicago, Illinois. Telephone conversation with author on August 22, 1980.

49. *Wall Street Journal* (April 30, 1979), p. 8.

50. Anne A. Scitovsky, Nelda McCall, and Lee Benham, "Factors Affecting the Choice Between Two Prepaid Plans," *Medical Care*, Vol. 16, No. 8 (August 1978), pp. 671-672.

51. Ron N. Forthofer, Jay H. Glasser, and Nancy Light, "Life Table Analysis of Membership in an HMO Retention," *Journal of Community Health*, Vol. 5, No. 1 (Fall 1979), p. 49.

52. Klaus Roghmann, et al., "Who Chooses Prepaid Medical Care," *Public Health Reports*, Vol. 90 (1975), p. 523.

53. John B. Christianson and Walter McClure, "Competition in the Delivery of Medical Care," *New England Journal of Medicine*, Vol. 301, No. 1 (October 1979), p. 813.

54. Kaiser-Permanente Medical Care Program, *Annual Report, 1979: Challenge of Change* (Oakland, Calif.: 1980), pp. 32-33.

55. Ibid., "Notes to Combined Financial Statements" (December 31, 1979, and 1978).

56. Greer Williams, *Kaiser-Permanente Health Plan: Why It Works* (Oakland, Calif.: Kaiser Foundation, 1971), pp. 25-26.

57. Anne R. Somers, ed., *The Kaiser-Permanente Medical Care Program* (New York: Commonwealth Fund, 1971), p. 76.

58. Williams, *Kaiser-Permanente*, p. 46.

59. Margaret Greenfield and Alfred Childs, "Prepaid Health Plans: California's Experiment in Changing the Medical Care System," *Public Affairs Report*, Vol. 17, No. 2 (Calif.: University of Berkeley, April 1976), pp. 1-8.

60. Rita R. Campbell, "Economics of Health and Public Policy" (Washington, DC: AEI-Hoover Institution, 1971), p. 26.
61. Harold S. Luft, "Assessing the Evidence on HMO Performance," *Milbank Memorial Fund Quarterly: Health and Society*, Vol. 58, No. 4 (Fall 1980), p. 517.
62. State of California, Health and Welfare Agency, "Annual Report to the Governor and Legislature on Prepaid Health Plans (PHB)" (June 1974), p. 3. (Mimeo)
63. "The Medi-Cal Program: 1966 through 1977," *Socioeconomic Report*, Vol. 18, No. 6 (San Francisco: California Medical Association, June 1978), p. 3.
64. Gerald T. Perkoff, *et al.*, "Lack of Effect of An Experimental Prepaid Group Practice on Utilization of Surgical Care," *Surgery*, Vol. 77, No. 5 (May 1975), p. 619.
65. Carol Greenfield, *et al.*, "Use of Out-of-Plan Services by Medicare Members of HIP," *Health Services Research* (Fall 1978), p. 256.
66. Lloyd Wollstadt, Sam Shapiro, and Thomas Bice, "Disenrollment from a Prepaid Group Practice: An Actuarial and Demographic Description," *Inquiry* (June 1978), p. 145.
67. Greenfeldt, *et al.*, "Use of Out-of-Plan Services," pp. 259, 251.
68. William R. Barnes, *et al.*, vs. Health Alliance of Northern California, Inc., No. 408962, Superior Court of California, Santa Clara County (December 5, 1978), pp. 3-4. (Mimeo)
69. Stephen Moore, "Cost Containment through Risk-Sharing by Primary-Care Physicians," *New England Journal of Medicine*, Vol. 300, No. 24 (June 14, 1979), p. 1360.
70. Edward A. Yelin, Curtis J. Henke, and Wallace V. Epstein, "Rheumatology Manpower in California," *Arthritis and Rheumatism*, Vol. 20, No. 3 (April 1977), p. 809.
71. Stephen Moore, "The Primary Care Network: A New Type of HMO for Private Physicians," *The Western Journal of Medicine*, Vol. 132 (May 1980), p. 420.
72. U.S. Congress, Senate, Committee on Finance Hearings, June 19–21, 1979, "Presentation of Major Health Insurance Proposals" (Washington, DC: Government Printing Office), Appendix, p. A-529.
73. Notes from conversation with Thomas O. Pyle, President, Harvard Community Health Plan, April 16, 1980.
74. Victor Zink, Statement to the U.S. Senate Subcommittee on Health (April 19, 1976), p. 6. (Mimeo)
75. This comparison is suggested by Uwe Reinhardt, "Comment," in Federal Trade Commission, *Competition in the Health Care Sector* (Washington, DC: Government Printing Office, 1978), p. 164.
76. For simplicity, "subscribers" is used here to represent all in the subscriber unit, usually a family. Clyde Pope, "Consumer Satisfaction in a Health Maintenance Organization," *Journal of Health and Social Behavior*, Vol. 19 (September 1978), pp. 293–98.

CHAPTER VII.

1. *1968 Source Book of Health Insurance Data* (New York: Health Insurance Institute, 1969), p. 18.
2. Marjorie S. Carroll and Ross H. Arnett, "Private Health Insurance Plans in 1977: Coverage Enrollment and Financial Experience," *Health Care Financing Review* (Fall 1979), p. 46.
3. John Helyar, "Colonial Penn Loses Anew to Prudential in Writing Health Policies for Retirees," *Wall Street Journal* (June 30, 1981), p. 6.

4. Kenneth Arrow, "Uncertainty and the Welfare Economics of Medical Care," *The American Economic Review* (December 1963), pp. 964-965.21.

5. "5 to 8 percent," in U.S. Congressional Budget Office, "Profile of Health Care Coverage: The Haves and Have-nots" (Washington, DC: Government Printing Office, March 1979), p. 9; "12-13 percent figure" in Marjorie Smith Carroll, "Private Health Insurance Plans in 1976: An Evaluation," *Social Security Bulletin*, Vol. 41, No. 9 (September 1978), p. 6.

6. The labor force includes the employed and the unemployed who are available and seeking work.

7. Stephen G. Sudovar and Patrice H. Feinstein, *National Health Insurance Issues: The Adequacy of Coverage* (Washington, DC: Roche Laboratories, December 1979), p. 26.

8. Robert M. Gibson and Charles R. Fisher, "Age Differences in Health Care Spending, Fiscal Year 1977," *Social Security Bulletin*, Vol. 42, No. 1 (January 1979), p. 12.

9. U.S. Department of Health, Education, and Welfare, "Research and Statistics Note," No. 19 (July 10, 1959), p. 3.

10. Wilbur J. Cohen, "Next Steps for Voluntary Health Insurance," in *Private Health Insurance and Medical Care: Conference Papers* (Washington, DC: Government Printing Office, 1968), p. 92.

11. Ruth S. Hanft, "National Health Expenditures, 1950–65," *Social Security Bulletin*, Vol. 30, No. 2 (February 1967), Table 7, p. 22.

12. *1980 Annual Report of the Board of Trustees of the Federal Hospital Insurance Trust Fund* (Washington, DC: June 17, 1980), p. 5. (Mimeo)

13. Robert M. Gibson and Charles R. Fisher, "National Health Expenditures, Fiscal Year 1977," *Social Security Bulletin*, Vol. 41, No. 7 (July 1978), p. 16.

14. *1980 Annual Report of the Board of Trustees of the Federal Hospital Insurance Trust Fund*, p. 17.

15. Richard A. Knox, "Hospitals: King Aide Produce [sic] Rate Deal," *Boston Globe* (June 19, 1980), p. 22.

16. *Ibid.*, p. 17.

17. As quoted in "HEW Proposes New Uniform Reporting Requirements," *National Health Insurance Report*, Vol. 10, No. 1 (March 21, 1980), p. 18.

18. *Medical Care Review*, Vol. 37, No. 5 (May 1980), p. 443.

19. U.S. Accounting Office, Elmer B. Staats, Comptroller General of the U.S., Statement on Report, "Costs Can Be Reduced by Millions of Dollars if Federal Agencies Fully Carry Out GAO Recommendations," House Committee on Interstate and Foreign Commerce, HRD-80-6 (Washington, DC: November 13, 1979), p. 20. (Mimeo)

20. *Ibid.*, p. 13.

21. Thomas P. Ferry, Marian Gornick, Marilyn Newton, and Carl Hackerman, "Physicians' Charges Under Medicare: Assignment Rates and Beneficiary Liability," *Health Care Financing Review* (Winter 1980), p. 49.

22. *Ibid.*, p. 50.

23. *Ibid.*, p. 53.

24. U.S. General Accounting Office, Elmer B. Staats, Comptroller General of the U.S., "Statement" HRD-79-111 (Washington, DC: Government Printing Office, September 6, 1979), p. 11.

25. U.S. Congress, House, Committee on Interstate and Foreign Commerce, Staff for the Subcommittee on Health and the Environment, "Data on the Medicaid Program: Eligibility of Services, Expenditures: Fiscal Years 1966–76," Print No. 18

(Washington, DC: Government Printing Office, January 1976), p. 43.

26. *Health: United States, 1979*, p. 259.

27. Daniel N. Price, "Cash Benefits for Short-Term Sickness, 1948–76," *Social Security Bulletin*, Vol. 41, No. 20 (October 1978), p. 7.

28. Sue C. Hawkins and Donald E. Rigby, "Effect of SSI on Medicaid Caseloads and Expenditures," *Social Security Bulletin*, Vol. 42, No. 2 (February 1979), pp. 7-8.

29. Robert M. Gibson, "National Health Expenditures, 1979," *Health Care Financing Review, 1980*, Vol. 2, No. 1, p. 7.

30. *Annual Report to the Governor and Legislature on Prepaid Health Plans (PHPs)*, California Health and Welfare Agency, Department of Health (June 1974), p. 21. (Mimeo)

31. *Health: United States, 1979*, p. 237.

32. "Medicare-Medicaid Anti-Fraud and Abuse Amendments," in *Weekly Compilation of Presidential Documents: Administration of Jimmy Carter* (Washington, DC: Office of the Federal Registrar, October 14, 1977), p. 1656.

33. Staats, "Costs Can Be Reduced," p. 17.

34. David Johnston, "Deukmejian Assails Investigative Cuts," *Los Angeles Times* (October 30, 1979), as reported in *Medical Care Review*, Vol. 36, No. 11 (December 1979), p. 1176.

35. Federal Trade Commission, "Medical Participation in Control of Blue Shield and Certain Other Open-Panel Medical Prepayment Plans," *Staff Report* (no publisher, no place, April 1979), and "Proposed Trade Regulation Rule," "For Commission Review Not for Official Publication" (Washington, DC: April 1979), p. 182. Hereafter referred to as *FTC Staff Report*.

36. *Blue Cross/Blue Shield Fact Book, 1978* (Chicago: Blue Cross and Blue Shield Association, 1979), pp. 3, 13.

37. For further analysis of this point, see Martin Feldstein, "The Welfare Loss of Excess Health Insurance," *Journal of Political Economy*, Vol. 81, No. 2 (March–April 1973), pp. 251-280.

38. H. E. "Ted" Frech, III, and Paul Ginsburg, "Imposed Health Insurance in Monopolistic Markets: A Theoretical Analysis," *Economic Inquiry*, Vol. 13, No. 1 (March 1975), p. 63.

39. *FTC Staff Report* (April 1979), Footnote 152, p. 183.

40. Marjorie Smith Carroll and Ross H. Arnett III, "Private Health Insurance Plans in 1977," *Health Care Financing Review* (Fall 1979), p. 18.

41. *Ibid.*, p. 13.

42. Roger D. Blair, Paul B. Ginsburg, and Ronald Vogel, "Blue Cross-Blue Shield Administration Costs: A Study of Non-Profit Insurers," *Economic Inquiry*, Vol. 13, No. 2 (June 1975), p. 239.

43. *Blue Cross/Blue Shield Fact Book, 1978*, p. 2.

44. *Ibid.*

45. Thomas L. Delbanco, Katherine C. Meyers, and Elliot A. Segal, "Paying the Physician's Fee," *New England Journal of Medicine*, Vol. 301, No. 24 (December 13, 1979), pp. 1315-1316.

46. *FTC Staff Report* (April 1979), pp. 185, 187.

47. U.S. Congress, House, Committee on Interstate and Foreign Commerce, Subcommittee on Oversight and Investigations, Pub. 95-68, "Conflicts of Interest on Blue Shield Boards of Directors," Ninety-fifth Congress, Session 2 (Washington, DC: Government Printing Office, 1978), p. 3.

48. *Staff Report to the Federal Trade Commission and Proposed Trade Regulation Rule*, Bureau of Competition, "Medical Participation in Control of Blue Shield and Certain Other Open-Panel Medical Prepayment Plans" (April 1979), p. 1, "unofficial." (Mimeo)
49. Deborah A. Stone, "The Probability of Monopoly Power in Federal Health Policy," *Milbank Memorial Fund Quarterly: Health and Society*, Vol. 58, No. 1 (Winter 1980), p. 51.
50. Clark Havighurst, "Antitrust Enforcement in the Medical Services Industry: What Does It All Mean?" *Milbank Memorial Fund Quarterly: Health and Society*, Vol. 58, No. 1 (Winter 1980), p. 93.
51. *Ibid.*, p. 101.
52. *Ibid.*, p. 102.
53. "Staff Report to the Federal Trade Commission and Proposed Trade Regulation Rule," *FTC Report* (April 1979). The FTC has not adopted this staff report.
54. California Medical Association, "Physician Supply in California: December 1978," *Socioeconomic Report*, Vol. 20, No. 3 (April–May 1980), p. 6.
55. Mark V. Pauly and Mark A. Satterthwaite, "The Effect of Provider Supply on Price," in *The Target Income Hypothesis*, U.S. Department of Health and Human Services, Pub. No. HRA-80-27 (Washington, DC: Government Printing Office, 1980), p. 26.
56. David Perlman, "A Medical Clinic for Laymen in San Francisco," *San Francisco Chronicle* (July 8, 1981), p. 2.
57. Lawrence G. Goldberg and Warren Greenberg, "The Competitive Response of Blue Cross and Blue Shield to the Health Maintenance Organization in California and Hawaii," *Medical Care*, Vol. 17, No. 10 (October 1979), p. 1025.
58. Sylvia A. Law, *Blue Cross: What Went Wrong?* (New Haven and London: Yale University Press, 1974), p. 25.
59. "Blues Must Disclose Rate Data, State Says," *Detroit Free Press* (March 31, 1979), p. 148:5a, as quoted in *Medical Care Review*, Vol. 36, No. 5 (May 1979), p. 470.
60. Law, *Blue Cross*, p. 60.
61. Carroll and Arnett, "Private Health Insurance Plans," pp. 4-5.
62. Marjorie Smith Carroll, "Private Health Insurance Plans in 1976: An Evaluation," *Social Security Bulletin*, Vol. 41, No. 9 (September 1978), p. 9.
63. Carroll and Arnett, "Private Health Insurance Plans," p. 5.
64. M. L. Barer, R. G. Evans, and G. L. Stoddart, *Controlling Health Care Costs by Direct Charges to Patients: Snare or Delusion?*, Occasional Paper 10 (Canada: Ontario Economic Council, 1979), p. viii.
65. *Ibid.*, p. ix.
66. *Ibid.*, pp. 74-75.

CHAPTER VIII.

1. Joseph G. Simanis and John R. Coleman, "Health Care Expenditures in Nine Industrialized Countries, 1960-76," *Social Security Bulletin*, Vol. 43, No. 1 (January 1980), p. 4.
2. *World Development Report* (Washington, DC: The World Bank, August 1980), p. 53.
3. U.S. Department of Health, Education, and Welfare, Public Health Service, Office of Health Research, Statistics, and Technology, National Center for Health Statistics, various issues of *Vital Statistics*; U.S. Department of Health, Education, and Welfare, Public Health Service, Office of the Assistant Secretary of Health, National

Center for Health Statistics, National Center for Health Services Research, PHS Pub. 781232 (Washington, DC: Government Printing Office, 1978); and *Health: United States, 1978, Health: United States, 1979,* and *Health: United States, 1980.*

4. Michael Grossman and Steven Jocobowitz, "Determinants of Variations in Infant Mortality Rates among Counties of the United States: The Roles of Social Policies and Programs," in *Abstracts,* World Congress on Health Economics, Leyden University, the Netherlands (September 9–11, 1980), p. 35. (Mimeo)
5. *Health: United States, 1980,* p. 193.
6. *Congressional Record (Daily Edition)* (January 15, 1975), p. S44.
7. "U.S. Final Mortality Statistics, 1978," U.S. PHS *Vital Statistics,* p. 11.
8. "Health: A Matter of Class," *The Economist* (September 6, 1980), pp. 52, 61.
9. *Health: United States, 1978,* p. 168.
10. *Ibid.,* p. 175.
11. *Ibid.,* p. 230.
12. *Ibid.*
13. *Health: United States, 1980,* p. 25.
14. U.S. Department of Health, Education, and Welfare, Public Health Service, Office of the Assistant Secretary for Health and Surgeon General, "Healthy People: The Surgeon General's Report on Health Promotion and Disease Prevention," PHS Pub. 79-55071 (Washington, DC: Government Printing Office, 1979), pp. 10-11, 18.
15. Richard Havlik and Manning Feinleib, eds., *Proceedings of the Conference on the Decline in Coronary Heart Disease Mortality,* U.S. National Institutes of Health, Pub. No. 79-1610 (May 1979), p. 299. (Mimeo). Hereafter referred to as *CHD Conference, 1979.*
16. O. W. Anderson and G. Rosen, "An Examination of the Concepts of Preventive Medicine," Series 12 (New York: Health Information Foundation's Research, 1960), pp. 18-19.
17. *Monthly Vital Statistics: Annual Summary for the U.S., 1978,* pp. 2-3.
18. *Ibid.,* p. 5. Figures for 1978 are estimates.
19. *Health: United States, 1978,* p. 167.
20. *CHD Conference, 1979,* p. 12.
21. *Health, United States, 1978,* Table 30, p. 188.
22. *Health: United States, 1980,* p. 201.
23. *Ibid.,* p. 207.
24. The difference for each was: 0.1 for Canadians; 0.2 for Swedes, the Swiss, and the Israelis; and 0.3 for the Japanese. *Health: United States, 1978,* pp. 168, 175.
25. *Health: United States, 1979,* p. 99.
26. *Health: United States, 1980,* p. 205.
27. *Ibid.,* p. 409.
28. *Ibid.,* p. 420.
29. "Healthy People," pp. 3-8.
30. *Ibid.*
31. Jonathan D. Quick, "Liberalized Abortion in Oregon: Effects on Fertility, Prematurity, Fetal Death, and Infant Death," *American Journal of Public Health,* Vol. 68 (October 1978), p. 1003.
32. Francis L. Hutchins, Norman Kendall, and John Robino, "Experience with Teenage Pregnancy," *Obstetrics and Gynecology,* No. 54 (July 1979), p. 2.
33. U.S. Department of Health and Human Services, "Trends and Differentials in Births to Unmarried Women: United States, 1970–76," *Vital and Health Statistics,*

Pub. No. 80-1914, Series 21, No. 36 (May 1980), pp. 3-4, 32. All other data in this section on illegitimate births are from the same source.

34. Inderjit S. Thind, *et al.*, "Infant Mortality in Newark, New Jersey: A Study of Sociolographic and Medical Factors," *Public Health Reports*, No. 94 (July–August 1979), p. 354.

35. "Healthy People," pp. 3-5.

36. *Health: United States, 1980*, p. 225.

37. Ezra Davidson, as quoted in "Pregnant Women and Newborns at Risk Are the Focus of Efforts Nationwide to Recognize Perinatal Services," *Special Report*, Robert Wood Johnson Foundation, Princeton, New Jersey, No. 2, 1978, p. 13.

38. U.S. Department of Health, Education, and Welfare, *Vital Statistics Report*, PHS 81-1120, Vol. 28, No. 13 (Washington, DC: Government Printing Office, 1979), p. 6.

39. U.S. Department of Health, Education, and Welfare, *Vital Statistics of the U.S., 1975*, Vol. 11, Mortality, Part A (Washington, DC: Government Printing Office, 1979), pp. 1-7.

40. *Health: United States, 1978*, pp. 234-235.

41. U.S. Bureau of Labor Statistics, "Press Release," 79-174 (March 12, 1979).

42. R. B. Haynes, D. L. Sackett, D. W. Taylor, *et al.*, Absenteeism from Work after Detection of Labelling of Hypertensive Patients," *New England Journal of Medicine*, Vol. 299, No. 14 (October 5, 1978), pp. 741-744.

43. Daniel E. Taylor, "Absence From Work: Measuring Hours Lost, May 1978," *Monthly Labor Review* (August 1979), p. 49.

44. "Healthy People," p. 6.

45. *Ibid.*, pp. 6-8.

46. *CHD Conference, 1979*, p. xxv.

47. "Healthy People," pp. 6-11.

48. *CHD Conference, 1979*, p. xxv.

49. "Controlling a Killer: Gains Are Made in Prevention, Treatment of Strokes," *Wall Street Journal* (July 18, 1979), p. 1.

50. Rita Ricardo-Campbell, "Your Health and the Government," in *The United States in the 1980s* (Stanford, Calif.: Hoover Institution Press, 1980), p. 332.

51. *CHD Conference, 1979*, p. xxv.

52. Gary D. Friedman, "Decline in Hospitalizations for Coronary Heart Disease and Stroke," in *CHD Conference 1979*, p. 112.

53. U.S. Congress, House, Committee on Science and Technology, Subcommittee on Science, Research, and Technology, *The Food and Drug Administration's Process for Approving New Drugs* (Washington, DC: Government Printing Office, November 1980), p. 36.

54. *Ibid.*, p. 37.

55. Haynes, *et al.*, "Increased Absenteeism," pp. 741-744.

56. *CHD Conference, 1979*, p. xxiii.

57. "Healthy People," pp. 6-20.

58. *Ibid.*, pp. 6-16.

59. *Monthly Vital Statistics Report* (February 11, 1977), p. 22.

60. "Cancer Facts and Figures, 1981" (New York: American Cancer Society, 1980), p. 5.

61. *Health: United States, 1978*, pp. 188-191.

62. *Health: United States, 1980*, p. 403.

63. Jean Mayer, Johanna T. Dwyer, Kathryn Dowd, and Laura Mayer, eds., *Food and*

Nutrition Policy in a Changing World (New York: Oxford University Press, 1979), p. 241.

64. *Ibid.*, p. 238.

65. *Ibid.*, p. 235.

66. U.S. H.H.S. *"Trends in Breast Feeding,"* in *Advance Data,* National Center for Health Statistics, PHS Pub. No. 80-1250, No. 59 (Washington, DC: Government Printing Office, March 28, 1980), p. 2.

67. White House, Office of the Press Secretary, *A Program for Economic Recovery,* "Reduce Middle-Upper Income Benefits" (Washington, DC: The White House, Office of the Press Secretary, February 18, 1981), Section 2, p. 1.

68. *Ibid.*, Section 2, p. 1.

69. Shan Pou Tsai, Eun Sul Lee and Robert Hardy, "The Effect of a Reduction in Leading Causes of Death: Potential Gains in Life Expectancy," *American Journal of Public Health,* Vol. 68, No. 10 (October 1978), p. 966.

70. Marc Lalonde, *A New Perspective on the Health of Canadians* (Ottawa, Canada: 1975), p. 31.

71. "Healthy People," p. I-9.

72. *Ibid.*, pp. I-6, I-10.

73. Thomas C. Chalmers and Alfred R. Stern, "The Staggering Cost of Prolonging Life," *Business Week* (February 23, 1981), p. 19.

CHAPTER IX.

1. *Inequalities in Health: Report of a Research Working Group* (Royal Stationers: Department of Health and Human Services, 1980), p. 48. (Mimeo)

2. The acute condition was defined as lasting less than three months, but involving either medical attention or restricted activity in the two weeks prior to the interview week.

3. U.S. Department of Health, Education, and Welfare, "Medical Care of Acute Conditions," Pub. No. 79-1557, Series 10, No. 129 (February 1979), p. 7.

4. Lu Ann Aday, Ronald Andersen, and Gretchen V. Fleming, *Health Care in the U.S.: Equitable for Whom?* (Beverly Hills and London: Sage Publications, Inc., 1980), p. 302.

5. Carroll and Arnett, "Private Health Insurance Plans," p. 14.

6. *Health: United States, 1980,* p. 284.

7. "Humana Increases Offer to Acquire Brookwood Health," *Wall Street Journal* (April 17, 1981), p. 4.

8. "Stanford to Repay $1.5 Million to Medicare," *San Francisco Chronicle* (July 16, 1981), p. 8.

9. Herbert S. Denenberg is known for his various *Shopper's Guides* to dentistry, health insurance, and hospitals. They were first published during 1972–73, causing an uproar among many providers. The full titles of two of the guides will indicate their content: Herbert S. Denenberg, *A Shopper's Guide to Surgery: Fourteen Rules on How to Avoid Unnecessary Surgery* (Harrisburg, Penna.: Pennsylvania Insurance Department, July 1972) (Mimeo) and Herbert S. Denenberg, *A Shopper's Guide to Dentistry: Thirty-two Rules for Selecting a Dentist and for Obtaining Good Dental Care With Representative Dental Fees Charged in Pennsylvania* (Harrisburg, Penna.: Pennsylvania Insurance Department, February 1973).

10. *The Washington Post* (March 30, 1979), p. 1.

11. Marilyn Chase, "City of Doctors," *Wall Street Journal* (March 13, 1980), p. 33.

12. For a recent example, see Cornelius Ryan and Kathryn Morgan Ryan, *A Private Battle* (New York: Fawcett Popular Library, 1980).
13. *Business Week* (August 1980), p. 126.
14. Jean T. May, Lois Michaels, and Frances W. Cohen, "The Pittsburgh Health Education Survey and *Tel-Med* Program Evaluation," Tenth International Conference on Health Education in London, England (September 1979). (Mimeo)
15. Federal Trade Commission, *News Summary*, No. 19 (Washington, DC: Government Printing Office, March 30, 1979), p. 3.
16. Federal Trade Commission, *News Summary*, No. 30 (Washington, DC: Government Printing Office, June 15, 1979), p. 2.
17. Federal Trade Commission, *News Summary*, "Keep Voice in Government Decision-Making, FTC Chairman Urges" (Washington, DC: Government Printing Office, July 20, 1979), p. 1.
18. U.S. Department of Health, Education, and Welfare, Food and Drug Administration, *Final Report of the Review Panel on New Drug Relations* (Washington, DC: Government Printing Office, May 1977), p. 5.
19. Irving Kristol, "Summer Notes and Footnotes," *Wall Street Journal* (July 18, 1977), p. 12.
20. Rita Ricardo-Campbell, *Drug Lag: Federal Government Decision-Making* (Stanford, Calif.: Hoover Institution Press, 1976), p. 34, fn. 70.
21. U. S. Department of Health, Education, and Welfare, Food and Drug Administration, *HEW News*, P79-28 (Washington, DC: Government Printing Office, October 11, 1979), p. 1.
22. *Ibid.*, p. 2.
23. U.S. Congress, House, Subcommittee on Science, Research and Technology, *The Food and Drug Administration's Process for Approving New Drugs* (Washington, DC: Government Printing Office, 1980), p. v.
24. *Ibid.*, p. 79.
25. *Ibid.*, pp. 79-80.
26. *Ibid.*, pp. 75, 30.
27. Alexander M. Schmidt, "Dimensions of Change in the FDA," Speech, Pharmaceutical Advertising Seminar (Chicago: September 13, 1973), p. 9.
28. Nelson S. Hartunian, Charles Smart, and Mark S. Thompson, "The Incidence and Economic Costs of Cancer, Motor Vehicle Injuries, Coronary Heart Disease, and Stroke: A Comparative Analysis," *American Journal of Public Health*, Vol. 70, No. 12 (December 1980), p. 1249.
29. Beulah Cypress, "Office Visits for Preventive Care . . . ," *Advance Data*, National Center for Health Care Statistics, No. 69 (April 1, 1981), p. 2.
30. John C. Goodman, *National Health Care in Great Britain: Lessons for the U.S.A.* (Dallas: Fisher Institute, 1980).
31. Karen Davis and Cathy Schoen, *Health and the War on Poverty: A Ten-Year Appraisal* (Washington, DC: The Brookings Institution, 1978), p. 65.
32. *Ibid.*
33. Richard E. Johnson and Daniel J. Azevedo, "Comparing the Medical Utilization and Expenditures of Low Income Health Plan Enrollees with Medicare," *Medical Care*, Vol. 17 (September 1979), pp. 953-966.
34. Goodman, *National Health Care in Britain*, p. 180.
35. U.K. Department of Social Services, *Working Group on Inequalities in Health*, Report to Patrick Jenkin, Secretary of State (Royal Stationers: Government Document, August 1980), pp. 95-98. Later referred to as *Inequalities in Health*.

36. David S. Salkever and Thomas W. Bice, *Hospital Certificate-of-Need Controls: Impact on Investment, Costs and Use* (Washington, DC: American Enterprise Institute, 1979), p. 75.

37. U.S. Congress (96th), First Session, *Congressional Quarterly Almanac*, Vol. XXXV, (1979) (Washington, DC: 1980), p. 475.

38. Arnold S. Relman, "Cat Scanners—Conferring 'the Greatest Benefit on Mankind,' " *New England Journal of Medicine*, Vol. 301, No. 19 (November 8, 1979), p. 1062.

39. Hal Lancaster, "CAT Scanners Put on Wheels to Cut Costs," *Wall Street Journal* (July 1, 1980), p. 23.

40. American College of Physicians, "Regents Approve Eight CEAP (Clinical Efficacy Assessment Project) Recommendations," *Observer*, Vol. 1, No. 6 (June 1981), p. 1.

41. *Ibid.*, pp. 16-17.

42. *Ibid.*, p. 9.

43. National Center for Health Technology, "Unofficial Summary" (Rockville, Maryland). (Mimeo, undated, 2 pages).

44. Rita Ricardo-Campbell, "Risk-Benefit/Cost Benefit: Improving Government Regulation of Approval of New Drugs," Presented at the World Congress on Health Economics, Leyden University, the Netherlands (Stanford, Calif.: Hoover Institution Press, September 1980).

45. U.S. Congress, Office of Technology Assessment, "Implications of Cost-Effectiveness Analysis of Medical Technology" (Washington, DC: Government Printing Office, 1980), p. 5.

46. James W. Varpel, "Early Death: An American Tragedy," *Law and Contemporary Problems*, Vol. XL, No. 4 (Durham, North Carolina: Duke University Press, Autumn 1976), p. 78.

47. James F. Fries, "Aging, Natural Death, and the Compression of Morbidity," *New England Journal of Medicine*, Vol. 303, No. 3 (July 17, 1980), p. 133.

48. "This is What You Thought about . . . A Patient's Right to Die," *Glamour* (June 1980), p. 23.

49. Ricardo-Campbell, "Risk-Benefit/Cost-Benefit," p. 8.

50. *Ibid.*, p. 11.

51. Ernest M. Gruenberg, "The Failures of Success," *Milbank Memorial Fund Quarterly: Health and Society*, Vol. 55, No. 1 (Winter 1977), pp. 19, 22.

52. John Roper, "Doctors' Dilemma Over Kidney Patients," *London Times* (May 15, 1978), p. 4.

53. Renee C. Fox and Judith P. Swazey, *The Courage to Fail* (Chicago: The University of Chicago Press, 1974), pp. 240-79.

54. Ronald Kartzinel, Acting Director, Division of Neuropharmacological Drug Products, U.S. Department of Health, Education, and Welfare, Federal Drug Administration. (Letter to author dated September 6, 1977.)

55. Guido Calabresi and Phillip Bobbitt, *Tragic Choices* (New York: W. W. Norton, 1978), p. 17.

56. U.S. Congress, House, Committee on Science, Research, and Technology, Subcommittee on Science and Technology, *The Food and Drug Administration's Process for Approving New Drugs* (Washington, DC: Government Printing Office, November 1980), p. 42.

57. For elaboration, see Ricardo-Campbell, "Risk-Benefit/Cost-Benefit," pp. 7-8.

58. Susan V. Lawrence, "Heart Transplants: Blessing or Boondogle," *Forum on Medicine*,

Vol. 3, No. 7 (July 1980), pp. 442-443.

59. *Ibid.* Stanford University Medical Center's criteria include: patient under fifty years of age, in good health except for Class IV end-stage cardiac disease, emotionally stable, supportive family to whom patient can return, enough money to pay his or her own and supportive family member's travel and living expense over the period of evaluation, operation, and post-operative care.

60. *New England Journal of Medicine* article, as reported in the *San Francisco Chronicle* (April 9, 1981).

61. Julian Le Grand, "The Distribution of Public Expenditure: The Case of Health Care," *Economica*, Vol. 45, No. 179 (August 1978), p. 137.

62. Mary-Ann Rozbicki, *Rationing British Health Care: The Cost/Benefit Approach*, U.S. Department of State, Executive Seminar, Twentieth Session (1977–78), p. 7. (Mimeo)

63. *Ibid.*, p. 8.

64. *Ibid.*, p. 9.

65. A. J. Culyer and J. G. Cullis, "Hospital Waiting Lists and the Supply and Demand of Inpatient Care," *Social and Economic Administration*, Vol. 9, No. 1 (Spring 1975), p. 19.

66. Anthony J. Culyer, *Need and the National Health Service: Economics and Social Choice* (London: Martin Robertson Publications, 1976), p. 110.

67. *Ibid.*, p. 111.

68. C. H. C. Thomas, "Personal View," *British Medical Journal*, Vol. 1, No. 5959 (March 22, 1975), p. 678.

69. Kjeld Kjeldsen, "Evaluation of the Impact of Various Diseases on Mortality," *Bulletin of World Health Organization*, No. 52 (1975) p. 369.

70. Goodman, *National Health Care in Britain*, pp. 101-102.

71. Rozbicki, *Rationing British Health Care*, p. 8.

72. *The Maui News* (August 11, 1980), p. A8.

73. Calabresi and Bobbitt, *Tragic Choices*, pp. 44-45.

74. "Implementing the End-State Renal Disease Program of Medicare," *Health Care Financing Grants and Contracts Report*, Project Directors Richard A. Rettig and Ellen L. Marks (Washington, DC: Government Printing Office, March 1981), p. 135. (Mimeo)

75. Goodman, *National Health Care in Britain*, p. 101.

76. Joanne Linnerooth, "The Value of Human Life: A Review of the Models," *Economic Inquiry*, Vol. 17 (January 1979), p. 57.

77. *Ibid.*, p. 72.

78. As quoted in "Can Government Place a Value on Saving a Human Life?", *National Journal* (February 17, 1979), p. 254.

79. U.S. Congress, Office of Technology Assessment, *The Implications of Cost-Effectiveness Analysis of Medical Technology* (Washington, DC: Government Printing Office, August 1980), p. 5.

80. *An Evaluation of Research Needs in Endocrinology and Metabolism: A Report to the National Institute of Health*, Sidney H. Ingbar, Chairman and Principal Investigator (Boston, Mass.: Learning Systems, Inc., December 1979), p. 13.

81. Martin J. Bailey, *Reducing Risks to Life: Measurement of the Benefits* (Washington, DC: American Enterprise Institute, 1980), p. 26.

82. *The Economist*, Vol. 275, No. 7135 (May 31–June 6, 1980), p. 113.

83. G. K. Wilcock, "Economic Aspects of the Demand for Total Hip Replacement in the Elderly," *Age and Aging*, Vol. 8 (1979), p. 32.

84. Rozbicki, *Rationing British Health Care*, p. 11.

85. *Ibid.*, p. 18.
86. Brian Watkin, "All Reasonable Requirements," *The Lancet* (May 12, 1979), p. 1022.
87. U.K. Department of Social Services, *Inequalities in Health*, Foreword, no page number.
88. *Ibid.*, p. 289.
89. "Priorities in the N.H.S.," *The Lancet* (March 25, 1978), 659.
90. Alan Maynard and Anne Ludbrook, "What's Wrong With the National Health Service?", *Lloyds Bank Review*, No. 138 (October 1980), pp. 30-31.
91. *Ibid.*, p. 31.
92. Jerome P. Kassirer, "The Principles of Clinical Decision Making: An Introduction to Decision Analysis," *Yale Journal of Biology and Medicine*, Vol. 49, No. 2 (May 1976), p. 155.
93. Murray Seeger, "Russ Abuse Emergency House Calls," *Los Angeles Times* (November 5, 1972), Section I, p. 12.

CHAPTER X.

1. *Special Analyses, Budget of the United States Government, Fiscal Year 1982* (Washington, DC: Government Printing Office, 1981), p. 229.
2. Alain Enthoven, *Health Plan: The Only Practical Solution to the Soaring Cost of Medical Care* (Reading, Mass.: Addison-Wesley, 1980).
3. Martin Feldstein, "A New Approach to National Health Insurance," *The Public Interest*, Vol. 23 (Spring 1971), pp. 93-105.
4. James F. Blumstein, "Constitutional Perspectives on Governmental Decisions Affecting Human Life and Health," *Law and Contemporary Problems*, Vol. 40, No. 4 (Autumn 1976), pp. 267-269.
5. U. S. Congress, Congressional Budget Office, *Catastrophic Health Insurance*, Budget Issue Paper (January 1977), pp. 2-3.
6. *Ibid.*, p. 6.
7. *Ibid.*, p. 8.
8. Joseph P. Newhouse, "The Demand for Medical Care Service: A Retrospect and Prospect," Working Draft, May 1, 1980 (Santa Monica, Calif.: Rand Corporation), p. 16. (Mimeo)
9. W. Mannin, C. Morris, L. Orr, *et al.*, "A Two-Part Model of the Demand for Medical Care: Preliminary Results from the Health Insurance Study," Working Draft, May 1980 (Santa Monica, Calif.: Rand Corporation), pp. 1-2. (Mimeo)
10. Deborah Randolph, "More Workers are Getting a Chance to Choose Benefits Cafeteria-Style," *Wall Street Journal* (July 14, 1981), p. 25.
11. Michael H. Cooper, *Rationing Health Care* (New York: John Wiley, 1975), p. 51.
12. Brandon S. Tenlewall, "Cost-Benefit Analysis and Heart Transplantation," *New England Journal of Medicine*, Vol. 37, No. 15 (April 9, 1981), p. 903.
13. Campbell, *Economics of Health*, p. 26.
14. Jane S. Williams, Claudia R. Sanders, Michael A. Riddiough, *et al.*, "Cost Effectiveness of Vaccination Against Pneumococcal Pneumonia," *New England Journal of Medicine*, Vol. 303, No. 10 (September 4, 1980), p. 553.
15. *Science*, Vol. 202 (December 15, 1978), p. 1175.
16. Haynes, *et al.*, "Increased Absenteeism," pp. 741-744.
17. *Health: United States, 1978*, p. 32.
18. U. S. Congress, Joint Committee Subcommittee Hearings, *Low Income Families,*

81st Congress, 1st Session, 1952, p. 162, as cited in R. R. Campbell and W. G. Campbell, "Compulsory Health Insurance," p. 3.

19. Charles E. Phelps, "Illness Prevention and Medical Insurance," *Journal of Human Resources*, Vol. 13, Supplement (1978), p. 183.

20. "Competition and the Quality of Medical Care," *American Medical News*, Vol. 24, No. 31 (August 14, 1981). (Editorial)

21. Ricardo-Campbell, "Your Health and the Government," pp. 303-304.

22. "Blue Cross' 'First Aid' for Chrysler," *The Peninsula Times Tribune* (February 6, 1981), p. E-4.

23. Fairfield/Westchester Business Group on Health, *First Annual Report: July 1, 1979–June 30, 1980* (1980), p. 10.

24. Robert Beck, "IBM Health Care Strategy: A Summary," Presentation made to the Price Advisory Committee of the Council on Wage and Price Stability, Washington, DC (April 16, 1980), p. 6. (Mimeo)

25. Alain Enthoven, "Health Care Costs: Why Regulation Fails, Why Competition Works: How to Get There from Here," *National Journal* (May 26, 1979), p. 885.

26. Harold S. Luft, "Health Maintenance Organizations, Competition, Cost Containment, and National Health Insurance," in *National Health Insurance*, ed. by Mark V. Pauly, p. 303.

27. Eli Ginzberg, "Competition and Cost Containment," *New England Journal of Medicine*, Vol. 303 (November 6, 1980), p. 1115.

28. *The Maui News* (August 11, 1980), p. A8.

29. Alan F. Westin, "Patient's Rights: Computers and Health Records," *Health Progress* (April 1977), p. 57.

30. Alan F. Westin, *Computer, Health Records, and Citizen Rights* (New York: Columbia University Press, 1977); U.S. National Bureau of Standards, Monograph No. 157 (Washington, DC: Government Printing Office, 1978), pp. xviii-xix.

31. This suggestion evolved during a discussion between the author and Mary Lee Ingbar, Professor of Family and Community Medicine, University of Massachusetts Medical Center.

32. Ricardo-Campbell, "Your Health and the Government," pp. 335-337.

33. Michael Waldholy, "Ailing Health Programs," *Wall Street Journal* (September 25, 1980), p. 48.

34. For a well-reasoned discussion on catastrophic health insurance, see Clark C. Havighurst, James F. Blumstein, and Randall Bovbjevg, "Strategies in Underwriting the Costs of Catastrophic Disease," *Law and Contemporary Problems*, Vol. 40, No. 4 (Autumn 1976), pp. 122-195.

35. Eric J. Cassell, "The Commodity View of Medicine," *Wall Street Journal* (April 30, 1979), p. 18.

INDEX

organ transplants, 285, 292, 305; and
dialysis, 292; immunosuppressive, 292;
and poor people, 316. *See also* Pharmaceutical companies; Pharmacists;
United States Food and Drug Administration
Duke University, 52
Dutton, Diana, 26
Dyckman, Zachary, 148

Ear infections, 16
Eastern United States, 148. *See also*
Northeastern United States
East Germany, 226, 227, 231
East South-Central states, 232
Eating. *See* Diet
Economists and economics, 5, 10, 15, 17,
19, 24, 25, 28, 29, 30, 31, 40, 41, 46, 49,
52, 60, 62, 63, 65, 68, 73, 80, 81, 90–103,
109, 113, 120, 129, 131, 137, 141, 147,
149, 154–55, 157, 163, 171, 189, 207,
212, 213, 214, 216, 220, 221, 222, 225,
226, 250, 255, 256, 267, 268, 275, 276,
278, 279, 280, 281, 288, 290, 292, 293,
295, 296, 297, 300, 301, 306, 311, 312,
315, 316, 317, 320, 324, 333
Education: on medical care, 8, 11, 13–14,
47, 73, 93, 97, 104, 122, 126, 129, 130,
131, 137, 150, 162, 164, 167, 175, 186,
203, 212, 215, 217, 232, 241, 242, 247,
250, 259–61, 290, 299, 305, 312, 314–18,
323, 329, 330–31; general, 8, 13, 25, 26,
28, 42, 61, 65, 67, 74, 101, 106, 112, 113,
114, 121, 122, 123, 125, 126, 128, 129,
173, 174, 197, 214, 229, 230, 233, 237,
247, 248, 257, 258, 269, 297. *See also*
Medical schools and training; Universities and colleges
Efficacy and medical devices, 273–75; and
drugs, 273
Ehrlich, Isaac, 96
Elderly people. *See* Aged people and
aging
Electrocardiograms, 57, 121, 122
Emergency medical care, 11, 19, 26, 29,
30, 31–32, 33, 34, 46, 49, 52, 70, 73, 90,
91, 92, 93, 94, 98, 103, 104–10, 111, 113,
115, 157, 164, 165, 202, 245, 251, 302
Emergency Medical Sources Systems Act
of *1973*, 107

Emphysema, 73
Emphysema Anonymous, 73
Employers Health Cost Committee of San
Diego, 321
Endocrine disorders, 102, 117
Energy, 92, 132
Engineering, 133
England. *See* Great Britain
Enthoven, Alain, 179, 306–8, 312, 326
Environment and environmental health,
14, 131, 132, 224, 243, 244, 245, 250, 277,
297, 318, 329
Epidemics, 67, 121
Epilepsy, 284
Ernst and Ernst, 81
Estrogen, 243
Ethics, 3, 15, 16, 29, 31, 92, 113, 114, 147,
163, 186, 252, 261, 265, 266, 275, 278,
279, 280, 283, 286, 294, 296, 308, 312,
333
Ethnic groups, 13. *See also specific people*
Europe, 3, 84, 85, 241, 245
Executive Order No. *12044*, 296
Exercise, 7, 72, 96, 97, 126, 127–28, 130,
224, 229–30, 235, 239, 240, 241, 249,
250, 258, 291, 316, 322
Expenditures for medical care. *See* Costs
of and expenditures for medical care
Experience-rating, 158, 162, 210, 326, 329
Experimental medicine, 33, 34, 106, 285
Eye glasses, eye examinations, and eye
care, 13, 97, 121, 122, 126, 129, 151, 156,
172, 202, 221, 261, 266

Fairfield/Westchester Business Group on
Health, 183, 262, 322
Families and family health, 11, 13, 22, 43,
44, 45, 72, 85, 88, 112, 143, 202, 203,
214, 244, 288, 298, 306, 307, 323, 327,
328. *See also* Income: family
Farms. *See* Rural areas
Fats, 127, 128, 239, 245
FDA. *See* United States Food and Drug
Administration
Federal Accounting Standards Board,
(FASB), 77, 198
Federal Bureau of Investigation (FBI), 206
Federal government. *See* United States
Congress and United States govern-
ment

113, 130, 134, 139, 140, 141, 143, 149, 158, 196, 257, 260, 265, 279, 284, 312, 324, 330
Medical societies, 62, 214, 256, 260, 328
Medicare, 7, 11, 12, 17, 19, 20, 21, 22, 26, 27–28, 33, 34, 36, 39, 50, 54, 55, 60, 64, 77, 80, 81, 84, 85, 86, 88, 92, 97, 98, 100, 102, 105, 113, 117, 126, 138, 141, 142, 159, 161, 162, 165, 168, 173, 175, 187, 188, 190, 192–201, 205, 206, 208, 210, 211, 212, 213, 219, 220, 222, 253, 254, 255, 257, 260, 266, 268, 272, 273, 274, 275, 276, 280, 281, 282, 283, 284, 285, 292, 303, 305, 309, 311, 312, 313, 314, 317, 320, 326, 327, 329, 330, 332
"Medigap" insurance, 188, 194
Mendocino County, Calif., 328
Mental illness. *See* Psychiatry, psychology, and mental illness
Metabolism, 15, 102, 117
Metropolitan areas. *See* Urban areas
Mexico, 231, 245
Michigan, 218, 322
Mid-Peninsula Health Service, 73
Midwestern United States, 77, 271
Midwives, 43, 53, 54, 55, 59, 60, 224
Migrant workers, 27, 191
Minneapolis, Minn., 160, 163, 165, 166, 167, 323–24
Minnesota, 160, 163, 165, 166, 167, 323–24
Minorities, 40, 227. *See also specific minorities*
Mississippi, 202
Missouri, 174
Monopolies, 43, 186, 210, 211, 212–13, 214, 215, 216, 219, 262, 301
Montana, 77
Montreal, Canada, 59
Morals and morality, 28–31, 32, 34, 92, 94, 95–98, 225, 226, 265, 291
Morbidity rates, 24, 51, 124, 126, 132, 149, 228, 229, 235, 236, 278, 315
Mortality rates, 24, 44, 51, 97, 124, 126, 127, 132, 149, 150, 175, 197, 224, 225, 226, 227, 228, 229, 236, 239, 240–41, 242, 243, 245, 249–50, 256, 289, 299, 313, 315, 316. *See also* Infant mortality rates
Motel chains, 81
Motor vehicle accidents. *See* Accidents

Multiphasic screening. *See* Screening
Multiphasic testing. *See* Testing and diagnostic procedures
Mutual Insurance, Ltd., 79
Myocardial infarctions. *See* Heart disease and heart surgery

Nashville, Tenn., 82
National Academy of Sciences, 239, 272
National Advisory Drug Committee (NADC), 263, 264
National Blue Cross Plan, 210
National Cancer Institute, 134
National Center for Health Care Technology (NCHCT), 105, 273, 274, 275, 282, 320
National Center for Higher Education Management Systems, 197
National health insurance. *See* Insurance, medical: national
National Health Service (NHS) (British), 9–10, 84, 113, 221, 222, 269, 287–89, 290, 298, 299, 301
National Health Service Corps, 39
National Institute of Medicine, 142
National Institute of Mental Health, 74
National Institute of Health (NIH), 134, 239
National Library of Medicine, 134
National Science Foundation, 42
Nebraska, 87
Neonatal mortality rate. *See* Infant mortality rates
Neoplasms. *See* Cancers; Tumors
Nephrology. *See* Kidney disease
Netherlands, 61, 84, 223, 226, 227, 238, 279, 293
Neurology and neurological diseases, 102, 117, 121, 134, 141, 265
Neustein, Daniel, 48
Nevada, 79
New England, 73
New Hampshire, 234
Newhouse, Joseph P., 19–20, 311
New Jersey, 82, 99, 131
Newspapers, 164, 167, 169, 186, 196, 206, 214, 257, 258, 281, 298, 302, 316, 324, 330
New York (city and state), 32, 41, 98, 99, 159, 160, 163, 166, 175–76, 183, 196,